THE AMERICAN NEGRO
HIS HISTORY AND LITERATURE

HISTORY OF SCHOOLS
FOR THE
COLORED POPULATION

ARNO PRESS and THE NEW YORK TIMES

NEW YORK 1969

General Editor
WILLIAM LOREN KATZ

PROBABLY NO WORK ON NEGRO EDUCATION DURING THE nineteenth century has been cited so frequently as the *Special Report of the Commissioner of Education on the Improvement of Public Schools in the District of Columbia, 1871*. Several generations of scholars have found it to be an invaluable resource. Emerging from its myriad details are most of the major issues and themes on Negro education that have developed during the one hundred years since it was written.

The *Special Report* was issued by the first United States Commissioner of Education, Henry Barnard, who organized the federal Bureau of Education in 1867. Its relevant Section C—"History of Schools for the Colored Population"—is in two approximately equal parts. Part I is a detailed account of the development of schools for Negroes in the District of Columbia from 1800 to 1861 and in Georgetown and Washington (which subsequently merged) from 1861 to 1868. Part II, covering much the same period, consists mainly of factual summaries of the legal status of schools for Negroes in each of thirty-five states and in the District of Columbia.

Carter G. Woodson relied heavily upon the *Special Report* in his *Education of the Negro Prior to 1861*. He described Part I as "exhaustive" and noted that the author, M. B. Goodwin, was alone among scholars investigating this "field of profitable research." He assessed Part II as "a mass of valuable materials, but neither comprehensive nor thorough."

The intimate details with which Goodwin reconstructs the development of schools for Negroes are fascinating. Here is a simple, straightforward account of the defeats and triumphs of a long series of efforts to conduct schools for the "colored population." The narrative is replete with names and places—e.g., "The Smothers School-House . . . built by Henry Smothers on the corner of Fourteenth and H Streets, not far from the Treasury building" —and with biographical and other facts about the persons involved, many of them former slaves who purchased their freedom and dedicated their lives to their people. "It is quite certain," says Goodwin, "that the most of what is gathered in these pages from the first half century of the District would have never been rescued from the past under any other auspices, and from the original, novel, and instructive nature of its character, it has been deemed best to go with much minuteness into details."

The dominant theme emerging from all his detail is the heroic struggle of black people for education. The first schoolhouse for Negroes, for example, was built about 1807 by "three men who ... at that time just emerged from the condition of slaves, and knew not a letter of the alphabet." Their lives and efforts, and those of scores of others who followed, are told here with great empathy: "There is an almost tragic pathos running through the tale of the patient sufferings and sacrifices which these humble and dutiful people have experienced, through so many years of oppression, in their struggle for knowledge."

(Incidentally, the story of the twentieth-century sequel to this early self-help movement in Negro education has never been adequately told. I refer to the massive, widespread and effective campaigns among rural Negroes in the South—especially during the two decades after World War I—in which millions of dollars were raised for purchasing land, constructing buildings, hiring teachers and extending school terms for Negro youth in "public" schools. Here is a fruitful field of research that still awaits its modern-day Goodwin.)

Reflected in the *Special Report* accounts of early Negro school developments in the District of Columbia and elsewhere are the shifting currents in American political history during the first seventy years of the nineteenth century. Liberal attitudes and practices toward the education of Negroes during the early 1800's gave way to harsh suppression—by mob action and by law—as the expanding slave system grew in power. This was especially true after the Nat Turner insurrection in 1831, which "spread terror everywhere in slave communities" and strengthened anti-Negro reaction in the North. During and after the Civil War, however—with the "beginning of the new order of things"—the Negro school movement burgeoned, with the assistance of dozens of missionary and philanthropic societies, thousands of volunteer teachers from the North, state and local legislatures and especially the federal government. Opposition to schools for Negroes persisted, but it was usually overcome through the concerted political action of the Negro people and their newfound allies. The progressive thrust of Reconstruction democracy was still strong at the time the *Special Report* was written, and one finds here no forecast of the impending defeat of the Negro people—and hence of Negro education—during the final quarter of the century.

The issues around which the struggle for Negro education developed after the Civil War are essentially those issues which rose to prominence with the renaissance of Negro education after World

War I. There were the questions of public support versus support of private agencies; segregated versus "mixed" schools; separate taxes on Negro-owned property for separate Negro schools; Negro control over separate Negro schools; vocational versus liberal education for Negroes; education to prepare for "repatriation" to Africa; and, pervasive throughout the country during the whole period, the question of equality of material and professional resources for schools serving Negro children.

Also at issue during this early period of Negro education was the still-persisting question of the educability of the Negro masses, a topic on which the conclusion of the *Special Report* is eloquent. It said that the facts of this study

> . . . put to flight a class of ethnological ideas that have been woven by philosophers into unnumbered volumes of vain theories. The great and imposing truth that the colored race has been for nearly seventy years on a grand trial of their capacity to rise in the scale of intelligence, such as has not elsewhere in the history of the world been granted them, seems to have entirely escaped observation. If these records are, as they are confidently believed to be, substantially accurate in all their details, the capabilities of the colored race to rise to superior mental and social elevation, and that too under the most appalling disabilities and discouragements, is illustrated on a conspicuous theatre, and with a completeness that cannot be shaken by any cavil or conjecture.

As subsequent developments have revealed, the author of the *Special Report* underestimated the resourcefulness of pseudoscience in the service of political reaction and racism. Almost a century later, the vain ethnological theories he thought had been put to rest continue to thwart the effective education of the masses of Negro children. Perhaps a reading of this report by school administrators and teachers—and also a few atavistic behavioral scientists—might help them to comprehend what the lessons of history would seem to make self-evident.

Doxey A. Wilkerson,
PROFESSOR OF EDUCATION
YESHIVA UNIVERSITY

C.

HISTORY OF SCHOOLS FOR THE COLORED POPULATION

———

I. DISTRICT OF COLUMBIA

II. STATES.

PART I.

HISTORY OF SCHOOLS FOR THE COLORED POPULATION IN THE DIS-
TRICT OF COLUMBIA.

SCHOOLS AND EDUCATION OF THE COLORED POPULATION.

I. *Historical development of schools for the colored population in the District of Columbia.*

PERIOD I.—1800 TO 1861.

193

PERIOD II.—1861 TO 1868.

1.—*Cities of Washington and Georgetown.*

2.—*Colored schools in Washington county.*

3.—*Colored schools in Alexandria.*

SCHOOLS OF THE COLORED POPULATION.

PERIOD I.—1801–1861.

The struggles of the colored people of the District of Columbia, in securing for themselves the means of education, furnish a very instructive chapter in the history of schools. Their courage and resolution were such, in the midst of their own great ignorance and strenuous opposition from without, that a permanent record becomes an act of justice to them. In the language of Jefferson to Banneker, the black astronomer, it is a publication to which their "whole color has a right for their justification against the doubts which have been entertained of them." Though poor, proscribed and unlettered, they founded, in their humble way, an institution for the education of their children within less than two years after the first school-house of whites was built in the city. The sentiment against the education of the colored classes was much less rigorous in the early history of the capital than it was a third of a century later. The free colored people were sometimes even encouraged, to a limited extent, in their efforts to pick up some fragments of knowledge. They were taught in the Sunday schools and evening schools occasionally, and respectable mulatto families were in many cases allowed to attend, with white children, the private schools and academies. There are scores of colored men and women still living in this District who are decently educated, and who never went to any but white schools. There are also white men and women still alive here, who went to school in this city and in Georgetown with colored children and felt no offence. Another fact important to be considered is that the colored people, who first settled in Washington, constituted a very superior class of their race. Many of them were favorite family servants, who came here with congressmen from the south, and with the families of other public officers, and who by long and faithful service had secured, by gift, purchase, or otherwise, their freedom. Others were superior mechanics, house servants, and enterprising in various callings, who obtained their freedom by their own persevering industry. Some, also, had received their freedom before coming to this city, and of these there was one family, to be referred to hereafter, which came from Mount Vernon. Still the number of those who could read, even of the very best class of colored people, was very small.

THE FIRST SCHOOL AND SCHOOL HOUSE.

The first school-house in this District, built expressly for the education of colored children, was erected by three men who had been born and reared as slaves in Maryland and Virginia. Their names were George Bell, Nicholas Franklin and Moses Liverpool. It was a good one-story frame building, and stood upon a lot directly opposite to and west of the house in which the mother of Daniel Carroll, of Duddington, then resided, and where the Providence Hospital now stands. It was built about the year 1807, and a school, under a white teacher, Mr. Lowe, was opened there as soon as it was finished. It was a full school, and continued several years, after which, for a time, the house was used as a dwelling. The following is a summary from the census of Washington taken in 1807, the year in which this colored school-house was built:

White males	2,139	Free black females	153
White females	2,009	Free mulatto males	95
Male slaves	409	Free mulatto females	120
Female slaves	479	Total white	4,148
Male non-resident slaves	55	Total free colored	494
Female non-resident slaves	61	Total slaves	1,004
Free black males	126	Total colored	1,498

It is seen from these figures that when this school was put into operation there was a population of 494 souls only to represent it that being the number of free colored persons. On the other hand, with a population of more than 4,000, the white residents had the year before built but two public school-houses for white scholars, one in the eastern and the other in the western section of the city, though there were three or four small private schools. The three men who built the school-house had at that time just emerged from the condition of slaves, and knew not a letter of the alphabet. Franklin and Liverpool were caulkers by trade, having come from the sea-coast in the lower part of Virginia, and were at work in the Navy Yard. How they secured their freedom is not clearly known, though the tradition is that Franklin, experiencing religion, was made free by his master, who was a member of the Methodist church, the discipline of which at that time admitted no slave to membership.* These two men worked at their trade all their lives, raised up their families with all the education their means would afford, and their grandchildren are now among the respectable colored people of this city.

THE BELL AND BROWNING FAMILIES.

George Bell was the leading spirit in this remarkable educational enterprise, and was conspicuous in all efforts for the benefit of his race in this community. He was the slave of Anthony Addison, who owned a large estate upon the borders of the District beyond the Eastern Branch, and his wife, Sophia Browning, belonged to the Bell family, on the Patuxent. When the commissioners were surveying the District in 1791 they received their meals from their cabin across the Eastern Branch, and the wife used often to describe the appearance of Benjamin Banneker, the celebrated mathematician and astronomer, who was one of the surveying party by invitation of the commissioners. She had a market garden and used to attend the Alexandria market every market day, though she had a family of three sons and a daughter. In this manner she saved four hundred dollars without the knowledge of her owner, who was Mrs. Rachel Pratt, (Bell,) the mother of Governor Pratt, of Maryland. This money was intrusted to a Methodist preacher, who bought the husband's freedom with it, and shortly afterwards, while the wife was dangerously sick, her freedom was bought for five pounds Maryland currency by the husband. These purchases were effected about six years before the building of the school-house. Two of the sons, born in slavery, the father purchased a few years later; the third was accidentally killed in Washington, and the daughter they could not buy, her mistress declining peremptorily to relinquish her, but making her free by her will at her decease, which occurred many years later in Georgetown. These children belonged, as did the mother, to Mrs. Pratt. The two boys were purchased "running"—while on the foot as runaways—the one for $750 and the other for $450. The first free-born child, widow Harriet Dunlap, a woman of much intelligence and singular clearness of memory, born in 1803, is still living and resides here, as do also Margaret, who was freed by Mrs. Pratt, and the two younger sons. The two sons that were purchased were both lost at sea. Mrs. Dunlap, and her next sister, Elizabeth, after the Bell school, as it may be called, closed, went for brief periods successively to schools taught by Henry Potter, an Englishman, by Anne Maria Hall, and Mrs. Maria Haley. There were several colored children in Mrs. Haley's school, and some complaints being made to the teacher, who was an Irish lady, the two Bell girls were sent to the school in Baltimore, taught by Rev. Daniel Coker, who subsequently, as a colored Methodist missionary, became conspicuously known throughout the Christian world by his wise and courageous work in the first emigration to Liberia. They remained at this school two years and a half, from 1812 to 1815. George Bell died in 1843, at the age of 82 years, and his wife some years later, at the age of 86. They left all their children not only with a good education but also in comfortable pecuniary circumstances. The mother was a woman of superior character, as were all the family. One sister was the wife of the late Rev. John F. Cook, and

---

* The Methodist Discipline as amended in 1784 prescribed among other rules the following two:

First. Every member of our Society who has slaves in his possession shall, within twelve months after notice given to him by the assistant, legally execute an instrument whereby he emancipates and sets free every slave in his possession.

Second. No person holding slaves shall in future be admitted into our Society or to the Lord's Supper, till he previously complies with these rules concerning slavery.

another was Mrs. Alethia Tanner, whose force of character and philanthropy gave her remarkable prominence here and elsewhere among her race, and commanded the respect of all who knew her. All of the Browning family belonged to Mrs. Rachel Pratt. Mrs. Tanner commenced her remarkable career by the purchase of her own freedom for $1,400. The last payment of $275 was made June 29, 1810, and her manumission papers from Mrs. Rachel Pratt bear date July 10, 1810. In 1826 she purchased her older sister, Laurena Cook, and five of the Cook children, four sons and a daughter. One of these sons, then sixteen years old, was afterwards known and respected for more than a quarter of a century by all classes in this community as an able and enlightened school teacher and clergyman. His name was John F. Cook. In 1828 she purchased the rest of the Cook children and their offspring as follows: Hannah and her two children, Annette and her two children, Alethia and her child, George Cook and Daniel Cook, comprising, in all, her sister with ten children and five grandchildren, paying for the sister $800, and for the children an average of $300 each. She also purchased the freedom of Lotty Riggs and her four children, and of John Butler, who became a useful Methodist minister; and in 1837 she purchased the freedom of Charlotte Davis, who is still living in this city. The documents showing these purchases are all preserved in the Cook family. Mrs. Tanner was alive to every wise scheme for the education and elevation of her race. It was through her efforts, combined with those of her brother in law, George Bell, that the First Bethel Church on Capitol Hill was saved for that society. When the house was put up at auction by the bank which held the notes of the society, these two individuals came forward, bid in the property, paid for it and waited for their pay till the society was able to raise the money. Mrs. Tanner, at her death in 1864, left a handsome property. Her husband died many years before, and she had no children. She was the housemaid of Mr. Jefferson during his residence at the capital, and Richard M. Johnson, who was her friend, appears as the witness to the manumission papers of Laurena Cook, her sister, and of John F. Cook, the son of Laurena, whose freedom she bought while Mr. Johnson was United States senator.

THE SCHOOL OF THE RESOLUTE BENEFICIAL SOCIETY.

After the Bell school-house had been used several years as a dwelling, it was in 1818 again taken for educational purposes, to accommodate an association organized by the leading colored men of the city, and for the specific purpose of promoting the education of their race. The courage of these poor men, nearly all of whom had but a few years previously emerged from bondage and could not read a syllable, cannot be justly estimated without recalling the fact, that at that period the free colored people were considered everywhere in the south as a nuisance, and very largely so through the north. The Savannah Republican newspaper, in 1817, in a carefully prepared article on the subject, said: "The free people of color have never conferred a single benefit on the country. They have been and are a nuisance, which we wish to get rid of as soon as possible, the filth and offal of society;" and this article was copied approvingly into leading, temperate northern journals. It will be seen from the announcement that this school was established upon the principle of receiving all colored children who should come, tuition being exacted only from such as were able to pay; that it was more nearly a free school than anything hitherto known in the city. The announcement of this school, which appeared in the columns of the Daily National Intelligencer, August 29, 1818, is full of interest. It clearly indicates, among other things, the fact that at that period there were some slave owners in this District who were recognized by the colored people as friendly to the education of their slaves; a sentiment, however, which, in the gradual prostitution of public opinion on the subject, was very thoroughly eradicated in the succeeding forty years. But what is of special significance in this remarkable paper is the humble language of apology in which it is expressed. It is plainly manifest in every sentence that an apology was deemed necessary from these poor people for presuming to do anything for opening to their offspring the gates of knowledge which had been barred to themselves. The document reads as follows:

"*A School,*

" Founded by an association of free people of color, of the city of Washington, called the

'Resolute Beneficial Society,' situate near the Eastern Public School and the dwelling of Mrs. Fenwick, is now open for the reception of children of free people of color and others, that ladies or gentlemen may think proper to send to be instructed in reading, writing, arithmetic, English grammar or other branches of education apposite to their capacities, by a steady, active and experienced teacher, whose attention is wholly devoted to the purposes described. It is presumed that free colored families will embrace the advantages thus presented to them, either by subscribing to the funds of the society or by sending their children to the school. An improvement of the intellect and morals of colored youth being the objects of this institution, the patronage of benevolent ladies and gentlemen, by donation or subscription, is humbly solicited in aid of the fund, the demands thereon being heavy and the means at present much too limited. For the satisfaction of the public, the constitution and articles of association are printed and published. And to avoid disagreeable occurrences, no writings are to be done by the teacher for a slave, neither directly nor indirectly, to serve the purpose of a slave on any account whatever. Further particulars may be known by applying to any of the undersigned officers.

"WILLIAM COSTIN, *President.*   "ARCHIBALD JOHNSON, *Marshal.*
"GEORGE HICKS, *Vice-President.*   " FRED. LEWIS, *Chairman of the Committee.*
"JAMES HARRIS, *Secretary.*   "ISAAC JOHNSON, ⎰ *Committee.*
"GEORGE BELL, *Treasurer.*   " SCIPIO BEENS, ⎱

"N. B.—An evening school will commence on the premises on the first Monday of October, and continue throughout the season.

☞ "The managers of Sunday schools in the eastern district are thus most dutifully informed that on Sabbath days the school-house belonging to this society, if required for the tuition of colored youth, will be uniformly at their service.

"*August* 29, 3*t.*"

This school was continued several years successfully, with an ordinary attendance of fifty or sixty scholars, and often more. The first teacher was Mr. Pierpont, from Massachusetts, a relative of the poet; and after two or three years, was succeeded by John Adams, a shoemaker, who was *the first colored man who taught in this District,* and who, after leaving this school, had another, about 1822, near the Navy Department. The Bell school-house was after this period used as a dwelling by one of Bell's sons, and at his father's decease fell to his daughter Elizabeth, the wife of Basil Sims. Soon afterwards Sims and his wife both died, leaving a handsome property for their children, which, however, was totally dissipated by the executor. The Bell school-house and lot were sold for taxes; the children when coming of age vainly seeking its recovery.

MR. HENRY POTTER'S SCHOOL.

The third school for colored children in Washington was established by Mr. Henry Potter, an Englishman, who opened his school about 1809, in a brick building which then stood on the southeast corner of F and Seventh streets, opposite the block where the post office building now stands. He continued there several years and had a large school, moving subsequently to what was then known as Clark's row on Thirteenth street west, between G and H streets north.

MRS. HALL'S SCHOOL.

During this period Mrs. Anne Maria Hall started a school on Capitol Hill, between the Old Capitol and Carroll row, on First street east. After continuing there with a full school for some ten years, she moved to a building which stood on what is now the vacant portion of the Casparis House lot on A street, close to the Capitol. Some years later she went to the First Bethel church, and after a year or two she moved to a house still standing on E street north, between Eleventh and Twelfth west, and there taught many years. She was a colored woman from Prince George's county, Maryland, and had a respectable education, which she obtained at schools with white children in Alexandria. Her husband died early, leaving her with children to support, and she betook herself to the work of a teacher, which she loved, and in which, for not less than twenty-five years, she met with uniform success. Her schools were all quite large, and the many who remember her as their teacher speak of her with great respect.

MRS. MARY BILLING'S SCHOOL.

Of the early teachers of colored schools in this District there is no one whose name is mentioned with more gratitude and respect by the intelligent colored residents that that of Mrs.

Mary Billing, who established the first colored school that was gathered in Georgetown. She was an English woman; her husband, Joseph Billing, a cabinet maker, coming from England in 1800, settled with his family that year in Washington, and dying in 1807 left his wife with three children. She was well educated, a capable and good woman, and immediately commenced teaching to support her family. At first, it is believed, she was connected with the corporation school of Georgetown. It was while in a white school certainly that her attention was arrested by the wants of the colored children, whom she was accustomed to receive into her schools, till the opposition became so marked that she decided to make her school exclusively colored. She was a woman of strong religious convictions, and being English, with none of the ideas peculiar to slave society, when she saw the peculiar destitution of the colored children in the community around her, she resolved to give her life to the class who seemed most to need her services. She established a colored school about 1810, in a brick house still standing on Dunbarton street opposite the Methodist church, between Congress and High streets, remaining there till the winter of 1820–'21, when she came to Washington and opened a school in the house on H street near the Foundry church, then owned by Daniel Jones, a colored man, and still owned and occupied by a member of that family. She died in 1826 in the fiftieth year of her age. She continued her school till failing health, a year or so before her death, compelled its relinquishment. Her school was always large, it being patronized in Georgetown as well as afterwards by the best colored families of Washington, many of whom sent their children to her from Capitol Hill and the vicinity of the Navy Yard. Most of the better educated colored men and women now living, who were school children in her time, received the best portion of their education from her, and they all speak of her with a deep and tender sense of obligation. Henry Potter succeeded her in the Georgetown school, and after him Mr. Shay, an Englishman, who subsequently came to Washington and for many years had a large colored school in a brick building known as the Round Tops, in the western part of the city, near the Circle, and still later removing to the old Western Academy building, corner of I and Seventeenth streets. He was there till about 1830, when he was convicted of assisting a slave to his freedom and sent a term to the penitentiary. Mrs. Billing had a night school in which she was greatly assisted by Mr. Monroe, a government clerk and a Presbyterian elder, whose devout and benevolent character is still remembered in the churches Mrs. Billing had scholars from Bladensburg and the surrounding country, who came into Georgetown and boarded with her and with others. About the time when Mrs. Billing relinquished her school in 1822 or 1823, what may be properly called

THE SMOTHERS SCHOOL-HOUSE

was built by Henry Smothers on the corner of Fourteenth and H streets, not far from the Treasury building. Smothers had a small dwelling-house on this corner, and built his school-house on the rear of the same lot. He had been long a pupil of Mrs. Billing, and had subsequently taught a school on Washington street, opposite the Union Hotel in Georgetown. He opened his school in Washington in the old corporation school-house, built in 1806, but some years before this period abandoned as a public school-house. It was known as the Western Academy, and is still standing and used as a school-house on the corner of I and Nineteenth streets west. When his school-house on Fourteenth and H streets was finished his school went into the new quarters. This school was very large, numbering always more than a hundred and often as high as a hundred and fifty scholars. He taught here about two years, and was succeeded by John W. Prout about the year 1825. Prout was a man of ability. In 1831, May 4, there was a meeting, says the National Intelligencer of that date, of "the colored citizens, large and very respectable, in the African Methodist Episcopal church," to consider the question of emigrating to Liberia. John W. Prout was chosen to preside over the assemblage, and the article in the Intelligencer represents him as making "a speech of decided force and well adapted to the occasion, in support of a set of resolutions which he had drafted, and which set forth views adverse to leaving the soil that had given them birth, their true and veritable home, *without the benefits of education.*" The school under Prout was governed by a board of trustees and was organized as and so continued two or three years. The number of scholars was very large, averaging a hundred and fifty. Mrs. Anne Maria Hall was the assistant teacher. It relied mainly for support upon subscription, twelve and a half cents a month only being expected from each pupil, and this amount was not compulsory. The school was free to all colored children, without money or price, and so continued two or three years, when failing of voluntary pecuniary support (it never wanted scholars) it became a regular tuition school. The school under Mr. Prout was called the "Columbian Institute," the name being suggested by John McLeod, the famous Irish schoolmaster, who was a warm friend of this institution after visiting and commending the scholars and teachers, and who named his new building in 1835 the Columbian Academy. The days of thick darkness to the colored people were approaching. The Nat. Turner insurrection in Southampton county, Virginia, which occurred in August, 1831, spread terror everywhere in slave communities. In this district, immediately upon that terrible occurrence, the colored children, who had in very large numbers been received into Sabbath schools in the white churches, were all turned out of those schools. This event, though seeming to be a fiery affliction, proved a blessing in disguise. It aroused the energies of the colored people, taught them self-reliance, and they organized forthwith Sabbath schools of their own. It was in the Smothers' school-house that they formed their first Sunday school, about the year 1832, and here they continued their very large school for several years, the Fifteenth-street Presbyterian Church ultimately springing from the school organization. It is important to state in this connection that

THE SUNDAY SCHOOL,

always an extremely important means of education for colored people in the days of slavery, was emphatically so in the gloomy times now upon them. It was the Sabbath school that taught the great mass of the free people of color about all the school knowledge that was allowed them in those days, and hence the consternation which came upon them when they found themselves excluded from the schools of the white churches. Lindsay Muse, who has been the messenger for eighteen Secretaries of the Navy, successively, during forty years, from 1828 to the present time; John Brown; Benjamin M. McCoy; Mr. Smallwood; Mrs. Charlotte Norris, afterwards wife of Rev. Eli Nugent; and Siby McCoy are the only survivors of the resolute little band of colored men and women who gathered with and guided that Sunday school. They had, in the successor of Mr. Prout, a man after their own heart,

JOHN F. COOK,

who came into charge of this school in August, 1834, about eight years after his aunt, Alethia Tanner, had purchased his freedom. He learned the shoemaker's trade in his boyhood, and worked diligently, after the purchase of his freedom, to make some return to his aunt for the purchase money. About the time of his becoming of age he dislocated his shoulder, which compelled him to seek other employment, and in 1831, the year of his majority, he obtained the place of assistant messenger in the Land Office. Hon. John Wilson, now Third Auditor of the Treasury, was the messenger, and was Cook's firm friend till the day of his death. Cook had been a short time at school under the instruction of Smothers and Prout, but when he entered the Land Office his education was at most only the ability to stumble along a little in a primary reading book. He, however, now gave himself in all his leisure moments, early and late, to study. Mr. Wilson remembers his indefatigable application, and affirms that it was a matter of astonishment at the time, and that he has seen nothing in all his observation to surpass and scarcely to equal it. He was soon able to write a good hand, and was employed with his pen in clerical work by the sanction of the Commissioner, Elisha Hayward, who was much attached to him. Cook was now beginning to look forward to the life of a teacher, which, with the ministry, was the only work not menial in its nature then open to an educated colored man. At the end of three years he resigned his place in the Land Office, and entered upon the work which he laid down only with his life. It was then that he gave himself wholly to study and the business of education, working with all his might; his school numbering quite a hundred scholars in the winter and a hundred and fifty in the summer. He had been in his work one year when the storm which had been, for some years, under the discussion of the slavery question, gathering over the country at large, burst upon this District.

THE SNOW RIOT,

or "Snow storm," as it has been commonly called, which occurred in September, 1835, is an event that stands vividly in the memory of all colored people who lived in this community at that time. Benjamin Snow, a smart colored man, keeping a restaurant on the corner of Pennsylvania avenue and Sixth street, was reported to have made some remark of a bravado kind derogatory to the wives of white mechanics; whereupon this class, or those assuming to represent them, made a descent upon his establishment, destroying all his effects. Snow himself, who denied using the offensive language, with difficulty escaped unharmed, through the management of white friends, taking refuge in Canada, where he still resides. The military was promptly called to the rescue, at the head of which was General Walter Jones, the eminent lawyer, who characterized the rioters, greatly to their indignation, as "a set of ragamuffins," and his action was thoroughly sanctioned by the city authorities.

At the same time also there was a fierce excitement among the mechanics at the Navy Yard, growing out of the fact that a large quantity of copper bolts being missed from the yard and found to have been carried out in the dinner pails by the hands, the commandant had forbid eating dinners in the yard. This order was interpreted as an insult to the white mechanics, and threats were made of an assault on the yard, which was put in a thorough state of defence by the commandant. The rioters swept through the city, ransacking the houses of the prominent colored men and women, ostensibly in search of anti-slavery papers and documents, the most of the gang impelled undoubtedly by hostility to the negro race and motives of plunder. Nearly all the colored school-houses were partially demolished and the furniture totally destroyed, and in several cases they were completely ruined. Some private houses were also torn down or burnt. The colored schools were nearly all broken up, and it was with the greatest difficulty that the colored churches were saved from destruction, as their Sabbath schools were regarded, and correctly regarded, as the means through which the colored people, at that time, procured much of their education.

The rioters sought, especially, for John F. Cook, who, however, had seasonably taken from the stable the horse of his friend Mr. Hayward, the Commissioner of the Land Office, an anti-slavery man, and fled precipitately from the city. They marched to his school-house, destroyed all the books and furniture and partially destroyed the building. Mrs. Smothers, who owned both the school-house and the dwelling adjoining and the lots, was sick in her house at the time, but an alderman, Mr. Edward Dyer, with great courage and nobleness of spirit, stood between the house and the mob for her protection, declaring that he would defend her house from molestation with all the means he could command. They left the house unharmed, and it is still standing on the premises. Mr. Cook went to Columbia, Pennsylvania, opened a school there, and did not venture back to his home till the autumn of 1836. At the time the riot broke out, General Jackson was absent in Virginia. He returned in the midst of the tumult, and immediately issuing orders in his bold, uncompromising manner to the authorities to see the laws respected at all events, the violence was promptly subdued. It was nevertheless a very dark time for the colored people. The timid class did not for a year or two dare to send their children to school, and the whole mass of the colored people dwelt in fear day and night. In August, 1836, Mr. Cook returned from Pennsylvania and reopened his school, which under him had, in 1834, received the name of

UNION SEMINARY.

During his year's absence he was in charge of a free colored public school in Columbia, Lancaster county, Pennsylvania, which he surrendered to the care of Benjamin M. McCoy when he came back to his home, Mr. McCoy going there to fill out his engagement.

He resumed his work with broad and elevated ideas of his business. This is clearly seen in the plan of his institution, embraced in the printed annual announcements and programmes of his annual exhibitions, copies of which have been preserved. The course of study embraced three years, and there was a male and a female department, Miss Catharine Costin at one period being in charge of the female department. Mr. Seaton, of the National Intelligencer, among other leading and enlightened citizens and public men, used to visit his school from year to year and watch its admirable working with deep and lively interest. Cook was at this period not only watching over his very large school, ranging from 100 to 150 or more pupils, but was active in the formation of the "First Colored Presbyterian church of Washington," which was organized in November, 1841, by Rev. John C. Smith, D. D., and worshipped in this school-house. He was now also giving deep study to the preparation for the ministry, upon which in fact, as a licentiate of the African Methodist Episcopal church, he had already in some degree entered. At a regular meeting of "The Presbytery of the District of Columbia," held in Alexandria, May 3, 1842, this church, now commonly called the Fifteenth Street Presbyterian church, was formally received under the care of that Presbytery, the first and still the only colored Presbyterian church in this District. Mr. Cook was elected the first pastor July 13, 1843, and preached his trial sermon before ordination on the evening of that day, in the Fourth Presbyterian church (Dr. J. C. Smith's) in this city, in the presence of a large congregation. This sermon is remembered as a manly production, delivered with great dignity and force and deeply imbued with the spirit of his work. He was ordained in the Fifteenth-street church the next evening, and continued to serve the church with eminent success till his death in 1855. Rev. John C. Smith, D. D., who had preached his ordination sermon and been the devoted friend and counsellor for nearly twenty years, preached his funeral sermon, selecting as his text, "There was a man sent from God whose name was John." There were present white as well as colored clergymen of no less than five denominations, many of the oldest and most respectable citizens, and a vast concourse of all classes, white and colored. "The Fifteenth-street church," in the words of Dr. Smith in relation to them and their first pastor, " is now a large and flourishing congregation of spiritually-minded people. They have been educated in the truth and the principles of our holy religion, and in the new present state of things the men of this church are trusted, relied on as those who fear God and keep his commandments. The church is the monument to John F. Cook, the first pastor, who was faithful in all his house, a workman who labored night and day for years, and has entered into his reward. 'Blessed are the dead who die in the Lord.' 'They rest from their labors and their works do follow them.' "

In 1841, when he entered, in a preliminary and informal way, upon the pastorate of the Fifteenth-street church, he seems to have attempted to turn his seminary into a high school, limited to 25 or 30 pupils, exclusively for the more advanced scholars of both sexes, and his plan of studies to that end, as seen in his prospectus, evinces broad and elevated views—a desire to aid in lifting his race to higher things in education than they had yet attempted. His plans were not put into execution, in the matter of a high school, being frustrated by the circumstance that there were so few good schools in the city for the colored people, at that period, that his old patrons would not allow him to shut off the multitude of primary scholars which were depending upon his school. His seminary, however, continued to maintain its high standard, and had an average attendance of quite 100 year after year till he surrendered up his work in death.

He raised up a large family and educated them well. The oldest of the sons, John and George, were educated at Oberlin College. The other three being young, were in school when the father died. John and George, it will be seen, succeeded their father as teachers, continuing in the business down to the present year. Of the two daughters the elder was a teacher till married in 1866, and the other is now a teacher in the public schools of this city. One son served through the war as sergeant of the 40th colored regiment, and another served in the navy.

At the death of the father, March 21, 1855, the school fell into the hands of the son, John F. Cook, who continued it till May, 1857, when it passed to a younger son, George F. T. Cook, who moved it from its old home, the Smothers House, to the basement of the Presbyterian church in the spring of 1858, and maintained it till July, 1859. John F. Cook, jr., who had erected a new school-house on Sixteenth street, in 1862, again gathered the school which the tempests of the war had dispersed, and continued it till June, 1867, when the new order of things had opened ample school facilities throughout the city, and the teacher was called to other duties. Thus ended the school which had been first gathered by Smothers nearly 45 years before, and which, in that long period, had been continually maintained with seldom less than 100 pupils, and for the most part with 150, the only suspensions being in the year of the Snow riot and in the two years which ushered in the war.

The Smothers House, after the Cook school was removed, in 1858, was occupied for two years by a *free Catholic school*, supported by "The St. Vincent de Paul Society," a benevolent organization of colored people. It was a very large school with two departments, the boys under David Brown and the girls under Eliza Anne Cook, and averaging over 150 scholars. When this school was transferred to another house, Rev. Chauncey Leonard, a colored Baptist clergyman, now pastor of a church in Washington, and Nannie Waugh opened a school there, in 1861, that became as large as that which had preceded it in the same place. This school was broken up in 1862 by the destruction of the building at the hands of the incendiaries, who, even at that time, were inspired with all their accustomed vindictiveness towards the colored people. But this was their last heathenish jubilee, and from the ashes of many burnings imperishable liberty has sprung forth.

About the time that Smothers built his school-house, in 1823,

LOUISA PARKE COSTIN'S SCHOOL

was established in her father's house on Capitol Hill, on A street south, under the shadow of the Capitol. This Costin family came from Mount Vernon immediately after the death of Martha Washington, in 1802. The father, William Costin, who died suddenly in his bed, May 31, 1842, was twenty-four years messenger for the Bank of Washington, in this city. His death was noticed at length in the columns of the National Intelligencer in more than one communication at the time. The obituary notice, written under the suggestions of the bank officers, who had previously passed a resolution expressing their respect for his memory, and appropriating fifty dollars towards the funeral expenses, says: "It is due to the deceased to say that his colored skin covered a benevolent heart," concluding with this language: "The deceased raised respectably a large family of children of his own, and in the exercise of the purest benevolence took into his family and supported four orphan children. The tears of the orphan will moisten his grave, and his memory will be dear to all those—a numerous class—who have experienced his kindness;" and adding these lines:

"Honor and shame from *no condition* rise;
Act well your part—there all the honor lies."

John Quincy Adams also, a few days afterwards, in a discussion on the wrongs of slavery, alluded to the deceased in these words: "The late William Costin, though he was not white, was as much respected as any man in the District, and the large concourse of citizens that attended his remains to the grave, as well white as black, was an evidence of the manner in which he was estimated by the citizens of Washington." His portrait, taken by the direction of the bank authorities, still hangs in the directors' room, and it may also be seen in the houses of more than one of the old and prominent residents of the city.

William Costin's mother, Ann Dandridge, was the daughter of a half-breed, (Indian and and colored,) her grandfather being a Cherokee chief, and her reputed father was the father of Martha Dandridge, afterwards Mrs. Custis, who, in 1759, was married to General Washington. These daughters, Ann and Martha, grew up together, on the ancestral plantations. William Costin's reputed father was white, and belonged to a prominent family in Virginia, but the mother, after his birth, married one of the Mount Vernon slaves by the name of Costin, and the son took the name of William Costin. His mother being of Indian descent, made him, under the laws of Virginia, a free born man. In 1800 he married Philadelphia Judge, (his cousin,) one of Martha Washington's slaves, at Mount Vernon, where both were born in 1780. The wife was given by Martha Washington at her decease to her granddaughter, Eliza Parke Custis, who was the wife of Thomas Law, of Washington. Soon after William Costin and his wife came to this city the wife's freedom was secured on kind and easy terms, and the children were all born free. This is the account which William Costin and his wife and his mother, Ann Dandridge, always gave of their ancestry, and they were persons of great precision in all matters of family history, as well as of the most marked scrupulousness in their statements. Their seven children, five daughters and two sons, went to school with the white children on Capitol Hill, to Mrs. Maria Haley and other teachers. The two younger daughters, Martha and Frances, finished their education at the Colored Convent in Baltimore. Louisa Parke and Ann had passed their school days before the convent was founded. Louisa Parke Costin opened her school at nineteen years of age, continuing it with much success till her sudden death in 1831, the year in which her mother also died. When Martha returned from the Convent Seminary, a year or so later, she reopened the school, continuing it till about 1839. This school, which was maintained some 15 years, was always very full. The three surviving sisters own and reside in the house which their father built about 1812. One of these sisters married Richard Henry Fisk, a colored man of good education, who died in California, and she now has charge of the Senate ladies' reception room. Ann Costin was for several years in the family of Major Lewis, (at Woodlawn, Mount Vernon,) the nephew of Washington. Mrs. Lewis (Eleanor Custis) was the granddaughter of Martha Washington. This school was not molested by the mob of 1835, and it was always under the care of a well-bred and well-educated teacher.

THE WESLEYAN SEMINARY.

While Martha Costin was teaching, James Enoch Ambush, a colored man, had also a large school in the basement of the Israel Bethel church on Capitol Hill for a while, commencing there in April, 1833, and continuing in various places till 1843, when he built a school-house on E street south, near Tenth, island, and established what was known as "The Wesleyan Seminary," and which was successfully maintained for 32 years, till the close of August, 1865. The school-house still stands, a comfortable one-story wooden structure, with the sign "Wesleyan Seminary" over the door, as it has been there for 25 years. This was the only colored school on the island of any account for many years, and in its humble way it accomplished a great amount of good. For some years Mr. Ambush had given much study to botanic medicine, and since closing his school he has become a botanic physician. He is a man of fine sense, and without school advantages has acquired a respectable education.

FIRST SEMINARY FOR COLORED GIRLS.

The first seminary in the District of Columbia for colored girls was established in Georgetown, in 1827, under the special auspices of Father Vanlomen, a benevolent and devout Catholic priest, then pastor of the Holy Trinity Church, who not only gave this interesting enterprise his hand and his heart, but for several years himself taught a school of colored boys three days in a week, near the Georgetown College gate, in a small frame house, which was afterwards famous as the residence of the broken-hearted widow of Commodore Decatur. This female seminary was under the care of Maria Becraft, who was the most remarkable colored young woman of her time in the District, and, perhaps, of any time. Her father, William Becraft, born while his mother, a free woman, was the housekeeper of Charles Carroll, of Carrollton, always had the kindest attentions of this great man, and there are now pictures, more than a century and a half old, and other valuable relics from the Carroll family now in the possession of the Becraft family, in Georgetown, which Charles Carroll of Carrollton, in his last days, presented to William Becraft as family keepsakes. William Becraft lived in Georgetown 64 years, coming there when eighteen years of age. He was for many years chief steward of Union hotel, and a remarkable man, respected and honored by everybody. When he died, the press of the District noticed, in a most prominent manner, his life and character. From one of the extended obituary notices, marked with heavy black lines, the following paragraph is copied:

"He was among the last surviving representatives of the old school of well-bred, confidential, and intelligent domestics, and was widely known at home and abroad from his connection in the company of stewards for a long series of years, and probably from its origin, and until a recent date, with the Union hotel, Georgetown, with whose guests, for successive generations, his benevolent and venerable aspect, dignified and obliging manners, and moral excellence rendered him a general favorite."

Maria Becraft was marked from her childhood for her uncommon intelligence and refinement, and for her extraordinary piety. She was born in 1805, and first went to school for a year to Henry Potter, in Washington, about 1812, afterwards attending Mrs. Billings's school constantly till 1820. She then, at the age of 15, opened a school for girls in Dunbarton street, in Georgetown, and gave herself to the work, which she loved, with the greatest assiduity and with uniform success. In 1827, when she was twenty-two years of age, her remarkable beauty and elevation of character so much impressed Father Vanlomen, the good priest, that he took it in hand to give her a higher style of school in which to work for her sex and race, to the education of which she had now fully consecrated herself. Her school was accordingly transferred to a larger building, which still stands on Fayette street, opposite the convent, and there she opened a boarding and day school for colored girls, which she continued with great success till August, 1831, when she surrendered her little seminary into the care of one of the girls that she had trained, and in October of that year joined the convent at Baltimore as a Sister of Providence, where she was the leading teacher till she died, in December, 1833, a great loss to that young institution, which was contemplating this noble young woman as its future Mother Superior. Her seminary in Georgetown averaged from 30 to 35 pupils, and there are those living who remember the troop of girls, dressed uniformly, which was wont to follow in procession their pious and refined teacher to devotions on the sabbath at Holy Trinity Church. The school comprised girls from the best colored families of Georgetown, Washington, Alexandria, and surrounding country. The sisters of the Georgetown convent were the admirers of Miss Becraft, gave her instruction, and extended to her the most heartfelt aid and approbation in all her noble work, as they were in those days wont to do in behalf of the aspiring colored girls, who sought for education, withholding themselves from such work only when a depraved and degenerate public sentiment upon the subject of educating the colored people had compelled them to a more rigid line of demarcation between the races. Ellen Simonds and others conducted the school a few years, but with the loss of its original teacher it began to fail, and finally became extinct. Maria Becraft is remembered, wherever she was known, as a woman of the rarest sweetness and exaltation of Christian life, graceful and attractive in person and manners, gifted, well educated, and wholly devoted to doing good. Her name as a Sister of Providence was Sister Aloyons. From the origin of this convent at Baltimore there has been connected with it a female seminary, which last year was incorporated as

ST. FRANCES ACADEMY FOR COLORED GIRLS.

In this connection it is not inappropriate to give some account of this school, which has done so valuable a work for the education of the colored people of this District and the country at large. For many years it was the only colored school within the reach of the colored people of this District, in which anything was attempted beyond the rough primary training of the promiscuous school, and there are women who still live in this District and elsewhere, whose well-bred families owe their refinements largely to the culture which the mothers a quarter of a century ago, or more, received in this female seminary. It was there that many of the first well-trained colored teachers were educated for the work in this capital.

St. Frances Academy for colored girls was founded in connection with the Oblate Sisters of Providence Convent, in Baltimore, June 5, 1829, under the hearty approbation of the Most Rev. James Whitfield, D. D., the Archbishop of Baltimore at that time, and receiving the sanction of the Holy See, October 2, 1831. The convent originated with the French Fathers, who came to Baltimore from San Domingo as refugees, in the time of the revolution in that island in the latter years of last century. There were many colored Catholic refugees who came to Baltimore during that period, and the French Fathers soon opened schools there for the benefit of the refugees and other colored people. The colored women who formed the original society which founded the convent and seminary, were from San Domingo, though they had some of them, certainly, been educated in France. The schools which preceded the organization of the convent were greatly favored by Most Rev. Ambrose Marechal, D. D., who was a French Father, and Archbishop of Baltimore from 1817 to 1828, Archbishop Whitfield being his successor. The Sisters of Providence is the name of a religious society of colored women who renounce the world to consecrate themselves to the Christian education of colored girls. The following extract from the announcement which, under the caption of "Prospectus of a School for Colored Girls under the direction of the Sisters of Providence," appeared in the columns of the daily National Intelligencer, October 25, 1831, shows the spirit in which the school originated, and at the same time shadows forth the predominating ideas pertaining to the province of the race at that period. The prospectus says:

"The object of this institute is one of great importance, greater, indeed, than might at first appear to those who would only glance at the advantages which it is calculated to directly impart to the leading portion of the human race and through it to society at large. In fact, these girls will either become mothers of families or household servants. In the first case the solid virtues, the religious and moral principles which they may have acquired in this school, will be carefully transferred as a legacy to their children. Instances of the happy influence which the example of virtuous parents has on the remotest lineage in this humble and naturally dutiful class of society are numerous. As to such as are to be employed as servants, they will be intrusted with domestic concerns and the care of young children. How important then it will be that these girls shall have imbibed religious principles and have been trained up in habits of modesty, honesty, and integrity."

It is impossible to conceive of language fuller of profound and mournful import than are these humble, timid words of this little band of colored women, who thus made known the exalted scheme to which they had given themselves. Why this tone of *apology* for embarking in as noble a service as ever entered into the plans of a company of women upon the face of the earth, the attempt to lift the veil of moral and intellectual darkness which they saw everywhere resting like death upon their sex and race?

The sisters purchased a three-story brick building on Richmond street, in which they started their work, but have since, in the admirable success of their enterprise, built large and ample structures, and their school was never in more efficient operation than at the present time. From the first it has been through all its years, almost forty in number, a well-appointed female seminary, amply supplied with cultivated and capable teachers, who have given good training in all the branches of a refined and useful education, including all that is usually taught in well regulated female seminaries. The number of Sisters connected with the convent and seminary has for very many years ranged from 30 to 35. The academy has always been well patronized, comprising girls from every part of the south as well before as since the war. The number the past year was some 170, of which about 45 were boarders, a large number being from Washington and Georgetown. Attached to the convent, also, is a free school for girls and an orphan asylum, and till last year they had for many years maintained also a school for boys. In 1862 some of these Sisters established a female seminary in Philadelphia, which has been very successful. There is also a colored female school in Washington under the care and instruction of teachers formerly attached to this sisterhood. For nearly a quarter of a century this seminary at Baltimore was the school in which the most of the colored girls of this District, who were so fortunate as to receive any of the refinements of school culture, resorted for their training from the founding of the convent down to 1852, when

MISS MYRTILLA MINER'S SEMINARY

for colored girls was initiated in Washington. This philanthropic woman was born in Brookfield, Madison county, New York, in 1815. Her parents were farmers, with small resources for the support of a large family. The children were obliged to work, and the small advantages of a common school were all the educational privileges furnished to them. Hop-raising was a feature in their farming, and this daughter was accustomed to work in the autumn, picking the hops. She was of a delicate physical organization, and suffered exceedingly all her life with spinal troubles. Being a girl of extraordinary intellectual activity, her place at home chafed her spirit. She was restless, dissatisfied with her lot, looked higher than her father, dissented from his ideas of woman's education, and, in her desperation, when about 23 years old, wrote to Mr. Seward, then recently elected governor of her State, asking him if he could show her how it was possible for a woman in her circumstances to become a scholar; receiving from him the reply that he could not, but hoped a better day was coming, wherein woman might have a chance to be and to do to the extent of her abilities. Hearing at this time of a school at Clinton, Oneida county, New York, for young women, on the manual-labor system, she decided to go there; but her health being such as to make manual labor impossible at the time, she wrote to the principal of the Clover-street Seminary, Rochester, New York, who generously received her, taking her notes for the school bills, to be paid after completing her education. Grateful for this noble act, she afterwards sent her younger sister there to be educated, for her own associate as a teacher; and the death of this talented sister, when about to graduate and come as her assistant in Washington, fell upon her with crushing force. In the Rochester school, with Myrtilla Miner, were two free colored girls, and this association was the first circumstance to turn her thoughts to the work to which she gave her life. From Rochester she went to Mississippi, as a teacher of planters' daughters, and it was what she was compelled to see, in this situation, of the dreadful practices and conditions of slavery, that filled her soul with a pity for the colored race and a detestation of the system that bound them, which held possession of her to the last day of her life. She remained there several years, till her indignant utterances, which she would not withhold, compelled her employer, fearful of the results, to part reluctantly with a teacher whom he valued. She came home broken down with sickness, caused by the harassing sights and sounds that she had witnessed in plantation life, and while in this condition she made a solemn vow that whatever of life remained to her should be given to the work of ameliorating the condition of the colored people. Here her great work begins. She made up her mind to do something for the education of free colored girls, with the idea that through the influence of educated colored women she could lay the solid foundations for the disenthralment of their race. She selected this District for the field of her efforts, because it was the common property of the nation, and because the laws of the District gave her the right to educate *free* colored children, and she attempted to teach none others. She opened her plan to many of the leading friends of freedom, in an extensive correspondence, but found especially, at this time, a wise and warm encourager and counsellor in her scheme in William R. Smith, a Friend, of Farmington, near Rochester, New York, in whose family she was now a private teacher. Her correspondents generally gave her but little encouragement, but wished her God speed in what she should dare in the good cause. One Friend wrote her from Philadelphia, entering warmly into her scheme, but advised her to wait till funds could be collected. "I do not want the wealth of Crœsus," was her reply; and the Friend sent her $100, and with this capital, in the autumn of 1851, she came to Washington to establish a Normal school for the education of colored girls, having associated with her Miss Anna Inman, an accomplished and benevolent lady of the Society of Friends, from Southfield, Rhode Island, who, however, after teaching a class of colored girls in French, in the house of Jonathan Jones, on the Island, through the winter, returned to New England. In the autumn of 1851 Miss Miner commenced her remarkable work here in a small room, about fourteen feet square, in the frame house then, as now, owned and occupied by Edward C. Younger, a colored man, as his dwelling, on Eleventh street, near New York avenue. With but two or three girls to open the school, she soon had a room-full, and to secure larger accommodation moved, after a couple of months, to a house on F street north, between Eighteenth and Nineteenth streets west, near the houses then occupied by William T. Carroll and Charles H. Winder. This house furnished her a very comfortable room for her school, which was composed of well-behaved girls, from the best colored families of the District. The persecution of those neighbors, however, compelled her to leave, as the colored family, who occupied the house, was threatened with conflagration, and after one month her little school found a more unmolested home in the dwelling-house of a German family on K street, near the Western market. After tarrying a few months here, she moved to L street, into a room in the building known as "The Two Sisters," then occupied by a white family. She now saw that the success of her school demanded a school-house, and in reconnoitering the ground she found a spot suiting her ideas as to size and locality, with a house on it, and in the market at a low price. She raised the money, secured the spot, and thither, in the summer of 1851, she moved her school, where for seven years she was destined to prosecute, with the most unparalleled energy and conspicuous success, her remarkable enterprise. This lot, comprising an entire square of three acres, between Nineteenth and Twentieth streets west, N and O streets north, and New Hampshire avenue, selected under the guidance of Miss Miner, the contract being perfected through the agency of Sayles J. Bowen, Thomas Williamson, and Allen M. Gangewer, was originally conveyed in trust to Thomas Williamson and Samuel Rhoades, of the Society of Friends, in Philadelphia. It was purchased of the executors of the will of John Taylor, for $4,000, the deed being executed June 8, 1853, the estimated value of the property now being not less than $30,000. The money was mainly contributed by Friends, in Philadelphia, New York, and New England. Catharine Morris, a Friend, of Philadelphia, was a liberal benefactor of the enterprise, advancing Miss Miner $2,000, with which to complete the purchase of the lot, the most, if not all which sum, it is believed, she ultimately gave to the institution; and Harriet Beecher Stowe was another generous friend, who gave her money and her heart to the support of the brave woman who had been willing to go forth alone at the call of duty. Mr. Rhoades, some years editor of the Friends' Quarterly Review, died several years ago, near Philadelphia. Mr. Williamson, a conveyancer in that city, and father of Passmore Williamson, is still living, but some years ago declined the place of trustee. The board, at the date of the act of incorporation, consisted of Benjamin Tatham, a Friend, of New York city, Mrs. Nancy M. Johnson, of Washington, and Myrtilla Miner, and the transfer of the property to the incorporated body was made a few weeks prior to Miss Miner's death. This real estate, together with a fund of $4,000 in government stocks, is now in the hands of a corporate body, under act of Congress approved March 3, 1863, and is styled "The Institution for the Education of Colored Youth in the District of Columbia." The officers of the corporation at this time are John C. Underwood, president; Francis G. Shaw, treasurer; George E. Baker, secretary; who, with Nancy M. Johnson, S. J. Bowen, Henry Addison, and Rachel Howland, constitute the executive committee. The purpose of the purchase of this property is declared, in a paper signed by Mr. Williamson and Mr. Rhoades, dated Philadelphia, June 8, 1858, to have been "*especially for the education of colored girls.*"

This paper also declares that "the grounds were purchased at the special instance of Myrtilla Miner," and that "the contributions by which the original price of said lot, and also the cost of the subsequent improvements thereof, were procured chiefly by her instrumentality and labors." The idea of Miss Miner in planting a school here was to train up a class of colored girls, in the midst of slave institutions, who should show forth, in their culture and capabilities, to the country and to mankind, that the race was fit for something higher than the degradation which rested upon them. The amazing energy with which this frail woman prosecuted her work is well known to those who took knowledge of her career. She visited the colored people of her district from house to house, and breathed a new life into them pertaining to the education of their daughters. Her correspondence with the philanthropic men and women of the north was immense. She importuned congressmen, and the men who shaped public sentiment through the columns of the press, to come into her school and see her girls, and was ceaseless in her activities day and night, in every direction, to build up in dignity and refinement her seminary, and to force its merits upon public attention.

The buildings upon the lot when purchased — a small frame dwelling of two stories, not more than twenty-five by thirty-five feet in dimensions, with three small cabins on the other side of the premises—served for the seminary and the home of the teacher and her assistant. The most aspiring and decently bred colored girls of the District were gathered into the school; and the very best colored teachers in the schools of the District, at the present time, are among those who owe their education to this self-sacrificing teacher and her school. Mrs. Means, aunt of the wife of General Pierce, then President of the United States, attracted by the enthusiasm of this wonderful person, often visited her in the midst of her work with the kindest feelings, and the fact that the carriage from the Presidential mansion was in this way frequently seen at the door of this humble institution did much to protect it from the hatred with which it was surrounded.

Mr. Seward and his family were very often seen at the school, both Mrs. Seward and her daughter, Fanny, being constant visitors; the latter, a young girl at the time, often spending a whole day there. Many other congressmen of large and generous instincts, some of them of pro-slavery party relations, went out there—all confessing their admiration of the resolute woman and her school, and this kept evil men in abeyance.

The opposition to the school throughout the District was strong and very general among the old as well as the young. Even Walter Lenox, who as mayor, when the school was first started, gave the teacher assurances of favor in her work, came out in 1857, following the prevailing current of depraved public sentiment and feeding its tide, in an elaborate article in the National Intelligencer, under his own signature, assailed the school in open and direct language, urging against it that it was raising the standard of education among the colored population, and distinctly declaring that the white population of the District would not be just to themselves to permit the continuance of an institution which had the temerity to extend to the colored people "a degree of instruction so far beyond their social and political condition, which condition must continue," the article goes on to say, "in this and every other slave-holding community." This article, though fraught with extreme ideas and to the last degree proscriptive and inflammatory, neither stirred any open violence nor deterred the courageous woman in the slightest degree from her work. When madmen went to her school-room threatening her with personal violence, she laughed them to shame; and when they threatened to burn her house, she told them that they could not stop her in that way, as another house, better than the old, would immediately rise from its ashes.

The house was set on fire in the spring of 1860, when Miss Miner was asleep in the second story alone, in the night time, but the smell of the smoke awakened her in time to save the building and herself from the flames, which were extinguished. The school girls, also, were constantly at the mercy of coarse and insulting boys along the streets, who would often gather in gangs before the gate to pursue and terrify these inoffensive children, who were striving to gather wisdom and understanding in their little sanctuary. The police took no cognizance of such brutality in those days. But their dauntless teacher, uncompromising, conscientious, and self-possessed in her aggressive work, in no manner turned from her course by this persecution, was, on the other hand, stimulated thereby to higher vigilance and energy in her great undertaking. The course of instruction in the school was indeed of a higher order than had hitherto been opened to the colored people of the District, as was denounced against the school by Walter Lenox in his newspaper attack. Lectures upon scientific and literary subjects were given by professional and literary gentlemen, who were friends to the cause. The spacious grounds afforded to each pupil an ample space for a flower bed, which she was enjoined to cultivate with her own hands and to thoroughly study. And an excellent library, a collection of paintings and engravings, the leading magazines and choice newspapers, were gathered and secured for the humble home of learning, which was all the while filled with students, the most of whom were bright, ambitious girls, composing a female colored school, which, in dignity and usefulness, has had no equal in the District since that day. It was her custom to gather in her vacations and journeys not only money, but everything else that would be of use in her school, and in this way she not only collected books, but maps, globes, philosophical and chemical and mathematical apparatus, and a great variety of things to aid in her instruction in illustrating all branches of knowledge. This collection was stored in the school building during the war, and was damaged by neglect, plundered by soldiers, and what remains is not of much value. The elegant sofa-bedstead which she used during all her years in the seminary, and which would be an interesting possession for the seminary, was sold, with her other personal effects, to Dr. Carrie Brown, (Mrs. Winslow,) of Washington, one of her bosom friends, who stood at her pillow when she died.

Her plan embraced the erection of spacious structures, upon the site which had been most admirably chosen, complete in all their appointments for the full accommodation of a school of one hundred and fifty boarding scholars. The seminary was to be a Female College,

14

endowed with all the powers and professorships belonging to a first-class college for the other sex. She did not contemplate its springing up into such proportions, like a mushroom, in a single night, but it was her ambition that the institution should one day attain that rank. In the midst of her anxious, incessant labors her physical system began so sensibly to fail, that in the summer of 1858, under the counsel of the friends of herself and her cause, she went north to seek health, and, as usual in all her journeys, to beg for her seminary, leaving her girls in the care of Emily Howland, a noble young woman, who came down here for the love of the cause, without money and without price, from the vicinity of Auburn, New York. In the autumn Miss Miner returned to her school; Miss Howland still continuing with her through the winter, a companion in her trials, aiding her in her duties, and consenting to take charge of the school again in the summer of 1859, while Miss Miner was on another journey for funds and health. In the autumn of that year, after returning from her journey, which was not very successful, she determined to suspend the school, and to go forth to the country with a most persistent appeal for money to erect a seminary building, as she had found it impossible to get a house of any character started with the means already in her hands. She could get no woman, whom she deemed fit to take her work, willing to continue her school, and in the spring of 1860, leasing the premises, she went north on her errand. In the ensuing year she traversed many States, but the shadow of the rebellion was on her path, and she gathered neither much money nor much strength. The war came, and in October, 1862, hoping, not vainly, for health from a sea voyage and from the Pacific climate, she sailed from New York to California. When about to return, in 1866, with vivacity of body and spirit, she was thrown from a carriage in a fearful manner; blighting all the high hopes of resuming her school under the glowing auspices she had anticipated, as she saw the rebellion and the hated system tumbling to pieces. She arrived in New York in August of that year in a most shattered condition of body, though with the fullest confidence that she should speedily be well and at her work in Washington. In the first days of December she came here in a dying condition, still resolute to resume her work; was carried to the residence of her tried friend, Mrs. Nancy M. Johnson, and on the tenth of that month, surrounded by the friends who had stood with her in other days, she put off her wasted and wearied body in the city which had witnessed her trials and her triumphs, and her remains slumber in Oak Hill cemetery.

Her seminary engaged her thoughts to the last day of her life. She said in her last hours that she had come back here to resume her work, and could not leave it thus unfinished. No marble marks the resting place of this truly wonderful woman, but her memory is certainly held precious in the hearts of her throngs of pupils, in the hearts of the colored people of this District, and of all who took knowledge of her life and who reverence the cause in which she offered herself a willing sacrifice. Her assistants in the school were Helen Moore of Washington, Margaret Clapp and Amanda Weaver of New York State, Anna H. Searing of New York State, and two of her pupils, Matilda Jones of Washington, and Emma Brown of Georgetown, both of whom, subsequently, through the influence of Miss Miner and Miss Howland, finished their education at Oberlin, and have since been most superior teachers in Washington. Most of the assistant teachers from the north were from families connected with the Society of Friends, and it has been seen that the bulk of the money came from that society. This sketch would be incomplete without a special tribute to Lydia B. Mann, sister of Horace Mann, who came here in the fall of 1856, from the Colored Female Orphan Asylum of Providence, R. I., of which she was then, as she continues to be, the admirable superintendent, and, as a pure labor of love, took care of the school in the most superior manner through the autumn and winter, while Miss Miner was north recruiting her strength and pleading for contributions. It was no holiday duty to go into that school, live in that building, and work alone with head and hands, as was done by all these refined and educated women, who stood from time to time in that humble persecuted seminary. Miss Mann is gratefully remembered by her pupils here and their friends.

Mention should also be made of Emily Howland, who stood by Miss Miner in her darkest days, and whose whole heart was with her in all her work. She is a woman of the largest and most self-sacrificing purposes, who has been and still is giving her best years, all her powers, talents, learning, refinement, wealth, and personal toil, to the education and elevation of the colored race. While here she adopted, and subsequently educated in the best manner, one of Miss Miner's pupils, and assisted several others of her smart girls in completing their education at Oberlin. During the war she was teaching contrabands in the hospital and the camp, and is now engaged in planting a colony of colored people in Virginia with homes and a school-house of their own.

A seminary, such as was embraced in the plan of Miss Miner, is exceedingly demanded by the interests of colored female education in this District and the country at large, and any scheme by which the foundations that she laid so well may become the seat of such a school, would be heartily approved by all enlightened friends of the colored race. The trustees of the Miner property, not insensible of their responsibilities, have been carefully watching for the moment when action on their part would seem to be justified. They have repeatedly met in regard to the matter, but, in their counsels, hitherto, have deemed it wise to wait further developments. They are now about to hold another meeting, it is understood, and it is to be devoutly hoped that some plan will be adopted by which a school of a high order may be, in due time, opened for colored girls in this District, who exceedingly need the refining, womanly training of such a school.*

The original corporators of Miss Miner's Institution were Henry Addison, John C. Underwood, George C. Abbott, William H. Channing, Nancy M. Johnson, and Myrtilla Miner. The objects as expressed in the charter " are to educate and improve the moral and intellectual condition of such of the colored youth of the nation as may be placed under its care and influence."

ARABELLA JONES'S SCHOOL.

About the time that Miss Miner commenced in the northern section of Washington, Miss Arabella Jones, a colored girl, who had just returned from the St. Frances' Academy at Baltimore, opened a female school on the island, called St. Agnes' Academy. She had been educated with the greatest care at home by her father, and had, besides, the benefit of her mother's instruction, a woman of extraordinary native sense, who was for a brief time a pupil of Mrs. Billing in her early girlhood, and from her youth through many years a favorite servant in the family of John Quincy Adams, commencing when he was Secretary of State. Miss Jones had a good English education, wrote and spoke with ease and propriety the French tongue, was proficient in music and in all the useful and ornamental needlework branches. Her father, though a poor man, had on her return from school purchased her a piano and a well-selected library, including a full set of the British poets in handsome binding, bought in London expressly to his order, among which was a specially handsome edition of Shakspeare, the favorite author of the daughter, who not only relished such works, but showed taste and talent in her own poetic effusions, which occasionally found their way into the public press. She taught with great delight and success, for several years, till better compensation was offered to her for her skill with the needle. She was a girl of decided talents, and had her high aims and education found a more fortunate field for display, she would have done more for her sex than fell to her lot to do. In 1857 she was married, and her subsequent life was clouded. She died in 1868 in the 34th year of her age, and was borne to the tomb with distinguished marks of respect without distinction of class or color. At the time of her death she had been appointed to a government clerkship.

MARY WORMLEY'S SCHOOL.

In 1830 William Wormley built a school-house for his sister Mary near the corner of Vermont avenue and I street, where the restaurant establishment owned and occupied by his brother, James Wormley, now stands. He had educated his sister expressly for a teacher, at great expense, at the Colored Female Seminary in Philadelphia, then in charge of Miss Sarah Douglass, an accomplished colored lady, who is still a teacher of note in the Philadel-

---

* Since the above was written, information has been received that Major General O. O. Howard has tendered to the trustees a donation of $30,000 from the building fund of the Freedmen's Bureau, and that they will immediately proceed to erect a first-class building for a female college.

phia Colored High School.   William Wormley was at that time a man of wealth.   His livery stable, which occupied the place where the Owen House now stands, was one of the largest and best in the city.   Miss Wormley had but just brought her school into full and successful operation when her health broke down, and she lived scarcely two years.   Mr. Calvert, an English gentleman, still living in the first ward, taught a class of colored scholars in this house for a time, and James Wormley was one of the class.   In the autumn of 1834 William Thomas Lee opened a school in the same place, and it was in a flourishing condition in the fall of 1835, when the Snow mob dispersed it, sacking the school-house, and partially destroying it by fire.   William Wormley was at that time one of the most enterprising and influential colored men of Washington, and was the original agent of the Liberator newspaper for this District.   The mob being determined to lay hold of him and Lee, they fled from the city to save their lives, returning when General Jackson, coming back from Virginia a few days after the outbreak, gave notice that the fugitives should be protected.   The persecution of William Wormley was so violent and persistent that his health and spirits sank under its effects, his business was broken up, and he died a poor man, scarcely owning a shelter for his dying couch.   The school-house was repaired after the riot and occupied for a time by Margaret Thompson's school, and still stands in the rear of James Wormley's restaurant.   During this period, and for some years previous,

MRS. MARY WALL'S SCHOOL

was doing a great service to the colored people.   Mrs. Wall, whose husband, Nicholas Wall, died some years before she came to this District, was a member of the Society of Friends, and a most benevolent, gentle, and refined woman.   They were Virginians, and were reared in affluence, but reverses at last limited her means, which she had used in her prosperous days with open hand in works of benevolence and charity.   In her widowhood she left her native State, and gave much of her subsequent life to the education of the colored children of this District.   As early as 1824 she had a school in a house which then stood on Fifteenth street, between the residences now owned by Senator Morgan and Representative Hooper.   This school-room was always crowded, and applications, by reason of limited room, were often refused.   The school-room accommodated about 40 pupils.   She continued her school here quite a number of years, and some of the most intelligent and enterprising colored men of Washington owe the best part of their education to this good woman, James Wormley and John Thomas Johnson being of the number.   Her high breeding and culture exerted the most marked influence upon the children of poverty and ignorance whom she thus took by the hand.   Many colored people of this District remember her school and her loving kindness, and bless her memory.   She belonged to the class of southern people, not small in her time, who believed in the education and improvement of the colored race.   William Wall, the distinguished merchant on Pennsylvania avenue, of the firm of. Wall, Robinson & Co., is a son of this truly Christian lady.

BENJAMIN McCOY'S, AND OTHER SCHOOLS.

About this time another school was opened in Georgetown, by Nancy Grant, a sister of Mrs. William Becraft, a well-educated colored woman.   She was teaching as early as 1828, and had a useful school for several years.   Mr. Nuthall, an Englishman, was teaching in Georgetown during this period and as late as 1833 he went to Alexandria and opened a school in that city.   William Syphax among others, now resident in Washington. attended his school in Alexandria about 1833.   He was a man of ability, well educated, and one of the best teachers of his time in the District.   His school in Georgetown was at first in Dunbarton street, and afterward on Montgomery.

The old maxim that " the blood of the martyrs is the seed of the Church," seems to find its illustration in this history.   There is no period in the annals of the country in which the fires of persecution against the education of the colored race burned more fiercely in this District and the country at large than in the five years from 1831 to 1836, and it was during this period that a larger number of respectable colored schools were established than in any other five years prior to the war.   In 1833, the same year in which Ambush's school was started, Benjamin M. McCoy, a colored man, opened a school in the northern part of the city, on L street, between Third and Fourth streets west. In 1834 he moved to Massachusetts avenue, continuing his school there till he went to Lancaster county, Pennsylvania, in the autumn of 1836, to finish the engagement of Rev. John F. Cook, who came back to Washington at that time and re-opened his school. The school at Lancaster was a free public colored school, and Mr. McCoy was solicited to continue another year, but declining, came back, and in 1837 opened a school in the basement of Asbury church, which, in that room and in the house adjoining, he maintained with great success for the ensuing 12 years. Mr. McCoy was a pupil of Mrs. Billing and Henry Smothers, is a man of good sense, and his school gave a respectable rudimental education to multitudes, who remember him as a teacher with great respect. He is now a messenger in the Treasury Department. In 1833 a school was established by Fanny Hampton, in the western part of the city, on the northwest corner of K and Nineteenth streets. It was a large school, and was continued till about 1842, the teacher dying soon afterwards. She was half-sister of Lindsay Muse. Margaret Thompson succeeded her, and had a flourishing school of some 40 scholars on Twenty-sixth street, near the avenue, for several years, about 1846. She subsequently became the wife of Charles H. Middleton, and assisted in his school for a brief time. About 1830 Robert Brown commenced a small school, and continued it at intervals for many years till his death. As early as 1833, there was a school opened in a private house in the rear of Franklin row, near the location of the new Franklin school building. It was taught by a white man, Mr Talbot, and continued a year or two. Mrs. George Ford, a white teacher, a native of Virginia, kept a colored school in a brick house still standing on New Jersey Avenue between K and L streets. She taught there many years, and as early perhaps as half a century ago.

THOMAS TABBS'S SCHOOL

was an institution peculiar to itself. Mr. Tabbs belonged to a prominent Maryland family, and was bred in affluence and received a thorough and polished education. He came to Washington before the war of 1812, and resided here till his death, which occurred 10 years ago. He at once commenced teaching the colored people, and persistently continued to do so as long as he lived. He was called insane by some, but there was certainly a method in his madness. When he could find a school-room he would gather a school, but when less fortunate he would go from house to house, stopping where he could find a group of poor colored children to instruct. At one period he had the shadow of a large tree near the Masonic Lodge at the Navy Yard for his school, and it was there that Alexander Hays, afterwards a teacher in Washington, but then a slave, learned his alphabet. Mr. Tabbs must have spent nearly fifty years in this mode of life, and there are many colored people, well advanced in years, who owe their tolerable education to the instruction of this kind-hearted, singular man. At one time he had a school on A street south, between Seventh and Eighth streets east, and at another had a large school, with an assistant, in the Israel Bethel church. He was an upright man, and the colored people of the older class in the eastern section of Washington remember him with respect and gratitude.

DR. JOHN H. FLEET'S SCHOOL

was opened in 1836, on New York avenue, in a school-house which stood nearly on the spot now occupied by the Richards buildings at the corner of New York avenue and Fourteenth street. It had been previously used for a white school, taught by Mrs. McDaniel, and was subsequently again so used. Dr. Fleet was a native of Georgetown, and was greatly assisted in his education by the late Judge James Morsell, of that city, who was not only kind to this family, but was always regarded by the colored people of the District as their firm friend and protector   John H. Fleet, with his brothers and sisters, went to the Georgetown Lancasterian school, with the white children, for a long period, in their earlier school days, and subsequently to other white schools. He was also for a time a pupil of Smothers and Prout. He was possessed of a brilliant and strong intellect, inherited from his father, who was a white man of distinguished abilities. He studied medicine in Washington, in the office of Dr. Thomas

Henderson, who had resigned as assistant surgeon in the army, and was a practising physician of eminence in Washington. He also attended medical lectures at the old Medical College, corner of Tenth and E streets. It was his intention at that time to go to Liberia, and his professional education was conducted under the auspices of the Colonization Society. This, with the influence of Judge Morsell, gave him privileges never extended here to any other colored man. He decided, however, not to go to Liberia, and in 1836 opened his school. He was a refined and polished gentleman, and conceded to be the foremost colored man in culture, in intellectual force, and general influence in this District at that time. His school-house, on New York avenue, was burned by an incendiary about 1843, and his flourishing and excellent school was thus ended. For a time he subsequently taught music, in which he was very proficient; but about 1846 he opened a school on School-house hill, in the Hobbrook Military School building, near the corner of N street north and Twenty-third street west, and had a large school there till about 1851, when he relinquished the business, giving his attention henceforth exclusively to music, and with eminent success. He died in 1861. His school was very large and of a superior character. One of his daughters is now a teacher in one of the public schools. While Dr. Fleet was teaching on School-house hill,

JOHN THOMAS JOHNSON'S SCHOOL,

on Twenty-third street west, near L north, in the same neighborhood, was also in very flourishing operation. Mr. Johnson is a well-known employé at the Capitol at the present time. He was born and educated in this District, and is a man of intelligence and force of character. He was a pupil of Mrs. Wall, of whose character, as an accomplished teacher and woman, he speaks with the deepest respect. He was also a scholar in Smothers's school and in Prout's. In 1838, when the persecution of the colored people of the District was still raging, he left the city, and on his route west, in search of a more tolerant latitude, stopped at Pittsburg, Pa., where, at the suggestion of Rev. John Peck and J. B. Vashon, esq., he offered himself as a candidate for teacher of the First District school of that city. He had two white competitors. The examination before the board of school managers resulted in the declaration that he was the best qualified for the place, and he accordingly took the position, and taught with eminent success for several years, to the astonishment and admiration of all interested in the school. He finally resigned his place for a more lucrative position as a steward on a Mississippi steamer. In 1843 he came back to his native city, and started a school, as stated in the commencement of this notice, with a zeal and boldness equalled by few of the most courageous of the colored men at that time, when their school-houses were at the mercy of the mob. Shielded by no law, he built a school-house and gathered a school, which, commencing with half a dozen, soon became very large—once numbering as high as 200 and more, and averaging from 150 to 170 well-dressed and well-behaved children, many of whom, now men and women grown, are among the best colored people of this District. He continued his school down to 1849, when he relinquished a work in which he had uniformly achieved decided success. As he was about to retire from the field,

CHARLES H. MIDDLETON'S SCHOOL

was started, in the same section of the city, in a school-house which then stood near the corner of Twenty-second street west and I north, and which had been used by Henry Hardy for a white school. Though both Fleet's and Johnson's schools were in full tide of success in that vicinity he gathered a good school, and when his two competitors retired—as they both did about this time—his school absorbed a large portion of their patronage and was thronged. In 1852 he went temporarily with his school to Sixteenth street, and thence to the basement of Union Bethel church on M street, near Sixteenth, in which, during the administration of President Pierce, he had an exceedingly large and excellent school, at the same period when Miss Miner was prosecuting her signal work. Mr. Middleton, now a messenger in the Navy Department, a native of Savannah, Ga., is free-born, and received his very good education in schools in that city, sometimes with white and sometimes with colored children. When he commenced his school he had just returned from the Mexican war, and his enterprise is especially worthy of being made prominent, not only because of his high style as a teacher, but also because it is associated with

THE FIRST MOVEMENT FOR A FREE COLORED PUBLIC SCHOOL.

This movement originated with a city officer, Jesse E. Dow, who, in 1848 and 1849, was a leading and influential member of the common council. He encouraged Mr. Middleton to start his school, by assuring him that he would give all his influence to the establishment of free schools for colored as well as for white children, and that he had great confidence that the councils would be brought to give at least some encouragement to the enterprise. In 1850 Mr. Dow was named among the candidates for the mayoralty, and when his views in this regard were assailed by his opponents, he did not hesitate to boldly avow his opinions, and to declare that he wished no support for any office which demanded of him any modification of these convictions. The workmen fail, but the work succeeds. The name of Jesse E. Dow merits conspicuous record in this history for this bold and magnanimous action. Mr. Middleton received great assistance in building up his school from Rev. Mr. Wayman, then pastor of the Bethel church, and afterwards promoted to the bishopric. The school was surrendered finally to Rev. J. Y. B. Morgan, the succeeding pastor of the church, who conducted the school as a part of the means of his livelihood.

ALEXANDER CORNISH AND OTHERS.

In the eastern section of the city, about 1840, Alexander Cornish had a school several years in his own house on D street south, between Third and Fourth east, with an average of 40 scholars. He was succeeded, about 1846, by Richard Stokes, who was a native of Chester County, Pa. His school, averaging 150 scholars, was kept in the Israel Bethel church, near the Capitol, and was continued for about six years. In 1840 there was a school opened by Margaret Hill in Georgetown, near Miss English's seminary. She taught a very good school for several years.

ALEXANDER HAYS'S SCHOOL,

was started on Ninth street west, near New York avenue. Mr. Hays was born in 1802, and belonged originally to the Fowler family in Maryland. When a boy he served for a time at the Washington Navy Yard, in the family of Captain Dove, of the navy, the father of Dr. Dove, of Washington, and it was in that family that he learned to read. Michael Tabbs had a school at that time at the Navy Yard, which he taught in the afternoons *under a large tree*, which stood near the old Masonic Hall. The colored children used to meet him there in large numbers daily, and while attending this singular school, Hays was at the same time taught by Mrs. Dove, with her children. This was half a century ago. In 1826 Hays went to live in the family of R. S. Coxe, the eminent Washington lawyer, who soon purchased him, paying Fowler $300 for him. Mr. Coxe did this at the express solicitation of Hays, and 17 years after he gave him his freedom—in 1843. While living with Mr. Coxe he had married Matilda Davis, the daughter of John Davis, who served as steward many years in the family of Mr. Seaton, of the National Intelligencer. The wedding was at Mr. Seaton's residence, and Mr. Coxe and family were present on the occasion. In 1836 he bought the house and lot which they still own and occupy, and in 1842, the year before he was free, Hays made his last payment and the place was conveyed to his wife. She was a free woman, and had opened a school in the house in 1841. Hays had many privileges while with Mr. Coxe, and with the proceeds of his wife's school they paid the purchase money ($550) and interest in seven years. Mr. Hays was taught reading, writing, and arithmetic by Mr. Coxe, his wife, and daughters, while a slave in their family. When the colored people were driven from the churches, in the years of the mobs, Mrs. Coxe organized a large colored Sabbath school in her own parlor, and maintained it for a long period, with the co-operation of Mr. Coxe and the daughters. Mr. Hays was a member of this school. He also attended day schools, when his work would allow of it. This was the education with which, in 1845, he ventured to take his wife's school in charge. He is a man of good sense, and his school flourished. He put up an addition to his house, in order to make room for his increasing school, which was continued down to 1857—16 years from its opening. He had also a night school and taught music, and these two features of his school he has revived since the war. This school contained from 35 to 45 pupils. Rev. Dr. Samson, Mr. Seaton, and Mr. Coxe often visited his school and encouraged him in his excellent work. Thomas Tabbs used also to come into his school and give him aid and advice, as also did John McLeod.

JOSEPH T. MASON'S SCHOOL, IN GEORGETOWN,

was established in 1840, in the rear of Mount Zion church, in a house near where the large free school building for colored children now stands. Mr. Mason was a scholar in Prout's school, and in that of the elder Cook. He was an admirable disciplinarian, and his school, which rarely fell below a hundred members, was conducted with more than common system and thoroughness for more than a quarter of a century, until he became insane, a year or two before the war.

THOMAS H. MASON'S SCHOOL

was commenced in 1859, in his father's house, on L near Twenty-first street west, and has continued without interruption to the present time. This school, prior to the war, averaged about 100, but during and since the war it has been about 50. He is well educated and a very excellent teacher, was a scholar under both Johnson and Fleet, and finished his education at Oberlin. His father was a cousin to Joseph T. Mason.

MR. AND MRS. FLETCHER'S SCHOOL

was opened about 1854, in the building in which Middleton first taught, on I near Twenty-second street. Mr. Fletcher was an Englishman, a well-educated gentleman, and a thorough teacher. He was induced to open the school by the importunities of some aspiring colored young men in that part of the city, who desired first-rate instruction. He soon became the object of persecution, though he was a man of courtesy and excellent character. His school-house was finally set on fire and consumed, with all its books and furniture; but the school took, as its asylum, the basement of the John Wesley Church. The churches which they had been forced to build in the days of the mobs, when they were driven from the white churches which they had aided in building, proved of immense service to them in their subsequent struggles. Mrs. Fletcher kept a variety store, which was destroyed about the time the school was opened. She then became an assistant in her husband's school, which numbered over 150 pupils. In 1858 they were driven from the city, as persecution at that time was particularly violent against all white persons who instructed the colored people. This school was conducted with great thoroughness, and had two departments, Mrs. Fletcher, who was an accomplished person, having charge of the girls in a separate room.

ELIZA ANNE COOK,

a niece of Rev. John F. Cook, and one of his pupils, who has been teaching for about 15 years, should be mentioned. She attended Miss Miner's school for a time, and was afterwards at the Baltimore convent two years. She opened a school in her mother's house, and subsequently built a small school-house on the same lot, Sixteenth street, between K and L streets. With the exception of three years, during which she was teaching in the free Catholic school opened in the Smothers' school-house in 1859, and one year in the female school in charge of the colored sisters, she has maintained her own private school from 1854 down to the present time, her number at some periods being above 60, but usually not more than 25 or 30.

MISS WASHINGTON'S SCHOOL.

In 1857 Annie E. Washington opened a select primary school in her mother's house, on K street, between Seventeenth and Eighteenth streets west. The mother, a widow woman, is a laundress, and by her own labor has given her children good advantages, though she had no such advantages herself. This daughter was educated chiefly under Rev. John F. Cook and Miss Miner, with whom she was a favorite scholar. Her older sister was educated at the Baltimore convent. Annie E. Washington is a woman of native refinement, and has an excellent aptitude for teaching, as well as a good education. Her schools have always been conducted with system and superior judgment, giving universal satisfaction, the num ber of her pupils being limited only by the size of her room. In 1858 she moved to the base- ment of the Baptist church, corner of Nineteenth and I streets, to secure larger accommoda- tions, and there she had a school of more than 60 scholars for several years.

A FREE CATHOLIC COLORED SCHOOL.

A free school was established in 1858 and maintained by the St. Vincent de Paul Society, an association of colored Catholics, in connection with the St. Matthew's church. It was organized under the direction of Father Walter and kept in the Smothers' school-house for two years, and was subsequently for one season maintained on a smaller scale in a house on L street, between Twelfth and Thirteenth streets west, till the association failed to give it the requisite pecuniary support after the war broke out. This school has already been mentioned.

OTHER SCHOOLS.

In 1843, Elizabeth Smith commenced a school for small children on the Island in Wash- ington, and subsequently taught on Capitol hill. In 1860 she was the assistant of Rev. Wm. H. Hunter, who had a large school in Zion Wesley church, Georgetown, of which he was the pastor. She afterwards took the school into her own charge for a period and taught among the contrabands in various places during the war.

About 1850 Isabella Briscoe opened a school on Montgomery street near Mount Zion church, Georgetown. She was well educated and one of the best colored teachers in the District before the rebellion. Her school was always well patronized, and she continued teaching in the District up to 1868.

Charlotte Beams had a large school for a number of years, as early as 1850, in a building next to Galbraith chapel, I street north, between Fourth and Fifth west. It was exclusively a girl's school in its latter years. The teacher was a pupil of Enoch Ambush, who assisted her in establishing her school.

A year or two later Rev. James Shorter had a large school in the Israel Bethel church, and Miss Jackson taught another good school on Capitol Hill about the same time. The above mentioned were all colored teachers.

Among the excellent schools broken up at the opening of the war was that of Mrs. Char- lotte Gordon, colored, on Eighth street, in the northern section of the city. It was in suc- cessful operation several years, and the number in attendance sometimes reached 150. Mrs. Gordon was assisted by her daughter.

In 1841 David Brown commenced teaching on D street south, between First and Second streets, island, and continued in the business till 1858, at which period he was placed in charge of the large Catholic free school, in the Smothers house, as has been stated.

CHURCHES, PAROCHIAL AND SUNDAY SCHOOLS.

No religious sect has, from the earliest history of this District, exhibited so true a Christian spirit towards the colored people as the Catholic. In Georgetown, Rev. Leonard Neale, D. D., the archbishop, who resided there at an early period, and his brother, Rev. Francis Neale, the founder and first pastor of Holy Trinity church, and Father Van Lommel, pastor of the same church in 1827, were all friends of the poor, showing no distinction on account of color. They established schools and gathered to them the ignorant and poor, both white and colored. Father Van Lommel himself taught a school in which the white and colored children were instructed together and gratuitously, in the house that Mrs. Commodore Decatur for many years afterwards occupied near the Georgetown college gate. That the Catholic church was true to the Christian doctrine of the unity of the human race and the equality of all mankind before the altar of worship, was shown in the labors of these representatives of its priesthood. In 1837, when the pro-slavery spirit was enjoying its greatest triumph in this country, Pope Gregory XVI issued his famous anti-slavery bull. He first quotes the bull of 1537, by Paul III, addressed to the Cardinal Archbishop of Toledo, and another, still more comprehensive, by Urban VIII, of 1636, to the collector Jurius, of the Apostolic Chamber of Portugal, "most severely castigating, by name, those who presumed to subject either East or West Indians to slavery; to sell, buy, exchange, or give them away, to separate them from their wives and children, despoil them of their goods and property, to bring or transmit them to other places, or by any means deprive them of liberty, or retain them in slavery," and then proceeds to reprobate, by "apostolical authority, all the above-described offences as utterly unworthy of the Christian name," and, "under the same authority, to rigidly prohibit and interdict all and every individual, whether ecclesiastical or laical, from presuming to defend that commerce in negro slaves," and to declare that, after mature deliberation in council of their Eminences, the Cardinals of the Holy Catholic Church, he was admonished "to invoke in the Lord all Christians, of whatever condition, that none henceforth dare to subject to slavery, unjustly persecute, or despoil of their goods, Indians, negroes, or other classes of men, or be accessories to others, or furnish them aid or assistance in so doing."

Father McElroy, now a resident of Boston, eighty-seven years old, whose life has been as full of pious and benevolent deeds as it is of years, was the assistant pastor of Holy Trinity church of Georgetown, D. C., with Father De Theux, who in 1817 succeeded Father Francis Neale. In 1818 Father McElroy established a Sunday school for colored children, and labored with the utmost devotion to gather the poor and despised children under his instruction. The school was held Sunday afternoon, and was a large and interesting institution. It continued two hours each day, and the children were taught spelling, reading, writing and christian doctrine. Young men and women of the first standing in Georgetown were the teachers, under the superintendence of Father McElroy, and the school was maintained with great efficiency for many years, especially during the service of Father McElroy, who was there five years, till he went to Frederick, Md., in 1822. There are many colored men and women still living in this District, now furrowed and gray with age, who learned to read and write in that school, including some who were slaves at the time.

The Catholic church was as free in all its privileges to the black worshipper as to the white, and in the sanctuary there was no black gallery. It was so in St. Patrick's church, in Washington, under its founder, Father Matthew of blessed memory, who had the friendship of Jefferson and other distinguished public men of his time, and who recognized the poorest and most benighted negro of his parish as inferior to none in all the privileges and duties of the church. The colored people in those days, in all the Catholic churches, not only knelt side by side with the highest personages, but the pews were also free to all. Father John Donelan, the founder of St. Matthew's church, was equally Christian in his impartiality, and this has been the general treatment which the colored people have received from the Catholic church, the cases in which a priest has attempted to make a distinction having been very few and exceptional. The older and more intelligent colored people of the District will fully sustain this statement. The Sisters of the convent in Georgetown have also trained many colored girls in the refined and solid attainments of a good education. The parochial instruction of the churches has always embraced all the children, and it is believed that St. Aloysius church, the last that was built before the war, has not been in the least behind the earlier churches in this respect. Colored people have always held pews there on the same floor with the whites, and there is a large free female colored school in the parochial school building connected with this church, in which there is also a white female school numbering some 250 pupils. The St. Mary's Catholic church at Alexandria in the earlier years manifested a similar Christian spirit, and has continued to do so. The colored people occupied the same floor with the white, and the free pews were occupied without discrimination of color.

When the colored people were excluded from all the Protestant churches of the District in the years of the mobs, the Catholic people stood firm, allowing no molestation of their colored worshippers. When the Sabbath schools for colored children were broken up in every Protestant church in the District, every Catholic church steadily retained its colored children under the usual Sunday instruction, and these schools embraced all ages, from the mere child to the hoary head.   The above brief statements will explain why the colored Catholics here organized but one Catholic church, St. Martin's, though forming a considerable part of the colored population of the District.

The Protestant churches in the District, like the Catholic, seem at first to have had no separate galleries; and children in the Sabbath school, white and colored, sat in the same room on the same seats.   This was the case in the First Baptist church in Washington, which was established in 1802, but at a later day this was changed, the galleries being assigned to the colored people.   But most of the Protestant churches went so far as gradually to limit them to the back seats in the galleries, which so mortified their self-respect as to drive them, in spite of their poverty, to build humble religious homes of their own.   When the new Baptist church was built on Tenth street, which was afterwards sold and converted into a theatre, afterwards known as Ford's Theatre, the gallery was given to the colored people.   This was satisfactory to the majority, but some of the more spirited chafed under the new arrangement.   The church, and its pastor, Rev. O. B. Brown, however, treated their colored members and worshippers with Christian charity.   The pastor was a large-hearted Christian minister, who knew no distinction as to the color of a person's skin at the altar of worship.   When they built on Tenth street, in 1833, the colored members bought the old church, corner of Nineteenth and I streets, for a chapel, in which to hold their social meetings.   Soon afterwards they employed Rev. Mr. Nickens to preach for them temporarily, which resulted in about thirty of the colored members seceding, and organizing a church by themselves.   These seceding members were expelled, and, as the church property was deeded to the *members of the church*, a controversy arose as to the title to the house, which is still litigated in chancery, between the mother church and her colored offspring.

Among the Methodists an alienation of feeling grew up at an earlier date than in the other churches.   As early as 1820 the colored members of the Ebenezer church, on Fourth street east, near Virginia avenue, erected a log building in that vicinity, not far from the present Odd Fellows' lodge, for their social religious meetings and Sabbath school.   About the same time some of the leading members, among them George Bell and George Hicks, already mentioned, becoming dissatisfied with their treatment, withdrew and organized a church in connection with the African Methodist Episcopal church.   At first they worshipped in Basil Sim's rope-walk, First street east, near Pennsylvania avenue, but subsequently in Rev. Mr. Wheat's school-house on Capitol Hill, near Virginia avenue.   They finally purchased the old First Presbyterian church, at foot of Capitol Hill, now known as the "Israel Bethel African Methodist Episcopal church."   Some years later other members of the old Ebenezer church not liking their confined quarters in the gallery, and otherwise discontented, purchased a lot corner of C street south and Fifth street east, built à house of worship, and were organized as the "Little Ebenezer Methodist Episcopal church."   About the year 1835 a third colonization from the original Ebenezer church took place.   Among other grievances, the colored members were dissatisfied with their white pastors because they declined to take the colored children in their arms when administering the rite of baptism.   In 1839 this alienation grew into an open rupture, when thirteen class leaders and one exhorter left the mother church, and, after purchasing a lot on the Island, erected a house and formed a colored church, independent of the Methodist Episcopal body, under the name of the Wesley Zion church, and employed a colored preacher.   Among the prominent men in this separation, still living, were Enoch Ambush, the well-known schoolmaster, and Anthony Bowen, who for many years has been an estimable employé in the Department of the Interior.   Mr. Bowen has been a local preacher for forty years, and under his guidance the St. Paul's colored church on the Island was organized, at first worshipping in E street chapel.

In a volume, by Rev. Benjamin T. Tanner, entitled "An Apology for African Methodism," published in Baltimore in 1867, the statement is made that while the Presbyterians, Lutherans, Congregationalists, and others have opened their Theological schools and colleges to colored men, the Methodist Episcopal denomination has refused them admission even in cases where the colored people have aided in establishing and supporting these schools.

In this connection it may not be inappropriate to refer to the formation of the "African Methodist Episcopal church."   "In November, 1787, the colored people belonging to the

Methodist Society of Philadelphia convened together in order to take into consideration the evils under which they labored, arising from the unkind treatment of their white brethren, who considered them a nuisance in the house of worship, and even pulled them off their knees while in the act of prayer and ordered them to the back seats. For these and various other acts of unchristian conduct they considered it their duty to devise a plan in order to build a house of their own, to worship God 'under their own vine and fig tree.'" The above extract is taken from the historical chapter of the "Book of Church Discipline" of the "African Methodist Episcopal church," and the chapter is signed by Bishop Wm. P. Quinn, Bishop Daniel A. Payne, Bishop Alex. W. Wayman, and Bishop Jabez P. Campbell. Among other prominent men of Philadelphia, Dr. Benjamin Rush was the friend of the colored people, and Bishop White also, who ordained one of their own number, after the order of the Protestant Episcopal church, as their pastor. In 1793 those of Methodist proclivities having concluded to build a church, Rev. Richard Allen gave them the land for the purpose, and with a few others aided them in the work. Francis Asbury, always their friend, and then bishop of the Methodist Episcopal church, officiated at the consecration, and the house was named "Bethel." Thus matters stood until 1816. During this period the colored people of Baltimore, Washington, and other places were oppressed as in Philadelphia, and in April, 1816, they called a general convention in that city, which organized the "African Methodist Episcopal Church." At the same time the first bishop was ordained, Rev. William Allen, who in the year 1799 had been ordained as preacher by Bishop Asbury of the "Methodist Episcopal church."

One of the local preachers of this church, Rev. Thos. E. Green, now connected with the "Pisgah chapel," Washington, when a child was bound out by the orphans' court to Jacob Gideon, a well-known citizen of Washington, and he expresses himself greatly indebted to Mr. and Mrs. Gideon for their kind treatment and the excellent instruction given him.

The number of colored people connected with Protestant Episcopal churches of the District has always been quite small. Christ church, Navy Yard, the oldest church of this denomination in the District, was as impartial and kind in the treatment of its colored worshippers as were the other Protestant churches in their early history. When the Sabbath school was organized the colored children were gathered into it, occupying seats upon the same floor with the white children, and this has been the usual custom of these churches. In their worship the gallery, or a portion of it, has been assigned to the colored worshippers, who, at the administration of the sacrament, are wont to descend and approach the altar when the white communicants have retired. The banishment of the colored members to the back seats at the sacramental table is not, however, peculiar to this church. The Methodist Episcopal people, even in New England, have done likewise. Not long before the war one of the most gifted colored men in the country entered the Elm street Methodist Church in New Bedford, intending to unite with the church, but what occurred while he was present made him depart without doing as he had intended. The following is his statement, [Rev. Mr. Bonney was at that time the pastor:] "After the congregation was dismissed the half dozen colored members descended from the gallery and took a seat against the wall most distant from the altar. Brother Bonney was very animated, and sung very sweetly 'Salvation, 'tis a joyful sound;' and after serving the emblems to all the 'white sheep,' raising his voice to an unnatural pitch and walking to the corner where his black sheep seemed to have been penned, he beckoned with his hand, exclaiming, 'Come forward, colored friends! Come forward! You, too, have an interest in the blood of Christ. God is no respecter of persons. Come forward and take this holy sacrament to your comfort.'"

In Georgetown there seems to have been less of Christian brotherhood in the Episcopal churches towards the colored people than in Washington. In 1821 Rev. Stephen H. Tyng, D. D., and Bishop Charles P. Mac Ilvaine, both then just entered into holy orders, were in Georgetown; the former being pastor of St. John's and the latter of Christ church. These gifted and devout young men knew no distinction in their holy office founded upon the color of the skin, and did not fail to indicate their sentiments on the subject. When Mr. Tyng was invited to the pastorate of St. John's, the vestry made some repairs upon their church. The colored people, who had hitherto entered the same front door with their white brethren and sisters in order to pass up into their gallery, were now furnished a new ingress and egress. A stairway on the outside of the church was run up to a gallery window, which was converted into a door. It is the tradition that Mr. Tyng declined to accept the arrangement on the ground that the faith, which he preached, acknowledged no back stairs to heaven for the humble poor. "The niggers' back stairs to heaven," as the stairway was called, was not used, and it is believed that the colored people entirely abandoned the church because of the project. There was a deep feeling at this period in Georgetown, growing out of this matter of the staircase and the well known views of these two pastors.

The first attempt to found a colored Episcopal church in this District was made in 1867, and the little "St. Mary's chapel" on Twenty-third street west and a small church and congregation are the results. They are not, however, furnished a pastor of their own race—it may be that they have none such in their ministry. This little band of colored people are doing well. They have a large and flourishing Sabbath school, and are using much self-denial and energy in the maintenance of the interests of education in connection with their organization. The pastor is Rev. John M. E. McKee.

The Unitarian church, founded in 1820, and also the Friends'.meeting and the Universalist church, have always been opposed to slavery, and never tolerated unchristian treatment of the colored people. The first named was a New England church in its spirit and membership, as it continues to be. The Orthodox Congregational church, resuscitated after the war or near its close, was always of like spirit.

The *Sabbath school* among the colored people in those times differed from the institution as organized among the whites, as it embraced young and old, and most of the time was given not to the studying of the Bible, but to learning to read. It was the only school which, for a time, they were allowed to enter, and was consequently of vital importance in the history of their education in the District. As the distinction of color in the church grew more prominent the colored Sabbath schools seem to have gradually lost favor, till in 1835 they were swept away as by a storm. The First Presbyterian church of Washington, which then worshipped in the edifice now occupied by the colored Israel Bethel church, at the foot of Capitol Hill, opened a Sunday school for colored people in 1826, which was held regularly every Sunday evening for many years, and in it many men and women, as well as children, learned their alphabet and to read the Bible. Michael Shiner, one of the most remarkable colored men of the District, who remembers almost everything that has occurred at the Navy Yard during his service of some 60 years there, is of this number. Rev. Reuben Post, then the pastor of the church, now Dr. Sunderland's, was the leader in this Sabbath school work, and his church and society fully supported him. There was a colored Sabbath school in the City Hall for a number of years prior to 1831. The Trinity church people were worshipping there in that period, and the school is believed to have been maintained mainly through the efforts of that society. Mr. C. H. Wiltberger and his wife, themselves slave-holders, were the teachers of the school from its organization till its dispersion at the time of the Snow riot.

Christ Church, at the Navy Yard, established a Sabbath school for colored persons some years before the war of 1812. Among those most active in its organization were Rev. Andrew Hunter, the chaplain; Rev. John Chalmers, pastor of the Methodist Ebenezer church; and Mr. John Coyle, an elder in the First Presbyterian church, and a man foremost in every humane and christian work. The school was first held in Christ church, but afterwards moved to a school-house on New Jersey Avenue, used by Rev. Mr. Hunter for a day school, opened by him about the year 1810. Here it was maintained for several years. Mr. Hunter, Mrs. Chalmers, Mrs. William Dougherty, and Mrs. Henry Ingle, the mother of Mrs. Wm. H. Campbell and Mrs. Harvey Lindsley, both of Washington, were the good women who entered heart and hand into these benevolent labors. There are still living in the District colored persons who learned to read and write under their instruction.

OBSERVATIONS AND CONCLUSIONS.

It has been seen that when the rebellion approached, John F. Cook, George F. T. Cook, Enoch Ambush, Miss Miner, Thomas H. Mason, Mrs. Charlotte Gordon, and the St. Vincent de Paul Society had each a very laige school in operation in Washington; Annie E. Washington had a fine select school for the younger class of pupils; Eliza J. Brooks and Elizabeth Smith had each a respectable school for primary scholars; 10 schools, with quite 1,100 scholars, in Washington. Isabella Briscoe, moreover, had quite a large school in Georgetown. In addition to these there were several small daily gatherings of children in private houses; also night schools, which were largely attended by colored men, women, and children.

In passing from the schools whose history embraces more than half a century under the old order of things, it is well to remark that the general character of both the schools and the teachers was of an inferior grade as compared with what followed, when the great band of accomplished teachers from the north came and took up the work in the District in the closing years of the war. Some of those earlier schools, however, have not been surpassed, it is believed, by any that have arisen under the new régime, and others were not much inferior to the old-fashioned district schools of the New England rural towns.*

It is worthy of observation, also, that in no case has a colored school ever failed for the want of scholars. The parents were always glad to send their children, and the children were always ready to go, even when too poor to be decently fed or clothed. When a school failed it was for want of money, and not for want of appreciation of the benefits of education. The same remarkable avidity for learning was then apparent as is now so manifest among the whole body of the colored population of this District.

The facts detailed in this narrative fully substantiate the following propositions:

First. The impression which prevails very generally that the colored people of this District before the war had no schools is unfounded and exceedingly unjust to them.

Second. Public sentiment in the earlier years of the District was not only tolerant of education among the colored people, but positively in favor of it, and it was a common thing for colored and white children to associate together in the same school.

Third. The attendance of colored children at school was as large before the war as it is now in proportion to the free colored population of the District at the respective periods.

Fourth. The colored people of the District have shown themselves capable, to a wonderful degree, of supporting and educating themselves, while at the same time contributing by taxation to the support of white schools, from which they were debarred, and that, too, when in numerous cases they had previously bought themselves and families from slavery at very great expense; their history furnishing an example of courage and success in the midst of trial and oppression scarcely equalled in the annals of mankind.

---

* NOTE.—Since the sketches of the early schools were written, the first prospectus of Miss Jones' school (see page 13) has come to hand, and it is given below as indicating the praiseworthy and honorable ambition of many of the colored people.

Prospectus of St. Agnes' Academy, for colored girls, under the direction of Miss Arabella C. Jones, Washington city, March 10, 1852.

The object of this academy is of great importance, particularly to those who are devoid of schools in their vicinity, and also to society at large. Here the poor are educated gratuitously, the orphans clothed, educated, and a good trade given them. Females in this age are naturally destined to become either mothers of families or household servants. As mothers, is it not necessary that they should be skilled in habits of industry and modesty, in order to transmit it to posterity? As domestics, should they not be tutored to the virtues of honesty, integrity, and sobriety? Last, though not least, many of our citizens of color are emigrating to Liberia, and it is necessary, as well-wishers of our race, that our children be well educated, in order to impart their knowledge to the illiterate. Shall we, my friends, go there to teach, or be taught? As emigrants from a land of intelligence, I answer, to teach.

TERMS:

Boarding and tuition, quarterly	$18 in advance.
French	5 "
Music	10 "
Bedding	2 "
Use of piano	1 "

Parents who are not able to educate their children can address a letter to the proprietor. Scholars are to be provided with one-half dozen towels, all toilet articles, a napkin ring, and desert spoon.

The school is situated in a locality known as the Island. A large house in the city will be procured if duly patronized.

PERIOD II.—1861-1868.

1, CITIES OF WASHINGTON AND GEORGETOWN.

RELIEF SOCIETIES AND FIRST CONTRABAND SCHOOLS.

The first attempt to gather contrabands into schools in Washington, though not the first in the District,, some schools having been opened in the county still earlier by colored teachers, was made by the *American Tract Society* of New York. Several of its agents were here early in March, 1862. Mr. N. Du Bois, a clerk in the Interior Department, who was an active man in the work, kept a careful diary of those times, from which it appears that on Sunday afternoon, March 16, 1862, a meeting of contrabands was called in Duff Green's Row, Capitol Hill, then crowded with this class of people, held as captured material of war   Rev. H. W. Pierson, for some time President of Cumberland College, Ky., as an agent of this Tract Society, called the meeting, and there were present some sixty men, women, and children, fresh from Virginia plantations, all eager to learn.   Mr. Pierson taught them with printed cards, having on them verses of scripture in large letters; and, using "the word method," was very successful, they being able, to their great delight, to read a whole verse in half an hour.   These meetings were followed up daily.   Two or three weeks later another school was started in the basement of the colored Union Bethel church, on M street, near Fifteenth street west, by Rev. George Shearer, who had come with Mr. Pierson from the Princeton Seminary as an associate.   Elizabeth Smith, who had many years maintained a colored school near this church, went to the first meeting, and attracting the notice of Mr. Shearer by her great interest in his "word method" of teaching, was at once drafted into the work as the leading teacher.   The school was held in the late afternoon and in the evening, two sessions daily, and she was always there, maintaining her own day school at the same time.   Dr. Lorenzo D. Johnson, then clerk in a government department, was also present before the close of the first meeting, and making known his great interest in the enterprise, was selected to superintend the work, which he did with the utmost devotion till he was appointed assistant surgeon and assigned to duty at Lincoln hospital in August, 1862, after the second battle of Bull Run.   There were many in those days whose philanthropy found expression in ardent words and eloquent resolutions; but Dr. Johnson was peculiarly a man of action.   This school speedily overflowed, and they went into the hall of the Bethel Society, in the rear of their church, continuing the excellent work till November, when it was found advisable to convert it into a day school with a regular teacher.   This was done by transferring the scholars to the house of Elizabeth Smith, who, opening an additional room, incorporated them with her own school.   Dr. Johnson paid her for the house and services fifteen dollars a quarter, while he continued to exercise authority over the school, down to June, 1863.   Subsequently she received nothing, though the school was continued through the war, aided to some extent by the African Civilization Society.

The Tract Society had its seat of operations at Duff Green's Row till July 5, 1862, when it took up its quarters at what were then known as McLellan barracks, a group of horse-stables, with some small officers' quarters, which were roughly transformed into the homes of the contrabands with their managers and teachers.   General James Wadsworth, then in command of the District, took the profoundest interest in the schools at that place, and was a very frequent visitor and their generous supporter.   The camp was at a later day called Camp Barker, and is now the seat of the fine schools and industrial operations of the New England Friends' Mission, at the junction of Twelfth street west, R north, and Vermont avenue.   The work here was prosecuted with great vigor and discretion, and on Thanksgiving day, 1862, they held the first public entertainment ever given by a contraband school in the District.   Senator Pomeroy, of Kansas, was present, and addressed them in favor of the scheme of a colored colony in Central America, which had then recently been recommended by President Lincoln.   Another remarkable occasion was when the Proclamation of Emancipation took effect, the whole congregated multitude of contrabands, young and old, awaiting upon their knees at midnight the signal of the moment between December

31, 1862, and January 1, 1863, which was to usher in their freedom! Scenes like this occurred in many other places in the District on that occasion. In June, 1863, the Tract Society divided its force, Mr. A. M. Sperry remaining in charge of the Camp Barker school; and one portion, under the charge of Rev. D. B. Nichols, going to Arlington Heights, where Freedmen's Village was then building. There they dwelt in tents, hovels, and out doors till the autumn, when they got into more comfortable quarters. It was at this village that the first thoroughly systematic and genuine contraband school was established within the sight of the national Capitol. The schools in Washington were always of a mixed character, comprising many scholars, young and old, who had long lived in the District, and who had gathered some scraps of knowledge. At Freedmen's Village a spacious school-house was erected, and in the late autumn of 1863, there was a school numbering some 250 children, all fresh from the plantations. Mr. H. E. Simmons, assisted by his wife, was the teacher, and he was a master of his business in the best sense of the term. The school attracted the attention of all really careful observers of the times in this District. Secretary Seward, with his wife and his daughter Fannie, were constant visitors there, as they had been in other years at Miss Miner's school. Mr. Seward went there with the foreign ministers and great public characters who visited the capital in those times, taking them into the school to show them a practical exemplification of the native powers of the negro in his most untutored condition. Senators and representatives also went there to see the marvellous spectacle, and those who watched the school most carefully were the most surprised, so signal were the results. This school at one time comprised some 400 contraband children, and was continued through the war, the work being turned into the hands of the American Missionary Society, 1865, and the village entirely broken up in 1868. Miss Sallie L. Daffin, a native of Philadelphia and a graduate of the "Institute for Colored Youth" of that city, a woman of superior talent, was one of the most useful teachers at the Freedmen's Village.

The National Freedmen's Relief Association, organized in Washington April 9, 1862, had two evening-schools, one at the Bethel church already noticed, and another at the Ebenezer church, under its general management and support that year. In November, 1863, they opened another day-school, in addition to that of Miss Smith's, with two teachers, and in December still another with two teachers, of whom one was colored. Mr. George T. Needham was one of the foremost in organizing and conducting both the evening and day schools at this time. This association was composed mostly of those persons resident in the District, who, realizing the great necessities developed by the war, united temporarily for the emergency, until more systematic and permanent aid could come from the north. The work they initiated was of the greatest service, and not the least portion of it was that of enlisting the sympathies of their friends in other parts of the country.

In June, 1863, *Dr. Johnson organized a school* at Lincoln hospital, seconded by Dr. Magee, the surgeon in charge. It was opened in the chapel, and Miss Laura Gates, of Pennsylvania, whose brother commanded the company of Veteran Reserves on duty there, was employed as teacher. She was allowed one ration from the hospital and $20 a month, which monthly allowance was paid by Dr. Johnson for two months. He also procured books and clothing from northern friends and contributions to pay the teacher. Another teacher was subsequently employed. The school was for the contraband people about the hospital, and comprised all ages, numbering about 50.

The American Tract Society of Boston was represented in the year 1862 and 1863 by their agent, Rev. J. W. Alvord, who rendered an important service in furnishing the excellent school and religious books, which the society had very wisely compiled and published for schools of that class then organizing in the District. Mr. Alvord was afterwards appointed to and still holds the responsible position of general superintendent of the educational work of the Freedmen's Bureau throughout all the southern States.

THE APPEAL TO THE COUNTRY.

In the vain hope that Congress would give substantial aid to the cause, the friends of colored schools had struggled through more than two years, doing something to meet the stupendous emergency. In the first months of 1864 the extraordinary condition of things was brought to the notice of the country through the public press. It was estimated that there were in the District and vicinity 30,000 or 40,000 colored people from the plantations, all anxious for instruction, while but 2,000 or 3,000, at most, were provided with the slightest privileges of an educational kind. A very large number of government clerks and other friends of the cause in Washington, who had been sustaining night schools through the previous year, at this time organized an "Association of Volunteer Teachers," and sent forth an appeal under its sanction, setting forth in clear and forcible language the facts in the case.. This appeal, dated April 16, 1864, was written by A. E. Newton, who had been in the work as a teacher and who was destined to be an eminently wise and conspicuous leader in the great work which was then opening in the District.

RELIEF SOCIETIES CONTINUED.

The American Missionary Association sent its agents in the summer of 1862, but finding the Tract Society of New York on the ground in full force they retired without further demonstrations that year. In February, 1864, they sent Mr. William J. Wilson, a well known colored teacher of Brooklyn, N. Y., to enter upon the work. He immediately started a school in the hall of Asbury church. Mr. A. M. Sperry, who, assisted by Miss Georgiana Willets, had been in charge of the Tract Society's work at Camp Barker after Mr. Nichols took charge at Freedmen's Village, being, with his assistant, ordered south by the society in June, 1864, surrendered his school to Mr. Wilson, who immediately assumed charge, with his wife as assistant, continuing energetically in that work till the camp broke up in the autumn of 1866. The school was held in the chapel which the Tract Society built, and which the Missionary Association purchased at this time. It had one spacious hall and two recitation rooms, and here a school averaging at least 250 scholars was kept up for more than two years, the number sometimes reaching 400 men, women, and children. It was probably the largest school ever seen in a single room in the District, and, considering its magnitude and miscellaneous nature, was eminently successful under the vigorous and intelligent management of those teachers, but it was not possible to attain such results as were developed under the system of graded schools organized in 1865 by the Pennsylvania and New York Relief Societies under Mr. A. E. Newton. Mr. Wilson went from Camp Barker to the Third street Baptist church in the autumn of 1866, opening there a large school, which was continued for one year by his wife and daughter under the auspices of the Missionary Association, and with excellent success. In November, 1864, this society had in operation the school at Camp Barker, a large school in Georgetown, another on the Island in Washington, and a fourth in Soldiers' Free Library, embracing 11 teachers, with two evening schools, in all embracing quite 1,000 scholars. This association was organized September 2, 1849, and originated in a dissatisfaction with the neutral policy of other missionary societies on the slavery question.

The Pennsylvania Freedmen's Relief Association, in response to the "teachers'" appeal, widely disseminated through the northern States, came resolutely upon the ground, and commenced operations in May, 1864, in the Union Wesley church, Twenty-third street west, and in June opened another school in the Zion Wesley church, Island, with two teachers in each, under the superintendence of Mr. Rogers, an excellent young man from Massachusetts, who died that season of typhoid fever. In the autumn they established a school in Galbraith chapel, L street between Fourth and Fifth, and still another in Georgetown in the Mount Zion church, the Miss Chamberlains taking in charge these two last-named schools. In the Mount Zion church school a second and third teacher were soon added. In December, 1864, the society bought a house and stable on L street near Nineteenth street west, and having fitted up the latter, with an industrial establishment attached, at a cost of about $3,000, opened two schools, using the house for the teachers' home. January 1, 1865, Mr. A. E. Newton became the superintendent, also opening their schools in Alexandria, and at this time and the following winter the society did the largest work of any organization, and did not withdraw from the field until 1868. Some of the first merchants and men of wealth of Philadelphia were at the bottom of these operations, among whom may be mentioned J. Miller McKim, an old anti-slavery man ; the brothers Marmaduke Cope and Francis R. Cope, Friends, well known for their works of benevolence. The president of the society was

15

Stephen Caldwell, at that period acting as president of the United States revenue commission. The secretary was James Rhoads, also conspicuous in many of the best efforts to improve the African race.

The Philadelphia Friends' Freedmen's Relief Association was here with like spirit in the same month, starting their first school in Union Wesley church, Twenty-third street west. They soon bought a lot on Nineteenth street near the boundary, and built a large school-house, costing $6,000, which before winter was filled with scholars under an admirable corps of teachers. The location, however, did not prove to be a favorable one, and in 1866 the lot and house were sold and the school given up.

The African Civilization Society was also at work in the early summer, opening a school in the hall of the Union Bethel church, on M street near Fifteenth street. In 1865 and 1866 Rev. Benjamin W. Arnett, colored and a native of Pennsylvania, conducted a large school supported by this society.

The Reformed Presbyterian Mission, in the course of the same summer, purchased a tract of land on First street west between N and O, (Island,) and erected sixteen dwellings, with a chapel for religious and educational purposes. This location was in the extreme southern section of the city, where the colored population was large and mostly made up of contra-bands, as it still continues to be. A large school was soon organized under the direction of Rev. J. Bayliss, who was succeeded by Rev. J. M. Armour. In the early part of 1867 Rev. J. M. Johnston was made superintendent, and in the autumn of that year the school was removed to a barrack building on Sixth street west near M street south. It is divided into four departments, with nearly 200 scholars, under the care of excellent teachers—Miss Sarah E. Moore, of East Craftsbury, Vermont; Miss Helen M. Johnston, Miss Kate E. Trumbull, and Miss Eunice A. Jameson, of Logan county, Ohio. Miss Moore entered upon the work in 1865, the others in 1867. Religious services and a large Sabbath school, under eight teachers, are held on Sundays. Nearly all the families represented in the school belonged to the slave population of Virginia, and the improvement that has been wrought in both children and parents by the persevering labors of this mission forms one of the most interesting and encouraging chapters in the educational work in the District.

The Old School Presbyterian Mission in 1864 opened a school in Georgetown, in the basement of the Presbyterian church on Bridge street, and another in Lincoln Hospital chapel, east of the Capitol. These were flourishing and useful schools, and were continued until February, 1867. The first superintendent was Rev. Mr. Aiken, who was succeeded by Dr. John A. E. Walk. Among the teachers in the Georgetown school was Miss Emma L. Crane, now in charge of the grammar school in the Brick school-house, Island.

In May, 1864, there were in operation 12 day schools, with 25 teachers and about 1,300 scholars; also, 36 night schools, with 36 teachers and about 1,350 scholars. The night schools were generally continued with interest through the year, though some of those depending on volunteer teachers expired from neglect. The Volunteer Association of Teachers did good service, but was disbanded in the spring of 1865. (This association was made up mostly of department clerks, and was quite distinct from that organized afterwards among the regular teachers of Washington, Georgetown, and Alexandria.) The night teachers were paid $10 a month through private contributions. In the autumn of 1864, and through the winter, aid came with great generosity from the north.

The New York Freedmen's Relief Association was actively engaged in the work in 1864 with a vigor not inferior to that of any other organization in the field. For three years their schools were widely known for the large and generous scale on which they were operated, and for their excellent character. Their M street school, as it was called, comprising from eight to ten departments, with an average attendance of over six hundred scholars, and directed by Mr. A. E. Newton, excited the deepest interest among all who were observant friends of the cause in those years. One of the first teachers sent by this association was Rev. B. W. Pond, of Maine, who opened a school early in the summer of 1864 in the basement of Asbury church, Eleventh and K streets. This was a pay school, a small charge for tuition being made, but many who were unable to meet this expense were admitted. In the following winter two portable houses were sent from Boston by the association, into which the school was moved after their erection on M street near Massachusetts avenue. In 1865 Mr. Pond was sent by the association to North Carolina as superintendent of their operations there, and he was succeeded by Miss Julia A. Lord, who was at that time teaching in the Lincoln Institute, on the Island. When the hospital barracks, near by, at the corner of M and Fourteenth streets, were taken by the association, Miss Lord was placed in charge of the grammar school, and the portable buildings were used for the large infant department. The grammar school furnished to the Howard University, when its preparatory department was opened in May, 1867, a larger number of scholars than any other school in the city. Of that department Miss Lord is now one of the principals.

The New England Freedmen's Aid Commission, supported by the Baptists of Boston, established the "Boston School," so called, corner of Nineteenth and I streets, in September, 1864. In November, 1864, this school was graded, Miss R. S. Capron, of Massachusetts, being its principal till the ensuing January, when Miss Lucy A. Flagg, a young lady of much talent and remarkable capability in her work, succeeded to the place, continuing there till her health failed in 1866. In the spring of that year the school was transferred to the American Baptist Home Missionary Society of Boston, and by them organized as a Normal school, and still later converted into "The Wayland Theological Seminary." The above Commission was a different organization from the New England Freedmen's Aid Society.

The New England Freedmen's Aid Society did an excellent work in taking charge of the first colored public school ever opened in the District, and at that time the only one. It was opened March 1, 1864, in the colored Ebenezer church, Capitol Hill, but in May, 1865, was removed to the school building erected for them on C street. They added two teachers and two schools, supporting the four teachers and filling the house with scholars, the average attendance being over 300. The first teachers were Miss Emma V. Brown, colored, one of Miss Miner's favorite scholars and also her assistant, and Miss Frances W. Perkins, of New Haven, Connecticut. Miss Brown was afterwards placed by the trustees in charge of the O street grammar school, which she conducted in a most praiseworthy manner, until failing health, last year, compelled her to resign. As is hereafter mentioned in connection with the history of the public schools, Miss Perkins was instrumental in obtaining funds for erecting this building, the first public school house in the District.

The New England Friends' Mission also came in 1864, and still continues its very excellent work. In the autumn of that year they purchased a large tract of land on Thirteenth street between R and S north, built a store, and furnished goods at cost to the colored people. In the following winter they opened schools in the government buildings, which were turned over to them, teaching a large school of women to sew and the children to braid straw. A day school was organized in the autumn of 1865, and in the winter a second was opened, the two comprising some 150 children, with two teachers. In 1866 and 1867 there were five teachers, with two hundred scholars. At the present time this school is arranged in four departments, under the care of Miss·H. S. Macomber, of New Bedford, Massachusetts, a lady of cultivation, and an admirable principal, with four excellent assistants, all ladies of refinement—Miss Mary C. Lawton and Miss Susan H. Pierce, of New Bedford; Miss Mary E. Oliver and Miss Mary E. Gove, of Lynn, Massachusetts. The important work of visiting the colored families and children at their homes is committed to Miss Sarah E. Wall, of Worcester, Massachusetts, who has labored here assiduously for five years for the good of the colored people. She is also in charge of the sewing department, an important branch of the industrial work. The school now numbers more than 250, and is full to overflowing, rendering it necessary to refuse many applications almost daily. A flourishing Sabbath school has also been maintained from the beginning, averaging about 150 scholars, with ten or twelve teachers. In 1865 more land was purchased and several houses erected, which were sold on easy terms, as intended, to industrious colored families, the monthly rent being credited as purchase money. The school is supported by the New England Friends' yearly meeting, and in an unobtrusive and judicious manner is accomplishing great and permanent good. Among its generous and active supporters from the first has been Hon. Joseph Grinnell, of New Bedford, who often comes to visit it, giving his personal attention to its support and management. The Trustees of the public schools have aided this school so far as to furnish fuel the past year. From the organization of the school in October, 1865, to June, 1867, Richard Battey, from Blackstone, Mass., was the superintendent; since which time Mr. and Mrs. John C. Gove, from Lynn, Mass., have had the general management. About two-thirds of the scholars are boys.

"*The Washington Christian Union,*" an organization of this city, now actively engaged in educational work among the colored people, originated in or grew out of the "Young Men's Unitarian Association, which was formed February 3, 1866, its object being general missionary and christian work among the needy of all classes. Early in 1867, as members of other denominations had for some time been their co-workers and given substantial aid, and also for the purpose of extending their work and making it more effective, it was judged advisable to adopt a new name for the Association, and invite the co-operation of all Christian and benevolent people. At the same time the pressing necessities existing among the freedmen in the District claimed all the resources and enlisted the sympathies of the "Union." Accordingly, on the 2d of May of that year, (1867,) a night school especially for adult colored persons, at first consisting of 15 scholars, but the number soon ranging from 100 to 150, was opened at the Lincoln Institute, or E street chapel, on the Island, and was conducted by volunteer teachers. In the autumn the Trustees of colored public schools gave them the use of two rooms in the new brick school-house corner of Ninth and E streets, into which they moved about November 1, the rent of the Lincoln Institute having been paid by the "Freedmen's Bureau." The school is still continued at the same place with gratifying success, though the number of scholars has somewhat decreased. Mr. W. H. Treadway, of the Treasury Department, has had the immediate charge of the school, aided by other members of the "Union."

The first superintendent appointed by the "Christian Union" was Mr. W. A. White, but he was soon succeeded by Mr. J. R. Fletcher, of the Treasury Department, who was then conducting an independent night school and a Sabbath school, in the Free Library building, Judiciary Square. In the autumn Mr. Fletcher was made and still continues General Superintendent of all the educational work of the society, and in January, 1868, his night school was formally included in its operations.

Another night school has just been opened (January, 1869,) in the O street colored school-house, which numbers over 200 scholars of all ages, children, parents, and grandparents seated together learning to read and write. The president of the Union, Mr. James M. Blanchard, late of the Patent Office, has charge of this school, assisted by nine or ten excellent teachers.

These night schools have done and are doing a very important work, most of those attending them being intelligent and ambitious adult scholars, who are unable to attend the day schools. All the labor of instruction and of general management has been done from the first by volunteer, unpaid teachers. The officers of the society are, James M. Blanchard, President; John E. Mason and J. M. Jayne, Vice-Presidents; F. S. Nichols, Secretary; W. H. Treadway, Corresponding Secretary.

The Universalists of Maine.—One of the best day schools in the District, though continued for less than two years, was that in the Lincoln Institute in 1867 and 1868, taught by *Miss Julia C. Chase*, of South Livermore, Maine, and supported by the *Universalists* of that State. The school numbered about 50, and perhaps in no school in the District have the scholars been more attached to their teacher or made more rapid progress. Miss Chase came in March, 1866, teaching through the remainder of that school year in the school of the New York Freedmen's Association, in the Capitol Hill barracks. In the following winter she opened her own school on the Island, and taught until June, 1868. Her success, like that of Miss Elwell in the Fourteenth street school, shows how much good can be accomplished by one faithful teacher. The Lincoln Institute building, or E street chapel, was built in 1858 by what is now known as the St. Paul's African Methodist Episcopal church, which in 1862 moved into their new edifice on E street between Ninth and Tenth streets.

Miss Elwell's school.—Among the teachers of the *New York Freedmen's Relief Association* school on M street, corner of Fourteenth street, in 1865 and 1866, was Miss Rebecca R. Elwell, of Hartford, Connecticut. In the autumn of 1867 she was engaged by the *Hartford*

Relief Society, and opened a school in Carroll Hall, on Fourteenth street near Pennsylvania avenue. The next year she moved down Fourteenth street nearer the canal, in the section known as "Murder Bay," where she still remains. Her school room is in a small Baptist church, and, without an assistant, she has charge of about 70 colored children, most of them belonging to the poorest classes, and gathered from the hovels and by-ways of the city. Among the benevolent operations of the District, there is no one demanding more self-denying labor than this ; but in the remarkable love of the scholars for their teacher, as well as in their improvement, she finds a rich reward. Her records show many rare cases of faithful attendance and good conduct, and the desire for knowledge among these more unfortunate colored children is fully equal to that shown among the more favored. Several of the boys, from ten to twelve years of age, have been marked only once or twice for either absence or tardiness during a whole year, and even those resulting sometimes from sickness. This school was last year organized as one of the public schools, the Trustees providing furniture, books, fuel, &c., but the salary is still paid by the Hartford Relief Society. Miss Elwell commenced her benevolent work early in 1865, in connection with the Pennsylvania Freedmen's Relief Association, on the Island.

The Associations maintained through the school year 1864–'65, in the two cities, 27 day schools, comprising 3,588 scholars under the charge of 64 teachers, and 18 night schools with 1,020 scholars and 46 teachers. Nearly all the Societies continued their labors during the two following years, and two additional Societies joined in the work.

The following tables give the names of most if not all of the Associations, and the extent of their operations. The numbers given are in some cases only general estimates or averages, but are based on trustworthy information, and even where the fullest records are preserved there were necessarily great fluctuations from month to month:

Schools of the Relief Societies, May, 1864.

	Schools.	Teachers.	Scholars.
National Freedmen's Relief Association, District of Columbia	5	11	500
American Tract Society, N. Y.................................	1	2	100
African Civilization Society	1	2	100
Reformed Presbyterian Mission, (one night school)	2	4	200
Pennsylvania Freedmen's Relief Association......................	1	2	150
Philadelphia Friends' Freedmen's Relief Association	1	2	150
Dr. L. D. Johnson, (one night school)	2	2	100
Trustees of Colored Public schools...........................	1	2	100
Volunteer Teachers' Association, (night schools).................	12	34	1,250
Total	26	61	2,650

Day Schools, 1864–'65.

	Schools.	Teachers.	Scholars.
Pennsylvania Freedmen's Relief Association	6	14	816
New York Freedmen's Relief Association	5	9	450
American Missionary Association, New York	4	11	732
Philadelphia Friends' Freedmen's Relief Association	2	6	360
African Civilization Society, New York	2	3	180
Old School Presbyterian Mission	2	5	350
Reformed Presbyterian Mission, Pittsburg	1	4	200
New England Freedmen's Aid Commission, Boston	2	4	160
New England Freedmen's Aid Society, Boston, [took charge of public school]	3	4	200
American Free Baptist Mission Society, New York	1	1	80
Private school, Miss Goodenow, Maine	1	1	60
Total	29	62	3,588

Night Schools, 1864–'65.

	Schools.	Teachers.	Scholars.
Volunteer Teachers' Association	10	22	500
Old School Presbyterian	2	7	100
American Missionary Association	4	8	270
Soldiers' Free Library	1	6	100
Reformed Presbyterian Mission	1	3	50
Total	18	46	1,020

During the above school year of 1864–'65, there were also in operation six private colored schools taught by colored teachers, with an average attendance of 340 scholars. It has been stated that the American Tract Society, N. Y., partially in the autumn of 1863 and finally in 1864, withdrew from their extended field of operations in Washington that they might concentrate their force at the Freedmen's Village, Arlington, where the need of humane and christian work was so great.

Day Schools, May, 1865. (*Near Washington.*)

	Schools.	Teachers.	Scholars.
American Tract Society at Freedmen's Village	1	3	242
Miss Emily Howland, near Arlington	1	1	100
Miss Atkinson, at Camp Wadsworth	1	1	50
Pennsylvania Freedmen's Relief Association at Alexandria	1	3	180
New England Freedmen's Aid Society	1	3	170
New York Freedmen's Relief Society	2	4	240
Government Superintendent of Freedmen	3	10	269
Reformed Presbyterian Mission, Xenia, Ohio	1	5	240
Private Colored Schools	8	12	600
Total	19	42	2,091

Day Schools, 1865–'66.

	Schools.	Teachers.	Scholars.
Pennsylvania Freedmen's Relief Association, Philadelphia	9	17	858
New York Freedmen's Relief Association, New York	8	12	604
American Missionary Association, New York	8	11	594
American Baptist Home Missionary Society, New York	3	7	284
Philadelphia Friends' Freedmen's Relief Association	2	6	376
New England Freedmen's Aid Society	4	4	315
New England Friends' Mission	2	3	180
Old School Presbyterian Mission, Pittsburg	2	5	373
Reformed Presbyterian Mission	1	3	186
African Civilization Society, New York	2	2	108
Bangor Freedmen's Relief Associaton	1	1	52
Total	42	71	3,930

In May, 1865, the Volunteer Teachers' Association was disbanded, and their ten *Night Schools,* with 625 scholars, were continued by the teachers of the day schools.

Day Schools, 1866–1867.

In the autumn of 1866 there was a consolidation of the three Relief and Aid Societies of New York, Pennsylvania, and New England, for the purpose of more systematic operations. They had their headquarters at New York city, with branch offices at Boston, New York, and Philadelphia. In 1866–'67 the records show as follows:

	Schools.	Teachers.	Scholars.
New York Branch Freedmen's Union Commission	15	17	1,041
Pennsylvania Branch Freedmen's Union Commission	15	17	849
New England Branch Freedmen's Union Commission	4	4	217
American Missionary Association	8	9	507
American Baptist Home Missionary Society	3	6	101
New England Friends' Mission	2	5	267
Reformed Presbyterian Mission	5	5	297
Bangor Freedmen's Aid Society	1	1	74
Theological Institute and University, Rev. Dr. Turney	2	5	75
St. Martin's Church, colored, Catholic	2	4	350
Trustees of Colored Schools	5	7	450
Total	62	80	4,228

In the autumn of 1867, these aid organizations nearly all concluded to withdraw from the field, upon the supposition that the Trustees of colored schools were able to fully assume their work. Mr. A. E. Newton, who had been for three years in the work, persistently urged otherwise, and the New York and Pennsylvania "branches," of which he had been the superintendent, consented to return each 8 teachers; the New England Friends, 5; the Reformed Presbyterian Mission, 2; the Hartford, the Bangor, and the Holliston, Mass. Associations each, 1; the Universalists of Maine, 1; the New England F. A. Commission and the Rochester Anti-Slavery Society, each a teacher of sewing. Total, 29. In February, 1867, there was 24 night schools in successful operation.

The following is a general estimate of the expenditures of the leading benevolent agencies:

Pennsylvania F. R. Association, (Pa. branch committee)	$32,500
New York F. R. Association, (N. Y. branch committee)	24,000
New England F. A. Society, (N. E. branch committee)	6,000
American Missionary Association	14,500
Philadelphia Friends	13,500
New England Friends	7,000
Reformed Presbyterian Mission	11,500
O. S. Presbyterian Mission	6,500
American Baptist Home Missionary Society, (including N. E. F. A. Commission)	8,000
African Civilization Society	3,000
American Free Baptist Mission	1,000
National F. R. Association, D. C. (contributed from the north)	1,500
American Tract Society	1,000
Miscellaneous contributions	5,000
Total Northern aid in the four years	135,000

This estimate, made by superintendent Newton, a man of great precision, does not embrace the very extensive donations of books, school furniture, and clothing. The expenditure was divided in the several years about as follows: 1863-4, $8,500; 1864-5, $39,000; 1865-6, $35,500; 1866-7, $35,000; 1867-8, $17,000. Total, $135,000. Add to this amount $25,000 contributed in books, school furniture, and clothing, which is undoubtedly an under estimate, and there is the sum of $160,000 which was, with open hands and hearts, poured into the noble and triumphant work of these years by the patriotic North, and that too while the same agencies were extending their beneficence in almost all parts of the south.

The character of the teachers sent into this work by these benevolent agencies was of the highest order, a large proportion of them young women of solid and refined culture, apt to teach, experienced in the vocation, and all deeply interested in the self-denying labor. Mr. Newton was the leading spirit, and was admirably fitted for the position. While a clerk in the Quartermaster's office he commenced his work as the teacher of a night-school. In January, 1866, he was appointed superintendent by the Pennsylvania Freedmen's Relief Association, subsequently receiving the same appointment from the New York Freedmen's Relief Association. Having resigned his clerkship, he gave himself wholly to the schools of these and other societies till, in the autumn of 1867, he was also made superintendent of the colored public schools by the trustees, fulfilling all these arduous and complicated trusts with extraordinary efficiency—giving place to a new superintendent, appointed by the trustees last year. The teachers in November, 1865, were organized into an association for the purpose of securing more system and harmonious action. This association met monthly, and the whole body of teachers—nearly all females—were invariably present, and their meetings were continued for two years, accomplishing a vast amount of good. The first teacher who had great success in bringing order out of chaos was Miss Lucy A. Flagg, of Massachusetts, who made the Boston school, corner of 19th and I street, in 1865, a model of order and thoroughness. The New York school, at the junction of 14th and M streets, was however the first of these schools in establishing something like a graded system in the true sense of the term. This school not only had better buildings than the Boston school, but it also had Mr. Newton from the first to the last as its special superintendent. In Miss Julia A. Lord, the principal of its highest department, it had also a teacher eminently fitted for her place, as in fact were all the other nine teachers during those years. Nor should the name of Eliza A. Chamberlain, of Massachusetts, be omitted, who came here in 1866 and entered into the work in Georgetown with the greatest zeal. Her superior qualifications find an ample witness in the school in which she still continues to act as principal in that city.

THE COLORED ORPHANS' HOME.

This is one of the most interesting and useful institutions of an educational nature connected with the colored people that has been established in this District. Its origin was singular. Late in the autumn of 1862, the contraband families, which had gathered in great numbers in the contraband camps of Washington, were transferred to Arlington Heights by order of the War Office. The order, which was to transfer all the *families*, was executed, leaving some 40 or 50 orphan children, belonging to *no family*, in the abandoned camps in utter desolation. This contraband camp was subsequently called Camp Barker, and was on the north side of the city, between Twelfth and Thirteenth streets. The ground is now occupied by the New England Friends' school. The benevolent women of the city immediately made these poor outcasts temporarily comfortable in the old camp, and went resolutely to work to provide for them a Christian home. They formed an association, and fed, clothed, sheltered, taught them, and ultimately built an asylum for them and other colored orphans. The original meeting was at the rooms of Mrs. James W. Grimes, January 31, 1863. Mrs. B. F. Wade, Mrs. James Harlan, Mrs. S. C. Pomeroy, Mrs. Henry Wilson, Mrs. A. H. Gibbons, Mrs. Daniel Breed, and Mrs. J. F. Potter, were present. Mrs. Pomeroy was selected to preside, and they proceeded directly to the work of establishing " an Asylum for aged and destitute Colored Refugees and Colored Orphans," of which classes there were multitudes then " collected in the contraband camps in and around Washington." The next meeting was at the residence of Sayles J. Bowen, February 5, when articles of association, presented by

Mrs. Gibbons, of New York, were adopted, and an organization effected, with the following officers: Mrs. Pomeroy, president; Mrs. Grimes, vice-president; Mrs. Mary E. Webster, of Connecticut, treasurer; Mrs. Daniel Breed, secretary. The association was incorporated by Act of Congress approved February 16, 1863; and on the same day an organization, under the charter, was effected at the residence of Daniel Breed; the officers above named as chosen under the temporary organization being all re-elected, together with the following board of managers: Mrs. Henry Wilson and Miss A. M. Hooper, Massachusetts; Mrs. Harriet Underhill, Mrs. Louisa Howells, Mrs. W. R. Johnson, Miss Mary A. Donaldson, and Mrs. Rufus Leighton, of Washington; and Miss Emily Howland, of New York. Since then the successive boards of officers have been as follows:

1864.—Mrs. T. D. Eliot, president; Mrs. A. M. Gangewer, vice-president; Mrs. W. R. Johnson, treasurer; Miss Emily Howland, secretary. Executive committee: Mrs. Henry Wilson, Mrs. A. H. Gibbons. Miss M. A. Donaldson, Mrs. L. Howells, Mrs. G. E. Baker, Mrs. Samuel Wilkinson, Miss Anna M. Hooper, Mrs. C. C. Leighton, Mrs. F. T. Brown Trustees: Sayles J. Bowen, A. M. Gangewer, George E. Baker.

1865.—Miss Margaret Robinson, president; Mrs. M. C. Hart, vice-president; Mrs. Germond Crandell, treasurer; Mrs. W. L. Nicholson, secretary. Executive committee: Mrs. Jas. M. Blanchard, Mrs. H. Underhill, Mrs. Geo. W. McLellan, Mrs. S. P. Bliss, Miss S. P. Searle, Miss Eliza Heacock, Mrs. Geo. B. Whiting, Mrs. Chas. Faxon, Mrs. Stephen D. Charles. Trustees: Geo. E. Baker, A. M. Gangewer, John Joliffe.

1866.—Mrs. B. F. Wade, president; Mrs. Geo. W. McLellan, vice-president; Mrs. Germond Crandell, treasurer; Miss Eliza Heacock, secretary. Executive committee: Mrs. S. C. Pomeroy, Mrs. Lyman Trumbull, Mrs. Susan Wilson, Mrs. Gen. O. O. Howard, Mrs. H. Underhill, Mrs. D. N. Cooley, Miss Louise S. Swan, Miss D. P. Baker, Mrs. Dr. Parker. Trustees: A. M. Gangewer, S. J. Bowen, Charles King.

1867.—Mrs. B. F. Wade, president; Mrs. Geo. W. McLellan, vice-president; Mrs. Germond Crandell, treasurer; Miss Eliza Heacock. secretary. Executive committee: Mrs. S. C. Pomeroy, Mrs. Lyman Trumbull, Mrs. W. F. Nelson, Mrs. Gen. O. O. Howard, Mrs. H. Underhill; Miss S. G. Searle, Miss L. S. Swan, Mrs. J. M. Blanchard, Mrs. R. M. Bigelow.

1868.—Mrs. S. C. Pomeroy, president; Mrs. Geo. W. McLellan, vice-president; Mrs. Germond Crandell, treasurer; Miss Eliza Heacock, secretary. Executive committee: Mrs. Gen. O. O. Howard, Mrs. Oakes Ames, Mrs. R. M. Bigelow, Mrs. H. Underhill, Mrs. W. F. Nelson, Mrs. H. E. Paine, Miss Louise S. Swan, Miss Sarah P. Searle, Mrs. J. M. Blanchard. Trustees: Sayles J. Bowen, Charles King, Geo. W. McLellan.

1869.—Mrs. S. C. Pomeroy, president; Mrs. George W. McLellan, vice-president; Mrs. Germond Crandell, treasurer; Mrs. Hiram Pitts, secretary. Executive committee: Mrs. Gen. O. O. Howard, Mrs. Rev. Sella Martin, Mrs. R. M. Bigelow. Mrs. Harriet Underhill, Mrs. W. F. Nelson, Miss Susan Walker, Miss Louise S. Swan, Mrs. W. F. Bascom, Mrs. J. Blanchard. Trustees: Sayles J. Bowen, Charles King, George W. McLellan.

The first donations to the association were received in April, 1863—$100 from James Arnold, of New Bedford, and $50 from Emily Howland, whose generosity had been for many years well-nigh omnipresent where money and work were demanded in behalf of the neglected race. The National Freedmen's Relief Association soon after gave the association $1,000. At a meeting of the executive committee or board of managers, May 8th, action was taken to secure a building, a committee being raised for that duty, and Daniel Breed was solicited to examine the title to a certain residence on Georgetown Heights: and on June 2 he reported to a meeting of the executive board that it stood in the name of Richard S. Cox, who had at the opening of the rebellion abandoned his property in Georgetown, gone to Virginia, and as a major in the confederate service taken up arms against the Union under circumstances peculiarly disgraceful and aggravating, being without the excuse of State allegiance urged by so many. This action was suggested by the Secretary of War, who, when the association called on him for a house in which to take care of these children, directed them to look up some place abandoned by those who had gone into the rebellion. Through the efforts of the society an order was at once issued by the Secretary of War, which on the 1st day of June placed the association in possession of a spacious residence of some dozen rooms, well furnished, with about 80 acres of land, including an excellent orchard. Mrs. Pomeroy, who was authorized to take possession of the premises by the Secretary of War, being sick upon what proved her death-bed, Mrs. Daniel Breed, the secretary, was deputed to act in her place in assuming the possession. Accordingly, she and her husband, Dr. Breed, entered the premises and made them their temporary quarters during the gathering in of the children and the organization of the institution. The house was occupied by a brother-in-law of R. S. Cox when seized by the military authorities. On the arrival of Dr. and Mrs. Breed the guard withdrew, and without human protection they safely passed the first night, though in imminent danger not only of violence but of their lives.

Soon after moving into their Home, a frame building was put up for a kitchen and cook-room, at a cost of $150, the work being done by "contraband carpenters;" and in the autumn of 1863 a laundry was built, and the carriage house fixed up for a dormitory. In the spring of 1866 water was introduced into the premises from the reservoir, which contributed much to the health of the inmates, who had previously suffered severely from diseases produced by want of cleanliness and proper sleeping apartments. The new build-dings, which had been erected by the Freedmen's Bureau, were at this time ready for occupation, and had been furnished with a good supply of bedsteads from the Office of Medical Stores of the War Department. New clothing was also furnished, and a thorough system instituted in everything, the excellent results of which were soon manifest in the condition of the children. Rations and a surgeon had been furnished, by the order of the Secretary of War, from February, 1864, down to the summer of 1865, and was continued through the month of May by the influence of Senator Pomeroy. In June, the attention of General O. O. Howard was called to the Home, who sent an inspector to examine the institution. The report was of the most commendatory nature, and the rations were continued through his orders, the association offering to receive any children the Bureau might intrust to them.

It was at this period that the association began to anticipate disturbance from R. S. Cox, who, having returned from the confederate army, was appealing to the President for pardon and the consequent restoration of the property then held by the Home. In July, 1866, Cox addressed a letter to the association, offering them $1,000 to vacate the premises, which proposition was declined. At this time the Attorney General assured the association that no pardon would be granted to Cox until an arrangement satisfactory to them should be effected. It was deemed advisable at that time to present a concise and exact statement showing the aggravated nature of Cox's disloyalty, and to present the same to the President, which was accordingly done. The paper was prepared in the form of a protest against the restoration of the property, and the main facts presented were these: That in 1861 Cox was a clerk in the Paymaster General's office, and, refusing to take the oath of allegiance, without resigning went south and served in the rebel army, with the rank of major, till the surrender of Lee. Cox held the commission of colonel of the 8th regiment of the District militia when he went south, having been placed at the head of that regiment by Floyd, just before the inauguration of President Lincoln, in place of Colonel Cruikshank, a man of undoubted loyalty and capability. In September, 1865, the Attorney General, Mr. Speed, issued an order for the process of confiscation, in the case of Cox, to proceed; and the association employed counsel to assist in the prosecution. It became evident, however, in the course of the winter of 1866, that Cox was receiving encouragement from the administration, and the earnest women interested in this Asylum resolved to go in person to the President, and present a statement of the strong claims of their Institution for protection in the possession of the property abandoned by its disloyal owner under circumstances which seemed to them to place him beyond the reach of all wise executive clemency. On the day fixed for the interview an assemblage of nearly a hundred ladies of the first social and intellectual standing in the National Capital gathered at the Executive mansion. The Secretary of War, Mr. Stanton, who believed in the righteousness of their purpose and who was an efficient friend of the Asylum in many emergencies, was present to give the ladies an introduction to the President. Mrs. Senator Trumbull was selected to make the appeal, and she performed the duty with remarkable clearness and force of statement and striking dignity of manner. She began by affirming that "treason is the greatest crime known to the law, and should be made odious," adroitly weaving her argument from the language in which the President had put himself on record so abundantly both in his own State and after becoming the Chief Magistrate of the country. After receiving a courteous but indefinite reply, the ladies withdrew, fully satisfied that an unconditional pardon would be granted to Cox. In the object sought and in the circumstances of the occasion, the delegation was one of the most remarkable that ever presented a petition at the Presidential mansion, and loyal men and women will long believe that it was deference to traitors which withheld a compliance with the request of the petitioners. In the summer the Attorney General signified to the association that he was in favor of pardoning Cox. It is due to Mr. Speed to say that, in taking this ground, he assigned as his reason that the class of rebels to which Cox belonged had been embraced in the President's scheme, and that he could see no just reason for making this an exceptional case. In June the pardon was granted, and on August 17 General Howard informed the association that the President had requested him to procure a place for the orphans, in order to restore the estate to Cox.

The association went immediately to the preparation of a new Home. They bought a valuable tract, consisting of five lots on the extension of Eighth street, in Washington, just beyond the boundary, paying $2,500 for the property; and the Freedmen's Bureau, under the guidance of General O. O. Howard, proceeded without delay to build a spacious, well planned, two-story frame structure for the Home. Congress, October 2, 1866, appropriated $5,000 for the use of the association, and from this sum they paid for the land. On the 6th of November, when the time given to move by the President had expired, the Secretary of War, seeing that the new Home was yet untenantable, assumed the authority to say that they should not be disturbed for another month. On the 7th of December Cox went to the Home, with officers, took off the doors and hinges, and removed all the furniture, rendering it unsafe and impossible for the occupants to remain. General Howard in this emergency offered to furnish them such quarters as could be found till the new Home was completed, but the association decided to move at once to the unfinished house. Cox laid claim to the frame building which had been built by the association, but the question was promptly settled by General Howard, who sent a sufficient force to remove it rapidly from the premises. Cox subsequently brought an action against the association for damages, in the sum of $10,000, although the association had expended $3,000 in improving the property, these improvements including the introduction of water into the buildings. The suit, however, was dropped. In the summer of 1867 the Bureau finished the house, which makes a very excellent Home. The grounds were, during the same period, terraced, and a fine lot for a garden separately enclosed, in which are raised sufficient vegetables for the family during the summer. The parlor was handsomely furnished last year by the exertions of Mrs. Madison, an efficient and benevolent colored woman of Washington, who gathered the money for the purpose among her friends. The haste with which the association was compelled to take its children to the new unfinished home in December, 1865, caused some unusual sickness, and, it was believed, hastened death in several cases. With this exception health has prevailed in the Asylum to an uncommon degree.

The Home is governed by a matron, who is subject to the direction of an executive committee, from whom she holds her office. The first matron was Mrs. Hull, chosen June 2, 1863, the day after the Home was moved to Georgetown, her service continuing only to the 25th of July following, when Miss Page, of Washington, took the place in the emergency. Miss Wilbur, of Rochester, was immediately elected; but declining, the office was filled by Miss Jeannette Jackson, who, assuming charge September 18, 1863, was exceedingly successful. The association, when, by reason of ill health, she resigned, January 27, 1864, expressed their deep sense of her superior work in a formal resolution of the executive board. It being at that time deemed desirable to have a man and wife in charge, Mr. J. B. Walt and wife were elected to the duties. They served acceptably for several months, resigning the charge to Mrs. Lucy L. Coleman, in the summer of 1864. In September, 1864, Mrs. Coleman resigned, and was succeeded by Miss Read, who also resigned January 16, 1865, Mrs. C. J. B. Nichols, of Connecticut, being elected as matron on the same day. Mrs. Nichols continued in charge with much capacity and success till, called to other duties, she resigned February 6, 1866. Her successor was Miss Eunice L. Strong, of Ohio, who filled the arduous place from February, 1866, to October, 1868, with the greatest fidelity and good judgment, her resignation causing universal regret among the friends of the asylum.

She was succeeded by Mrs. Olive Freeman, who is managing the affairs of the institution with much wisdom and success at the present time.

No assistant matron was employed in the Home till the Educational Commission of Boston, in May, 1864, kindly volunteered to send Mrs. Carr to the institution for that duty. Mrs. Carr remained in the Home in various duties till February, 1866. In this period Miss Seymour served for a time as assistant matron, resigning in June, 1866, by reason of ill health. Subsequently Mrs. Songers, of New York, was filling that position, and in 1867 she was in charge of the industrial school. In June, 1866, the Young Ladies' Christian Union, of Worcester, Massachusetts, sent Miss Hattie Stickney, of New Hampshire, to the Home as assistant matron, and still continue to support her in that position, which she fills with the highest success and approbation.

The Providence Colored Orphan Asylum in April, 1863, offered to adopt into their asylum in Rhode Island 12 colored children—orphans desired—which proposition was accepted, the children being sent as soon as suitable selections could be made.

The school was organized early in June, 1863, as soon as the children were gathered into their home on Georgetown Heights, and it has been continued till now with the utmost efficiency and success. Miss Emma Brown, a very capable colored young lady of Georgetown, took charge of the school when it was first organized, and continued there with admirable success during all her summer vacation, she being at that time a teacher in one of the Washington free schools. Miss Maria R. Mann succeeded her in September, 1863, remaining till January 11, 1865. During her service much exertion was used to secure a good school-house, the school at first being held in the parlor, and subsequently in a very inconvenient temporary structure. In the autumn of 1863 Miss Mann visited Boston under the sanction of the asylum, and in its service received from Boston friends $600 in money, besides many school-books, maps, cards, and some school charts. She also purchased about 30 second-hand school desks at $2 50 each. The school-room at Georgetown, as already stated, was always inconvenient, small, and exposed to interruptions by persons passing through the house.

In December, 1863, the school numbered 22 children, and in the beginning of January, 1864, there were 37 scholars, at which time the asylum, which had now been at Georgetown six months, contained two aged women and 62 children. In May succeeding there were but 40 children, ranging from one year or less to twelve years of age, quite one-third being at that time, as previously, below the school age. The temporary buildings in the form of barracks—dining room, laundry, school-room, and dormitory—had been completed when the new year, 1864, opened. It is proper to state that when Miss Maria R. Mann's connection with the school was dissolved, in January, 1865, she deemed it just to withhold from the Home the funds and property which she had collected in Boston and elsewhere for school purposes, including a portable school-house sent from Boston, which had been for some months stored in Washington. In this action she was sustained by her friends who had contributed largely to the funds.

Miss Mann was succeeded temporarily by Miss Harding and Mrs. Carr, but in February the Freedmen's Aid Society of Worcester, Massachusetts, through the kind offices of Mrs. A. P. Earle of that city, sent Miss Sarah Robinson as a teacher, paying her salary. Under her care the school was maintained in its excellent condition and numbered at that period 46 scholars.

At the close of the summer term, June, 1865, Miss Robinson was compelled to relinquish her work by reason of ill health, much to the regret of the asylum. At the opening of the autumn term, however, the institution had the excellent fortune to secure the services of Miss Susan Towle, of Bangor, Maine. The Bangor Freedmen's Aid Association, learning that Miss Towle was giving her services, and thinking it unjust for her to do so, offered to pay her a salary, which they still continue to do.

The number of boys in the Home at the close of 1866 was 42, the number of girls 34; the number of children received during the year 1867 was 168, and the number remaining at the close of the year was 87. At the close of the year 1868 there were 89 inmates, (boys 53, girls 27, aged women 9,) some 25 being below school age. This is, without any exception, one of the best conducted and most admirable colored schools within the District. The school-room is spacious, handsomely supplied with furniture, convenient, cheerful in its appearance, in a healthy location, and the scholars, some 50 or 60 in number, progressing with uncommon rapidity. There is an industrial department connected with the school, in which the children are taught sewing, knitting, and straw-braiding, the large children being also each day employed in the labors of the household.

The institution is not limited to receiving orphan children, but also offers a home to destitute children at the request of the parents, on their making a written surrender of their claim; also on the request of one parent, in case of gross neglect or habitual drunkenness on the part of the other. The trustees are also authorized to bind out such children as may be deemed capable of learning trades, or of becoming useful in other occupations. The school is so divided that each child who is old enough attends the school daily. During the last year the school, in all its branches, has been managed by Miss Towle.

This institution has struggled hard to maintain its work and build a Home for a class whose claims upon the benevolent are very great. The women who have engaged in this noble work cannot all be mentioned in this condensed history. Many of them are seen in the lists of the officers, nearly all of whom were active, though some of the most efficient of the band do not appear in those lists. It will be deemed only a meed of justice, however, to mention Miss Eliza Heacock, of Philadelphia, whose unremitting work for several years as secretary is recognized by all who are familiar with the history of the association. Her fidelity in the preservation of the records, which in the struggles through which the Asylum has passed has been neither a small nor unimportant duty, extended to many other labors, contributing to the welfare, pecuniarily and otherwise, of the institution.

The Society of Friends in various States deserve to be mentioned for their large contributions in money and in laborers. Of those who started the institution none were more laborious and effective than Mrs. S. C. Pomeroy, Mrs. John F. Potter, Mrs. Daniel Breed, and Mrs. Lyman Trumbull, all of whom have passed to their reward, their mantles falling, it can be truly said, upon those who are still carrying onward wisely and well this elevated Christian enterprise.

The Freedmen's Bureau has been the arm of strength to the association in every emergency, and what these children of desolation are to do when the rations of the Bureau cease does not yet appear, though it is not to be doubted that they and their Home will be maintained by the government and by the fostering hands of humane men and women.

It was feared that the aid from the Freedmen's Bureau would be withdrawn January 1, 1869, under the limitations fixed by act of Congress to take effect at that date in the powers and work of the Bureau; but this misfortune has been for a time deferred by the action of the Commissioner in annexing the Home to the freedmen's hospital of the District, "so far as may be necessary for providing medical attendance, medicine, and rations for the inmates." At no distant day, however, the association will have to depend entirely on private benefactions.

Though attention has been almost exclusively directed to this Asylum as a home for the orphan, there have been aged and infirm women in its care from the first month of its existence, a very few in the first years, not usually in any period numbering above a dozen at a time.

Both Mrs. Potter and Mrs. Pomeroy died in 1863, the first year of the association. The annual report says:

"There were with us in the beginning two leading minds, especially distinguished by unselfish devotion to this holy cause; Mrs. Potter, of Wisconsin, and Mrs. Pomeroy, of Kansas, two of the originators of this enterprise, have passed from works to reward. Mrs. Potter left us early, but not until the good work had felt the impetus of her earnest spirit. The loss of our president, Mrs. Pomeroy, we have great reason to deplore. The Home has been justly called her monument. Declining the rest and change she needed, she remained with us during the summer's heat to aid in our work, still laboring with us even when life was waning, and her parting spirit sent us back a blessing with the prophet words, 'the Home will succeed.' We remember her words : ''Tis for a race, for millions we are working; let us forget ourselves.'"

In 1866 the association " sustained the loss of another of its original projectors and most earnest friends," Mrs. Gulielma Breed, of Washington. The annual report further adds :

" After a life of active usefulness in various departments, and many years of heroic and unflagging devotion to the cause of the oppressed and downtrodden, she was called to her reward. In the day when the record of those who have ministered unto Christ in the person of his needy ones shall be made up, many a sable son and daughter of Ethiopia will rise up and call her blessed."

Last year (1868) the association was again called to mourn over the death of a distinguished member, Mrs. Trumbull. The report continues :

" During the past year one of the earliest and warmest friends of the association, Mrs. Lyman Trumbull, of Illinois, has been called to her heavenly home. Although some months previous to her decease she had withdrawn from our membership, we knew that it was not from want of sympathy with our cause, but that her position as president of another and equally important charity claimed all the attention that her delicate health permitted her to bestow. As a beloved and valued officer of the association, and a liberal contributor to its funds, a friend wise in counsel, gentle and lovely in spirit, her name will ever be held in grateful remembrance by those who had the pleasure of being connected with her in this work of labor and love. ' The sacred memory of the just shall flourish though they sleep in dust.' "

MISS WASHINGTON AND MISS JONES.

Miss Washington's excellent school has already been referred to under Period I. Subsequently she moved to a house on L street near her mother's, remaining there till 1861, when she opened a school in the hall over the feed store of Alfred Jones, in company with Matilda Jones, a daughter of the owner of the building. Miss Jones was one of the most talented of Miss Miner's scholars, and was her assistant in 1859. She went to Oberlin through Miss Miner's influence. They continued the school with eminent success three years, averaging more than a hundred scholars through that period. In the spring of 1864 Miss Jones went back to Oberlin to finish her studies, and Miss Washington went in September to the Baptist church corner of Nineteenth and I streets, to take charge of the Boston School when it was first opened. When, afterwards, this school was under the charge of Miss Capron and Miss Flagg, Miss Washington became an assistant under these white teachers, and Miss Jones, returning in 1865 from Oberlin, joined the school as associate with Miss Washington, the three ladies making a corps of teachers not surpassed by any other in the District. Miss Jones became subsequently the wife of Rev. S. W. Madden, pastor of the First Baptist church in Alexandria. When the Boston School was disbanded in 1867, Miss Washington became connected with the public schools, in which she is still doing admirable service as a teacher.

ST. ALOYSIUS' SCHOOL FOR GIRLS.

There are in the District but five colored schools exclusively for girls. Mrs. Ellen B. Wood came here from Philadelphia, where she had been teaching many years, and started a school in 1863 on Fifteenth street, opposite Scott square, in the western part of the city ; moving to E street north, between First and Second streets west, in 1864, and thence to the corner of Third street west and G street north in 1867. The school has now taken up its home in two very good rooms, recently finished for the purpose, in the Parochial School building connected with St. Aloysius church, under the auspices of which the school is now conducted. Mrs. Wood was born in Hayti, but coming early to Philadelphia was educated with white children in that city, excepting in French, which she learned in a colored school under a Haytien teacher. She taught a mixed colored and white school in Camden, New Jersey, for a period, and afterwards built up a large colored school in Philadelphia, which numbered a hundred pupils, when it was surrendered into the hands of the Sisters of Providence in 1862. Her work in Washington has grown from a few pupils into a large school with two departments, the average number being about 80 girls. The assistant, Elizabeth Brown, a native of Philadelphia, was educated at the convent in Baltimore, where she spent five years at St. Frances Academy. She is well-educated, and competent to teach Latin, French, and music, as well as the primary branches. This school is free to all who are unable to pay.

SAINT MARTIN'S SCHOOLS.

St. Martin's school for girls is under the charge of two teachers from Baltimore. The principal, Mary S. Noel, was a member of the sisterhood of the Baltimore convent, but has been detached to engage in teaching. The assistant, Miss Julia Smith, was educated at the St. Frances Academy. St. Martin's school was established in the summer of 1866 through the exertions of Rev. Charles T. White, D. D., pastor of St. Matthew's church, and is not yet fully systematised. The female academy, which is designed to be a seminary of the higher grade, has hitherto, for want of accommodations, been conducted in connection with the parochial female school of St. Martin's (colored) church. It is now in contemplation to have them separated. These schools at present occupy a large building at the junction of L street north and Vermont avenue; the academy comprising at the present time more than 40 and the parochial school 45 pupils. There is also an academy for boys and a parochial school for boys, each numbering about 30 scholars. The principal is Mr. John McCosker, who was educated at the Georgetown College. A small night school for adults is also kept up.

MISS MANN'S SCHOOL.

After Miss Mann gave up the charge of the Orphan Asylum school in Georgetown, in January, 1865, she established a private school, near the corner of 17th and M streets, for older colored children of both sexes, intending to give it the character of a Normal school, as far as the material of the school would allow. In the summer of 1867, however, the Trustees arranged with Miss Mann to connect the school with the public schools of the District, giving it the rank of a high school. It now numbers about fifty scholars, those more advanced being sent to it both from Georgetown and Washington. It has been conducted with system, thoroughness, and energy, and there are several girls of the school, who will soon be fitted to act as teachers. At the opening of the year 1869, its connection with the public schools was dissolved by the action of the Trustees, and it is therefore at present a private and independent school.

J. R. FLETCHER'S SCHOOLS.

In the spring of 1864 Mr. J. M. Perkins started an evening school and a Sabbath school in the Soldiers' Free Library building in Judiciary Square; both which passed into the hands of Mr. J. R. Fletcher, of the Treasury Department, in the following autumn. Mr. Fletcher is an enthusiastic and thorough teacher, and familiar with the best methods of the Massachusetts schools. Under his excellent management the schools rapidly increased, and soon reached their present numbers, about 75 in the evening school and 110 in the Sabbath school; three-fourths of whom were slaves before the war. The free contributions from the scholars have paid for a part of the expenses, and he has been aided in part by one or two Aid Societies and by his personal friends, in addition to what he himself has expended. For example, the American Tract Society of Boston furnished the fuel during the first winter and the American Missionary Association the second winter, and the Unitarian Church has made some contributions. Teachers of different denominations have aided him, as he desired to make it a *union* and unsectarian work. In January, 1868, Mr. Fletcher having previously been made general Superintendent of the schools under the direction of the "Washington Christian Union," his night school was included in their work, they assuming the responsibility of making up any deficit that might arise in the support of the school. It has been his aim to draw to the school older and more advanced pupils, and he has recently organized an adult class of 25 scholars in the hope, eventually, of establishing a thorough Normal course, and fitting such a class, or a portion of them, to be useful and well informed teachers—at present one of the most important objects in the education of the colored people. The Sabbath school is one of the most flourishing and best organized in the District, and is quite independent of any aid or church society. It is called the "Puritan Free Mission Sabbath School."

JOSEPH AMBUSH'S AND OTHER SCHOOLS.

Joseph Ambush, a colored man, free born, opened a school in 1862, July 1, on New York avenue between Fourth and Fifth streets, which soon averaged, during a part of the year,

75 scholars, and now averages nearly that number. Mr. Ambush's father was a slave. He himself attended John F. Cook's school, and for many years was a servant in the family of Commissary General George Gibson, in whose family he received a good deal of instruction. In 1867 he moved his school to the school room connected with Asbury church, corner of Eleventh and K streets. More than half the scholars belong to contraband families, most of them quite poor, but they all appear very well, and the school is well conducted. Mr. Ambush is a nephew of Enoch Ambush, already mentioned. He speaks of General Gibson and his family as being very kind to him, and always ready to aid him in his efforts to get an education.

Mrs. C. W. Grove, in 1863, came from New York city and opened a private school on I street between Nineteenth and Twentieth streets. In the following summer she was employed by the Pennsylvania Freedmen's Aid Society in their school in Galbraith chapel, where she remained until June, 1867, when she was engaged by the Trustees of the colored public schools, at first teaching in the school on Twenty-fourth and F streets, and afterwards in the M street school. About the last of December, 1868, her connection with the public school ceased by order of the Trustees, and she soon opened a private school on Twenty-third street near the Circle.

Mrs. Louisa Ricks, who came to Washington from Texas, opened a school for girls about two years ago in the barrack building on I street near Seventeeth street west. She is assisted by Miss Eva Dickinson from Connecticut, who teaches music on the piano, the school being provided with a good instrument. The scholars number about 50, and 16 are taking music lessons.

January 4, 1869, Rev. Chauncey Leonard, pastor of the Second Baptist church, (colored,) opened a day school at the corner of Third and G streets, and has an average attendance of fifty-five scholars of both sexes, with one assistant teacher. Most of the scholars pay a small tuition fee, but the receipts do not cover the expenses of the school, and the balance is paid by Rev. Mr. Leonard, in addition to his services as teacher.

COLFAX INDUSTRIAL MISSION.

This institution owes its origin to an unpretending association of the teachers of the Sabbath school at Wisewell barracks, which held its first meeting November 7, 1867, at those barracks, on the corner 7th and O streets. The Sabbath school was organized by these teachers in the autumn of 1866, the American Tract Society having discontinued its work at that place in the previous spring. The Sabbath school was under the superintendence of John A. Cole, and still remains under his supervision. The leading purpose of the teachers was to maintain an Industrial school, which had been supported by the Tract Society. On the 20th of May, 1868, with the plan of securing a more permanent place for their school, they adopted a constitution and entered into a full organization, with the following officers: John A. Cole, President; Charles H. Bliss, Vice President; S. C. Hotchkiss, treasurer; Miss J. M. Alvord, secretary; John A. Cole, Rev. G. A. Hall, Samuel Barron, John H. Cook, Charles H. Bliss, trustees. The committee who prepared the constitution consisted of E. Whittlesey, Charles H. Bliss, Rev. J. W. Alvord. At the same meeting a committee, consisting of Mr. Alvord, Rev. John Kimball, and Mr. Wolcott, was appointed to make inquiries and report as to a lot upon which to build a house. They reported, at a meeting, May 9th, 1868, that a suitable lot had been found, and that the American Missionary association would furnish the requisite funds for its purchase. The lot, about one hundred feet square, on the corner of R and Eleventh streets, was purchased for $2,500, and the Missionary Association furnished $1,600 in part payment. Messrs. Cole, Bliss, and Barron were added to the committee, and they were now recognized as the building committee.

The edifice, which was opened with the new year, is about 45 by 95 feet, two stories, and is composed of the same material as the Howard University. It was erected by the Freedmen's bureau and when completed will have cost about $20,000. The lower story consists of one school room capable of seating eight or nine hundred persons, with two recitation rooms, the upper story comprising a large industrial room, and some eight or ten smaller rooms for various kinds of industrial employment.

The Sunday school of this Association has an average attendance of more than six hundred scholars of all ages, and the industrial school, held every Saturday, averages about 200 girls, who are taught various kinds of work upon cloth, as well as useful occupations connected with house-keeping. These schools are in the care of an association of ladies with the following officers: Mrs. C. P. Bliss, President; Mrs. E. W. Robinson, Vice President; Miss Ella Cole, treasurer, Miss J. M. Alvord, secretary. These schools were moved to the new building on new year's day, 1869, and the American Missionary Association took it in charge, furnishing a missionary, Rev. G. N. Marden, of Orland, Maine, who conducts the benevolent work. The Colored Mechanic's Association is to have its headquarters here, and besides the schools and Sunday worship, there are to be lectures upon useful subjects. Miss Ella Cole, formerly of the Christian Commission, is at present in the service of the Missionary association. A night school has been organized, and is attended by over 200 scholars, who pay a small tuition fee, 25 cents a month. The Trustees propose to establish an Industrial school for boys, with shops and utensils for teaching useful trades; also a school for adult women. Mr. John A. Cole is the present Superintendent of the Institution. The Executive Committee consists of the Trustees, with eight others, E. Whittlesey, Rev. J. W. Alvord, Rev. John Kimball, Rev. G. N. Marden, S. C. Hotchkiss, A. S. Pratt, A. P. Eastman, Warren Brown. Steps have been taken to secure a charter for the institution.

MISS WALKER'S INDUSTRIAL SCHOOL.

Among the Industrial schools for the freedmen, that of Miss Susan Walker is a prominent and very useful one. Though strictly outside the city limits, it may very properly be included among the schools of Washington. Miss Walker is a cousin of Rev. James Walker, D. D., for many years president of Harvard College, and a sister of Judge Walker, the late eminent lawyer and jurist of Cincinnati, and at one time a partner of Chief Justice Chase. On the breaking out of the war she devoted herself to the welfare of the soldiers in hospitals and to the freedmen, being one of the first who in 1862 went to Port Royal for the relief of the freedmen, who had gathered there in great numbers and were in a suffering condition. In 1865 she was urged, and in September was formally appointed, to organize an industrial school among the freedmen at Campbell barracks, near the terminus of the Seventh street railroad. December 1 the school was opened in one of the barrack buildings, and soon Miss Walker had under training, six hours a day, about 70 scholars, mostly women, who were taught various kinds of plain sewing, she preparing the work for them, cutting the garments, &c., in the evening. As these women could not afford to take the time even for instruction, unless receiving some remuneration, Miss Walker adopted the plan of paying them proportionately from the articles of clothing made. In September of the next year, 1866, a regiment of cavalry took up its quarters near her school, causing her great annoyance and much anxiety, as well as disturbing the school work. The officer in command gave her assurance of the fullest protection, but the soldiers finally broke into the school-house, and destroyed or took away private property and private papers, a summary way of declaring their creed on the subject of educating contrabands. In November the school was removed to Wisewell barracks, and speedily reorganized with an increase of scholars. The general plan and purpose of Miss Walker in this most unpretentious but most useful work are best seen in the following extract from her report of 1866 and 1867: "During the session of three months instruction and employment were given to 315 women and 12 men and boys; 819 garments, consisting of every variety of clothing for men, women, and children, were made in the school. The Bureau furnished material for 70 pairs of pants, 60 pairs of drawers, and 57 shirts, for the making of which $60 were received. The surgeon-in-chief of the Bureau paid from eight to ten rations per month for work done for the hospital. These rations were divided as part payment among the women, who during the winter desired food rather than clothing; 600 garments were also given as additional payment. Service places in and around Washington were found for 100 women, and 30 others were provided with employment out of the District. The Bureau provides school room and fuel. The teacher gives her time and service, and provides material from such sources as she can command. The resul*s of the two years are most gratifying. With few exceptions the women had but recently exchanged the shovel and the hoe for the needle and thimble. They had not ventured to use the scissors. In a few weeks, however, they have learned to cut and make a variety of garments. During the first school year ten freedwomen, 'field hands' in slavery, cut and made, economically and neatly, 300 pairs of men's pants. Others have learned to do fine sewing, and have made fine linen shirts in the best manner. To-day a woman came to thank me for teaching her, as she now earns $3 a week with her needle. She prefers it to the shovel. The school was commenced with the desire that, if possible, no money should be expended for teaching. With the exception of one month, during which a refugee from New Orleans was placed in the school as an assistant, the teaching and charge of the school has been a free gift, gladly offered. As fast as women learn to be useful they are required to teach others. The purpose of the school is *to help the freedwomen to help themselves.* It is not so much to furnish employment and do a large quantity of work, as to teach them how to do well whatever they undertake. The object is to aid them to become self-supporting and independent; to encourage in them habits of industry, economy, and cleanliness; to elevate them in character and condition; and to inspire an ambition for self-improvement." In August, 1867, Miss Walker, to secure a permanent location for her school, bought a lot near the spot where she first opened it, and on this lot the Bureau erected a commodious building, to which the school was moved in April, 1868. It is situated near the base of the ridge of land on which the Howard University is built. In the first four months of that year, while still at Wisewell barracks, 1,745 garments were made specially for the Bureau, which supplied the material. During the last year Miss Walker has given one hour a day to instructing a portion of the scholars in reading and writing. The importance of this and every well-managed industrial school, in advancing the best interests of the freedmen, can hardly be over-estimated. Mrs. Doolittle, wife of Prof. M. H. Doolittle, of the Naval Observatory, established and carried on in Georgetown in 1865–'66 a large and very successful industrial school for freedwomen, giving instruction to 120, mostly adults, and there are others who have done and are doing much good in this important department of benevolent work.

THE TWO NATIONAL THEOLOGICAL INSTITUTES AND UNIVERSITIES.

The first attempt to organize an institution to train colored men for the ministry was commenced in January, 1865, by Rev. Edmund Turney, D.D., a Calvinist Baptist clergyman of some eminence in the denomination. Dr. Turney came here in that month, and through his activity a meeting was held in the First Baptist Church, on the first day of February, to discuss the subject, and at an adjourned meeting on the 13th of the same month the plan of a seminary, under the name of the "National Theological Institute for Colored Ministers," was completed, and Dr. Turney was elected president. It was chartered by Congress, under that name, May 10, 1866; and by an amendatory act, March 2, 1867, the institution was expanded into a University, embracing in its designs of culture "others than those connected with the Christian ministry." This enlargement produced a rupture in the association. The Boston Baptist people, mostly clergymen, wished the institution to be confined exclusively to the education of ministers and teachers, and a portion of the executive committee of the corporation, claiming to be the executive board, and acting in harmony with the Boston friends, met at Newark, New Jersey, in May, 1867, and by formal vote resolved to hold the new powers "in abeyance," to transfer the "institute" and the seat of its operations from Washington to Boston, which transfer in a circular they subsequently announced had been done. The portion of the executive committee in favor of the "university" plan resisted the Newark movement, and carrying the question to the Court of this District were fully sustained by its decisions in their resistance, the Court deciding that the corporation by the terms of its charter, must reside here, and ordering the funds of the corporation, which had been tranferred to Boston, to be returned. The decision of the Court is as follows:

"The corporate functions of said corporation were, by said act, intended to be exercised in said District, and that the books, funds, and assets of said corporation should be within the jurisdiction of this Court," and it ordered that "the defendants, or such of them as hold or have control of said books, funds, and assets beyond said jurisdiction, return the same to the said jurisdiction, to the end that the same may be subject to the further order of this Court," May 26, 1868. The Court has no knowledge at this time, January, 1869, that the order has been obeyed.

In March, 1867, the Freedmen's Bureau turned over to the institution ten thousand dollars from the refugees and freedmen's fund, under the act of Congress authorizing the Bureau to assist in the establishment of institutions of learning for the benefit of the colored people. It is understood, however, that the Bureau took the ground that it was authorized so to do under the amendment, which transformed the institution from a Theological Seminary into a school of general culture. This donation is the bone of contention between these two rival parties, who are aiming at the same beneficent object.

Meanwhile the Boston section of the double-headed University, which, like Dr. Turney's, claims to be "The National Theological Institute and University," completed their organization. This new school was put into operation last autumn, under the instruction of Rev. G. M. P. King, a young man of excellent qualities, from the State of Maine, and, with a female assistant, he has now in his school upwards of 40 men, ranging from 18 years of age up to 45, and a small class of girls who are preparing to become teachers. The Soldiers' Free Library Building, on Judiciary Square, is their school house, and a large barrack building on I street, near Seventeenth, is the home of the young men—serving for dormitories and study rooms, with cooking quarters and dining hall attached—all fitted up in a comfortable manner, capable of accommodating 35 students. Sixteen are studying for the ministry.

The first two years of Dr. Turney's work in this District attracted much attention, and the success with which he trained his theological class received the marked commendation of all friends of the cause here and elsewhere. His operations, down to March 1, 1867, gave the Boston friends special satisfaction, as appears from the very high encomiums which were at that period accorded to him by nearly all the leading Baptist clergymen of Boston and vicinity, in a circular issued by the managers of the enterprise. Dr. Turney's University scheme embraces the plan of a central school in the District of Columbia, with subordinate institutions of a normal, preparatory, and industrial character, established at desirable points throughout the south. During his first year his work here included a series of night-schools for men and women, who were intending to teach or preach, and this work he prosecuted with great assiduity, showing faith in his cause and in the mode chosen to promote it. In March, 1868, his second year, he opened a day school in a large building on Louisiana avenue, near Seventh street, and continued it till September, 1867, when it was removed to a spacious government structure, corner of Twenty-second street west and I north, where it has been to the present time. This school was large, some 45 in number, at its opening, and has so continued. About thirty-five young men are pursuing Theological studies. The system of subordinate schools in the region bordering upon the city and District has been maintained from the beginning with persistency, and his friends here and abroad are firm in his support. This University is the first one, designed specifically for freedmen, ever incorporated in the country. In August, 1867, he published a plan of a "Female Collegiate Institute," with a full board of instruction. Dr. Turney has an evening school in his school building of about 30 scholars, not including theological students, and in February, 1869, he opened another evening school in the Fifth Colored Baptist church on Vermont avenue, commencing with 30 men, many of whom had been his pupils. This school is under his personal instruction. In the same building a school for colored women, now numbering 25 scholars, is held two afternoons a week, under the management of Dr. Turney, but taught by Miss Lavinia Warner, colored. On Capitol Hill he has established an afternoon school, numbering about 25 scholars, including some of his theological students, one of whom, Washington Waller, has the personal charge of the school, which is taught five afternoons in the week. This same teacher has an evening school of about 15 scholars in the small colored Baptist church on Fourteenth street, at "Murder Bay." John Johnson, another of Dr. Turney's scholars, has a small evening school in the Pennsylvania Friend's building, on Nineteenth street west, near the boundary. Dr. Turney has also a school five evenings in the week at Freedmen's Village, Arlington, under his direction. Robert S. Laws, a scholar in the Wayland Theological Seminary and who preaches at Arlington, has the supervision of this school, which averages about 100 scholars. Mrs. Ellen Reeves, sister of Mr. W. Syphax, is the teacher. This is the only school now at Arlington, but a day school is about to be started under the direction of Dr. Turney, with Miss Julia Howard, a white teacher from Boston, as the instructor. In organizing and encouraging these night and afternoon schools, Dr. Turney has been doing a very useful work.

WAYLAND THEOLOGICAL SEMINARY.

This institution had its origin in the " Boston School," which was established in the basement of the First Colored Baptist Church, corner of Nineteenth and I streets, in September, 1864, by the New England Freedmen's Aid Commmission, an association of prominent benevolent persons of the Baptist denomination in Boston, and is not to be confounded with the New England Freedmen's Aid Society. The seminary was eminently successful, being very fortunate in its teacher, Lucy A. Flagg, and her assistants. Early in 1866 the above named Aid Commission arranged with the American Baptist Home Missionary Society to take the school, and in May the Commissioner of the Freedmen's Bureau offered that society a large government building for its use. The offer was accepted ; a fine lot adjoining the church was purchased by the society ; the barrack structure was transferred to the lot by the Bureau, and the school opened in the autumn as a Normal School. In July, 1867, it was converted into a Theological Seminary proper, under the remarkably judicious charge of Reverend S. B. Gregory, President, assisted by Mrs. S. B. Gregory and Miss Sarah Utley, all from New York State, and it has been doing a work, for the past two years, of great value to the cause, securing the respect of all who have enjoyed or observed its mode of instruction. The present number of students is about 36.

When the American Baptist Home Missionary Society was putting the Wayland School into operation in the spring of 1866, the managers of the " National Institute and University" solicited the society to assume the charge of the University, and make Dr. Turney president. The proposition was accepted by the society, but Dr. Turney declined to co-operate with the Home Missionary Society. This is believed to be a correct statement of the very unfortunate course of events which have resulted in the establishment in Washington of three separate Theological schools, under the auspices of one religious denomination. It should be stated however, that " The Wayland Seminary" is not identified with the very unfortunate alienation.

THE HOWARD UNIVERSITY.

The originators of this institution were a small band of men earnestly enlisted in the work of elevating the colored race. They were all northern men, and nearly all of them connected with the New Congregational Church and Society of Washington. The credit of originating the scheme belongs to Reverend B. F. Morris, of Cincinnati, Ohio, who was at that time in government employment in the District, and who subsequently, in a fit of melancholy, committed suicide at Springfield, Ohio. Mr. Morris was the son of Thomas Morris, one of the early anti-slavery men, a native of Virginia, who, while a senator in Congress from Ohio, from 1833 to 1839, was one of the bold, able, and foremost champions of freedom. Isaac N. Morris, a member of the House of Representatives from Illinois, during the thirty-fifth and the thirty-sixth Congress, and Jonathan D. Morris, who was a member of the thirty-first Congress from Ohio, are sons of Thomas Morris. Reverend B. F. Morris possessed a mind of remarkable originality, and was a man of generous and philanthropic sentiments. His original idea was to found an institution to train colored men for teachers and preachers. He presented his plan to his pastor, Reverend Charles B. Boynton, D. D., who entered cordially into the scheme, and subsequently to other friends. At this time Mr. H. A. Brewster also was considering a plan for a missionary association, with the same object in view, and how the project of the latter was turned to the purposes of the former, appears in the proceedings of the preliminary meetings, of which the following is a condensed history :

On the 20th of November, 1866, the first meeting was held, which initiated this great educational enterprise, and was suggested at a prayer meeting of the Congregational church held in the Columbia College Law Building, at which time Mr. Brewster made remarks on the importance of doing something for the education of the colored race. Some twenty persons were present, nearly all members of the newly organized Congregational church, and in sympathy with Mr. Morris, who had come to the meeting to assist in turning the work in that direction. The record of this meeting says: "By invitation of H. A. Brewster a meeting was held at his house for the purpose of considering missionary interests as related to the prerogatives and responsibilities of the First Congregational church, and, if found expedient, to devise ways and means for the promotion of the same." Reverend Charles B. Boynton, D. D., a'ter opening the meeting with prayer, called upon Reverend Benjamin F. Morris, who set forth his plan of a theological seminary, having in view the training of colored men for the ministry, Mr. Brewster having previously explained the purpose of the meeting. The views of Mr. Morris, which he stated to be "the result of reflection and consultation with other brethren," were unanimously accepted, the name of "Howard Theological Seminary" being adopted for the institution, and the following officers elected: Chairman of meeting, H. A. Brewster; Secretary, E. M. Cushman; Trustees of seminary, O. O. Howard, C. B. Boynton, D. B. Nichols, B. F. Morris, H. A. Brewster, H. Barber, J. B. Hutchinson, R. H. Stevens, Henry Wilson, Samuel C. Pomeroy, B. C. Cook; committee on organization, C. B. Boynton, B. F. Morris, D. B. Nichols. In the course of the meeting, General Howard offered to build a seminary structure from the educational funds of the Freedmen's Bureau if the association would furnish a lot; and Mr. Brewster thereupon gave his verbal guarantee that the lot should be secured. At the second meeting, December 6, the report of the committee on organization was submitted by Mr. Nichols, and on his motion the name of the seminary was changed to that of "The Howard Normal and Theological Institute for the education of Teachers and Preachers." This change of name originated with Senator S. C. Pomeroy, who urged the establishment of a Normal Department, which appears to have especially contributed to the change of plan from a school of Theology to that of a school of general learning. Senator Pomeroy urged, among other arguments in favor of the normal feature, that it would place the seminary in a position to share in the bounty which Congress was destined, as he believed, to bestow for the encouragement of this class of professional schools. This was apparently the controlling idea in his mind in suggesting the expansion of the plan. Mr. Nichols seems to have been the foremost to favor Mr. Pomeroy's views; and it should be added that the motions in the meeting pertaining to the name of the institution in all its modifications, including its final and permanent form, are to be mainly accredited to him. It should still further be stated that in his report on organization, presented at this meeting, Mr. Nichols used the term "collegiate" in the name which he proposed for the institution, though nothing appears indicating the idea of any distinct enlargement of the range of culture beyond what had been previously contemplated. The suggestions of Senator Pomeroy seem to have so modified the views of all the others that the report of Mr. Nichols did not assume any formal importance in the organization of the institution, though it embodied some excellent features, which were adopted. Prof. Silas L. Loomis, M. D., now connected with the Medical department of the University, who was present at the second meeting, urged the establishment of a department to train the students in letter writing, and suggested a professorship of Belles Lettres to that end. He also suggested, in connection with a plan of medical instruction, the name of Howard to be applied to the institution. The fact seems to be that both the name and the plan were gradually developed in the general discussion at the meetings and elsewhere, and that neither the one nor the other originated with any one individual. The original purpose was to build a school essentially Congregational in its character, and exclusively under the control and guidance of the Washington Congregational church, and much resistance was encountered, as the plan developed, by those who became the advocates of an expanded scheme. Senators S. C. Pomeroy and Henry Wilson seem to have been among the most judicious and influential actors and counsellors in the whole task.

The following committees were then elected: Finance, J. B. Johnson, H. A. Brewster, W. G. Finney; building and grounds, O. O. Howard, S. C. Pomeroy, H. Barber—S. L. Loomis being added at the next meeting; library, D. B. Nichols, B. F. Morris, E. Ketchum. At the third meeting, December 18, the various committees reported; that upon building and grounds being authorized to purchase the property near the terminus of the Seventh street railroad, as proposed. A committee, consisting of Senator Wilson, Senator Pomeroy, and Hon. B. C. Cooke, was chosen to obtain a charter. The Board of Trustees was increased to 15 by the addition of W. F. Bascom, C. H. Howard, E. H. Robinson, and E. M. Cushman, a still further increase being made at the next meeting by the addition of S L. Loomis. J. B. Johnson, and W. G. Finney. At the fourth meeting, January 8, 1867, the following officers were elected: C. B. Boynton, President Board of Trustees; H. A. Brewster, Vice President; E. M. Cushman, Secretary; J. B. Hutchinson, Treasurer; D. B. Nichols, Superintendent of institution and Librarian. At this meeting, after remarks by C. H. Howard, C. B. Boynton, and H. A. Brewster, on the subject of the name of the institution, on motion of D. B. Nichols, seconded by Dr. Boynton, who urged with much earnestness the propriety of sending down the name of Howard to the coming centuries in connection with the institution, the name was again changed to that of "The Howard University," under which it was chartered. Measures were also adopted looking to the organization of a Medical and Law department.

At the second meeting of the Board of Trustees the establishment of an Agricultural department was a topic of discussion. General O. O. Howard introduced the matter of the "Miner Institution," which incorporated and holding property in the city of Washington. has in view purposes cognate to those of the Howard University, and suggested the leasing of the property of that institution at six per cent. per annum upon the purchase price. At this meeting. in connection with the report of S. L. Loomis, embracing a plan of a Medical department, and on motion of D. B. Nichols it was made a condition of eligibility to a place in the board of instruction in the University that the candidate "furnish satisfactory evidence of Christian character." This provision was subsequently struck out and the following substituted: "Resolved, That every person elected to any position in the Howard University shall be a member of some Evangelical church," a change which, it is understood, the Trustees have determined to modify.

At the sixth meeting, being the third of the Board of Trustees, Dr. Boynton presented the outlines of the charter of the Michigan University as a basis for that of the Howard University. General O. O. Howard then presented the bill which Senator Wilson had introduced into the United States Senate to incorporate the Howard University; General O. O. Howard and Senator Wilson being appointed a committee to revise and present it in its revised form to Congress. The question whether provision by the charter should be made for the admission of females, was freely and with lively interest discussed at this time, the prevailing sentiment being that no distinction should be made. General O. O. Howard was among those not favoring the admission of females. It was also voted to lease the property purchased by the bounty funds at $1,200 per annum, lease to date from January 26, 1867; and that a Normal and Preparatory school be forthwith opened.

The original purpose in founding this Institution was to educate the colored race exclusively; to train men for preachers, teachers and missionaries, both in this country and in Africa. This was distinctly set forth in the plan of organization. as reported by Reverend D. B. Nichols at an early preliminary meeting. Senator Pomeroy and Dr. Boynton took ground in favor of the expanded scheme as embodied in the charter, which was drafted by Dr. Boynton, and which extends the privileges of the institution to both sexes and all colors. It has already been stated that General Howard was averse to this feature, which contemplated the union of the sexes and colors in the school, and so expressed himself at the time the provisions of the charter were discussed. It is an interesting fact to observe that while Oberlin College embarked on its work as a school for white scholars, and was changed to embrace colored, the Howard University started as exclusively a colored school, and was soon enlarged, and opened its door to all. It is perhaps hardly necessary to add that General O. O. Howard has been from the beginning, through all its stages, the great sustaining pillar of the enterprise.

Subjoined is the charter as it was passed by Congress and sanctioned by the President, March 2, 1867:

"ACT to incorporate the Howard University.

" *Be it enacted by the Senate and House of Representatives of the United States of America in Congress Assembled*, That there be established, and is hereby established, in the District of Columbia, a University for the education of youth in the liberal arts and sciences, under the name, style, and title of ' The Howard University.'

" SEC. 2. *And be it further enacted*, That Samuel C. Pomeroy, Charles B. Boynton, Oliver O. Howard, Burton C. Cook, Charles H. Howard, James B. Hutchinson, Henry A. Brewster, Benjamin F. Morris, Danforth B. Nichols, William G. Finney, Roswell H. Stevens, E. M. Cushman, Hiram Barber, E. W. Robinson, W. F. Bascom, J. B. Johnson, and Silas L. Loomis be, and they are hereby declared to be a body politic and corporate, with perpetual succession in deed or in law, to all intents and purposes whatsoever, by the name, style, and title of "The Howard University," by which name and title they and their successors shall be competent at law and in equity to take to themselves and their successors, for the use of said University, any estate whatsoever in any messuage, lands, tenements, hereditaments, goods, chattels, moneys, and other effects, by gift, devise, grant, donation, bargain, sale, conveyance, assurance, or will ; and the same to grant, bargain, sell, transfer, assign, convey, assure, demise, declare to use and farm let, and to place out on interest, for the use of said University, in such manner as to them or a majority of them shall be deemed most beneficial to said institution ; and to receive the same, their rents, issues and profits, income and interest, and to apply the same for the proper use and benefit of said University ; and by the same name to sue and be sued, to implead and be impleaded in any court of law and equity, in all manner of suits, actions, and proceedings whatsoever, and generally, by and in the same name, to do and transact all and every the business touching or concerning the premises : *Provided*, That the same do not exceed the value of fifty thousand dollars annual net income over and above and exclusive of the receipts for the education and support of the students of said University.

" SEC. 3. *And be it further enacted*, That the first meeting of said corporators shall be holden at the time and place at which a majority of the persons herein above named shall assemble for that purpose; and six day's notice shall be given each of said corporators, at which meeting said corporators may enact by-laws, not inconsistent with the laws of the United States, regulating the government of the corporation.

" SEC. 4. *And be it further enacted*, That the government of the University shall be vested in a Board of Trustees of not less than thirteen members, who shall be elected by the corporators at their first meeting. Said Board of Trustees shall have perpetual succession in deed or in law, and in them shall be vested the power hereinbefore granted to the corporation. They shall adopt a common seal, which they may alter at pleasure, under and by which all deeds, diplomas, and acts of the University shall pass and be authenticated. They shall elect a President, Secretary, and a Treasurer. The treasurer shall give such bonds as the Board of Trustees may direct. The said Board shall also appoint the professors and tutors, prescribing the number, and determining the amount of their respective salaries. They shall also appoint such other officers, agents, or employés as the wants of the University may from time to time demand, in all cases fixing their compensation. All meetings of said Board may be called in such manner as the Trustees shall prescribe, and nine of them so assembled shall constitute a quorum to do business, and a less number may adjourn from time to time.

" SEC. 5. *And be it further enacted*, That the University shall consist of the following departments, and such others as the Board of Trustees may establish : First, Normal ; second, Collegiate ; third, Theological ; fourth, Law ; fifth, Medicine ; sixth, Agricultural.

" SEC. 6. *And be it further enacted*, That the immediate government of the several departments, subject to the control of the Trustees, shall be intrusted to their respective faculties ; but the Trustees shall regulate the course of instruction, prescribe, with the advice of the professors, the necessary text-books, confer such degrees and grant such diplomas as are usually conferred and granted in other universities.

" SEC. 7. *And be it further enacted*, That the Board of Trustees shall have the power to remove any professor or tutor, or other officer connected with the institution, when in their judgment the interests of the University shall require it.

" SEC. 8. *And be it further enacted*, That the Board of Trustees shall make an annual report, making an exhibit of the affairs of the University.

" SEC 9. *And be it further enacted*, That no misnomer of the said corporation shall defeat or annul any donation, gift, grant, devise, or bequest to or from the said corporation.

" SEC. 10. *And be it further enacted*, That the said corporation shall not employ its funds or income, or any part thereof, in banking operations, or for any purpose or object other than those expressed in the first section of this act; and that nothing in this act contained shall be so construed as to prevent Congress from altering, amending, or repealing the same.

" Approved March 2, 1867."

The corporators held a meeting March 19, 1868, and organized in the choice of a Board of Trustees, President, Secretary, and Treasurer, and a committee to prepare a code of by-laws— the executive committee, under the by-laws, being chosen at a subsequent meeting, May 6, 1867. This committee originally consisted of Charles B. Boynton, D. D., President of the

University and *ex officio* chairman; O. O. Howard, William F. Bascom, and E. W. Robinson; and to them were confided the supervision of the building operations and financial affairs of the corporation.

The following is a list of the trustees and other officers of the institution, together with dates of their election:

Trustees.—Hon. Samuel C. Pomeroy, United States senator from Kansas, March 19, 1867; Rev. Charles B Boynton, D. D., Chaplain of the House of Representatives, and pastor of First Congregational church, Washington, D. C., March 19, 1867; Major General Oliver O. Howard, United States army, March 19, 1867; Hon. Burton C. Cook, member, from Illinois, of the United States House of Representatives, March 19, 1867; Brigadier General Charles H. Howard, United States volunteers, March 19, 1867; J. B. Hutchinson, esq., March 19, 1867; Henry A. Brewster, esq, March 19, 1867; Rev. Benjamin F. Morris, March 19, 1867; Rev. Danforth B. Nichols, March 19, 1867; William G. Finney, esq., March 19, 1867; Roswell H. Stevens, esq., March 19, 1867; E. M. Cushman, esq., March 19, 1867; Dr. Hiram Barber, March 19, 1867; Rev. E. W. Robinson, March 19, 1867; William F. Bascom, esq., March 19, 1867; James B. Johnson, esq., March 19, 1867; Dr. Silas L. Loomis, March 19, 1867; General George W. Balloch, March 19, 1867; Rev. Henry Highland Garnett, late pastor of the Fifteenth Street Presbyterian church, of colored people, Washington, D. C., April 8, 1867; Rev. Byron Sunderland, D. D., pastor of the First Presbyterian church, Washington, D. C., April 22, 1867; Rev. D. W. Anderson, pastor First Baptist church, of colored people, Washington, D. C., April 6, 1868; Judge Hugh L. Bond, Baltimore, May 4, 1868; Rev. J. W. Alvord, May 4, 1868.

Trustees resigned.—Rev. Charles B. Boynton, D. D., January 11, 1868; J. B. Hutchinson, esq., March 2. 1868; E. M. Cushman, esq., March 2, 1868.

Trustee deceased.—Rev. Benjamin F. Morris, June 28, 1867.

Presidents of the University.—Rev. Charles B. Boynton, D. D., March 19, 1867; resigned and ceased to act as Trustee, August 27, 1867; Rev. Byron Sunderland, D. D., August 27, 1867.

Secretaries of the Board.—E. M. Cushman, esq., March 19, 1867; resignation accepted December 20, 1867; E. W. Robinson, elected December 29, 1867.

Treasurer of the Board.—General George W. Balloch, March 19, 1867.

Collegiate Department.—General Eliphalet Whittlesey, Professor of Rhetoric and Belles-lettres, September 21, 1868; William F. Bascom, A. M., Professor of Greek and Latin, September 22, 1868.

Law Department.—Hon. A. G. Riddle, December 29, 1868; John M. Langston, esq., Professor, October 12, 1868.

Medical Department.—The President, *ex-officio* chairman; Silas L. Loomis, M. D., Dean; Joseph Taber Johnson, M. D., Secretary and Treasurer. Faculty.—Silas L. Loomis, M. D., Professor of Chemistry and Toxicology, May 4, 1868; Robert Reyburn, M. D, Professor of Anatomy, May 4, 1868; Joseph Taber Johnson, M. D., Professor of Materia Medica and Therapeutics, May 4, 1868; Lafayette C. Loomis, M. D., Professor of Physiology and Microscopy, September 21, 1868; Alexander T. Augusta, M. B., Demonstrator of Anatomy, September 21, 1868.

Standing Committee on Agriculture.—D. B. Nichols, October 12, 1868; J. W. Alvord, October 12, 1868; General George W. Balloch, October 12, 1868.

This committee was appointed with a view to the improvement of the university reservation, to the employment of students who may desire by labor to defray in part their expenses, and to the ultimate complete organization of the Agricultural Department. The need of an Education Society, to give aid to deserving and indigent youth—especially colored youth, who are almost without exception poor—is felt by the Board; but for the present the subject of aiding students, particularly by providing them labor, is referred to this committee.

Librarian.—Danforth B. Nichols, April 8, 1867.

Preparatory and Normal Department.—Principals.—E. F. Williams, from May 2, 1867; John H. Combs, September 10, 1867; A. L. Barber, April 13, 1868. Female Principal, Miss Julia A. Lord, June 25, 1867.

At the late meeting, December 29, 1868, the board elected Brigadier General Charles H. Howard to the chair of modern languages, which he declined, and at the same time a committee was chosen with the purpose in view to secure, if possible, the services of Major General O. O. Howard as President of the University. It should be here stated that the Presidency of the Board of Trustees and the Presidency of the University, originally constituting a single office, have been separated.

The University site.—The site for the university was purchased by the trustees of John A. Smith, for $147,500. The price was originally fixed at $150,000, the number of acres being by estimate 150. Thomas Coyle, however, holding the right by lease to take sand from the hill for a term of years, the owner of the land, after a protracted negotiation, finally made the proposition to deduct $2,500 from the price on account of the encumbrance, and this offer was accepted. The deed was made April 28, 1866, but was not finally executed and delivered till May 25, ensuing. The Trustees subsequently paid Thomas Coyle $5,000 for a surrender of his lease. The terms of the purchase were $20,000 cash, the balance payable in 10 equal annual instalments, and the interest on the whole unpaid principal payable semi-annually. Originally, 50 acres were appropriated for university grounds. Subsequently 10 acres were added, and still later an additional 10 acres for the park was set aside, making in all, in round numbers, 70 acres. The remaining 80 acres were laid off in lots, and mostly sold, making it certain that their proceeds will pay the entire original purchase.

The University buildings.—These buildings consist of a spacious university edifice proper four stories high, imposing in external appearance, commodious in its internal plan, and standing upon a commanding and handsome as well as healthy location, looking down upon the city and a broad expanse of the country, including many miles of the winding Potomac. There is also an ample dormitory, capable of accommodating the teachers and 300 scholars with board and lodging; three stories and basement, with every appointment belonging to a first-class structure for such purpose. A very large and commodious medical building is erecting on the premises, three stories in height, and corresponding in architecture and appearance with the other structures. The Normal and Preparatory department moved into the apartments in the University building, designed for that purpose, early in November last, and the teachers and students entered the dormitory with the opening of the new year of 1869. In the appendix will be found a note upon the material of which the buildings are made.

The cost of the university structure and dormitory, when fully completed, will be quite $100,000. The Freedmen's Bureau is building these, as also the medical building, in pursuance of an act of Congress approved March 2, 1868, authorizing the Bureau thus to aid the cause of education from the freedmen and refugees' fund, the aid in this case being justified by the fact that the University is intended to embrace within its benefits the children of freedmen and refugees. "The refugees' and freedmen's fund" embraces all moneys belonging to the government which come into the custody of the Bureau through the incidents of the war, comprising among other items those arising from rents, fines, and sales of old property. The name is used to distinguish it from the regular appropriation. Other fine school structures, similar to these university buildings, though not in any case on so large a scale, have been erected at important points in the south from the same funds. These buildings are held in the actual or constructive possession of the government, to await the direction of Congress, the expectation being that the Commissioner will be ordered to surrender them as the property of the associations upon whose lands they stand, with the limitation that they are to be forever used for educational purposes. Where the principle of the common law is restrained by no statute, it is clear that the government has no valid claim upon these buildings, as they become a part of the realty.

Normal and Preparatory Department.—This department was opened on the second day of May, 1867, in a comfortable building which, with three acres of land, had been purchased by the authorities of the Freedmen's Bureau, by deed dated December 21, 1866, for the sum of $12,000. The funds used in this purchase consisted of the retained bounty which accumulated under an order of Major General B. F. Butler, issued in 1864, at the period when State agents from the north were enlisting colored soldiers in his department in Virginia and North Carolina during the war. The purpose of the order was to save for these enlisted soldiers and their families a portion—one-third—of the large State bounty which they were receiving and wasting in dissipation. When General Howard took charge of freedmen's affairs, this retained fund, then in the hands of numerous officers, was immediately ordered into the custody of the Bureau, to be held for the benefit of the colored race, and subject to the call of legal claimants. This building and land were purchased with money from this fund, and has been rented since January 1, 1867, to the Howard University at $1,200 per annum. The most of this retained bounty, which, when called into the possession of the Bureau, amounted to some $150,000, has since been paid to the legal claimants, reducing the amount in August last to about $30,000; and if the portion invested in this property shall ever be legally claimed it will be at once refunded, the investment being exceedingly judicious in a pecuniary as well as in every other point of view. This money is not in any sense public funds, and is not so regarded at the Treasury Department. It is simply money belonging to colored soldiers, held in trust, subject to their call; and its investment in a mode not only to return fair interest but also to aid in educating the colored race, can be deemed by just men only in the light of a wise and beneficent disposition of the matter on the part of General O. O. Howard. The house was well repaired by the Bureau, and since the school has vacated the premises they have been occupied by the Medical Department.

The Normal and Preparatory Department has been eminently successful. It opened with five scholars in May, 1867, and so rapidly increased in numbers that it became necessary to employ a second teacher, the first quarter closing with an excellent school, the whole number for the period on the register being 83, of whom 26 were females, not including a night school of 11 scholars, under a good teacher. At the close of the first quarter the principal, Rev. Edward F. Williams, a graduate of Yale College and Princeton Theological Seminary, who had given the very highest satisfaction, resigned, in order to embark in his profession, and was succeeded by John H. Combs, A. M., a graduate of Williams College, who served from October, 1867, till April, 1868, when he gave place to A. L. Barber, a graduate of Oberlin, and a gentleman eminently adequate to the position. Miss Julia A. Lord, of Portland, Maine, the female principal, has continued to serve in this position, with the same superior efficiency which distinguished her labors in the colored grammar school of Washington, from which she was called to this place. The total number of students for the year ending in June, 1868, was 127, and the exercises of the first anniversary fully satisfied the expectations of the most sanguine friends. The fall term of 1868 proved still more satisfactory, commencing with more than 60 scholars and the number soon reaching 110, most of whom are pay scholars. Of the whole number only 12 are white. The school, since taking possession of its new and very handsome and commodious quarters in the university building, has put on new strength, and an assistant teacher, a colored young man of good qualifications, has been added to the corps of instruction. The large classes in grammar, philosophy, arithmetic, algebra, and other advanced English branches, as well as the three classes in Latin, numbering in all about 30, and a small class in Greek, progress with as much rapidity and thoroughness as do scholars in the same branches in other schools of this advanced grade, and this statement is based upon extensive personal knowledge of this as well as other schools of the higher class in the District. Tuition is free to such as cannot afford to pay.

The Medical Department.—The Medical Department was organized by the election of three members of its faculty in the early part of May, 1868, and in the month of September a fourth professorship was filled. The list of the university officers and faculties, to be found on a previous page, furnishes the facts in these cases. In September, also, Dr. Alexander T. Augusta, a distinguished colored physician of Washington, was elected as Demonstrator of Anatomy. Dr. Augusta is a gentleman of decided abilities, and is thoroughly educated in his profession. He is a native of Norfolk, Virginia, free-born, and served his apprenticeship as a barber in that city, subsequently working as a journeyman at his trade. In his boyhood he learned by stealth to read a little, and subsequently acquired, while working at his trade, some additional knowledge. At a later period he read medicine for a time in the office of a respectable physician in Philadelphia, but he could get no access to the medical college of that city by reason of his color. He went to California to get money to prosecute his purpose, and was highly successful. On his return he made another effort to find entrance to a Medical College, and was repulsed both in Philadelphia and in Chicago. He finally went to the University of Toronto, and was cordially welcomed to the Medical College of that very distinguished institution, second to no university in British America, and after some half a dozen years of laborious academic, classical as well as professional study he received the degree of Bachelor of Medicine, with the full honors of the college. During the war he was a surgeon in the army, and while stationed at Savannah, Georgia, in charge of a hospital in that city, he was repeatedly associated in professional relations with medical gentlemen of the first eminence in that city, who treated him with uniform courtesy. They often came to his hospital to observe cases interesting to the profession, and to join with him in uncommon surgical operations; facts honorable alike to both parties. Dr. Augusta is the only colored gentleman connected with the medical faculty, so far as it has yet been organized, and for this reason, as well as for the essential interest which marks his career, reference is here made to him. It is a suggestive fact that after such struggles to gain access to a medical school for his own culture, he should thus be called as a teacher in the first school of medical science founded for his race in America.

The first session of this Department was inaugurated in a lecture by Professor L. C. Loomis, which, in order to accommodate the very large audience certain to be called forth on the novel occasion, was delivered in the audience room of the new Congregational church. The session was announced to open on the 28th of October, but arrangements were not complete for the lecture till the succeeding week, and it was delivered November 4, 1868. Since that date the course of lectures has proceeded regularly, three each day of the week, distributed among the six members of the faculty. The class numbered six in December, and a considerable accession was expected with the beginning of the winter session, at the opening of the new year. The college is at present occupying the large building on Seventh street, recently vacated by the Normal and Preparatory Department when that school took up its permanent residence in the university edifice. This is a temporary arrangement, for two or three months only, while the very spacious and handsome medical college structure near that location is finishing. On the same square two large edifices are nearly completed, into which the Freedmen's general hospital—Campbell hospital, as it is commonly called—comprising several hundred patients, is to be transferred, from the old barrack buildings situated in that immediate vicinity. This hospital, which is freely open to the medical students of the college for purposes of instruction, contributes vastly to the value of the course of instruction.

The present course of lectures embraces in its plan Chemistry, Anatomy, Materia Medica, Physiology, and clinical lectures upon operative Surgery—the four main fundamental branches of medicine—and an attendance upon the course, together with study and recitations under a respectable practising physician during the entire year, will be regarded by the University as equivalent to one year in the Medical College. Very superior and ample chemical apparatus, and a complete cabinet of Materia Medica have recently been received.

Other Departments.—The Trustees appointed a committee, June 25, 1867, to report a plan for the organization of a Theological Department, but no action has yet been made public. Initiatory steps were also taken toward establishing a Law Department, and, in October last, John M. Langston, a graduate of Oberlin, a colored gentleman of superior attainments, was elected professor. December 30, 1868, the trustees publicly announced that the Department was organized, and a regular course of lectures would commence January 4, 1869, the faculty to consist of Professor Langston and Hon. A. G. Riddle, an eminent lawyer of Washington, and formerly a member of Congress from Ohio. On the evening of March 31, 1869, the first session of this Department closed with public exercises, in which the class of 15 colored and one white student all participated. The essays and discussions showed much study and thought, and were highly respectable as literary productions, most favorably impressing all who heard them. These students represent nearly a dozen States, and several are liberally educated. They all showed a manly grappling with their work, and the professors have ample reason to be satisfied with the opening term.

PUBLIC SCHOOLS AND EARLIEST LEGISLATION FOR THE CRISIS.

The abolition of slavery in the District of Columbia took effect on the 16th of April, 1862, and on the 21st of May, a little more than a month later, Congress, believing that with their freedom the subjects of slavery must be educated for their new condition, passed an Act requiring "ten per centum of taxes collected from persons of color in Washington and Georgetown to be set apart for the purpose of initiating a system of primary schools for the education of colored children" residing in these cities. This Act made the boards of Trustees of the two cities the custodians, in their respective cities, of the funds arising both from this tax and from contributions, the two species of funds however to be kept separate. The special friends of colored schools in the District, entertaining solicitude as to the execution of this law in good faith by the Trustees of the public schools, communicated their apprehensions to the friends of the cause in Congress, and on the 11th of July ensuing Congress passed another Act, under which the work of establishing colored schools was confided to a "Board of Trustees for Colored Schools for Washington and Georgetown." This board, consisting of three members, is appointed by the Secretary of the Interior, the term of one member expiring annually. The members of the first board, who held the office by the terms of the law one, two, and three years, respectively, were Daniel Breed, Zenas C. Robbins, and S. J. Bowen. Under this Act the municipal authorities of the two cities accredited to the colored school fund for the first two years as follows:

	1862.	1863.	Total.
In Washington	$256 25	$410 89	$667 14
In Georgetown		69 72	69 72
Total for the two cities			736 86

In 1862 no separate registry was kept of the taxes of colored people in either city, and the sum accredited for that year in Washington was a rough estimate. In 1863 there was a separate registration, but the friends of the colored schools regarded it as incomplete, and the fund not at all equal to what was justly due, as they had confidently expected full $3,000 annually.

The Act of 1862 thus proving a failure, another Act was passed and approved June 25, 1864, repealing the ten per centum clause of the Act of 1862 and providing, instead of that feature, that such a proportion of all the school funds raised in Washington and Georgetown should be set apart for colored schools as the number of colored children might bear to the whole number of children, taking the last reported census of children *between the ages of six and seventeen* as the basis of the calculation. It was also provided that the moneys accruing from fines, penalties, and forfeitures under United States laws in the District should be apportioned for school purposes in the same manner. This Act was also, like the other, construed by the municipal authorities in such manner as to deprive the colored schools of a large portion of the funds which the friends of those schools believed the act intended to give them. On the 23d of July, 1866, Congress further enacted that the previous Act should "be so construed as to require the cities of Washington and Georgetown to pay over to the Trustees of the colored schools of said cities such a proportionate part of all moneys received or expended for school or educational purposes in said cities, including the cost of sites, buildings, improvements, furniture, and books, and all other expenditures on account of schools, as the colored children, between the ages of six and seventeen years in the respective cities, bear to the whole number of children, white and colored, between the same ages; that the money shall be considered due and payable to said Trustees on the first day of October of each year; and if not then paid over to them, interest at the rate of ten per centum per annum on the amount unpaid may be demanded and collected." This Act seems to have accomplished the purpose for which it was designed, the funds which it brought into the hands of the Trustees in 1867 enabling them to inaugurate something in the nature of a system of public colored schools in the two cities. The main object of the bill was to provide for the establishment of primary free schools throughout the county of Washington, in the District, outside of the two cities. It was prepared by Senator Patterson, of New Hampshire, at that time a member of the House, and it was a section incorporated in it pertaining to the division of the school money in the cities of Washington and Georgetown that first effectually placed in the hands of the colored people the funds that belonged to them. To Senator Patterson belongs the honor of obtaining this meed of justice for this long abused class.

THE FIRST PUBLIC COLORED SCHOOL

in the District of Columbia was opened on the 1st of March, 1864, in the Ebenezer Church, the original colored church of Washington—the earliest sanctuary of their religion thus becoming the earliest home of their free public school. Miss Emma V. Brown, of Georgetown, an educated, capable colored girl, was appointed the teacher, at a salary of $400, and Miss Frances W. Perkins, a generous, spirited young woman, from New Haven, Connecticut, went into the work with Miss Brown, at first without compensation, though she was soon supported by the New England Freedmen's Aid Society of Boston. The school commencing with 40 scholars, rose immediately to more than 100, and the house was soon so thronged that many applicants were daily refused. It was through the exertions of this volunteer teacher, Miss Perkins, that in 1865

FIRST PUBLIC SCHOOL-HOUSE FOR COLORED CHILDREN.

in the District was built. Through her solicitations, in the summer of 1864 and while at work in the Ebenezer Church, a woman of large benevolence in New Haven, Connecticut, Mrs. —— Parker, placed at her disposal $1,000, to aid in building a house for this school. The Trustees, encouraged by this donation, gathered what they could from other sources, and after securing with some difficulty a lot, 42 by 120 feet, for the purpose, on C street south, between Second and Third streets, Capitol Hill, erected in the winter a frame building, 42 feet square, two stories, and two school-rooms on each floor. The school was moved into it May 1, 1865, on which occasion there were formal dedication exercises, an address being delivered by Rev. Henry Highland Garnet, D. D., then pastor of the Fifteenth street Presbyterian Church, now president of Avery College, Allegheny City, Pennsylvania.

PUBLIC SCHOOLS CONTINUED.

These schools, which began in the Ebenezer church in a single room, with two teachers, in March. 1864, and in the spring of 1865 moved into the first school house built for public schools in the District, were increased by the Aid Societies to four schools and as many teachers in 1866, and to five schools with seven teachers by the Trustees in the summer of 1867. In the autumn of the last named year the Trustees commenced their school year with 31 teachers, four more being soon added, making for nearly the whole of that year 35 teachers, while through the winter and spring months the number was 41, the Aid Societies furnishing at the same time 28, making a total of 69 teachers. The average number through the school year of 1867–'68, was 61.

The largest number of public schools sustained by the Trustees in the school year of 1867–'68, was 41 ; average number 39 ; largest number by other parties 25 ; average number 21 ; largest number of scholars belonging to the schools in any month, (February,) 2,969 ; average number belonging to the schools from November 1 to June 30, 2,826 : average attendance for the same period, 2,523 ; per cent. of average attendance in all schools for the year, 89. In these statistics the schools of the Trustees and of the societies are combined, as they were all under the control of Mr. Newton and all subjected to the same regulations. It will be seen that the attendance, considering the material, was very excellent, and such was the case during all the years of his superintendence. The following figures are important in this connection:

Total colored population in Washington, November, 1867	31,937
Total colored population in Georgetown, November, 1867	3,284
Total	35,221
Increase since 1860 in Washington	20,954
Increase in Georgetown since 1860	1,349
Total	22,303
Number of colored children between the ages of 6 and 17, in Washington	8,401
Number of colored children between the ages of 6 and 17, in Georgetown	894
Total	9,295

It thus appears that the largest number of scholars in school in any month last year was much less than one third the number of colored children in the District between the ages of 6 and 17, and when it is considered that very many above 17 years of age are embraced in the number in school, it seems safe to say that not more than one third of the children within the specified ages were at any time last year attending school, including both public and private. It may be added that the records of the present year present a still more painful condition of things growing out of the withdrawal of nearly all foreign aid.

Recapitulation of Census returns.

The following statement shows the movement of the population of the District, including the town and county of Alexandria before their retrocession to Virginia.

Year.	Whites.	Free colored.	Slaves.	Total.
1800	10,066	783	3,244	14,093
1810	16,079	2,549	5,395	24,023
1820	22,614	4,048	6,377	33,029
1830	27,563	6,152	6,119	39,836
1840	30,657	8,361	4,696	43,912
1850	37,941	10,059	3 687	51,687
1860	60,764	11,131	3,185	75,080
1867	88,327	38,663	....	126,990

As Alexandria, with the other portion of the District as originally constituted south of the Potomac, was retroceded to Virginia in 1846, the population of the retroceded territory in 1850 is subjoined, also the population of the cities of Washington and Georgetown separately for 1850 and 1860.

	White.	Free colored.	Slaves.	Total.
1850.				
Alexandria	7,299	1,413	1,382	10,094
Washington	29,730	8,158	2,113	40,001
Georgetown	6,080	1,561	725	8,366
Remainder of District	2,131	340	849	3,320
1860.				
Washington	50,139	9,209	1,774	61,122
Georgetown	6,793	1,358	577	8,733
Remainder of District	3,827	564	834	5,225

It will be seen from the above figures that the free colored population of the two cities in 1860 was 10,567, and as in that year there were full 1,200 colored children in the schools of the cities, it follows that there was about one child in school to nine of the free colored population. In 1867, the colored population of the two cities was 35,221. With the same proportion of children in school as in 1860, there would be with this population, about 3,900 under instruction, which is very nearly the number now in the schools of the cities. This shows that the facilities for instruction are about the same now for the colored children as before the war. The school-houses and methods of instruction, however, are now much better than in 1860, but the proportion of children actually reached by the privileges seems to be without enlargement.

SCHOOL PROPERTY BELONGING TO TRUSTEES OF PUBLIC SCHOOLS.

The schools, when the Northern societies came here during the war, were at first held in the basements and lecture halls of colored churches. A few school-houses were soon built in a temporary way, and as the war drew near its end the barrack buildings were liberally turned over by the government for such use, and these buildings still constitute the largest portion of the school accommodations. These school rooms were rough and inconvenient, and still continue to be so. The houses built last year are, however, furnished with modern school furniture, as were a few of the old buildings previously, and these are quite commodious and comfortable. The following is a general description of the school property belonging to the trustees of colored schools at this time:

District 1.—Square 182, M street, near 17th. Land about 22,800 feet. Temporary frame building, 48x72 feet two stories; 8 rooms, 444 seats.

District 2.—Square 511, O street, between 4th and 5th. Land about 8,640 feet. Brick school-house 45x88 feet, two stories; eight rooms each 22x38 feet; 444 seats.

District 2.—Square 935, corner 12th street east and D north. Land about 10,000 feet; donated by government. Frame building, four rooms; would seat 200 scholars.

District 3.—Square 762, C street south, between 2d and 3d streets east. Land about 6,300 feet; frame building, four rooms, 200 seats.

District 4.—Square 412, corner 9th and E streets south. Land about 8,000 feet; brick house, same as in district two.

District 4.—Square 663, Delaware avenue, between H and I streets south. Land about 7'550 feet; temporary frame building belonging to government, two rooms, would seat 200 scholars.

District 5.—Georgetown, east street. Land about 5,800 feet; frame building; two stories, eight rooms, 444 seats; bad location; the best that could be obtained for the purpose when bought.

The two brick houses (the one in district 2, and the other in district 4) were built last year, the contract price being some $7,200 each, and when furnished and ready for occupation cost each not far from $9,000. Erected in haste they are not what, with more time, the authorities would have made them. Besides the above specified lots and buildings, the Trustees are erecting a four-story brick edifice which they have appropriately named " The Stevens School-House," in honor of Thaddeus Stevens, of Penn. The name was suggested by Mr. William Syphax, then chairman of the board, in the following resolution, offered by him September 4, 1868 : " *Resolved*, That the New school-house on Twenty-first street be called the ' Stevens School-house' in honor of the late Hon. Thaddeus Stevens, of Pennsylvania, the champion of free schools for all." The building is located in square 72, 21st street, between K and L, on a lot embracing about 11,765 feet. House 48x88 feet ; 12 rooms with the one story for a hall, or 16 rooms without hall, each room seating 60 scholars. The original plan was to make the lower story a hall, to be let for public purposes, but it is believed that the Trustees will decide to use this very desirable part of the building for school purposes, which will accord with the law governing the use of the school funds. The cost of the house, finished and furnished, including lot, will probably be about $35,000. The house, furniture, and lot in Georgetown may be estimated at $5,000; the house, furniture, and lot on M street at $4,000 ; and the house, furniture, and lot on C street, Capitol Hill, at $3,500.

TRUSTEES OF THE COLORED SCHOOLS.

The following shows the names of those who have served as Trustees together with the period of their service. The act of Congress establishing the board, provides that they shall be appointed by the Secretary of the Interior. The original board was appointed July 1, 1862, consisting of S. J. Bowen, Daniel Breed, and Zenas C. Robbins. Mr. Bowen served two terms of three years each, and was succeeded last year (1868) by William Syphax, a well-known and intelligent colored citizen of Washington, who is doing his work with fidelity and excellent judgment as chairman of the board. He was born at Arlington, on the estate of Mr. Custis, who manumitted the mother and family when this son was a child, giving them a house and small tract of land on the border of the estate, which was confirmed to them by the Thirty-ninth Congress. Mr. Breed served two terms, the first being a term of one year, and was succeeded by Albert G. Hull, the present City Collector, whose term expires in 1869. Mr. Robbins served one term of two years and was succeeded in the next term of three years by Rufus Laten, resigned, Stephen J. W. Tabor, resigned, J. McClary Perkins, removed, and G. E. Baker, who completed the term. Alfred Jones, a prominent colored merchant of Washington, was appointed in 1867, his term expiring in 1870, and is the treasurer of the board.

THE TEACHERS.

The Trustees at this time, January, 1869, report fifty schools in successful operation, forty-three in Washington and seven in Georgetown. The superintendent, Mr. George F. T. Cook, had been ten years the teacher of a large colored private school in Washington when appointed to his new position, and is well educated. The schools are all in charge of female teachers, fifty in number, of whom twenty-five are white and twenty-five colored. The majority of the white teachers have been in these schools from the beginning of the new order of things, in 1865, and are remarkably capable and efficient. There are also some very superior colored teachers. Without in any degree disparaging others, mention may properly be made of Miss Sarah L. Iredell, who has charge of the school in what is known as the brick school house on the Island, (Washington.) She was educated at the Institute for colored youth in Philadelphia, where she graduated with the highest honors. The character of her scholarship is by no means ordinary or superficial, as the classical course of that excellent Institution includes the reading of Virgil's Aeneid, the Odes of Horace, Cicero's Orations, the Greek Testament, and Xenophon's Anabasis.

Among the superior colored teachers, the name of Miss Emma Brown may be given. She has already been mentioned in connection with the Georgetown schools, and was educated at Oberlin. There are also other colored teachers, educated at the above-named places, or at the Baltimore convent, or elsewhere, who, in ability and attainment, are quite equal to holding important positions in their profession. Eighteen of the colored teachers are natives of this District, the others being from the north, as also are all the white teachers. Sixty scholars are assigned to each teacher under the regulations of the Board of Trustees, but in some localities this number is exceeded. The school rolls now show an average of about fifty-five to each school, making a total of about 2,750 on the rolls, with an average attendance of about 2,500. There are eight schools in each of the three large school-houses and in the new building, the Stevens school house, there will be twelve. December 1, 1868, was the time fixed for the completion of the Stevens school house, but at this date, January, 1869, much remains to be done, and owing to want of funds, the Trustees have been obliged to suspend some portions of the work. This is greatly to be regretted, as the building is so much needed. If opened at the time expected, every room would have been at once occupied, to the great benefit of those schools and scholars for whom it is intended.* The teacher in each of these buildings, who has the care of the highest school, has also the special direction of all the schools in the building. The pay of the teachers is fixed at $50 per month, with $8 per month additional for those who are in charge of the large buildings. The Trustees, conceding this compensation to be inadequate to secure and retain first-rate teachers, hope ere long to be able to make it larger.

It should be especially stated that the Trustees have made it a principle in selecting teachers, to seek for those having the best qualifications, without regard to color, subjecting all alike to a rigid examination. In a circular issued September 10, 1868, the Trustees say:

"It is our determination to elevate the character of the schools by insisting on a high standard of qualifications in the teachers. This can be done only by employing the best teachers that our money will procure, irrespective of color. While we think it right to give preference in our schools to colored teachers, *their qualifications being equal,* yet we deem it a violation of our official oath to employ inferior teachers when superior ones can be had for the same money. It is no discredit to admit that the number of colored teachers, at least in this District, who can compete successfully with those of the hitherto more favored class, especially those from the northern States, is at present small. When our young men and women shall have enjoyed equal advantages for a sufficient length of time, we may expect this will be changed. The present duty of the Trustees plainly is to employ the best teachers who offer themselves.

---

* NOTE.—Since the above was in type this school-house has been completed and opened.

17

"The children of the people of color, for the most part, can attend school for but a few years, when they must seek employment by which to obtain a livelihood: it is, therefore, of the highest importance that they should make the most of their brief time in school. They should have the best of teachers and the best methods. The methods of teaching have, within the past few years, been as much improved as have those of travel by the introduction of steam. Teachers, who may have the same amount of learning, differ greatly in their ability to teach and train young minds. A skilful teacher, using the best modern methods, will accomplish more in one year, and do it far better, than a poor teacher will accomplish in three years. We deem it, therefore, little short of a *crime* against those for whose education we are made responsible to knowingly employ inferior teachers when better ones can be had, however worthy and deserving the former may be in other respects."

CHARACTER OF THE SCHOOLS.

Of these public schools, five are classified as grammar schools. There was some extravagance in the representations which attended the earlier efforts in the contraband schools. The avidity for instruction and the advancement made by these wild children from the plantations filled the northern teachers, who engaged in the interesting work of first gathering them into places of instruction, with so much astonishment and enthusiasm that in the novel and exciting work unreasonable expectations were in some degree indulged. There were also many children of the District who mingled in those early free schools, who had already been rudely taught some of the first elements. The teachers, not knowing that there were many of this class in the District, oftentimes supposed that the children learned under their instruction what in fact they had learned before. With these considerations fully in view, however, it may still be justly affirmed that the progress of these colored children has been equally as rapid as that of the white. They seem to succeed in mathematics and other studies, which demand the exercise of the reasoning faculty, quite as well as do the children of the lower classes among the white population, and the schools in all the grades justify the best hopes which have been cherished by their friends, furnishing abundant grounds for faith in the capacity of the race to rise to the highest range of intellectual culture, and most certainly of faith in their capacity to become sufficiently intelligent to discharge well the prerogatives of good citizens. The whole body of white teachers, who have taught colored children in this District, since the war, are unanimous in the opinion that the black children learn just as rapidly and thoroughly as do children of any other color. Thoughtful, fair minded men and women, who have carefully watched these schools are compelled, no matter what their prepossessions, to corroborate this judgment of the teachers. These statements are made with deliberation, and are authorized by the result of very large personal observation of the schools, as well as large personal acquaintance with the teachers, on the part of the person who makes them. These facts impose upon the country an imperative and stupendous work. They show that we have a million of colored children, almost entirely untaught, yet capable, and intensely eager to learn. These children must be educated or the country can scarcely stand. How can you build the house of which you have never laid the foundation. Take no timely precaution against the contagion to which youth is exposed, and no future care will cure the malady. Emphatically is this the case with these children, who have come up out of servitude and are subjected to the most untoward home influences. They will soon be out of the reach of a teacher. Once they are grown they will never submit again to become children. So sensible of this were the wise Lacedemonians that when they were required to give fifty children as hostages they chose rather to give fifty of the most eminent men in the State, whose principles were already formed, than children to whom the want of early instruction would be a loss entirely irreparable. It would be, according to the beautiful expression of Pericles, like cutting off the season of spring altogether from the year.

SCHOOL FUNDS AND THE FREEDMEN'S BUREAU.

In has been seen in these pages that much assistance, both in money and material, and in many forms has been contributed to the work of colored education in the District by the Freedmen's Bureau. In the annual reports of the Bureau these contributions to the cause are designated as derived from funds bearing different names, and as the nature of these funds is not well understood a concise statement of their origin may be found useful in this connection.

Refugees and Freedmen's Fund.—When the war closed there were found large sums of money in the hands of various military officers, the accumulations resulting from incidents of the conflict. When the Freedmen's Bureau was organized these funds were all called into the custody of its accounting officer, and to distinguish them from those derived from the regular appropriations by Congress for the support of the Bureau, are described by the Commission as the Refugees and Freedmen's funds, derived from miscellaneous sources. The chief of these sources were the tax on cotton, wages retained from the freedmen employed by the government during the war, for the relief of destitute freedmen's families, fines in the provost courts, taxes levied upon the planters and men of wealth in New Orleans, and other parts of Louisiana, for the support of colored schools, proceeds of confiscated property, marriage certificates, and contracts. During the first year after the war closed a considerable amount was received from the produce of farms and other abandoned lands, from rents of buildings and lands held as abandoned, in all amounting to nearly a million of dollars. The taxes upon cotton, wages of Freedmen withheld, fines in provost courts, and donations above specified, and moneys from sales of confiscated property, marriage certificates, and contracts, are generalized in the reports as the Freedmen's fund, but are all embraced under the name of Refugees and Freedmen's fund. This fund, which has been constantly receiving additions, from the miscellaneous sources, as well as suffering depletions from its donations, was reduced in August last to about $16,000. In the general appropriation act, approved March 2, 1867, is the following clause: "*Provided*, That the Commissioner be hereby authorised to apply any balance on hand at this date, of the Refugees and Freedmen's fund, accounted for in his last annual report, to aid educational institutions actually incorporated for loyal refugees and freedmen." Under this provision contributions have been made to such institutions in this District, as follows:

The Howard University, Congregationalist, $25,000; National Theological Institute University, Baptist, $10,600; St. Martin's Female Academy, Catholic, $2,000.

Retained Bounty Fund.—This is a fund which accumulated under an order of Major General B. F. Butler, issued in 1864, while he was in command of the department embracing a portion of Virginia and North Carolina. It was an order fraught with wisdom. This department was, at the time, thronged with State agents, offering very large bounties for contraband recruits to fill the State quotas. This order required the State agent or other person not enlisting recruits under the direct orders of the War Department, to pay one third of the bounty, in case of each recruit, into the hands of the superintendent of recruiting, and that, in default of such payment, the recruit should have his papers so certified that he could not be counted in any State quota. The object was to save the money for the benefit of the recruit and his family. When General Howard came to take charge of the Bureau, he very discreetly ordered all the fund, which had been scattered in the hands of many officers, into the custody of the Bureau. It amounted at that time to $115,236 49, and was embraced under the general name of Refugees and Freedmen's fund, but as it is in no sense public money, but essentially funds belonging to individuals, held in trust by the government, it has been kept separate and paid over to the legal claimants as fast as found. The balance still unclaimed, at the close of August last, was $24,963 83. The Bureau has used $12,000 of this unclaimed sum in the purchase of the building in which the preparatory department of the Howard University was at first held, and in which the medical department is now temporarily located. It is leased to the University at an annual rent of ten per cent on its cost, thus aiding the cause of the colored race, at the same time that a liberal interest is accumulating on the fund. The property has largely enhanced in value since the purchase.

School Fund.—This has been treated as a local fund by the Bureau, each assistant committeeman expending it in the district in which it may have accrued. It is derived from a provision in the act of Congress of July 16, 1866, which declares that " the commissioner shall have power to seize, hold, lease or sell all buildings and tenements, and any lands appertaining to the same, or otherwise formerly held under color of title by the late so-called confederate states and not heretofore disposed of by the United States, and buildings or lands held in trust for the same by any person or persons, and to use the same, or appropriate the proceeds derived therefrom, to the education of the freed people." Nothing has been received from this source in this District, and nothing expended.

The General appropriation.—The act of March 2, 1867, appropriated "for buildings for schools and asylums, including construction, rental, and repairs, five hundred thousand dollars." It is from this appropriation that the assistance in erecting houses has been extended in various ways to the Trustees of Public Colored Schools of the District, and to nearly all the private enterprises in the District looking to the education of the colored people. Among the donations to the public schools of the District were two sums of twenty-five hundred dollars each, given in aid of the two branch school buildings erected in Washington in the autumn of 1867. Liberal assistance has also been given these schools in the form of lumber and old barrack buildings. From this appropriation also the Howard University buildings are erecting, and the Colfax Industrial building, and aid has been given to nearly all the schools of the District which have the education of the colored people specially in view.

LEGISLATION 1868-'69.

In the early part of July, 1868, some of the friends of education in Washington conceiving it to be for the interest of the schools to have them all, both white and colored, under the supervision of a single board of trustees, proposed to the Committee on the District in the Senate to transfer all the duties of the trustees of colored schools in Washington and Georgetown to the trustees of white schools, abolishing the board of trustees of colored schools, but leaving the schools themselves without any change in relations and condition. The members of the committee in the Senate understanding from the representations that this plan was in accordance with the wishes of the leading colored people of the two cities, through Mr. Patterson, of New Hampshire, presented to the Senate July 3d the following bill, which was passed without discussion or dissent:

"*Be it enacted by the Senate and House of Representatives of the United States of America in Congress assembled,* That the several acts of Congress authorizing the appointment and defining the duties of a board of trustees of colored schools in the cities of Washington and Georgetown, in the District of Columbia, be, and the same are hereby, so modified as to transfer all the duties heretofore imposed by said acts on said trustees of colored schools to the trustees of public schools in said cities. All laws and parts of laws inconsistent herewith are hereby repealed."

It should be stated in justice to Mr. Patterson that he had nothing to do with the matter in committee, and presented the bill under the suggestions of the other members of the committee who more especially had the matter in charge. When this action of the Senate was announced the colored people specially interested in the schools went immediately to the Committee on the District in the House and made their remonstrance against the measure, and the bill, sent to the Committee on the District in the House, lay there till February last, the colored people, and in fact most of those originally proposing the measure to the Senate, supposing, as it appears, that it would receive no further attention. It was, however, February, 1869, reported to the House, and passed, as in the Senate, without debate or opposition. Its passage, however, created great excitement among the colored people of the District, the great mass of whom seemed to be utterly opposed to the measure. They held a public meeting and took formal action expressive of their views, and on the succeeding Sabbath the matter was presented in all the colored churches of the two cities, an overwhelming majority being found unqualifiedly opposed to the act. At the public meeting above referred to, held in the Israel Bethel church February 9, 1869, at which Mr. John F. Cook presided, the following resolutions were passed:

"Whereas by an act of Congress of May 21, 1862, provision was made for initiating a system of primary schools for the education of colored children in the cities of Washington and Georgetown, and the execution of the law was committed to the boards of trustees of public schools; and whereas by said boards positively refusing said executive trust, it was made necessary that Congress, by another act July 11, 1862, should place the execution of the law in charge of a separate board of three trustees of colored schools, to be appointed by the Secretary of the Interior; and whereas that officer, in such appointments, has rendered perfect satisfaction to us as a people, and we have been generally satisfied with the faithfulness of said trustees of colored schools in the discharge of this trust; and whereas the act recently passed by Congress transferring this duty from the trustees of colored schools to the trustees of public schools, thus subjecting it to the chances of being again refused, or at least being negligently or indifferently executed by persons whose positions are held by tenure of local politics and the prejudices consequent thereunto: Therefore,

"*Resolved*, That we, the colored citizens of Washington and Georgetown, D. C., deeply regret the action of Congress in making this transfer of the schools for colored children to the trustees of public schools until some more perfect system can be established in the District of Columbia."

"*Resolved*, That we, the colored citizens of Washington and Georgetown, District of Columbia, do hereby tender our thanks to Messrs. Albert G. Hall, Alfred Jones, and William Syphax, trustees of our schools, for the faithful performance of the trust committed to them, and do assure them of our hearty co-operation in all their efforts to promote the educational interests of our children."

The above resolutions were passed by almost a unanimous vote. The only opposition made to the action was based upon the idea that it was indiscreet for the colored people to array themselves against the action of Congress, which was controlled in its measures by the friends of the colored race. The measure in itself was not defended at all. Similar resolutions were adopted at crowded meetings held at the Nineteenth street Baptist church, at Asbury chapel, Union Bethel church, the Third Baptist church, the Ebenezer church, and other churches. The last meeting was held at the Fifteenth street Presbyterian church to take final action on the matter. The pastor, Rev. J. Stella Martin, addressed the congregation, and the following resolution was adopted, but one person voting in the negative:

"*Resolved*, That we are in favor of free schools and equal school rights, under a school system embracing white and colored children, and therefore we deprecate any legislation that does not abolish *in toto* the present system, built upon distinctions of race and color. We especially deprecate the bill transferring the powers from the board for colored schools, because it leaves it optional with the board to be appointed under that bill, should it become a law, to continue colored schools ; and also because the apportionment of the proposed board will be controlled by local politics, which one year may put in our friends, and the next year our enemies, which last, having the power of keeping up distractions in schools, gives every reason to believe they will use that power. We therefore petition Congress most respectfully to reserve all legislation on the subject till such time as they can pass a bill which will make us in the matter of school rights equal with all others *before the law;* that we may not be dependent upon personal favor in a matter so vital, nor exposed to political hostility in circumstances where we are powerless."

On the 13th of February, 1869, the President returned the bill without his signature, with his reasons as follows:

" The accompanying paper (preamble and resolutions of the colored people on the subject) exhibits the fact that the legislation which the bill proposes is contrary to the wishes of the colored residents of Washington and Georgetown, and that they prefer that the schools for their children should be under the management of trustees selected by the Secretary of the Interior, whose term of office is for four years, rather than subject to the control of bodies whose tenure of office, depending merely upon political considerations, may be annually affected by the elections which take place in the two cities.

"The colored people of Washington and Georgetown are at present not represented by a person of their own race in either of the boards of trustees of public schools appointed by the municipal authorities. Of the three trustees, however, who, under the act of July 11, 1862, compose the board of trustees of the schools for colored children, two are persons of color. The resolutions transmitted herewith show that they have performed their trust in a manner entirely satisfactory to the colored people of the two cities, and no good reason is known to the Executive why the duties which now devolve upon them should be transferred as proposed in the bill.

" With these brief suggestions, the bill is respectfully returned, and the consideration of Congress invited to the accompanying preamble and resolutions.

"ANDREW JOHNSON.

" WASHINGTON, D. C., *February* 13, 1869."

With the facts which had been disclosed in relation to this matter in view, Congress declined to act further upon the measure, and thus it ended.

SUMMARY.

Private and incorporated educational institutions for colored persons, Washington and George-town, January, 1869.

Name.	Location.	Sex.	Scholars.
Howard University, Normal and Preparatory Department.	Seventh street and boundary...	Mixed...	112
Howard University Law school		Males ...	16
Howard University Medical school		Males ...	8
Howard University Collegiate Department		Male	1
Wayland Theological Seminary	Nineteenth and I streets	Males ...	36
National Theological Institute and University, Rev. E. Turney, D. D.	I street, near Twenty-third	Males ...	45
National Theological Institute and University, Rev. G. M. P. King.	Judiciary Square	Mixed...	50
New England Friends' Mission school	Thirteenth street west, and S ...	Mixed...	250
Colfax Industrial school	R and Eleventh streets	Girls	200
Miss Walker's Industrial School	Near boundary, Fifth street	Women .	70
Orphan Asylum school	Eighth street, near boundary...	Mixed...	55
St. Aloysius's Parochial school	First street, between I and K...	Girls ...	80
St. Martin's Academy	Vermont Avenue and L street..	Girls	40
St. Martin's Parochial school	Vermont Avenue and L street..	Girls	45
St. Martin's Academy	Fifteenth street, bet. L and M..	Boys ...	30
St. Martin's Parochial school	Fifteenth street, bet. L and M ..	Boys ...	30
Reformed Presbyterian Mission school	Sixth street west near M south..	Mixed...	200
Miss Maria R. Mann's school	Seventeenth and M streets	Mixed...	50
Miss E. A. Cook's school	Sixteenth street, bet. K and L..	Mixed...	30
Thomas H. Mason's school	L street, near Twenty-first west.	Mixed...	50
Joseph Ambush's school	Eleventh and K streets	Mixed...	65
Mrs. C. W. Grove's school	Twenty-third street and Circle..	Girls ...	20
Mrs. Louisa Ricks's school	I street, near Seventeenth	Girls ...	50
Rev. E. Turney's school—Miss L. Warner, teacher	Baptist Church, Vt. Avenue	Women .	25
Rev. E. Turney's school—W. Waller, teacher	Fourth street east, near D south.	Mixed...	15
Rev. Chauncey Leonard's school	Third and G streets	Mixed...	55
Total			1,628
NIGHT SCHOOLS.			
Colfax Industrial school	R and Eleventh streets	Mixed...	212
Washington Christian Union	O street, bet. Fourth and Fifth.	Mixed...	200
Washington Christian Union	E street, Island	Mixed...	50
J. R. Fletcher's school, (Washington Christian Union) ...	Judiciary Square	Mixed...	75
Rev. E. Turney's school	I street, near Twenty-third	Men	30
Rev. E. Turney's school	Baptist Church, Vt. Avenue	Men	30
Rev. E. Turney's school—W. Waller, teacher	Baptist Church, Fourteenth st ..	Men	15
Rev. E. Turney's school—John Johnson, teacher	Nineteenth st. west, near b'dry.	Men	20
Rev. E. Turney's school—Mrs. Ellen Reeves, teacher....	Arlington*	Mixed...	100
St. Martin's school	Fifteenth street, bet. L and M..	Males ...	15
Rev. Chauncey Leonard	Corner Third and G streets	Mixed...	25
Henry Thorps	Near Navy Department	Males ...	20
Total			792

* Not in the District.

Colored Public Schools, Washington and Georgetown, January, 1869.

Location.	Buildings, property of—	No. of rooms.	No. of teachers.	Grade.					Average attendance.
				Primary.	Secondary.	Intermediate.	Grammar.	Mixed.	
M street, near Seventeenth street	Trustees	8	8	2	2	2	1	1	400
Corner Seventeenth and I streets	Government	4	3	1	1	1			162
Corner Twenty-fourth and F streets	Government	4	2	1	1				100
Fourteenth street, near canal	Rel. denomination ...	1	1	1					70
Corner Thirteenth and S streets	N. E. Friends	4	5	2	1	1		1	220
L street, near Sixteenth street	Private	1	1						50
O street, between Fourth and Fifth streets ...	Trustees	8	8	3	2	2	1		400
C street south, near Second street east	Trustees	4	4	1	1	1	1		220
Corner D street north and Twelfth street east.	Government	4	1					1	60
Corner E street south and Ninth street west .	Trustees	8	8	3	2	2	1		400
Delaware Avenue, H and I streets south	Trustees	2	2	1				1	160
Georgetown, East street	Trustees	8	7	3	2	1	1		350
Total		56	50	18	12	10	5	4	2,532

Teachers of Colored Public Schools.

Names.	White.	Colored.	Location of schools.	State.	Began teaching in the District.
Miss Sarah G. Brown	1	....	M street, near Seventeenth street..	Massachusetts ...	1867
Mrs. Anna P. Spencer	....	1	....do	New Jersey	1868
Miss M. E. Brooks	....	1	........do	Maryland	1868
Miss Helen A. Simmons	1	....	........do	Connecticut	1865
Mrs. M. C. Hart	1	....	........do	Massachusetts ...	1868
Miss Mary E. Garrett	....	1	........do	Dist. Columbia...	1868
Miss Laura V. Fisher	....	1	........do	...... do.........	1867
Miss Abby S. Simmons	1	....	........do	Connecticut	1865
Miss Annie E. Washington	....	1	Corner Seventeenth and I streets .	Dist. Columbia...	1857
Miss C. A. Jones	....	1	........do	...... do.........	1867
Miss Lucy A. Barbour	....	1	........do	...... do.........	1867
Miss Mary F. Kiger	....	1	Corner Twenty-fourth and F sts..	...... do.........	1867
Miss G. I. Fleet	....	1	........do	...... do.........	1867
Miss R. H. Elwell	1	....	Fourteenth street, near canal.....	Connecticut	1865
Miss H. S. Macomber	1	....	Corner Thirteenth and S streets...	Massachusetts ...	1867
Miss Mary E. Oliver	1	....	........do	...... do.........	1867
Miss Mary E. Gove	1	....	........do	...... do.........	1866
Miss Mary C. Lawton	1	....	........do	...... do.........	1868
Miss S. H. Pierce	1	....	........do	..... do.........	1867
Mrs. Nancy Warrick*	....	1	L street, near Sixteenth street	Dist. Columbia...	1861
Miss Emma J. Hutchins	1	....	O st., bet. Fourth and Fifth sts. ..	New Hampshire .	1868
Miss Laura W. Stebbins	1	....	........do	Massachusetts ...	1864
Mrs. F. H. Disbrow	1	....	........do	...... do.........	1866
Miss C. F. Withington	1	....	........do	Dist. Columbia...	1868
Miss Annie L. Foote	....	1	........do	...... do.........	1867
Miss Annie M. Wilson	....	1	........do	New York.......	1868
Miss Maria A. Dorster	....	1	........do	Massachusetts ...	1865
Miss Rachel J. Cook	....	1	........do	Dist. Columbia...	1867
Miss K. G. Crane	1	....	C st. south, near Second st. east....	Maine	1865
Miss Sarah Purvis	....	1	........do	Pennsylvania....	1868
Miss Christiana Nichols	....	1	........do	Dist. Columbia...	1868
Miss Helen M. Gordon	1	....	Cor. D st. north and Twelfth st. east.	Massachusetts ...	1865
Miss Grace A. Dyson	....	1	Cor. E st. north and Ninth st. west.	Dist. Columbia...	1867
Miss E. L. Crane	1	....	........do	Vermont	1865
Miss Sarah L. Iredell	....	1	........do	Pennsylvania....	1868
Miss M. R. Nason	1	....	........do	Massachusetts ...	1867
Miss Emma Prentiss	1	....	........do	Ohio	1868
Mrs. E. J. Brooks	....	1	........do	Dist. Columbia...	1867
Miss G. Withington	1	....	........do	Massachusetts ...	1867
Miss Mary R. Goines	....	1	........do	Dist. Columbia...	1867
Miss Mary E. Reed	....	1	........do	...... do.........	1868
Miss Eliza G. Randall	1	....	Delaware av., near H st. south...	Vermont	1867
Miss Anna V. Tompkins	....	1	........do	Dist. Columbia...	1868
Miss E. A. Chamberlain	1	....	East street, Georgetown...........	Massachusetts ...	1864
Miss P. T. Chamberlain	1	....	........do	...... do.........	1864
Miss C. W. Moore	1	....	........do	New Jersey......	1868
Miss Julia Luckett	....	1	........do	Canada	1868
Miss Mary A. Coakley	....	1	........do	Dist. Columbia...	1868
Miss Sophia P. Parsons	1	....	........do	New York.......	1865
Miss Martha C. Simms	....	1	........do	Dist. Columbia...	1868
Total	25	25			

* Mrs. Warrick, an excellent colored teacher, has been already mentioned under her maiden name of Nancy Waugh, as teacher with Rev. Chauncey Leonard in the Smother's school-house, at the time it was destroyed by incendiaries in 1863. Soon after that event she opened a private school in the Nineteenth-street Baptist church, subsequently removing it to L street, near Sixteenth street, where she continues to teach, having from 40 to 50 scholars. During most of the present school year, 1868–'69, her school-house has been used by the Trustees of the colored public schools, as they were needing more room, and she was also employed by them to conduct the school. In April, 1869, she resumed her private school.

2. COLORED SCHOOLS OF WASHINGTON COUNTY.

LEGISLATION—1856, 1862.

The earliest attempt to establish a system of free schools in the District outside the cities was embraced in an Act of Congress approved August 11, 1856. This Act, however, was not to become valid unless approved by "a vote of the majority of those persons residing and paying taxes within the limits of the District in which the poll is opened," the act providing for the division of the territory into seven school districts. The result was the rejection of the act in every district. The women, who were entitled to the franchise under the act, generally voting, it is believed, with the majority. The 36th section provided that "those who are for this act shall write on their ballots ' school,' and those opposed 'no school.' " It resulted that those who wrote "no school" had it all their own way, and as this was the first experiment in giving the franchise to women by Congress the result is the more curious. Mr. De Vere Burr, of district 5, was one of the commissioners under the law of 1856 and a warm friend of the cause. In that district three women voted, Mrs. Ann McDaniel, a large tax payer, who voted "school," and Mrs. Emily Beall and Mrs. Washington Berry, who voted "no school."

Thus the matter rested till March 19, 1862, when Mr. Grimes, chairman of the District committee of the Senate, introduced into that body a copy of the act of 1856, with the section making it optional with the voters of the districts to accept its provisions omitted. It was referred to the District committee, who made no changes in its provisions, except such as restricted the taxation exclusively to property owned by white people. This exemption was not a new proposition in the Senate, as the same principle was asserted in a bill for the encouragement of free schools in Washington, which passed the Senate in May, 1858, but which went to the House District Committee, and was there buried. It proposed in substance to create a new school fund amounting to $50,000 from the fines and forfeitures in the District, and to pay annually from the United States treasury to the support of the schools of the city as much as the city raised for the same purpose annually, not exceeding $20,000 a year. When this bill was reported to the Senate by Mr. Brown, of Mississippi, chairman of the District Committee, Mr. John P. Hale, May 15, 1858, moved an additional section in amendment as follows: "*And be it further enacted*, That all taxes levied on the estates of colored persons in the city of Washington shall be devoted to the support of schools for the education of colored children, under the direction of the government of the city." In offering the amendment Mr. Hale, in terms of conciliation, but of melancholy significance, appealed to the reason and humanity of the party then reigning in that body as follows:

"I desire to state that several of these individuals have spoken of it to me as a case of extreme hardship that the colored population here are taxed for the support of schools—and it forms no inconsiderable amount of the taxes contributed—and whilst they are compelled to pay taxes, their children have not the slightest benefit of the schools. I do not propose to establish any mixed schools or anything else, but to donate the taxes collected from this class to the education of their own children under the direction of the city government, and it seems to me to be a matter of such plain justice that it will hardly be denied. *They are an oppressed and degraded people*, and I think it hardly comports with the magnanimity of their superiors to collect their money and to use it to educate their own children. I hope that this proposition will commend itself to the chairman (Mr. Albert G. Brown, of Mississippi) of the District Committee."

Senator Brown, with large and enlightened ideas pertaining to free schools for his own race, was not willing to give the slightest aid, even indirectly, to encourage free schools for the colored race. "The city authorities have never made provision for the education of colored people," said he, "and I do not believe they ever will." He would not consent to tax the colored people to aid in their enlightenment, but would exempt their property from taxation for support of education. Mr. Hale, anxious to secure any relief, however small, the dominant power would give, immediately offered the following modification of his amendment, which was accepted without debate:

"SECTION —. *And be it further enacted*, That the estates of colored persons in the District of Columbia shall be entirely exempted from all taxes levied for schools and school-houses in the District."

The Act of May 20, 1862, which, as has been stated, was copied mainly from the act of August 11, 1856, embraced amendments confining the taxation for white schools and school-houses to property belonging to white persons, in accordance with Mr. Hale's amendment, though confined to the territory outside the cities. This bill, referred to the District Committee March 19, 1862, was reported March 24 by the chairman, Mr. Grimes, with the modifications above indicated, and when the bill was under discussion in final debate, April 4, he offered as an amendment the following, which was adopted as the thirty-fifth section of the act:

"SECTION 35. *And be it further enacted*, That the said levy court may, in its discretion, and if it shall be deemed by said court best for the interest and welfare of the colored people residing in such county, levy an annual tax of one-eighth of one per cent. on all the taxable property in said county outside the limits of the cities of Washington and Georgetown, owned by persons of color, for the purpose of initiating a system of education of colored children in said county, which tax shall be collected in the same manner as the tax named in section thirteen of this act. And it shall be the duty of the trustees elected under section nine to provide suitable and convenient rooms for holding schools for colored children, to employ teachers therefor, and to appropriate the proceeds of said tax to the payment of teachers' wages, rent of school rooms, and other necessary expenses pertaining to said schools; to exercise a general supervision over them, to establish proper discipline, and to endeavor to promote a full, equal, and useful instruction of the colored children in said county. It shall be lawful for such trustees to impose a tax of not more than fifty cents per month on the parent or guardian of each child attending such schools, to be applied to the payment of the expenses of the school of which such child shall be an attendant, and in the exercise of this power the trustees may from time to time discontinue the payment altogether, or may graduate the tax according to the ability of the child and the wants of the school. And said trustees are authorized to receive any donations or contributions that may be made for the benefit of said schools by persons disposed to aid in the elevation of the colored population in the District of Columbia, and to apply the same in such manner as in their opinion shall be best calculated to effect the object of the donors, said trustees being required to account for all funds received by them, and to report to the commissioners in accordance with the provisions of section twenty-two of this act."

The Act was entitled, "An Act to provide for the public instruction of youth in primary schools throughout the county of Washington, in the District of Columbia, without the limits of the cities of Washington and Georgetown," the same as the act of 1856. Both acts provided for the appointment of "seven intelligent inhabitants of the said county," outside the cities, by the levy court as school commissioners, and for the division by them of the territory under their jurisdiction into seven school districts, which districts were empowered to raise money by taxation to build school-houses and supply furniture. The levy court was required annually to impose a tax of one-eighth of one per cent. on all the assessable property in said territory "owned by white persons." The individual districts were enjoined to choose three district trustees to manage the district affairs, and a district collector. In case any district should persist in disregarding the requirements of the Act, the money annually raised by the assessment of the levy court, of which one-seventh belonged to each district, was to be held two years from the refractory districts, and then to be divided equally among the districts which had complied with the conditions of the Act. It was soon found that this legislation was so imperfect that little would be accomplished under it for white schools, while for the creation of a system of public schools for the colored people it would contribute no real assistance at all. It failed to benefit the colored people because it did not embrace in its provisions the principle vital to the free school system—that the taxable property of the State should provide for the education of all the children of the State without regard to the individuals to whom the property may belong, the children of poverty and of affluence standing on an absolute equality in all the rights and the privileges of the schools. The Act of 1862 was based upon ideas wholly averse to this theory. The Act of 1856 contemplated only the white race. The Act of 1862 embraced in its provisions both the white and the colored races, but in providing for the separate assessment of the property belonging to the two races it ceased to be a *common school* law in any just sense of the term. The provision in the amendment introduced by Mr. Grimes authorizing the commissioners in their discretion to fix a limited tuition to be paid in the colored schools by such as were able to pay, and which was also embraced in a section of the bill pertaining to white schools, was another feature tending directly to foster the idea of caste and to degrade the free school system in the public estimation. It was a feature, moreover, which had been tried in the white public schools of Washington for the first third of a century of their history, and repudiated as a calamitous experiment years before the passage of this act. The commissioners early saw that the act was exceedingly defective. At a special meeting of the board February 14, 1863, Dr. C. H. Nichols, the president of the board, after stating that in his judgment the existing law could not be made effectual in the erection of the school-houses essential to the establishment of the schools contemplated in the act, presented the draught of a bill which he had prepared as a substitute for the existing act, to be put into the hands of the District Committee. The bill was read section by section and approved by the members present at that meeting. In May, 1863, Dr. Nichols retired from the board, but his bill seems to have been placed in the hands of the District Committee of the Senate. On the 28th of January, 1864, at a meeting of the board, Mr. S. P. Brown, from the committee on the school act, reported a new bill, which had been prepared by Mr. C. H. Wiltberger. February 1, 1864, this bill was taken up, and, after discussion, adopted with some amendments, and the committee instructed to place it in the hands of the Senate District Committee.

THE ACT OF 1864.

This act, which is the existing school law for the whole District, originated in a bill brought into the Senate December 21, 1863, and one of the two bills already mentioned as in the hands of the District Committee. On the 9th of February, 1864, Mr. Grimes submitted the Wiltberger bill, with some modifications, as a substitute for the bill No. 26, already before the Senate, and on February 18 it was discussed at some length in the Senate and passed without any opposition, the only controversy being upon the expediency of allowing the commissioners $4 per day for actual service as was provided in the bill, the provision being finally by general assent discarded. The bill went to the House February 19, was referred to the District Committee February 26, and was reported back to the House April 28 by Hon. James W. Patterson, then chairman of the District Committee of that body, with amendments, constituting substantially a new bill. On the 8th of June, when the Senate bill came up in the House, Mr. Patterson moved the adoption of his bill in the way of a substitute for that of the Senate, and said:

" As this bill has not been printed, perhaps I ought to say a word in explanation, especially as it is an important bill for the District. It will be observed by comparing the Senate bill (No. 26) with the substitute reported by the House Committee that there are several minor amendments, some of them intended to perfect the bill, and others designed to bring it into complete conformity with the best results of the experience in those States where systems of education have been most liberally and successfully sustained. In the 20th section we have endeavored to give efficiency to the system by requiring all penalties and forfeitures imposed for violation of the laws of the United States to be paid into the hands of certain officers, who are made the custodians of this fund and are required to expend it for school purposes. But the most important feature of the amendment is to be found in the 17th and 18th sections, and in the proviso to the 19th section, which provides for separate schools for the colored children of the District. To accomplish this we have provided that such a proportion of the entire school fund shall be set apart for this purpose as the number of colored children, *between the ages of six and seventeen*, bears to the whole number of children in the District. These are the principal points of difference between the Senate bill and the substitute reported by the Committee for the District of Columbia. I may say that the committee were unanimous in their approval of these provisions, and I trust that that foreshadows the unanimity in the House. We may have differences of opinion in regard to the policy to be pursued in respect to slavery, but we all concur in this, that we have been brought to a juncture in our national affairs in which four millions of a degraded race, lying below the average civilization of the age and depressed by an almost universal prejudice, are to be set free in our midst. The question now is, what is our first duty in regard to them? I think there can be no difference of opinion on this, that it is our duty to give to this people the means of education, that they may be prepared for all the privileges which we may desire to give them hereafter." The bill was adopted without opposition June 8, 1864. The following are the sections to which Mr. Patterson called attention, and which constitute the only legislation of solid substance ever enacted by Congress for the establishment of colored schools in the District, embracing in their provisions the cities as well as "the county parts:"

"SECTION 17. It shall be the duty of the said commissioners to provide suitable and convenient houses or rooms for holding schools for colored children; to employ and examine teachers therefor, and to appropriate a proportion of the school funds, to be determined by the numbers of white and colored children between the ages of six and seventeen years, to the payment of teachers' wages, to the building or renting of school-rooms, and other necessary expenses pertaining to said schools; to exercise a general supervision over them, to establish proper discipline, and endeavor to promote a thorough, equitable, and practical education of colored children in said county. It shall be lawful for said commissioners to impose a tax of not more than fifty cents per month for each child on the parents or guardians of children attending said schools, to be applied to the payment of the expenses of the school of which said child shall be an attendant; and in the exercise of this power the commissioners may, from time to time, discontinue the payment altogether, or may graduate the tax according to the ability of said tax-payers and the wants of the school: *Provided*, That no child shall be excluded from such school on account of the inability of the parent or guardian to pay said tax. And said commissioners are authorized to receive any donations or contributions that may be made for the benefit of said schools by persons disposed to aid in the elevation of the colored population in the District of Columbia, and to supply the same in such manner as in their opinion shall be best calculated to effect the objects of the donors, said commissioners being required to account for all funds received by them, and to report to the levy court in accordance with the provisions of section nine of this act.

"SEC. 18. The first section of the act of Congress entitled 'An act providing for the education of colored children in the cities of Washington and Georgetown, District of Columbia, and for other purposes,' be and the same is hereby repealed; and that from and after the passage of this act it shall be the duty of the municipal authorities of the cities of Washington and Georgetown, in the District of Columbia, to set apart each year from the whole fund received from all sources by such authorities, applicable under existing provisions of law to purposes of education, such proportionate part thereof as the number of colored children between *the ages of six and seventeen years* in the respective cities bear to the whole number thereof, for the purpose of establishing and sustaining public schools in said cities for the education of colored children; that the said proportion shall be ascertained by the last reported census of the population of said cities made prior to said appointment, and shall be regulated at all times thereby; and that the said fund shall be paid to the trustees appointed under the act of Congress approved July eleven, eighteen hundred and sixty-two, entitled 'An act relating to schools for the education of colored children in the cities of Washington and Georgetown, in the District of Columbia,' to be disbursed by them in accordance with the provisions of said act.

"SEC. 19. One-fourth part of all the moneys now in the hands of the marshal of the District of Columbia, or of any other officer of said District, which have accrued from fines, penalties, and forfeitures imposed for the violations of the laws of the United States within said District, shall be by such officer or officers paid to the 'board of commissioners of primary schools of Washington county, District of Columbia,' one-fourth part to the mayor of the city of Georgetown, and the remaining two-fourths thereof to the mayor of the city of Washington; the said sums, so paid to the said commissioners and the said mayors, to constitute in their hands funds for the support of primary schools within the said county and public schools in said cities in the proportions aforesaid. And it shall be the duty of said marshal and other officers to pay over every three months, from and after the passage of this act, all money coming into their hands in the manner aforesaid, to the said board of commissioners of primary schools and to the said mayors, in the proportions aforesaid, for the use of the said primary and public schools, any law to the contrary notwithstanding: *Provided*, That the funds thus obtained for educational purposes shall be applied to the education of both white and colored children, in the proportion of the numbers of each between the ages of *six and seventeen years* as determined by the latest census report that shall have been made prior to such appointment; and the mayors of the aforesaid cities of Georgetown and Washington are hereby authorized and instructed to pay over such part thereof as may be applicable, under the provisions of this section and the proviso thereto, to the education of colored children in the aforenamed cities, to the trustees appointed under the act of July eleventh, eighteen hundred and sixty-two, entitled 'An act relating to schools for the education of colored children in the cities of Georgetown and Washington, in the District of Columbia,' to be used for the education of colored children according to the provisions of law; and the aforenamed officers failing to pay over the moneys as aforesaid shall be liable to the penalty imposed by the second section of the act of Congress approved July twelfth, eighteen hundred and sixty-two, entitled 'An act to provide for the payment of fines and penalties collected by and paid the justices of the peace in the District of Columbia under the acts of Congress approved the third and fifth of August, eighteen hundred and sixty-one, and for other purposes.'"

THE SCHOOL FUNDS.

The act of 1864, as the bill came from the hands of Mr. Patterson and became a law, embraces the true ideas of the free school system as enunciated with such terseness and force by Mr. Grimes and Mr. Morrill. Under its operations the friends of common schools were inspired with new energy, and the colored schools were now immediately brought into consideration as an established fact in the county. The provision authorizing the commissioners to impose a tuition upon children whose parents might be able to pay is retained in the law of 1866, and must have found place in Mr. Patterson's very excellent bill through inadvertence in the collating of the various bills which came before him.

The old board of commissioners and its officers were continued under the new law, and some of the members took hold of the work imposed upon them with much energy and public spirit, while others seem to have done nothing. There was soon disclosed in the board a decided difference of opinion as to the interpretation of the act. Some members of the board understood it to provide for the division only of that portion of the school fund derived from fines and forfeitures between the white and colored schools according to the number of white and colored scholars, while that portion derived from taxation was to be divided exclusively among the white schools. Other members believed that the entire fund should be divided between the white and colored schools. At a meeting of the board December 15, 1864, Commissioner Wiltberger proposed the issue of an order directing the funds derived from taxation to be used exclusively for white schools. Pending the discussion on this question, Mr. Miller offered the following :

"Resolved, That this board take a vote to determine whether the colored schools are entitled to a proportion of the school fund arising from taxes under the law of Congress approved June 25, 1864."

The result of the vote was, two yeas—George Mathiot and David Miller; three nays— C. H. Wiltberger, B. W. Keyser, and B. T. Swart. The resolution offered by Mr. Wiltberger, to the effect that the fines should be divided according to the number of scholars between the white and colored schools, and that the money from taxation should be used exclusively for the white schools, was then adopted. At the next meeting of the board, February 2, 1865, Mr. Miller offered a resolution affirming the following opinion of the levy court, dated January 9, 1865 :

"Resolved, That in the opinion of this court the school commissioners of the county of Washington, District of Columbia, are required by the act of Congress approved July 25, 1864, to appropriate the money derived from all sources, and constituting the school fund for the support of schools for white and colored children residing in said county in the proportion that said white and colored children between the ages of six and seventeen years have to each other in numbers according to the last census."

Of the four commissioners present at this meeting, Messrs. Miller and Mathiot voted in the affirmative, and Messrs. Swart and Wiltberger in the negative. Mr. Wiltberger, on the other hand, produced a written opinion from Joseph H. Bradley, sr., arguing at some length that the terms of the act confined the distribution of the funds for the benefit of colored schools exclusively to that portion derived from the fines, penalties, and forfeitures. Meanwhile the levy court took more distinct action, declaring to the board in a resolution that any distribution of the funds which did not give the colored schools the same share of the moneys accruing from taxation that was conceded by the board to them from the fines, penalties, and forfeitures would be deemed by the court an unlawful distribution. Soon after this action of the levy court the board, at a meeting April 20, 1865, on motion of Mr. Wiltberger, voted, without dissent, to divide the school money as instructed by the levy court from and after July 1, 1864, and this decision was executed.

In the work of 1864 and 1865, under the new act, the commissioners became sufficiently acquainted with the magnitude of the enterprise to be made sensible that the funds accruing under the provisions of that act were entirely inadequate to the demands of the cause. For white schools a house had been built in district No. 2 in 1864; a house in No. 1 and in No. 6

in 1865, while for the colored schools the commissioners had attempted nothing in the matter of building houses at all. Although at first the white people were to a very large extent opposed to schools and school-houses, and hostile to the school act, there were always some sterling friends of the cause in every district, while, under the operations of the schools for two or three years, many others had become friendly to the free school system. The colored people, who were originally unanimous for the schools, had year after year grown more and more anxious and restless in their destitution. Under the pressure upon them, the commissioners at a meeting May 3, 1866, appointed a committee to present their case to Congress. The committee reported June 7, 1866, that they had waited on Mr. Grimes, chairman of the District committee, who gave them no encouragement. They asked for ($5,000) five thousand dollars, and in the civil appropriation bill approved July 28, 1866, the sum of ($10,000) ten thousand dollars was appropriated " for the payment in part for the purchase of sites and the erection of school-houses in the county of Washington, in the District of Columbia." This money, which had mostly come into the hands of the commissioners late in the autumn of 1866, the last requisition being received by them in February, 1867, was nearly all expended for school-houses in 1866. At a meeting of the board January 3, 1867, it was voted to divide the appropriation between the white and colored schools according to the number of scholars, as it had been decided to divide the other funds. They assumed that this required one-third to be set aside for colored schools—the number of children five years old and under twenty, white, 1,203; colored, 574, being the basis of distribution. This appropriation, it would appear from the records, was not divided by the commissioners as it came into their possession, the portion belonging to each class being kept by itself with its accruing interest, but was used in common, no account being taken of the periods in which the disbursements for the white and the colored schools were made, and the same has been the rule with the rest of the school funds. Otherwise the application of the funds seem to have been justly made upon the basis above stated. The resolution approved March 29, 1867, requiring a new enumeration of the children of the District, was enacted specifically to place the colored people in a more equitable position in the distribution of the school funds than they occupied under the census of 1860. This census was completed on the 11th of November, 1867, and the school act of November 25, 1864, had provided that in the division of school funds the proportion should "be ascertained by the last reported census," prior to the distribution. Inasmuch, therefore, as there was no specific distribution, the expenditures being made from a fund in common, it would only be just, in making up the final settlement of the account between the two classes of schools when the building operations, still incomplete, shall be finished, to give the colored people the benefit of the new census.

Two school-houses for colored schools were built in 1866 and two in 1867, and in the spring of 1868 the commissioners found their treasury again empty, with their schools well filled with children and more houses imperatively demanded. At a meeting of the board February 6, 1868, a motion was made to close all the schools at the end of the month. This was amended, making it conform to the terms of a resolution passed August 1, 1867, providing for their close April 1, 1868, but allowing the teachers who desired to continue, taking their chances for pay when there should be funds in the treasury, and the motion was in this form passed, six in the affirmative and one in the negative. Soon after this time another application was made to Congress for relief, and with the prospect of success the schools were continued, and maintained through that school year without any foreign aid, the teachers being generally promptly paid. On the 20th of July, 1868, Congress made a second appropriation of ($10,000) ten thousand dollars " for the purchasing of suitable sites for the erection of additional school-houses, and for the maintenance of schools in the county of Washington, outside of the limits of the cities of Washington and Georgetown, the same to be expended under the direction of the levy court of the county of Washington, subject to the approval of the Secretary of the Interior." This appropriation has been about three-fourths expended—$4,000 to pay teachers and $2,728 50 for a colored school-house in district 7, and several hundred dollars on the colored school-house in district 1. The levy court approved of the above use of the $4,000, with the understanding that it should be refunded, and they increased the tax from ¼ per cent. to 7-20 in order to meet the emergency.

The District of Columbia contains about fifty-two square miles exclusive of the bed of the Potomac, the westerly boundary of the District being the Virginia shore of the river at low water mark. The two cities contain less than fifteen square miles. This gives at least thirty-seven square miles in the county outside the cities. The school districts vary in size, ranging in area from about four to six square miles, the smallest of the seven being No. 3, the others being each from about four and a half to about five and a half square miles in area. The school-house in district No. 1 is some two and a half miles, and in No. 2 less than that distance, beyond the limits of Georgetown, and in the other districts the houses range from a mile and a quarter to double that distance from the limits of Washington, around the borders of which they are ranged. There has been no change in the division into school districts, originally fixed in 1862, except a small alteration early made in the line between No. 6 and No. 7. The division of the county is based upon the plan made in the act of 1856, the language of which act has been successively copied into the two subsequent acts. The population has not only very largely increased since that date, but it has also been entirely revolutionized as to its chief localities. Another consideration, and that which especially concerns the subject in hand, is the fact that the division in 1856 was made by Congress with exclusive reference to the *white* population. In any subsequent legislation the particulars here suggested should be carefully considered. The decennial census soon to be taken, it is to be hoped, will furnish a detailed enumeration of the population, the children of the prescribed school age, the area and the taxable property of each of the school districts, as well as like facts in detail pertaining to Washington and Georgetown. The census report of 1860 does not give the area of the District of Columbia, and no census since the retrocession of Alexandria has given it correctly. In the census of 1860 the enumeration of the population is quinquennial, and consequently the number of children between 5 and 20 instead of 6 and 18 years of age was assumed as the basis of calculation in the division of the fund distributed prior to the census of November, 1867, and this basis is still adhered to, but there can be no doubt whatever that all moneys accruing to the school fund subsequent to the census of November 11, 1867, including the $10,000 given by Congress, should be divided on the basis of that census, which gives a percentage in the county of Washington of 38.89 in the place of 32.35 under the census of 1860.

Census returns, November 11, 1867.

Corporations, &c.	School districts.	White.	Colored.	Total.	Between 6 and 17 years.			School age percentage.	
					White.	Colored.	Total.	White.	Colored.
Between Potomac and Rock Creek.	1, 2.	1, 516	538	2, 054	....	....	....	....	....
Between Rock Creek and Eastern Branch.	3, 4, 5.	2, 441	1, 299	3, 740	....	....	....	....	....
Between Eastern Branch and Maryland line.	6, 7.	1, 746	1, 605	3, 351	....	....	....	....	....
Total county of Washington.	....	5, 703	3, 442	9, 145	1, 494	951	2, 445	61. 10+	38. 89+
Washington city	....	74, 115	31, 937	106, 052	17, 801	8, 401	26, 202	67. 94+	32. 05+
Georgetown	....	8, 509	3, 284	11, 793	2, 152	894	3, 046	70. 65+	29. 34+
Total in District	....	88, 327	38, 663	126, 990	21, 447	10, 246	31, 693	....	....

Census returns, 1860.

Corporations, &c.	White.	Colored.	Total.	Between 5 and 20 years. White.	Colored.	Total.	Per cent. of those between 5 and 20 years. White.	Colored.
County of Washington	3,827	1,398	5,225	1,203	574	1,777	67.64+	32.35+
City of Washington	50,139	10,983	61,122	16,079	4,014	20,093	80.02+	19.97+
Georgetown	6,798	1,935	8,733	2,307	702	3,009	76.66+	23.33+
Total in District	60,764	14,316	75,080	19,589	5,290	24,879		

Population by single years, between 6 and 17, (school age.)—Census returns, Nov. 11, 1867.

Corporations, &c.	6. White.	Colored.	Total.	7. White.	Colored.	Total.	8. White.	Colored.	Total.	9. White.	Colored.	Total.
Washington	1,579	513	2,092	1,709	626	2,335	1,758	699	2,457	1,588	601	2,189
Georgetown	213	58	271	188	58	246	198	61	259	195	69	264
County	124	79	203	126	90	216	135	103	238	106	79	185
Total District	1,916	650	2,566	2,023	774	2,797	2,091	863	2,954	1,889	749	2,638

Corporations, &c.	10. White.	Colored.	Total.	11. White.	Colored.	Total.	12. White.	Colored.	Total.	13. White.	Colored.	Total.
Washington	1,709	805	2,514	1,369	623	1,992	1,423	902	2,325	1,347	736	2,083
Georgetown	169	89	258	175	66	241	186	91	277	176	86	262
County	129	105	234	110	54	164	135	104	239	116	73	189
Total District	2,007	999	3,006	1,654	743	2,397	1,744	1,097	2,841	1,639	895	2,534

Corporations,&c.	14. White.	Colored.	Total.	15. White.	Colored.	Total.	16. White.	Colored.	Total.	17. White.	Colored.	Total.	General total.
Washington	1,356	781	2,137	1,311	716	2,027	1,372	765	2,137	1,280	634	1,914	26,202
Georgetown	169	76	245	163	83	246	169	89	258	151	68	219	3,046
County	136	77	213	143	70	213	128	61	189	106	56	162	2,445
Total District	1,661	934	2,595	1,617	869	2,486	1,669	915	2,584	1,537	758	2,295	31,693

MRS. CARROLL'S SCHOOL, (DISTRICT NO. 6.)

The first colored school in the District, outside of the limits of the two cities, was established by Mrs. David Carroll in August, 1861, and it was the first established in the District specially intended for educating slave children. The earliest contraband school opened in Washington was not started till the spring of 1862. David Carroll was one of the founders of the colored Presbyterian church of Washington, an original elder in the church, a man of property and superior character. This family went out to the farm-house belonging to Mr. Cornelius T. Boyle, beyond Benning's bridge, across the Eastern Branch, and took up their residence, shortly after the first battle of Bull Run, with a view of buying the farm. The next Sabbath after they became occupants of the premises, Rev. Selby B. Scaggs, a white Methodist preacher and a farmer in that neighborhood, locked up the chapel in which he was wont to preach, and when the people came to the church they found him patrolling, key in hand, in front of the house, and declaring that he would have no more praying for the President and the success of the Union arms on his premises. It appeared that the pious officers and soldiers from the neighboring forts had taken part in the Sabbath services and given this offence to the pastor. In this emergency the colored people were invited to hold their services and Sabbath school at the Boyle farm-house on that day. They did so, and David Carroll addressed them, urging the building of a church in which the prayer for the Union would be justified. John Payne, a colored farmer, offered a lot on his farm, and contributions to start the building operations were gathered, to the amount of fifty dollars, on the spot. They also fixed upon a neighboring grove for a temporary place of worship, and a stand and seats were erected there in camp-meeting style the ensuing week. The next Sunday Rev. Mr. Simpson, a private in company F, of the 10th New York heavy artillery, on duty at Fort Meigs, preached the inauguration sermon in the grove; also the dedication sermon in their new house just three months from that day. Mr. Deane, a white resident, kindly allowed the colored people to take all the timber for the church from his woodland, which had been prostrated by military orders. The weather on every Sunday of the three months was fair, and this is recounted by these people as a special providence to them. The Sunday school, which had been maintained with the greatest interest at the Boyle farm-house, was moved into the new house with the transfer of the meeting from the grove, and from that time the house has been crowded with scholars, old and young, many of them coming five or six miles to enjoy the weekly privileges. The first teachers were mostly Christian soldiers from the forts, but those who were the early scholars have now the entire management of the school, including the superintendent, John H. Jackson, son of Rev. Nathaniel Jackson, an intelligent colored preacher, who owns a place in that neighborhood and was one of the leaders in building the house, which they named Jones Chapel, in honor of another colored preacher who owns a small farm in that vicinity, and who is widely known in the District as a venerable and industrious man. Most of the early scholars have become members of this church. It is worthy of remark that this colored church and school, which have done so much good to these down-trodden people, were organized and for a time maintained upon the premises of one of the most extreme and uncompromising men who plotted treason in this District before the war and went foremost into the rebellion, serving as surgeon in the rebel army through the conflict. The books for the Sabbath school were at first procured by contributions taken up in the church and school, but afterwards, Mrs. Carroll, who at first had the entire charge of the school, procured them from the managers of the Soldiers' Free Library in Washington. The officers and soldiers contributed generously and gave great encouragement to the work in all its stages.

The day school.—Mrs. Carroll opened a day school in the Boyle house with twenty children the same week in which she started the Sunday school. The number rapidly increased to double that number, and as the colored people from the Maryland plantations pressed inside the District the school filled nearly the whole house, numbering at some periods nearly or quite a hundred. Mrs. Carroll's daughter by a former husband, Miss Rebecca T. Gordon, was assistant in the school, which was continued with undiminished success till April, 1865. Mr. Carroll having died the previous year, the family returned to their house in Washington.

The school was then taken in charge by Miss Ellen M. Jackson, the daughter of Rev. Nathaniel Jackson, and transferred to her father's house. She was soon, however, compelled by failing health to suspend her work, and died in that summer. There was no day school, therefore, through the summer and autumn, but in January, 1866, Mr. A. E. Newton, the superintendent of the schools in Washington and Georgetown, visited that locality and promptly established a school in the Jones Chapel, employing Frederick A. Lawton, a white man from the north, as the teacher. There was at this time more open hostility to colored schools than had been manifested during the war when the military forces held control. No white family in the neighborhood would board a teacher of a colored school at this time, and there was no colored family in suitable condition to receive a boarder. Mr. Lawton found a home with Mr. Tabor, a Union man, who had fled from Virginia with his wife and built a rough shelter in a forest a mile from the chapel. Mr. Tabor, a native of New York State, was a man of intelligence who had seen better fortunes, and his wife was a woman of refinement. They had lost everything, and purchasing a piece of land here they were living in such a shanty as they were able to build in their poverty. Mr. Lawton and the family suffered with cold the first winter, but the house was improved in the summer, and he lived with them during the two years in which he taught the school. Mr. Lawton was supported the first year wholly by an association of Universalists of Auburn, New York, through the New York Freedmen's Relief Association, and in part by the same association the second year, 1867–'68, the commissioners of primary schools assuming most of his support in the latter named school year. His school during the two years averaged at different periods from 40 to 60 scholars. Mr. Lawton was elected teacher by the school commissioners August 16, 1866, but as the pay, $37 50 per month, voted by the school board April 5, 1866, to all teachers, male and female, of colored schools, was so manifestly inadequate, Mr. Newton, in order to retain his services and to continue the school with efficiency, added $10 per month from the funds of the association.

Mrs. Carroll, well known as one of the capable colored teachers of Washington for twenty-five years, under the name of Charlotte Gordon, was born and grew to womanhood a slave in Alexandria. Her owner, Mrs. Mary Fletcher, a good woman, believed in educating her servants and practiced her faith. She sent this child, Charlotte Pankus, to the best schools accessible to colored children in that city from the earliest school age. Sylvia Morris, Alfred Parry, and Joseph Ferrell were the excellent colored teachers whose schools she attended. Ferrell, of whom mention has been elsewhere made as a man of remarkable abilities, was sent to the penitentiary accused of furnishing passes to his enslaved brethren who run for freedom. He was sentenced for a term of seven years, and coming out at the end of this term, was immediately seized on a second accusation and sentenced to a second term of five years. Charlotte Pankus, with others of his old scholars, was in the court-house in Alexandria when Thompson Mason, whose slaves were "caught running" with the forged passes, made his violent and vindictive argument for the second conviction. Ferrell subsequently had a school in Washington, and died here some years ago, persisting on his death-bed that he was innocent of the offence. This girl attended also for nearly two years an admirable school for colored girls which was maintained in Alexandria by the Sisters of Charity, who at the same period had a large boarding school for white girls in that city. Sisters Agnes Annina and Mary Frances are remembered by her as the teachers of the colored school. Miss Edmunds, who had a boarding school in the city at that period, and Benjamin Hallowell, the eminent Quaker schoolmaster, both befriended her, the latter named teacher instructing her in Latin, of which she acquired some knowledge. She began to teach when a mere girl in Alexandria, and had a school there at the time of the Snow riot in Washington in 1835. Some years later her owner, with the desire to make her free, sent her to Washington without registration in order that she might acquire her freedom by the operation of the registry law, and she was in Washington when Alexandria was retroceded in 1846. Before this period she married Wm. H. Gordon, who a few years later went to California and died there, leaving her with a family of small children, whom she raised in a respectable manner by her industry and intelligence as a teacher. Her first school in Washington was in a house on I near Eleventh street, west, where she taught six years, with an average of some forty scholars. From this place she moved her school to New York avenue, near Thirteenth street, into one of the houses of the locality known in that day as "Cover Tan Yard," where she had an average of about fifty scholars for five or six years, till about 1858, when she moved to Eighth between N and O streets, in the northern section of the city—a location then known as "Nigger Hill," at that time and now the centre of a large colored population. Her school here was very large, and in 1860 she occupied two adjoining small brick buildings, which were filled with scholars, her daughter being assistant. She established also a Sabbath school in connection with this school, and several white ladies took great interest in its progress, giving their personal aid as teachers and contributing to secure books. Among the most devoted friends of the school was Mrs. Mitchell, a Virginia lady, who gave her warm friendship to the work as a teacher from the beginning to the end of the school, which continued several years. Mrs. Mitchell is still a resident of Washington, an inmate of the family of her son-in-law, H. M. Binckley, esq., the Assistant Attorney General under the late administration. The day school was crowded when the war broke out, and was dispersed in the spring of 1861 when the soldiers began to throng the city, the small children, of which the school was mostly composed, being intimidated by the tramp of the armies. She had on her list at that time nearly a hundred and fifty scholars. This school was only briefly alluded to in the notices of schools in operation in the District, given in the previous pages. In 1861 she was married to Mr. Carroll, and the work which she did in the cause of enlightening her race during the war was perhaps the most useful of her life. David Carroll was born a slave, owned by Charles Carroll, of Carrolltown, but was early put to a trade and manumitted.

THE SCHOOLS, SCHOOL LOTS, AND SCHOOL-HOUSES.

District No. 1—Tenallytown.—At a meeting of the Board May 3, 1866, the commissioner of this district, R. W. Carter, a distinguished merchant of Washington, was instructed to hire a house at a rent not exceeding $5 per month. Nothing seems to have been further done, from the records, till April 4, 1867, when Mr. J. S. Lloyd was chosen teacher, whose first monthly report, June, 1867, shows six boys and seven girls on his list. He taught 13 months at $45 per month, and is now under the new schedule receiving $50. He is an efficient teacher, his school numbering about 40, with an average attendance of 24 scholars. Mr. Carter first came into the Board in April, 1866, and was elected president of the Board in the ensuing July, a position which with great public spirit and efficiency he still holds. He had recently purchased a country seat at Tenallytown, and entered into the objects of the Board with great interest, determined to secure for that community what they had hitherto not enjoyed—free schools. The project required courage. Among the mass of the white community there was no desire for schools of any kind, while the very few who felt the need of educational facilities generally regarded it vain to attempt anything of the kind in that population. The result has been the establishment of two admirable schools, one white and the other colored. A colored Methodist church has been formed, with a flourishing Sabbath school; also, a Catholic church. The colored school-house was built in the summer of 1867, and Mr. Carter has watched the school in all its stages with a generous fidelity that has left nothing to be desired. Public sentiment, which, not friendly to white schools three years ago, was extremely hostile to the education of the colored people, has been revolutionized, and schools of both classes are now approved by all, the opposition being very limited and emanating mostly from a vulgar class.

District No. 2.—It has already been stated that action was taken to buy a school lot in this district, which lies between district No. 1 and Rock Creek, at a meeting of the Board November 30, 1865. At a subsequent meeting, February 1, 1866, it was voted to hire a house at a rent of $4 per month, and the commissioner immediately opened a school, with Mary Boffey as teacher, who commencing with six boys and three girls in March, 1866, soon had a room full. She continued in the school seven months at $37 50 per month, and nine months at $45, the new building, costing $960 exclusive of fencing and stone, being completed in this period. She was succeeded by the present efficient teacher, Mr. B. M. Martin, who taught 13 months at $45 per month, which has been this year increased to $50; though it should be noted that in excluding the vacation this increase of the monthly pay is really a reduction of the annual compensation. This school has averaged under the present teacher about 26 scholars, with 68 names on the roll.

District No. 3.—In this district the first movement for a school originated in the meeting of the Board May 3, 1866, which authorized the commissioner of the district to hire a house for a colored school at a rent not exceeding $7 per month. Mr. Carpenter, the commissioner, immediately rented a barrack building, and opened a school the week in which it was authorized. He employed Harvey Smith, who commenced in May with two boys and six girls, and taught four months at $37 50 a month, 22 months at $45, and has the regular pay of $50 this year. The school-house of the same plan and cost of that in district No. 2 was finished in the summer of 1866, and was well filled with scholars. At the present time the average attendance is about 30, as it was through last year, with 56 names on the roll. When the school was first organized there was the same prevailing hostility to the work in this as in the two districts west of Rock Creek. It was impossible to purchase a school lot of a white man in the district. The lot was purchased of a colored man. In this district the records of the Board show complaints from Francis Hamilton, a teacher of a colored school in June, 1867, that the white scholars of that district were insolent and abusive to the inoffending children of the colored school. There was also a complaint of the same character preferred to the Board at that meeting from J. H. Voorhees, the teacher of the colored school of the adjoining district, No. 4, against the white school of his district. These disgraceful persecutions, however, have mostly ceased, and higher, more generous, and enlightened ideas are prevailing. Mr. Carpenter has done much to inculcate correct views, and has given great satisfaction as a commissioner.

District No. 4—Soldiers' Home.—At a meeting of the Board April 26, 1866, Henry Queen, then and now the commissioner of the district, was authorized to hire a house at $7 a month, provide benches, and employ a teacher for a colored school; and Mr. A. Bolton opened a school, numbering at first 10 scholars, five boys and five girls, May 1, 1866, teaching four months at $37 50 per month and one month at $45. He died in October, and was succeeded by J. H. Voorhees, who still is giving much satisfaction in the school. He taught 20 months at $45 and now receives $50. The school has numbered about 70 the last two years, with an average attendance of 23 scholars. The school-house, of same pattern and cost of those in districts 2 and 3, was built in 1867 on a lot purchased of Mary Walker in April of that year. It is located near the Soldiers' Home, and in the vicinity of the residence of C. H. Wiltberger, who was commissioner from 1862 to 1866, and who has devoted great attention to the schools, both white and colored, in his district and in the county. Public sentiment in this district was originally more enlightened and tolerant of education among the colored people than in the districts already noticed, and at the present time there seems to be a spirit of kindness prevalent toward its colored school. Its progress is the cause of satisfaction and not of offence to the white population. Mr. Wiltberger has been the secretary of the Board of commissioners from its organization in 1862 to the present time, and the facts in this chapter pertaining to the work which has been done under the operations of the successive school acts have been drawn in a very large measure from the remarkably careful and laborious record which he has preserved. Very rarely absent from a meeting of the Board, he has kept an account of every important transaction, the value of which to the cause of common schools in the county it is scarcely possible to overestimate. Nor is this all the valuable work he has done. He has annually compiled from the monthly returns of the teachers a careful summary of the facts communicated in those returns, and has preserved copies of them, while the original papers transmitted to the levy court are not to be found. While a majority of the persons who have successively been appointed commissioners seem to have totally neglected the duties of the office, Mr. Wiltberger has been vigilant and unwearied in his exertions to awaken the people of his own school district to a just appreciation of the school system, and has given cordial support to the education of the colored people, although he originally dissented from the views of the levy court as to the meaning of the school act touching the distribution of the school funds.

District No. 5.—In this district no colored school has been established. The colored population is so scattered that the commissioners have not deemed it discreet either to open a

school or to build a house. At a meeting of the Board January 3, 1867, a committee, consisting of David Miller and John E. Chappel, was authorized to select a site for a house,
but after looking the matter carefully over it is understood that they declined to proceed,
doubting the expediency of building a house under the circumstances. In 1868 further
action was taken, and at a meeting of the Board July 2, 1868, it was voted to condemn a
certain lot which had been selected and could not be amicably purchased. This order, however, was not carried out, mainly because of the violent hostility among the white residents
of the district to colored schools, and therefore no lot has yet been selected. This district
extends along the westerly side of the Eastern Branch.

District No. 6.—The colored school which was established in 1861 in the limits of this
district, which lies upon the easterly side of the Eastern Branch, has been fully sketched
down to the period when it was assumed by the commissioner under the caption of "Charlotte
Carroll's school." At a meeting of the Board January 18, 1866, the school at Jones's chapel
was accepted as a public school, and the wages of the teacher, Frederick A. Lawton, fixed
at $37 50 per month. At a previous meeting, January 4, 1866, it had been voted to pay Mr.
Lawton the above specified wages under the condition that the house should be furnished
with no expense to the commissioners. The report of the school for that month showed an
average attendance of 26 boys and 16 girls. The Board, October 4, 1866, authorized the
purchase of a lot for a school-house in this district at the rate of $200 per acre, and the com-
missioner purchased half an acre of Jacob Paine, a colored man owning a small farm in that
district. The house was completed late in the autumn of 1866. Mr. Lawton taught eight
months at $37 50 per month, and a year at $45. L. H. Smith, a son of the teacher in district
No. 3, succeeded Mr. Lawton, teaching 10 months at $45, and is still in the school giving
good satisfaction under the prescribed pay of the present year. The whole number of
scholars enrolled the year ending July 15, 1868, was 103, with an average attendance through
the year of 36. The school-house is 20 feet by 40 feet in dimensions. Mr. W. B. Lacey,
the present commissioner, is an active and efficient officer.

District 7, No. 1—Good Hope schools.—The second effort to start schools in the county for
the colored people was made in the Good Hope church, on the east side of the Eastern Branch,
a mile or more from the Navy Yard bridge. Mr. G. F. Needham, a clerk in the Post Office
Department, went over there early in the spring of 1864 and aided Miss Eliza H. Stanton,
of Virginia, who had been sent into this field as a teacher by the New York National Freedmen's Relief Association, in organizing a school in that chapel, a comfortable brick church
built by the African Methodist people before the war. Miss Stanton had a large school, and
managed it with energy and success, receiving for her services $30 per month, barely enough
to pay her board and lodging. The opposition to the work at that time in that vicinity was
exceedingly bitter. No white family would receive this refined woman into their house, and
the colored people were too poor and shelterless in their condition to do so. She was compelled to walk into the city, which broke down her physical powers in the course of the
summer, compelling her to disband her school. An illustration of the prevailing temper at
that period is found in the following reply which was made to Miss Stanton's application for
board by a family still living in that neighborhood: "If you are mean enough to teach
niggers, you may eat and sleep with them." The family has learned wisdom since then,
and would feel mortified now, as they should feel, to see their names in this connection.

In the autumn of 1865, shortly after Miss Stanton relinquished her work, Mr. A. E. Newton, the superintendent of the schools of the relief societies in the cities of Washington,
Georgetown, and Alexandria, took measures to revive her school, employing Mr. Addison
Wheeler, of Connecticut, as teacher, who began his labors in a night and day school in the
winter of 1865–'66. Mr. Wheeler at first found quarters with a lieutenant stationed at Fort
Wagner, in the vicinity, and Mr. Newton secured an order from the War Office when the fort
was abandoned which resulted in the transfer of the officers' small barrack building to the
Good Hope church lot. It was turned over to the control of the Freedmen's Bureau, and the
colored men each gave one day with all the teams they owned for its removal. The Bureau
gave some assistance and Mr. Newton paid $20. In this house Mr. Wheeler lived alone for
some time, cooking his own food, till he found good board at the table of a colored man by

the name of Payne in the neighborhood. The school was continued by Mr. Wheeler, with some interruptions caused by ill-health, through the year, and when the present remarkably superior teacher, Rev. J. S. Dore, came upon the ground in the spring of 1866 to engage with him in the work the school numbered about 60 scholars.

This new teacher has done his work with such extraordinary wisdom and energy, through evil report and through good, that his name merits a prominent place in this record. Mr. Dore, a native of Maine and a student in Waterville College in that State, at the opening of the war early embarked as a private soldier in the contest; subsequently becoming chaplain of the 6th New Hampshire veteran volunteers, continuing in that capacity through the war. Sent into this educational work by the Freedmen's Relief Association of Portland, Maine, he reached Washington early in April, 1866, and at once commenced a new era at the Good Hope school. In less than one month after entering upon his duties the school was increased from 60 to 145, and the school district No. 7 had been canvassed by him, disclosing the fact that it contained upwards of 300 children of the lawful school age. A night school was at the same time opened, meeting five nights a week, and soon numbering 90 men and women. A very large Sabbath school was also organized, the first ever held in the place, and is still with unabated efficiency maintained, with a Sabbath school library of several hundred volumes. At the close of the term, July 15, 1866, Mr. Wheeler retired, leaving the whole work in the hands of Mr. Dore. During the vacation of six weeks, Mr. Dore having entered into contract with the owner of an unfinished building to complete it for its use a year, vacated the small barrack building, which was fitted up for a school-room. Mr. Newton at the same time obtained permission of the War Office to take possession of a hospital structure at Fort Baker, and the Bureau moved it to the Good Hope chapel lot near the other barrack building, and converted it into two coarse but comparatively comfortable school-rooms, provision being thus secured for the schools without resorting to the chapel.

The first help from the School Commissioners is indicated by the following action of the Board at their regular meeting May 18, 1865: "Commissioner John Fox, of the 7th district, submitted to the board a monthly report (April) of a colored school in the 7th district taught by Addison Wheeler, and asked that said school be recognized by this Board and money appropriated, payable out of the colored fund, for the support of said school; when, on motion of Commissioner David Miller, (district No. 6,) it was resolved that the sum of $25 per month be fixed as the pay of Mr. Addison Wheeler as teacher of the school for colored children in the 7th district, and that the sum of $50 per annum be appropriated for rent of house, (Good Hope chapel,) payable quarterly." Pursuant of this resolution, on the 2d day of November, the Board voted to pay the first half year's salary ($150) to Mr. Wheeler and $25 for rent of the chapel, constituting the first money voted by the Board for the support of colored schools. At the examination of Mr. Dore's school July 15, 1866, two of the commissioners were present for the first time in any colored school, and the results so impressed them that at the next meeting of the Board, August 16, upon the representation of these members, Mr. Dore was elected teacher of the colored school in district No. 7 at a salary of $450, the same as was paid to the female teachers, while at that date the salary for male teachers in the white schools was $750. On the 1st of September, however, the Board raised the salary of male teachers of white schools to $900, and of female teachers in either white or colored to $540, male teachers of colored schools ranking in salary with the women. Mr. Dore was at this time offered the white school at Uniontown, in the adjoining district, No. 6, at $900, but preferred to remain in the Good Hope school. The New York branch of the National Freedmen's Aid Commission made his salary up to $600.

The Good Hope school opened September 1, 1866, with three teachers and three departments. Miss Jennie S. Palmer, of Cooperstown, New York, and Miss Leah Wither, of Abbott, Maine, (now Mrs. J. S. Dore,) both supported by the New York branch of the National Freedmen's Aid Commission, being Mr. Dore's assistants. These teachers carried their schools, which were always full, through the year with a systematic intelligence and fidelity that commanded the respect of opponents and attracted the admiration of friends. In addition to the large and flourishing night and Sabbath schools, a sewing school was maintained through the year, the term closing with an examination of remarkable excellence

July 15, 1867. At a meeting of the Board September 3, 1867, it was voted to raise the salary of Mr. Dore to $600, in consideration, as the resolution set forth, that his school was extraordinary in size, having numbered in the past season more than three hundred scholars. The next school year opened September 1, 1867, with Miss Flora A. Leland, of Ashland, Massachusetts, in place of Miss Jennie S. Palmer, resigned. Miss Leland, who proved to be a most superior teacher, as her school at Barry farm now abundantly testifies, was employed by the school commissioners at a salary of $450, and Mr. Dore's salary was increased to $900 by a contribution of $300 from the New York branch of the Freedmen's Union Commission.

The Good Hope school took possession of the new two story school-house, built for that purpose the past season, on the 22d of March, 1869. This house stands upon a spacious lot some fifty rods from the Good Hope chapel, and in one of the most commanding and delightful places in that region of the county. The house is about 26 by 38 feet on the ground, and is well finished inside and out. It is to be regretted that the commissioners allowed so good a house to be furnished with such very poorly shaped and made pine furniture. Such desks and seats are not evidence of enlightened ideas, and it is safe to say do not meet the full approbation of all the commissioners. The school rooms, about 25 feet square, are much too small for the number of desks placed in them, and it is unfortunate that at least one-third of the dozen feet used for ante-rooms was not embraced in the school rooms. The house, however, is a credit to the district, and is probably the best that has been built by the commissioners. This school is intended to accommodate some of the scholars in district No. 6, who reside near it. It is but just to make special mention of Dr. W. W. Godding, of the Insane Asylum, who, as commissioner for district No. 7, has made the cause of the schools, both white and colored, a labor of love. In full sympathy with the teachers and all friends of the colored schools, he has for years been their wise and enlightened counsellor and friend in all their trials and triumphs. The lot on which the house is built was sold to the commissioners by Mr. Dore, the teacher, near whose residence it stands. The school numbers about a hundred, nearly equally divided between Mr. Dore and Mrs. Dore, the assistant, filling the two school rooms quite full. The work which has been done in this district by these teachers at Good Hope and at Barry farm is very marvellous. The people upon whom they have wrought, the ignorant and despised from the plantations, to a very large extent have been clothed with new life under their ministrations. When the Good Hope school was founded it was as rare to find a colored person in the region who could read as it is now to find one who cannot read. Nearly all the old people as well as the young have learned to read, at least enough to use the Testament. Industry prevails, and there are but two or three recipients of the public charity in the whole neighborhood at the present time.

District 7, No. 2—The Howard schools.—The Barry farm, comprising about 375 acres, adjoining the estate of the St. Elizabeth Insane Asylum, south of the Eastern Branch, was purchased in the early part of 1868, by the Freedmen's Bureau. It was divided into house lots of one acre each and offered to the freedmen at cost, the Bureau furnishing each lot owner a portion of the lumber for a house. The payment for the lot was to be made within two years, and in equal monthly instalments, with an express stipulation that the lot is forfeited by failure to comply with these terms. The estate was purchased with funds which the Freedmen's Bureau, in pursuance of an act of Congress, March 2, 1867, deposited in the hands of three trustees for that purpose. The object of establishing such a fund was, as expressed in the special order of the Bureau, "to relieve the immediate necessities of a class of poor colored people in the District of Columbia by rental of land by sale, with deferred payments, or in such other way as their trustees judgment shall direct for this purpose, provided all proceeds, interest, or moneys received from rental or sale over and above necessary expenses shall be annually transferred" to said institutions.

The trustees are O. O. Howard, John R. Elvans, and S. C. Pomeroy, and they paid for the farm $52,000. The estate made 359 lots, of which 300 had been sold prior to October, 1868, and 40 of these had been forfeited. The lumber for 185 houses had been at that date issued by the Bureau and the most of the dwellings built. The enterprise, designed to stimulate these poor people with courage and industrious habits, has proved eminently successful. The Freedmen have entered with great ambition into the idea of securing a home, and have formed on this farm an enterprising, industrious village. They have built a Baptist church, and have purchased the lot upon which they are about to build a Methodist church. They also bought one of the acre lots upon which the Bureau erected in the closing months of 1867, a large one story school house, at a cost of some $1,500, about 75 feet long and 25 wide, comprising two excellent school rooms and capable of accommodating sixty scholars, with the requisite ante-rooms. There is also a flourishing night school in operation, for some time under the instruction of Charles Douglass, a son of Frederick Douglass. The proceeds of this property are to go ultimately to the colored schools of the District, of Virginia, and of North Carolina, one third part to each.

The Howard school at Barry farm, in Uniontown, or, as the place has been recently named, Anacostia, was opened January 1, 1868. Mr. Dore at this time consolidated his three schools at Good Hope into two, and leaving them in care of Mrs. Dore and Miss Leland, went down to " Anacostia " and organized the Howard school in the new house, remaining there through the month. On the first of February Miss Leland took charge of the Howard school, which soon numbered some 90 scholars, and Mr. Dore resumed the care of his Good Hope schools. Good Hope and the Howard schools are perhaps a little more than a mile apart. Miss Leland is a most superior teacher. Her large room has always been full and her school is one of the best in the District of Columbia. The children, nearly all from the plantations a few years ago, are clad with care, many of them nicely dressed, and there is a neatness and order about the school which, combined with the brightness and correctness apparent in the recitations, makes it a school meriting this special notice.

On the 20th of April, 1868, a primary school was organized in the other room of the Howard school-house, and Miss F. E. Hall employed as teacher by the Pennsylvania branch of the Freedmen's Relief Commission at $40 per month. Both the departments were crowded through the season. Miss Hall commenced with 40 and closed the school year July 30, 1868, with 60 scholars. When the new school year opened in September, 1868, Miss Leland's room was at once filled, and as the Aid Society had withdrawn its assistance and the commissioners could not assume another teacher, more than half the children at Barry farm were shut from the school room, which they would gladly fill. In this emergency, through the intervention of Rev. John Kimball of the Bureau, the Pennsylvania Relief Commission was induced to appropriate $20 a month to this school for another year. Miss Hall, interested in the school and the industrial scheme of the Barry farm, on learning these facts came back from Auburn and re-opened the school December 21, 1868, and both these schools have thus been maintained through the winter. The colored population of this place is increasing, and it is a matter of serious consideration how their educational wants are to be met the ensuing year when the small foreign aid now received will be certainly withdrawn. The uniformity of attendance in both branches of this admirable school is remarkable, showing unmistakably the deep interest which these humble people indulge in their privileges.

It has been seen that in all the districts except the fifth the colored people have been furnished respectable school privileges. The school-houses in the 1st, 2d, 3d, and 4th districts are frame buildings, one story, about 24 by 30 feet in dimensions, well finished and alike. The house in the 6th district is 20 by 40 feet, and the Good Hope house in the 7th district, has been stated, is 25 by 38 feet and two stories. The furniture in them all is of pine, manufactured by a carpenter of the county. The school lots have been fenced in a respectable manner and outhouses built. Most well-informed friends of these schools will regret that better houses have not been built, and certainly that better furniture has not been purchased.

The Board paid the rent of Good Hope church, at $7 per month, for Addison Wheeler's school, commencing May 1, 1865, and continuing until November, when the houses from the Bureau were ready, and this was all that was done in that school year towards providing school-houses for colored schools, except an appropriation of $69 to plaster one of the rooms at Good Hope and $39 for furniture. The next action was at a meeting after the new school year opened, November 30, 1865, when it was voted to authorize " the commissioner of the 2d district to purchase a lot of half an acre for the purpose of erecting a school-house thereon for a colored school, the sum to be paid for the lot not to exceed $80." In accordance with this action a lot was bought of John Mayer January 4, 1866, and December 6, ensuing, $960 was voted for building the school-house. In this same district a lot comprising one acre was purchased for a white school, under a vote of the board August 20, 1865, for $150, and November 9 following $1,080 was appropriated for the house, and $216 80 April 5, 1866, for furniture, $600 being voted the next year to build a vestibule and $340 for fencing. This district seems to be a fair example of the discrimination between the two classes which prevails in the county pertaining to the school lots and houses. The rule has been to buy an acre for a white and half an acre for a colored school lot, and to expend several hundred dollars more for a white than for a colored school-house. In district No. 4 the house for the colored school cost $960, but that for the white school cost $1,570, and this is about the ratio on which expenditures have generally been made.

Rev. John Kimball was present at the meeting of the Board April 5, 1866, and in behalf of the Freedmen's Bureau proposed to aid the commissioners in securing some of the barrack buildings at the dismantled forts in the county for colored school-houses. The Board thankfully accepted the proposition, and at once voted to use $125 for securing materials in this way for each district in which a house was needed. Mr. Kimball failed to secure the buildings, but offered to contribute $25 for each house that the commissioners would purchase at the auction sale of these government buildings. This suggestion was not adopted, though the purchase at least of one of the buildings at Fort Stevens was pressed upon them with much solicitude. Mr. Kimball, a native of New England, having served through the war as a chaplain, came to this District as superintendent of schools, at the establishment of the Freedmen's Bureau, for the territory comprising the District of Columbia, Maryland, and West Virginia, the State of Delaware having been subsequently added. This responsible place he has filled with a vigor and sagacity that have commanded universal commendation. In Washington and Georgetown he was the cordial and wise colaborer of Mr. A. E. Newton in laying the foundations of the free schools, which are doing such a wonderful work for the colored people in those cities at the present time, and this brief tribute is the least that can be said of his beneficent labors in this incidental notice.

COMPENSATION OF TEACHERS.

It has been seen that in the first aid extended to the colored schools by the commissioners Addison Wheeler, a white man from Connecticut, was in 1865 paid $25 per month as a teacher. The commissioners, at a meeting January 4, 1866, voted to authorize the commissioner in district No. 4 to pay a teacher $60 per month to instruct a white school and to pay $37 50 to a teacher of a colored school, " provided the commissioner is satisfied of the competency of the teacher and that the use of a building be obtained without cost to the Board." If the competency of the teacher were to be estimated by the price fixed for his services, the Board might well have raised the doubt suggested in their proviso. April 5, 1866, on motion of R. W. Carter, the Board fixed the pay of all female teachers at $37 50. August 16, 1866, the pay of all female teachers and of all male teachers of colored schools was raised to $45 per month. September 6, 1866, the pay of male teachers of white schools was increased from $62 50 to $75 per month, commencing September 1, 1866. The pay of assistant teachers was fixed at $35 per month. This rate of compensation was continued through the school year ending in July, 1867.

At a meeting of the Board August 1, 1867, B. D. Carpenter, the commissioner of district No. 3, presented a proposition, which was laid on the table, " to pay the male teachers of the colored schools the same salary as we pay the male teachers of the white schools ; " his resolution going on to affirm the very sensible idea that " while we require the same amount of labor and qualifications we feel " (or rather should feel, as the action of the Board upon the proposition shows that the majority did not, in fact, so feel,) " we cannot withhold this act of common justice." At the meeting of the Board October 3, 1867, Mr. Carpenter's resolution was taken up, and while under discussion Dr. W. W. Godding offered an amendment, fixing the pay of all male teachers at $65 per month. Henry Queen, commissioner of district No. 4, offered also an amendment, providing for the exclusive employment of female teachers. Both motions to amend, together with the original resolution, were rejected.

In the early months of 1868 the subject of systematizing the rates of teachers' pay was much discussed. January 2, 1868, Mr. Lacey introduced the following resolution at the meeting of the board: "*Resolved*, That the wages of the teachers of white schools shall be reduced to $60 per month, to take effect 30 days from date." And at the next meeting the resolution was referred to a special committee, who were instructed to report a graded system of wages. This committee, consisting of W. B. Lacey, L. H. Whitney, and B. D. Carpenter, reported July 2, 1868, fixing the scale as follows: Male principal of white schools, $75; male principal of colored schools, $60; female teachers of white and colored schools, $50; assistant teachers, $35; school year, nine months, from September 15 to June 15; teachers to be paid by the month and for the time of actual service only. After the appropriation of $10,000 was made by Congress, July 20, 1868, for the aid of these schools, the proposition was introduced at a meeting of the Board August 6, 1868, to fix the vacation, as hitherto, at six weeks, commencing July 15, and to pay the above scale of wages 12 months in the year as had been the custom. The subject was referred to a select committee, who reported September 3, 1868, to pay this scale for ten months in the year. At the meeting December 3, 1868, a proposition was made to confer with the levy court, and to suggest $65, $60, $50, and $35 as the graded scale. These protracted efforts resulted in no definite action, and the teachers were paid as in the previous year. The pay the current school year, 1868–'69, is as follows: Male teachers of white schools, 75; male teachers of colored schools, $50; female teachers, $50; assistants, $35. The colored school at Good Hope is an exception. The Board at a meeting September 3, 1868, voted that the pay of J. S. Dore should be "the same as in white schools for the current year." This action of the Board, however, is understood to be based upon the extraordinary services of Mr. Dore, and in no sense a recognition of equality between the teachers of white and colored schools. It should be stated that hitherto the teachers have been paid for the whole year, 12 months, not deducting the usual vacations, but this year they are to be paid only for actual service.

It is difficult to reconcile the discrimination in the remuneration of the teachers of the white and colored schools which is perceived in these details, though the present Board of commissioners in their action in many respects seem to be justly and generously disposed in the discharge of their duties towards the colored schools. It will not be disputed by any persons of enlightened views in regard to education that the colored schools demand as good qualifications and as much labor as the white of the same grade, and this is the principle affirmed in the resolution of Mr. Carpenter, which was rejected by the Board, as already stated, though it should be added, in justice to the Board, that at least three of the seven members were at that time, as they are now, in favor of Mr. Carpenter's proposition. In this connection, also, it is worthy to be stated to the credit of the Board that when Dr. Godding, June 6, 1867, moved "to expend $200 in premiums for the schools, to be apportioned according to the number of scholars, and *the premiums to be in the white and colored schools alike*," the proposition was adopted without dissent as to the mode of distribution.

By action of the Board December 5, 1867, the teachers were allowed to dismiss their schools one day each month in order to attend the regular meetings of the Teachers' Institute. July 2, 1868, the time was limited to one day each quarter. These meetings are held at room 13 in the old National Intelligencer Building, corner of Seventh and D streets, and the use of the room is given by the Board. The Institute is left entirely to the management of the teachers, but it is required to make a report of proceedings to the Board with the names of those attending. The application for the above privilege was made by Mr. J. S. Lloyd, teacher of colored school in district No. 1, and praise is due both to him and the Board for effecting an arrangement so conducive to the prosperity of so useful an organization as the Institute.

THE COMMISSIONERS AND TRUSTEES.

The present commissioners have done much in the last two years for the colored schools, and some have been exceedingly efficient throughout their service. The fact that the act of Congress allows them no compensation should, perhaps, be suggested, when it is said that in some cases they have *done nothing*. The trustees, of whom there are two in each district, in charge of the local matters of the individual districts, are represented to be, as a general rule, exceedingly inefficient, and in the most of the districts it is almost impossible to find good men who will consent to serve. These remarks apply to the present as well as to the past. The following are the commissioners at the present time: District No. 1, R. W. Carter, president of the board; district No. 2, B. T. Swart; district No. 3, B. D. Carpenter; district No. 4, Henry Queen; district No. 5, L. H. Whitney; district No. 6, W. B. Lacey; district No. 7, W. W. Godding. Charles H. Wiltberger, who has been the clerk of the board from its organization, receives a salary of $300 per annum, and Nicholas Callan, who, as the clerk of the levy court, is made by the act treasurer of the school fund, receives a salary of $100 per annum.

SUMMARY.

Colored public schools in Washington County, January, 1869.

District.	Teacher.	Opened.	Scholars.		Average attendance.		Total expenses.	
			1866–'67.	1867–'68.	1866–'67.	1867–'68.	1866–'67.	1867–'68.
1	J. S. Lloyd	June, 1867...	40	40	21	24	....	....
2	B. M. Martin	March, 1866..	73	68	18	26	....	....
3	Harvey Smith	May, 1866 ...	87	56	33	30	....	....
4	J. H. Voorhees.........	May, 1866 ...	36	70	13	23	....	....
5	No school.							
6	L. H. Smith	Aug., 1861...	117	103	35	36	....	....
7	Rev. J. S. Dore, No. 1 ..	March, 1864..	319	255	106	28	....	....
	Mrs. J. S. Dore							
7	Miss F. A. Leland, No. 2.	Jan., 1868 ...	....	169	....	80	....	....
	Miss F. E. Hall	April 1868...						
			672	761	226	306	$9,010 60	$5,709 93

The school in district 6, and school No. 1, district 7, (the Good Hope school,) were not established by the Trustees, but the former passed into their hands January, 1866; the latter, May, 1865. All the teachers named above are white.

School property of colored schools in Washington County, January, 1869.

District 1.—Lot ¼ acre, $174. Frame house, $974 77; built 1867. Furniture, $78 50.
District 2.—Lot ½ acre, $95 50. Frame house, $968; built 1866. Furniture, $184.
District 3.—Lot ½ acre, $134 25. Frame house, $971 20; built 1866. Furniture, $52 75. Fencing, $235.
District 4.—Lot ⅝ acre, $253 50. Frame house, $1,101 20; built 1867. Furniture, $256. Fencing, $285.
District 5.—None.
District 6.—Lot ⁴⁵⁄₁₀₀ acre, $104 75. Frame house, $1,164; built 1866. Furniture, $175 80. Fencing, $165.
District 7, *No.* 1.—Lot ¾ acre, $300. House, $1,978 50. Furniture, $200. Fencing, $275.
District 7, *No.* 2.—Lot owned by colored people, and building by Freedmen's Bureau.
The above figures do not include certain improvements made since the buildings were completed and occupied.

3. COLORED SCHOOLS OF ALEXANDRIA.

EARLIEST SCHOOLS.

The fact that the city of Alexandria, with the county in which it is situated, was for nearly half a century an important portion of this District, makes its history during that period important to the completion of this record. By act of Congress, February 27, 1801, it was provided that the laws of the State of Virginia as they existed at that date should "continue in force in that part of the District of Columbia which was ceded by the said State to the United States," and the same of that portion ceded in like manner by the State of Maryland. In neither of these States was there at that period any statute *forbidding the instruction of persons of color, whether bond or free.* It was not till nearly a third of a century after this period that the shocking laws utterly prohibiting the instruction of the colored classes were enacted in Virginia. It has been already remarked in other connections in these records that many of the most humane and enlightened men and women throughout the south, in the beginning of this century, like Mr. Jefferson, believed in the right of the colored people of all conditions to some education, and this affirmation finds exemplification in the history of Alexandria.

Schools for colored children seem to have been established in that city about 1809, not far from the year in which such schools were first opened in Washington and Georgetown. Perhaps the earliest was the one taught by Mrs. Cameron, a white Virginia lady, who had for some years a primary school for colored boys and girls on the corner of Duke and Fairfax streets, in the house now owned and occupied by Dr. Murphy. Mrs. Tutten, a white Virginia lady, also had a school about that period in a house on the corner of Pitt and Prince streets. Both these schools were in operation some time prior to the opening of the war of 1812. Immediately after this war

A FREE COLORED SCHOOL

was founded by an association of free colored people, who received cordial aid and encouragement from the enlightened and benevolent white people of the city. The school was held in the Washington Free School Building on Washington street, then not used for a white school, and was taught by Rev. James H. Hanson, white pastor of the Methodist Episcopal church, colored. It was conducted on the Lancaster system and averaged nearly three hundred scholars. The association was composed of the most substantial colored people of the city, and was maintained with great determination and success for a considerable period. There are colored men and women of good education still living in Alexandria who attended this school.

ALFRED H. PARRY,

born a slave in Alexandria in 1805, went to Mr. Hanson's school, and when a mere boy began himself to teach in a small way. An attempt being made to separate the mother and child by sale, the parent seized her offspring in her desperation and threw it into the Potomac, from which it was with difficulty rescued alive. The mother soon afterwards purchased both her own freedom and that of her child, the latter for $50. Mr. Parry taught many years in Alexandria. At first he had only a small night-school, which gradually increased so much as to attract the attention of the mayor, Bernard Hooe, in 1837, who called Parry before him and declared his school to be an "unlawful assembly." In Alexandria the schools were subjected to annoyance and restraints under the provisions of the city ordinance prohibiting all assemblages, day or night, "under the pretence or pretext of a religious meeting, or for any amusement." It was this provision that Mayor Hooe read to Parry when called before him. Parry plead for his school on the ground of his well-known good character, and the mayor replied that his assent to such a school would not be given though he knew the teacher to be as pure as the angel Gabriel." Parry, however, persisted, hired a white man to be present at his night-school, and the mayor, without assenting, endured the institution.

Parry soon opened a day-school, which was kept up through the severest period of the persecution which followed the Nat Turner insurrection in South Hampton county and the riots in Washington and other cities, from 1831 to 1835. Here he taught until he went to Washington, in 1843—the school-house last used by him being between Duke and Wolf streets, on a hill, and known as "Mount Hope Academy." His scholars numbered from 75 to 100, composed of both sexes. Many slave children attended his school under written permits from their owners; "I am willing that my servant, A. B., should attend the school of Alfred H. Parry," being substantially the form of the permission which met the requisitions of the law. The owners paid the tuition. The excitement in the times of the riots does not seem to have inflamed the people of Alexandria as it did in Washington, though the colored schools and churches were all closed for a time. Mr. Parry's wife was born at Ravensworth. Her mother, Kitty Jones, was one of the Mount Vernon servants, belonging to Washington, who made her free before the birth of the daughter, and she was brought up in the family of Jonathan Butcher, a good Quaker of Alexandria. Parry, now resides in Washington.

OTHER SCHOOLS.

Sylvia Morris, a colored woman, had a primary school for about twenty years on Washington street, in her own house, near the Lancaster school. It was at some periods quite large. She was teaching at the time of the Nat Turner insurrection, and continued her school up to the retrocession of Alexandria in 1846.

Mr. Nuthall, an Englishman, had a flourishing school for two or three years, from 1838, in the First Baptist colored church, but the opposition was so strong at that time that he discontinued it, and subsequently taught in Georgetown.

A few years before this period, about the time when General Jackson was first elected President, a white man by the name of Sargent taught on Duke street and in several other localities. Also, Joseph Ferrell, a colored man of decided abilities, had a school for some years on an alley between Duke and Prince streets. He was a baker by trade and a leading spirit among the colored people, but was sent to the penitentiary for assisting some of his race in escaping from bondage.

SABBATH SCHOOLS.

The first colored Sabbath school in Alexandria was established about 1818, in the Second Presbyterian (white) church, the Friends opening a similar school about the same time. In these schools the scholars, old and young, were taught to read. The colored people had chapels in which they held their prayer and social evening worship, but in the regular Sabbath ministrations they occupied the galleries in the white churches. Soon after the Sabbath schools were established in the white churches for the colored people they began to open them in their own chapels, the white people coming into them to assist. At the love feasts in the Methodist churches the white and colored communicants were accustomed to speak without discrimination; also at confirmation in St. Paul's church, and it is believed in the other Episcopal churches, the bishop placed his hand alike upon the head of the black and the white communicant. At the sacrament of the Lord's Supper, however, the colored were not allowed to participate till the whites had communed, and this continues to be the custom in all the Protestant white churches.

THE RETROCESSION AND THE RESULTS.

When Alexandria city and county were retroceded to Virginia by act of Congress, July 9, 1846, Sylvia Morris's long-established school was in a flourishing condition, and there were several smaller schools for little children taught in private houses. The hostility to the instruction of the colored people had become so strong that the children were obliged to conceal their school books on the street, and to dodge to and fro like the young partridges of the forest. But when the laws of Virginia took effect, by the ratification of the retrocession (1846) on the part of the State, matters became still worse, for the constables of the city were at once ordered to disperse every colored school, whether taught by day or night, on the week-day or on the Sabbath, and the injunction was most zealously executed. Every humble negro cabin in which it was suspected that any of these dusky children were wont to meet for instruction was visited, and so stern and relentless was the rule that the free colored people dared only in a covert manner to teach even their own children, a colored person not being allowed to read openly in the street so much as a paragraph in a newspaper. Some used to meet in secluded places outside the city, and, with sentinels posted, hold their meetings for mutual instruction, those who could read and write a little teaching those less fortunate. In 1845 they organized a colored masonic lodge, the charter being received from the Grand Lodge of Pennsylvania.* The city authorities, however, forbade their meetings within the limits of the city, and they were wont to meet beyond the city, with sentinels at outposts, as in the assemblages for learning to read and write.

Thus all the education which they could give their children was such as was dispensed by stealth in dark corners, except those who were able to send their sons and daughters to Washington and elsewhere, as many, by the most extraordinary exertion, continued to do through the next 14 years. But under the iron despotism of the "Virginia black code," as will be seen hereafter, those who sought their education abroad were expatriated, for the law strictly forbade such ever to return with their intelligence to their homes under penalty of fine or stripes. Many of the free colored people fled precipitately to Washington and to the north at the time of the retrocession, and those who remained courageously struggled under their ignominious burdens, praying day and night, as they now say, for the great deliverance, which the Lord, in his own good time, has brought them.

Schools were established in Alexandria by the benevolent societies about the same period they were opened in Washington, and for the last five years the colored children of the city have had vastly better school privileges than the white—a turn in the wheel of fortune abundantly suggestive of philosophic reflection.

THE FIRST SCHOOLS FOR CONTRABANDS.

The earliest schools for contrabands in the country were opened in Alexandria, and, to the honor of the colored people be it said, were established wholly by themselves. They were private, in part pay schools, and a very large majority of the scholars, from first to last, were contrabands.

The colored schools of Alexandria under the old order of things were summarily terminated, it has been seen, when the retrocession was consummated, July 9, 1846, and henceforth, for 15 years, the colored people in that city were, so far as stern municipal law and relentless public sentiment and public officers could compass the wretched purpose, shut up to ignorance. There were, however, in that city, as elsewhere in Virginia, those who held to the faith of the Virginians of an earlier day, and who gave their servants some education.

Among the few colored girls who had grown up under such training in Alexandria was Miss Mary Chase. The family retreating with the tide of the rebellion when the ill-fated Ellsworth so bravely planted there the standard of the Union, May 24, 1861, she was left behind, and, quickly appreciating the nature of the wonderful events passing before her eyes, she courageously set to work for the good of her race. September 1 of that year (1861) she started a school called the "Columbia Street School," near Wolf street, and continued it, with much usefulness, down to 1866, when nearly all the pay schools were absorbed in the better organized free schools of the benevolent societies. Her school numbered 25 scholars June 30, 1865, and this was about her usual number, of whom quite two-thirds had been slaves.

The second contraband school was the "St. Rose Institute," a day and evening school, on West street, between King and Prince. It was established October 1, 1861, by Mrs. Jane A. Crouch and Miss Sarah A. Gray, both colored, and natives of Alexandria. It averaged about 40 scholars, nearly all having been slaves. Miss Gray was one of Miss Miner's scholars; was also at the St. Frances Academy of the Baltimore convent, and is a superior scholar as well as teacher. She afterwards assisted Rev. Mr. Robinson in his school, but is at the present time teaching a flourishing private school of her own in Alexandria, num-

---

*NOTE.—The first Grand Lodge among the colored people of this country was organized in Boston in 1784, under a charter received from the masons of England.

bering from 60 to 70 scholars. Her father is a well known and respected citizen of that place. Mrs. Crouch, also an excellent teacher, received a part of her education at the Baltimore convent.

The third contraband school was organized January 1, 1862, by Rev. C. Robinson, an able colored Baptist clergyman, subsequently assisted by the American Free Baptist Mission Society of New York, and also by the American Baptist Home Missionary Society. The school was held in a room connected with the "Second Baptist" or "Beulah" church, of which Mr. Robinson is the present pastor, and which he organized in 1863; then and now composed entirely of persons manumitted by the emancipation proclamation. Mr. Robinson was born in Brunswick, Virginia, but has no knowledge of either of his parents. He received his collegiate and theological education at the "Ashmun Institute," now the Lincoln University, (Oxford, Penn.;) was supported by "The New Jersey Baptist State Educational Society," and was ordained in the First Baptist church at Newark. At the opening of the war he was teaching at Philadelphia, as the laws of Virginia did not permit him to return, he having left it for the purpose of getting an education. When the war swept down that barrier he at once returned, and opened his school, which he called the "First Select Colored school." The first teachers were, besides himself, Rev. G. W. Parker, Miss Amanda Borden, and Mrs. Robinson, all colored. The attendance was very large, and in 1862 the number registered was 715, though the average of regular scholars was much less. In December, 1864, the records show an average of 280. As the free schools were introduced the number necessarily diminished. In the autumn of 1865 the teachers were George H. Steemer, (colored,) Miss Martha J. Emerson, and Miss Louisa Avery, young ladies from New Hampshire and excellently fitted for their work. The next year it was made an entirely free school, and Miss Sarah A. Gray, already mentioned, Miss Lavinia Lane, and Miss Martha Winkfield were added to the corps of teachers, the average attendance being about 125. Before the close of that year the number of teachers was reduced to two, Miss Gray and Miss Clara Gowing, (colored,) Mr. Robinson not having at any time withdrawn his general superintendence of the school. In 1868 he resumed the direct charge. The number of scholars is now (January, 1869,) 100; average attendance, 90. Theological Department, 30; Normal Department, 30; Primary Department, 40. The teachers are A. Lewis, Rev. J. M. Dawson, Rev. J. Thomas, Rev. L. W. Brooks, and George H. Steemer, all colored. This school has for two years been under the auspices of a society afflicted with the ponderous title of "*The Home and Foreign Educational Missionary and Commission Society.*" From the beginning the "Beulah Normal and Theological school" has constituted one of the departments, the public examinations of which are held every summer. In the two years ending July, 1868, the above-named society had contributed to the school $728 33. The supporters of the society are men of wealth in Philadelphia, New York, and Boston, of whom the most liberal have been Hon. Wm. E. Dodge, of New York; the late J. P. Crozer, of Philadelphia; and A. H. Reese, of Chester, Pennsylvania. The society has educated eight missionaries, who are now teaching and preaching at the south, most of whom were ordained in the Beulah church. The following is a brief summary taken from the records of Mr. Robinson's school:

1862, scholars registered, Primary Department	700
Normal and Theological Departments	15
1863, scholars registered, Primary Department	708
Normal and Theological Departments	20
1864, scholars registered, Primary Department	558
Normal and Theological Departments	28
1865, scholars registered, Primary Department	400
Normal and Theological Departments	30
1866, scholars registered, Primary Department	380
Normal and Theological Departments	60
1867, scholars registered, Primary Department	300
Normal and Theological Departments	88
1868, scholars registered, Primary Department	40
Normal and Theological Departments	60

It should be mentioned that a large evening school has also been kept up from the origin of this enterprise.

The fourth contraband school in Alexandria was started in November, 1862, by Leland Warring, himself a contraband, who has since become a preacher under the instruction and by the assistance of Rev. E. Turney, D. D. At that time Warring could read and spell pretty well, and such limited knowledge as he possessed he was generously moved to impart to his brother contrabands less favored. It is an interesting fact that this school was opened in the Lancaster school-house, which was erected in Alexandria through the beneficence of Washington. This house was at the time filled with families of contrabands, and to Warring it offered a good place for beginning his work. He soon had a prosperous school of over 50 children, and continued the work in that place until the following February, 1863, when the school came under the charge of the government "superintendent of contrabands," and was moved to the "Freedmen's Home," in the barrack buildings.

The above-named four schools were wholly or in part pay schools, and started and conducted by colored persons.

The first white woman who went to Alexandria to labor for the contrabands was Miss Julia A. Wilbur, of Rochester, New-York. She arrived in October, 1862, and was sent by the *Ladies' Anti-slavery Society* of that city to assist the contrabands in whatever way seemed to her best. She immediately established sewing schools or working centres, and, being a woman of fortitude and sagacity, she accomplished in many ways an immense amount of good for the poor desolate beings to whom she gave her exertions. She was supplied with money and a large amount of useful contributions, and it is the testimony of all who have known her work that it has been done in a most judicious manner. She was constantly among the schools in Alexandria, and contributed a great deal by her fine intelligence and excellent sense in giving wise direction to the efforts of the many teachers of limited education. She still continues her labors for the colored people, mostly, for the last year or two, in Washington and Georgetown. Miss Wilbur was a teacher in Rochester at the time Miss Miner was teaching in a public school in that city, about 1846.

SCHOOLS ORGANIZED IN 1863.

The first free contraband school organized in Alexandria *by whites and conducted by white teachers* was "The First Free Colored Mission Day School " at the "Freedmen's Home," corner of Prince and Royal streets. As has been already stated, it was composed in part of the one opened in the autumn of 1862 by Leland Warring in the Lancaster school-house. In the winter of 1862–'63 Rev. Albert Gladwin, of Connecticut, came to Alexandria under the direction of the "*American Baptist Free Mission Society*" of New York. He was quite active among the contrabands in getting them into religious meetings and into schools, some of which he started. He was not himself a teacher, nor did he work in such a manner as to win the particular respect of those who were teachers. He was a man of very limited education, but understood very well how to appropriate to his purposes the intelligence of others. Soon after arriving he was appointed "Superintendent of Contrabands" by the military authorities, and this gave him large sway among this class of poor creatures, who were at this period congregated in great numbers in that city. The school was opened February 23, 1863, and the teachers were at first Miss M. C. Owen, Miss Mary A. Collier, Miss Elmira Keltie, and Rev. Mr. Owen, all white. Mr. Gladwin was also accustomed to get the services of convalescent soldiers detailed as teachers ; among whom were Corporal A. Borten, colored, and T. McKenzie Axe, who was quite prominent as an assistant. Some of the soldiers so detailed were very ignorant and some very inhuman. The number of scholars in attendance December 31, 1864, was 139, all contrabands ; in June, 1865, it was 75; in March, 1866, it was 110, then in charge of Miss Owen and Lovejoy S. Owen. In April it was disbanded. Mr. Gladwin had been discharged in January, 1865.

The female teachers of this school were excellent, and Miss Mary A. Collier, who entered the school when it was started at the Freedmen's Home or Barracks, and continued till she died, in the midst of her work, in December, 1866, was a truly noble example of heroic Christian philanthropy. She was the daughter of Dr. Collier, of Chelsea, Massachusetts, who was long the city missionary of Boston. Possessed of rare talents and the best intel-lectual culture, an author of repute, and reared in the tenderness of a refined home, she came into this work with all her heart, labored day and night, literally working herself to death. This is the uniform testimony of those who observed her incessant and self-sacrificing devo-tion. Miss Collier was sent by the American Baptist Home Missionary Society.

" *Union Town school*," corner of Union and Wolf streets, was organized May 2, 1863, under the instruction of Corporal L. A. Bearmor and Mrs. Nancy Williams, a colored woman. This was a free school. Number of scholars December 31, 1865, all contrabands, 80. In June, 1866, it was taught by Mrs. Christiana Richards, numbering 35 scholars.

The " *Primary school*," day and evening, was started September 1, 1863, on Princess, between Pitt and St. Asaph streets, by Wm. K. Harris and Richard H. Lyles, both colored. The number of scholars, all contrabands, December 31, 1866, was 77. In January, 1866, it had been changed to a "select school," and averaged about 30 scholars. In June, 1865, the number was 60, with one teacher, R. H. Lyles. This was a pay school.

" *Newtown school*," day and evening, was started at the west end of Cameron street, partly free, November 2, 1863, by two colored teachers, Anna Bell Davis and Leannah Powell, and was continued in 1865 by Miss Davis, who commenced teaching while, as a contraband, she was sheltered at the slave-pen prison, a portion of which at the beginning of the war had been transformed into a rude home for the Virginia contrabands who flocked into the city. Having acquired a little education while a slave, Miss Davis bought some books and opened a school in the prison, charging a tuition fee of 50 cents a month. Mr. Hill, a colored man, had a school of 50 scholars during a part of that year.

The *Sickles Barracks school*, a Reformed Presbyterian (Xenia, Ohio) Mission school, was organized by Rev. N. K. Crow, from Illinois, November 16, 1863, in a Methodist church, corner of Princess and Patrick streets. This church, abandoned by its congregation at the opening of the war and for some time used for hospital purposes, was now, by order of Gen-eral Heintzelman, turned over to this mission for school purposes. It was subsequently purchased by the colored people for a church for $3,000. Mr. Crow opened his school with eight scholars, and five days afterwards it numbered 120. He immediately opened an even-ing school of young men and women, which numbered from 90 to 130. Mr. Henry Fish, of Massachusetts, and his niece, Miss Mary Cleveland, were his first assistants; Rev. W. G. Scott, from New York, soon aiding him as teacher, and continuing in the school with great efficiency till 1868, being in charge of the operations for several years after Mr. Crow left. Mr. Samuel Young, from Philadelphia, then a theological student and now a clergyman, was one of the early teachers. He was succeeded in 1864 by Mr. S. K. Stormont, who remained till June, 1866, when he and Miss Cleveland were succeeded by Miss Jemima Silli-man and Miss L. Alcorn, who still continue in the schools. Miss Maggie Silliman, who came into the schools October, 1864, is also one of the admirable corps of teachers. Miss Jennette Darling, of New York city, was one of the excellent teachers in 1864 and 1865. At the close of 1864 the day school numbered about 150. The average attendance in December, 1865, was 160; in December, 1866, it was 136, and 156 in March, 1867.

June 1, 1863, a small school, day and evening, was opened at No. 81 Prince street by Charles Seals, colored, the day school numbering 20, all contrabands.

October 1, 1863, Mrs. Mary Simms, colored, started an evening school on Duke street, which in December, 1864, numbered 17 scholars, all contrabands, and, like that of Mr. Seals, a pay school.

SCHOOLS ORGANIZED IN 1864.

January 11, 1864. " *The Jacobs Free School*," corner of Pitt and Roanoke streets, supported by " *The New England Freedmen's Aid Society*."—Dr. J. R. Bigelow, surgeon in charge of contrabands in Alexandria, in his round of duty one Sunday morning, in August, 1863, visiting that particular section of the city called "Petersburg," and observing a one-legged negro standing near one of the small shanties that had been quite recently built, found on entering into conversation with him that he was a contraband shoemaker, who had built the first house in that settlement at a cost of $39. After a short colloquy he asked the dusky son of Crispin if he could sing. To which he replied with one of the grand old devotional hymns, which was sung in an inspiring manner. Others soon gathered, and joined as a chorus. When the singing was ended a large audience had congregated. and this homeless and almost houseless throng Dr. Bigelow addressed in a brief speech. promising to come the next Sunday and again speak to them. At the third of these singular Sunday meetings, held in the open air, a contribution to build a house for a school was proposed, when a contribution was taken up for the object, resulting in the collection of $200 on the spot, and all from contrabands. With this money they went immediately to work, and before winter had a large roughly-finished house for their school and meetings, costing $500, and known as the "Jacobs school." It was so named in honor of Mrs. Harriet Jacobs and her daughter Louisa, who were sent from New York by the Society of Friends in that city in January, 1863. This mother and daughter, born in slavery in Edenton, North Carolina, escaped from bondage some years before the war, and a book written by the mother, and edited by Mrs. Lydia M. Child, entitled "Linda," has made their history familiar to many. They made many friends in New York and other places at the north; and among those whose cordial hospitality they enjoyed, were Mr. N. P. Willis and his family, with whom Mrs. Jacobs visited Europe. She collected some funds to aid in building and furnishing the school-house. Miss Jacobs has just been placed in charge of a school in the Stevens school-house. The first teachers were Miss Louisa Jacobs and Miss S. V. Lawton, also colored. December 31, 1864, it numbered 170 scholars, and June 30, 1865, the number was 135, nearly all contrabands. In 1865 the teachers were Mr. J. S. Banfield, (white,) Miss S. V. Lawton and her sister, Miss E. M. Lawton; in 1866 Mr. Henry T. Aborn (white) and the Miss Lawtons; in 1867 Mrs. E. P. Smith and Miss Hattie R. Smith, both white. The Miss Lawtons came from Cambridge, Massachusetts, and are well educated.

January 18. "*Freedmen's Chapel,*" an evening school, corner of Pitt and Roanoke streets.—The teachers were Rev. W. M. Scott, Mary A. Collier, and Elvira Keltie, all white. Average number through the year about 150. The two Scotts, Rev. W. M. Scott and Rev. W. G. Scott, already mentioned, were able, untiring, and unselfish laborers.

April 4. *Fort William school;* day and evening; Mrs. Elmira Dean, with colored assistant, Mr. J. Hodge. Day school averaged about 40.

April 18. "*First National Freedmen's school,*" under auspices of the "New York Freedmen's Relief Association; day and evening; Mr. Henry Fish, Mrs. Melissa Fish, and Miss Harriet E. Mitchel, colored. Enoch Bath was subsequently added as a teacher. First located north of Cameron, between Payne and West streets, but in 1865 on corner of Queen and Payne. December 31, 1864, day school numbered 170 scholars; attendance averaging through 1865 about 125. This was "a part pay school." Nearly all contrabands.

May 1. "*St. Patrick's school;*" St. Patrick street; Miss Harriet Byron Douglass, colored; pay school; about one-third contrabands. Number of scholars December 31, 1864, 35; and June 30, 1865, 28.

June 14. "*Second National Freedmen's school,*" on Wolf, between Pitt and Royal streets; Rev. M. F. Sluby and Miss Laura Phenix, both colored. It was "a part pay school" under Mr. Sluby, but free under Miss Orton In December, 1864, this school had an average attendance of about 70 scholars, very few contrabands, which continued at about that average through 1865. In 1866 it rose to 100 in some months, but at the close of that school year, in June, the average attendance for the month was but 41. At the beginning of the next school year the school was in charge of Mr. I. C. Blanchard and Miss Carrie S. Orton; the average attendance for December, 1866, being 70. In January, 1867, this was raised to the rank of a "high school," under the charge of Miss Orton, principal, and Miss Susan Dennis, assistant, and was from first to last a higher style of colored school than had been known in Alexandria. It had an average attendance, in January, 1867, of 40 boys and 28 girls. It was now supported by the *North Shore and Portland, Maine, Aid Societies.* The school increased in numbers and in interest through the year.

September 5, 1864. "*Primary school,*" on St. Asaph street, south of Gibbon. Teachers, Miss M. F. Simms and Miss M. M. Nickens, both colored. A small contraband pay school. On the same day the "*Washington street school,*" No. 65 Washington street, was opened by

19

Miss L. V. Lewis and Miss A. M. Thompson, both colored; a pay school, numbering 70 scholars, and continuing through the year, and all contrabands. June 30, 1865, it was taught by Miss A. M. Thompson, colored, numbering 37 scholars. Rev. Leland Warring, colored, opened a small *evening pay school*, all contrabands, September 7, and September 20 Mr. G. S. Mell started the "*Home evening school*," a small pay school, mostly contrabands. Both schools held in barrack buildings. Mr. Mell subsequently started a small pay day school called the "*Washington Square school.*"

Rev. Chauncey Leonard, chaplain of L'Ouverture Military Hospital, had a flourishing school there through the winter of 1864–'65.

SCHOOLS ORGANIZED IN 1865 AND 1866.

The Pennsylvania Freedmen's Relief Association organized its first school January 9, 1865, in Zion Wesley church, on Columbia near Wolf street, under the charge of Miss Caroline W. Moore, Miss R. S. Capron, and Miss Mary F. Nickens, the latter a colored teacher. Attendance June, 1865, was 150. The association thinking it best to concentrate its strength in Washington, withdrew from Alexandria in the latter part of the same year, leaving their operations in good hands.

The New York Freedmen's Relief Association organized the "Third National Freedmen's school" November 20, 1865, on Alfred street near Wilkes. under Miss Emma E. Warren, who was succeeded in February, 1866, by Miss Cornelia Jones and Miss Mary S. Rowell, the latter going into another school soon and giving place to Miss Helen Vaughan. Average attendance under Miss Warren, about 50 ; under her successors, two schools, the attendance in each was nearly 50. Miss Rowell went into the "*Fourth National school*," which was organized November 25, 1865, on West between Prince and Duke streets. In June, 1866, the six departments had an average attendance of 246, with 320 on their combined rolls. The teachers were at that date Helen Vaughan, Mary S. Rowell, Frances Munger, Emma E. Warren, and Kate A. Shepard. Miss H. N. Webster was in the school at its organization, and Charles A. Libby was in charge in May, 1866. This school had at first four departments, with an average attendance of about 200.

The *Fifth National school* was opened December 1, 1865, near the corner of Union and Franklin streets, under Rev. Edward Barker and Mr. Enoch Bath. In June, 1866, this school had been moved to Water street, and the average attendance that month was 85.

There was a large school started at *Camp Distribution* in 1865, and continued down to 1868. Julia Benedict and Frances Rouviere were the original teachers, continuing till 1867, when Thomas Corwin took the school, which averaged about 35 scholars.

In the autumn of 1866 there were two schools opened at *L'Ouverture Hospital*, one taught by Miss L. A. Hall and the other by Helen Robertson; also two in *Barrack buildings*, one by Mary E. Fales, the other by Elmira S. Jones; another at *Battery Rodgers* by Emily J. Brown and Emma R. Hawley, all white teachers. In February, 1867, Miss Hawley's department was organized into a district school, and supported by the "*Penn Yan, N. Y. Aid Society.*" The above-named teachers were white, and the schools were supported in 1866–'67 by the New York branch of the Freedmen's Aid Commission, with an average attendance of nearly 250 scholars.

CHURCHES AND SABBATH SCHOOLS.

As the war advanced the contraband hamlet called "Petersburg," and already mentioned, became populous, at one period numbering some 1,500 people, with several hundred houses. They soon formed a Baptist church, and Rev. G. W. Parker, colored, who was teaching with Rev. C. Robinson in the "Select Colored School," became their pastor, and still continues with them in that relation. In due time, as the church and society increased, the necessity for better accommodations became apparent, and a Methodist white church edifice, which had been left empty by the owners, many of whom had gone into the rebellion, was purchased for the very small sum of $3,000, their pastor going north and collecting funds for this object. Up to that time the Jacob's school-house had been used for religious meetings, as well as for school purposes. Just as they were about to move into the church building they had purchased the school-house was destroyed by a violent storm. This church, the Third Baptist, (colored,) is in a flourishing condition, and numbers 600 members. They are now preparing to enlarge the building. The Sabbath school is very large, and, under the care of some half a dozen white persons of Christian benevolence, is one of the most interesting and effective educational institutions in Alexandria. The name of the place was changed when General Grant took command of the army from "Petersburg" to "Grantville," in honor of that event, the contrabands alleging that as Peter Grant, the founder of their settlement, was of the same name, in making the change they would be "killing two birds with one stone."

Before the war there were but two colored churches in Alexandria, the "First Baptist" and the "African Methodist Episcopal." They did not, however, have pastors of their own color, colored preachers being allowed to officiate only in the presence of a white minister or person detailed by him for that duty, and even in those cases the colored clergyman was not permitted to enter the pulpit. Rev. Philip Hamilton, a highly respected and well known local preacher of the Methodist church, was always subjected to this restraint. It was when on his way from Washington to Alexandria to preach in that church that Rev. Frost Pullett was once arrested as a free negro, the laws of Virginia forbidding a free negro or mulatto coming into the State.

There are now six churches of colored people in that city, the "African Methodist Episcopal" and five Baptist churches. The "First Baptist church" was organized more than 40 years ago, and the pastor is Rev. B. F. Madden. The "Second Baptist," or "Beulah church," was organized in 1863 by Rev. C. Robinson, the present pastor. This people bought a lot and started their house, the pastor, like Mr. Parker, going north and gathering funds to complete the building. This church is large and flourishing. These two colored pastors, it has been seen, started the "Select Colored School," in January 1, 1862, and they taught together till the "Petersburg" church bought their new house. The "Fourth Baptist," or "Shiloh" church, was organized about 1863, at "Newton"—L'Ouverture Hospital—the military hospital for colored soldiers, which was located in the yard of Price & Birch's old slave prison, used during the war as a prison for deserters. The ancient sign "Price, Birch & Co.," in dim characters, remained upon the front of the gloomy structure through the war; the windows with their iron grates, the lofty brick enclosure, and every aspect of the three-story spacious structure, suggesting the lacerated human hearts and bodies, the manacles, the chains, the auction-block, and all the manifold forms of anguish which such a shocking receptacle brings before every humane and reflecting mind. The pastor of the "Shiloh" church is Rev. Leland Warring, a colored man, who, like the others, was a teacher during the war. There is still another Baptist colored church, the "Zion Baptist," located in the vicinity of the railroad tunnel. These churches have each a flourishing Sabbath school, in which old and young unite in learning to read and in the study of the Bible.

It should have been previously stated that the Sisters of Charity, about 45 years ago, maintained for some years a small but very excellent school for colored girls, at the same period in which they had a large boarding school for white girls, in the large brick building then known as "The Old Brig," on the corner of Duke and Fairfax streets, in Alexandria. These Sisters also maintained a very large Sunday-school for colored children, in which they were instructed in spelling, reading, and in Christian doctrine. At this period the Friends also sustained a large Sunday-school in their meeting-house, in which refined women of prominent standing in the city were wont to teach the colored people, young and old, to spell and read and to write also, the last-mentioned branch being little tolerated in a colored school at any period in Virginia. In the Episcopal and Presbyterian churches the colored people were taught the catechism, rarely if ever to read at all.

SCHOOLS IN OPERATION JANUARY 1, 1869.

There are two colored school-houses in the city, six rooms in each; the Pitt street house, finished in April, 1867, and the Alfred street house, finished in the following November. The lots upon which these houses stand were purchased by the colored people, in 1866.

They held public meetings to rouse their people to the importance of the subject; concentrated their efforts, and raised the money in their poverty, paying $800 for the first lot, and about that sum for the other. The Freedmen's Bureau built the houses, which are very comfortable, and of a capacity each to seat 400 scholars; the estimated value of the Alfred street house and lot being $7,500; that of the other, $6,000.

In the Alfred street building there are now (January, 1869) in operation five schools, under the following teachers: Miss E. D. Leonard, Massachusetts; Miss Maggie L. Silliman, Miss Jemima Silliman, and Miss Lydia Alcorn, Pennsylvania; and Miss Savira Wright, Massachusetts. The Misses Silliman and Miss Alcorn are supported by the Reformed Presbyterian mission, and the others by the New York branch of the A. F. U. Commission.

In the Pitt street building there are also five schools, with five teachers and an assistant teacher, as follows: Miss M. E. Stratton and Miss Fannie A. Morgan, Connecticut; Miss Rosetta A. Coit, New York; Miss Mary E. Perkins; Miss Laura V. Phenix and Miss Mary M. Nickens, the latter a colored teacher. These 10 schools have an average attendance of about 420 scholars, with 500 or more names on the rolls. In the two private schools there are 170 more, making 670 registered scholars. Rev. C. Robinson's school numbers 100; Miss Sarah A. Gray's about 70. Miss Gray and the other colored female teachers mentioned above were born and brought up in Alexandria; the former, however, received her thorough education at the Baltimore Convent.

Rev. Richard Miles and his daughter have recently opened a school a few miles south of Alexandria, and about a mile from "Camp Distribution," a place well known during the years of the war, and where now there is a settlement of colored people, who are trying to support themselves by renting and tilling small pieces of land, varying in extent from five to 50 acres. Some of the scholars in Mr. Miles's school come a distance of three miles.

SUMMARY.

	Scholars.		Scholars.
Scholars registered, September, 1861, to December 31, 1864	3,732	Average attendance, January, 1866	1,594
		Scholars registered, January, 1867	975
Average attendance, December, 1864	1,646	Average attendance, January, 1867	645
Scholars registered, January to June, 1865	1,643	Scholars registered, January, 1868	1,086
		Average attendance, January, 1868	835
Average attendance, June, 1865	1,036	Scholars registered, January, 1869	777
Scholars registered, January, 1866	2,215	Average attendance, January, 1869	608

Colored population of Alexandria, 1865.

Children 14 years old and under	2,635	Slaves before the war	5,050
Children over 14 and under 20	1,144	Free before the war	2,713
Total colored population	7,763	Mulattoes	3,831
Number able to read	1,734	Blacks	3,932

REMARKS.

The above summary shows some falling off of numbers in the last two years. This is to be attributed in part to the improvement of the schools, the inferior ones being absorbed in the larger and better, and also to the moving away of many contrabands, who at first crowded in great numbers to Alexandria from the northern part of the State. It must, however, be acknowledged that the indefatigable labors of the various relief societies in gathering the children into the schools are sadly missed, and that at present the average attendance should be larger, and the school accommodations much increased. The Freedmen's Bureau has been and still is of great service, but this will soon be withdrawn; and with no public school system in the city or the State, and in the midst of a population where hardly a single resident has the least sympathy with any work for the elevation of the colored race, and where most are strongly and even bitterly opposed to such efforts, the prospect for this unfortunate class is far from encouraging.

The Friends in Alexandria who maintained their allegiance to the Union were among the most effective workers in the cause of colored schools, joining hands heartily with their brethren from the north. It is, however, a remarkable fact that the only case in which the great body of the Friends connected with any Friends' meeting in the country supported the rebellion, was that at Alexandria. Most of them went south, and the meeting was broken up. This shows how extreme was the disloyalty which reigned in that city.

Mr. Newton, already referred to as the efficient superintendent in 1865–'66 of the Washington and Georgetown schools, under the care of the New York and Pennsylvania freedmen's relief societies, took, for a time, a general supervision of the schools at Alexandria, at the request of the different benevolent associations. At that time semi-monthly meetings of all the teachers were held alternately in Washington and Alexandria, there often being as many as 125 present. These gatherings, or conferences, were productive of great good. This association of teachers was quite distinct from the "Volunteer association," so called, already noticed.

Most of the teachers now employed have been in the arduous work for years, and it is only those able to endure the severest toil who have not broken down under it. The very great number of young women who have come here with faith, fortitude, and health, and broken down, is well known to those who have been familiar with these schools, and shows that it has been a self-sacrificing field of labor. It is certain, also, that abler, better-educated, and more refined young women never entered into any benevolent enterprise than those who have given such signal success to this great educational undertaking in the District of Columbia and vicinity. The schools and teachers of Alexandria are substantially the same in character as those of Washington and Georgetown, and the remarks of a general nature already made apply equally to them. The scholars are about as well advanced and show the same aptitude and zeal in the one city as in the others.

As has been stated, the first three schools organized in Alexandria for colored instruction, after the war opened, were taught by colored persons. Colored schools in any form were sufficiently odious to the mass of the old white residents of that city: but when the northern white men and women entered upon the work the bitterness was very intense. When Rev. N. K. Crow with his band of associates went there to open their school, in November, 1863, no white family in the city would give them food or lodging. They found a home, however, with an excellent old colored man, H. H Arnold, now more than 80 years old, but smart as an ordinary man at 50, who had seen General Washington in 1799 at Christ church in that city, and was raised in the Scott family, in Dinwiddie county. Being of Indian extraction on his mother's side, he was free-born. Arnold was the body-servant of Lieutenant General Scott for thirty-seven years from 1811 to the close of the Mexican war, and he describes many a rough-and-tumble scuffle they had together when boys on the family plantation. This reminds one of the story told of Richard Henry Lee, in the memoir by his grandson: "Knowing he was to be sent to England, [to be educated,] it was his custom to make a stout negro boy fight with him every day. To his angry father's question, 'What pleasure can you find in such rough sport?' the son replied: 'I shall shortly have to box with the English boys, and I do not wish to be beaten by them.'" Arnold being in New York city at the time of the riots of 1863, was protected in General Scott's house, and was the only colored man that followed the remains of this great soldier to their last resting place.

Mr. Crow's school was persecuted, and the children often stoned by the white children; and every form of contempt was visited upon the refined and cultivated teachers by the white parents. This animosity has gradually abated, but still largely pervades the society, especially in the ranks of the impoverished classes of the aristocracy, who are smarting under the loss of wealth in human souls and bodies. In January, 1865, Miss Caroline W. Moore could find no decent white family who would receive her, and the colored people were too poor to furnish her proper accommodations: and she with her assistant, Miss R. S. Capron, were for some time compelled to board in Washington. It was her school that was complained of as a nuisance, though an exceedingly well-conducted institution. She presented her case to the mayor in person, and he discreetly dismissed the complaint.

THE AMERICAN TRACT SOCIETY AND LABORS OF DR. PIERSON.

Since the main portion of this report was written, fuller information has come to our hands in regard to the important initiatory and pioneer work among the freedmen by Rev. Dr. H. W. Pierson, acting as agent of the American Tract Society. The several schools organized by him were not only the foundation of all that was afterward accomplished, but the work was without precedent, the field an untried one, and formidable obstacles presented themselves at the outset, in the melancholy physical and mental condition of the freedmen themselves, in a public sentiment, strong and fierce, opposed to their enlightenment, and in the black code of the District, at that time in full force and bristling with enactments in hostile array against such a benevolent and Christian work.

The opening of the war at once drew the attention of the whole north to the rapid release of the slaves from bondage, wherever our troops reached slave soil, and as quickly the great question arose, What shall be done for them? At this juncture it was inevitable that many eyes should be turned to the Tract Society, with its complete organization and ample resources, and appeals were poured in on every side that it would move in this work. Dr. Pierson had resided many years at the south, as the Tract Society's superintendent of colportage in Virginia, as agent of the American Bible Society in Kentucky, and as President of Cumberland College, in that State. On graduating at the Union Theological Seminary in New York city, in 1848, Dr. Pierson was appointed by the American Board of Foreign Missions as missionary to Africa, but partial loss of health, owing to a disease of the lungs, prevented him from going. The following winter he went to Hayti as agent for the Bible Society. He may be truly called the life-long friend of the colored race, and in many other ways than those above referred to has he labored in their behalf in most of the southern States. To many Dr. Pierson is known as the author of a valuable work on the private life of Jefferson, the substance of which formed the subject of lectures delivered by him before the New York Historical Society and the Smithsonian Institute. On leaving Kentucky in 1861, he was so impressed by the wonderful opening offered to philanthropic men and women for effectually reaching the poor slaves with the means of instruction, and was so convinced that it was the duty of the Tract Society to enter energetically upon the work, that he proceeded to New York and communicated personally with the secretaries upon the subject. He then went to Washington, and was introduced to Hon. Salmon P. Chase, then Secretary of the Treasury, by Rev. J. C. Smith, of Washington, so well known for his devotion to the best interests of the colored population of the District, a devotion wisely directed and fearlessly shown through those many years when obloquy, persecution, and danger attended it. Dr. Pierson was cordially received by Secretary Chase, and, after several interviews with him as to the best method of organizing a plan for educating and aiding the freedmen, he was introduced by him to Mr. E. L. Pierce, of Boston, who had already been sent south by the government to make investigations in regard to the condition of the colored people within our lines, and had just arrived in the city. Mr. Chase desired them to confer very fully on the subject, and Dr. Pierson presented his plan of sending to the freedmen *teaching colporteurs*, which was cordially approved by Mr. Pierce. In a letter written soon after, Dr. Pierson says: "I was very anxious that the American Tract Society should embark in this work, as my former connection with the society made me fully aware of its great facilities for usefulness in its buildings, presses, and organization. I had been so absorbed in my own labors that I had taken no part in the discussion and excitements that it had passed through on the slavery question, but I knew that its receipts had fallen off about $100,000 on account of the withdrawal of those who had disapproved of its course on this subject. In my free conversations with the secretaries, I told them that they could in no way secure the sympathy of the warm friends they had lost as by entering upon educational and religious labors among the colored people."

It may be stated here that early in the winter of 1861–'62, a plan was under consideration among many prominent and wealthy philanthropic and Christian men in New York to organize a National Society whose leading object it should be to establish schools among the freedmen, as no efficient society then existing seemed prepared to take up the work. One feature of this plan was to enlist, as far as possible, the services of the army chaplains and soldiers, at such points as was practicable.

February 6, 1862, Rev. Dr. Smith wrote Dr. Pierson as follows: "Last evening I had a talk with Secretary Chase at his house. I found him much interested about the contrabands and he wants to do something effectively with and for them, and *at once,* something that will unite different denominations and benevolent men *in a society* or association like to the American Tract Society, with auxiliaries in other cities. The object will be to furnish teachers for the contrabands, have schools, and in every way seek to elevate them, 'for' said. the Secretary, 'whatever may be the *political* results of our present troubles, these contrabands will be on another footing than heretofore.' He says *immediate* steps ought to be taken, and he will co-operate in every way possible in the enterprise. The heart of Mr. Chase is in the thing. I told him you were the man to execute the whole business, and he has read your two letters. There are no funds of the government that can be used, but the *power* of the government can be had, and will be, if the work can go on. We do not want books and tracts so much as we want *men* to go and be with the contrabands. Do see as many men as you can. The whole work is simple and ought to be pushed now. Secretary Chase attaches all importance to it, and will give it his full and noble aid."

Early in the winter the Tract Society as well as the Bible Society donated their publications for the use of the freedmen, and the former society prepared several tracts for their special needs. The Secretary, Mr. Eastman, wrote under date of February 8, 1862, to Rev. Dr. Smith, as follows:

"MY DEAR SIR: Dr. Pierson has showed us your letter to him and we had an interview with him last evening. All I can say now is that we are deeply interested in the subject and are ready to do whatever we can to serve and promote the general object as we understand it. We have not, however, any plan fully matured, but will confer further on the subject. In the mean time I would say that in addition to our Tract Primer and Infant Primer, of which with other publications we have already sent the amount of 100,000 pages to Fortress Monroe and Port Royal especially for the colored people, we have now in press 24 small tracts in large type, which we have got up on purpose for them. These will be ready in a week. We shall add to the number as the work goes on. We cannot now tell all that we can do, but you will hear from us again in a few days."

Later in February Dr. Pierson addressed to the Tract Society the following letter:

"NEW YORK, *February* 25, 1862.

"GENTLEMEN: I enclose herewith a letter written by myself to Mr. Edward L. Pierce, special agent of the Treasury Department, and his reply. It has seemed to me that a great door and effectual is here opened for the beneficent labors of your society. I am aware that the labors required are somewhat different in character, though not in spirit, from those that have been for years performed by your colporteurs in the moral wastes of every part of the country.

"You are aware that the American Sabbath School Union has just published a 'Bible Reader,' composed exclusively of selections from the Bible, accompanied with a series of cards embracing the most recent and philosophical improvements in the work of imparting elementary instruction, and so arranged that groups of a hundred or more can be taught in concert to read much more rapidly than by former systems. Dr. Packard informs me that he thinks that, as a rule, adults can be taught to read the Bible by this system in a month. Moreover, the Reader is so arranged that by the time it has been mastered the pupil will be thoroughly informed as to the essential truths of our holy religion. I desire you to bring this whole matter before your committee and inform me as to these two points: First, Can your society superadd to its work that of teaching the contrabands to read the word of God? Second. Will you commission colporteurs for this work? If you give me an affirmative answer to these questions I will communicate further with the government agents, to whom this work has been intrusted. From my extended travel in the southern States, and residence there for many years, I feel a very deep interest in their welfare. A great educational and religious work, in the providence of God, is now thrown upon the great Christian heart of the country, and it seems to me that your society is called upon to enter upon it, but of that you must be the judge. Pardon me if, in my intense solicitude for these children of our common Father, so many thousands of whom have heard from my lips the message of salvation, I charge you to consider this matter prayerfully and maturely, and that you act upon it in view of the account you must render to Him who has said ' inasmuch as you have done it unto one of the least of these you have done it unto me.' "

On the 28th of February Dr. Pierson was commissioned by the Tract Society to visit Washington and other points for the purpose of establishing schools for the freedmen, and report to them further openings for similar operations. In a letter he thus briefly sketches his first experience after arriving in Washington :

" I soon learned that most of the contrabands who had passed through our lines and reached the city were assembled at the navy yard and in a building in Duff Green's row, near the Capitol. March 14, I visited Commodore Dahlgren, then in command at the navy yard, and presented a letter of introduction from Rev. J. C. Smith, stating my object and office. He received me most cordially, and indorsed my letter with these few but hearty words : ' *The commandant says certainly.*' He then directed Lieutenant Parker to send me whatever aid I desired. I told him I only wished to have the chapel opened and lighted, and all the contrabands in the yard notified to meet me there at 7 o'clock that evening. At the appointed hour I found a dusky group, such as I had seen on hundreds of plantations, awaiting my arrival and most anxious to enjoy the richest of all the privileges secured to them by their new-found freedom. It was a moment of indescribable interest—a pivotal point in their history as well as my own. At any previous period of our history such a meeting on any of the plantations from which they had escaped would have been criminal in the highest degree. I had myself seen a poor Irishman in the hands of the sheriff, who told me his prisoner had been convicted of teaching negroes to read, and he was taking him to Richmond to serve out the years in the penitentiary, for which he had been sentenced. Now I had no fear of the penitentiary, nor they of 'stripes well laid on.' My method of teaching was very simple, and the same in all the schools subsequently established, and intended expressly for adults. I began with the first verse of the Bible, printed on a card in letters so large that all could easily see it, and hung upon the wall. Without attempting to teach or even name the letters, I began with the words, requiring them to repeat each in concert several times, until well distinguished from the others, and in this way a short verse was learned in half an hour. With this ' word method,' instruction in the letters and in spelling was afterwards combined. At the navy yard Master C. V. Morris and his wife and daughter took the deepest interest in my labors, and rendered valuable aid in teaching. I called also on Mrs. Attorney General Bates, Mrs. Senator Trumbull, Mrs. Senator Grimes, and many other ladies of like social position, and received from them all assurances of sympathy, and from many personal co-operation in the work. As the work assumed larger proportions and the old slave laws were unrepealed, I thought it best to secure military protection. On receiving Mr. Shearer's commission from the Tract Society, I called upon Brigadier General James S. Wadsworth, military governor of the District, accompanied by Rev. J. C. Smith. He received us most kindly, and listened with the deepest interest and sympathy to our explanations of the routine of the work. I then handed him Mr. Shearer's commission, and requested him to place upon it such military indorsement as he judged best. He took it and wrote, as nearly as I can remember, ' The bearer is authorized to visit, instruct, and advise the colored people in this District, under the military protection of the government.' This paper secured access to all prisons, jails, camps, &c., in the District, and was of the greatest value in the prosecution of the work.

" On Sunday, March 30, I lectured in the Ebenezer church, (colored,) Georgetown, explained the nature of the work, and gave notice that I would meet them on an evening in the latter part of the week to organize a school. On Thursday, April 3, a statement appeared in the Star, that, in consequence of a report in circulation in Georgetown that a political lecture would be delivered to the colored people in that church on Wednesday evening, ' considerable excitement resulted, and threats were made to lynch the lecturer,' and that on that evening a large crowd of whites had gathered in a menacing attitude about the church. Also learning from private sources that a large number of young men had organized to break up such a meeting, I applied to the mayor and directed his attention to the article. He had seen it. I told him the nature of the work I was doing, and that I had called entirely out of regard to him and the foolish young men who had not comprehended the change that had taken place since the war began. I showed him the above paper indorsed by General Wadsworth, and assured him that if necessary I should call on the military for protection. I then made a similar visit to the chief of police. They both assured me that I would not be molested, and I was not.

"I have labored, as you know, not a little in the moral wastes of the land, and have seen many tears of gratitude and heard many thanks, but I have never seen anything that would be compared to the eagerness of these people to learn to read the word of God, or their gratitude for my labors in their behalf. One gray-headed old woman said, 'I never expected to live to see this—to read the blessed Bible. God is as good as His word, sisters; God is as good as His word. Hain't He told us He would sanctify us by His spirit and His word? We have felt His spirit right in here (laying her hand upon her heart) a long time, and now He has sent this man here to teach us, and ain't His word coming right along?'"

BANNEKER, THE ASTRONOMER.

Benjamin Banneker, the celebrated black astronomer and mechanician, was born near the village of Ellicott's Mills, Maryland, in 1732. His father was a native African, and his mother the child of native Africans. His mother was free at her marriage, and soon purchased her husband's freedom. She was a Morton, a family noted for intelligence. Prior to 1809 free people of color voted in Maryland, and it was one of that family, Greenbury Morton, who, not knowing the law of that year restricting the right of voting to whites, made the famous impassioned speech to the crowd at the polls when his vote was refused. Benjamin Banneker worked upon his father's farm. When nearly a man grown he went to an obscure and distant country school, learning to read and write and to cipher as far as Double Position. He had great inventive powers, and made a clock from the instruction he obtained from seeing a watch. He was also a profound and accurate observer of nature, men, and things. In 1787 George Ellicott, a gentleman of education, furnished him some works of the higher class on mathematics and astronomy, which he devoured with avidity, and which opened a new world to him. Astronomy was henceforth his absorbing study. He lived alone in the cabin upon the farm which his parents, who were dead, had left him, and was never married. In 1791 he made an almanac, which was published in Baltimore, and the publication being continued annually till he died in 1804, at 72 years of age. Benjamin H. Ellicott, of Baltimore, took great interest in this remarkable man, and some quarter of a century ago gathered up the fragments of his history, which were embraced with other facts in regard to him in a memoir, prepared and read by John H. B. Latrobe, esq., before the Maryland Historical Society. Banneker sent the manuscript, in his own handwriting, of his first almanac to Thomas Jefferson in 1791, with a long and manly letter, to which Mr. Jefferson made prompt and kind reply, thanking him for the letter and almanac, and added "Nobody wishes more than I do to see such proofs as you exhibit that nature has given to our black brethren talents equal to those of the other colors of men, and that the appearance of a want of them is owing only to the degraded condition of their existence both in Africa and America," concluding as follows: "I have taken the liberty of sending your almanac to Monsieur de Condorcet, secretary of the Academy of Sciences at Paris, and member of the Philanthropic Society, because I consider it a document to which your whole color had a right for their *justification against the doubts which have been entertained of them.*" It is noteworthy that Mr. Jefferson calls the colored people "our black brethren;" elsewhere in his writings he calls them fellow-citizens. This almanac was extensively circulated through the middle and southern States, and its calculations were so exact and thorough as to excite the attention and admiration of the philosophic and scientific classes throughout Europe, especially Pitt, Fox, Wilberforce, and their coadjutors, who produced the work in the British Parliament as an argument in favor of the abolition of slavery and the cultivation of the black race. Banneker was buried near Ellicott's Mills, and a few years ago the colored people honored themselves in raising a monument there to the memory of his great genius and fine character.

In the interesting debate in the Senate in March, 1864, on Mr. Sumner's amendment to the bill incorporating the Metropolitan railroad, (Washington city,) providing that there should be no exclusion of any person from the cars of said road, Mr. Reverdy Johnson, in his reply to Senator Saulsbury's depreciation of the colored race, referred to Banneker in the following words : "Many of those born free have become superior men. One of them was employed in Maryland in surveying several of our boundary lines—Mason and Dixon's particularly—and some of the calculations made on that occasion, astronomical as well as mathematical in the higher sense, were made by a black Maryland man who had been a slave."

A SABBATH SCHOOL IN GEORGETOWN.

Since closing the earlier period of this history it has been discovered that a colored Sabbath school was established in the old Lancaster school-house in Georgetown as early as 1816, and was continued many years. Mr. Joseph Searle was the superintendent of the male department, and his sister, Miss Ann Searle, of the female, both being at that time teachers in a seminary in the city. The various Protestant churches sent teachers to aid in the humane work, and among those specially interested were Francis S. Key, Captain Thomas Brown, John McDaniel, Robert Ober, Daniel Kurtz, and a large number of excellent ladies. Francis S. Key not only taught in the school, but often made formal addresses to the scholars.

THE AFRICAN EDUCATION SOCIETY.

A society under the above title was organized December 28, 1829, by friends of the colored race in Washington and Georgetown. In the words of the constitution, its object was "to afford to persons of color destined to Africa such an education in letters, agriculture, and the mechanic arts as may best qualify them for usefulness and influence in Africa." The intention was to establish an institution for the above purpose. A house in Washington, near the Georgetown bridge, was rented, and a slaveholder in the vicinity offered the free use of a farm for practical instruction in agriculture, and for aiding in the support of the institution. Mr. Isaac Orr, a graduate of Yale College of the class of 1818, at that time connected with the Colonization Society, was appointed secretary, with authority to collect funds and organize the school. In the Columbia Gazette, published at Georgetown, and in the National Intelligencer of July 3, 1830, it was announced that the society would open their institution September 1; the sum of $500 being sufficient to establish a scholarship. Among the managers were Rev. Walter Colton, chaplain in the navy, and Rev. R. R. Gurley, still a resident of Washington; but notwithstanding the high character of those originating this organization, and notwithstanding its wise provisions which could not fail to meet the approval of practical and sensible men, such was the prevailing sentiment of that time—the gloomiest period for the colored people in all their history—that the society failed to obtain funds sufficient for a permanent basis of operations. The following extract from the address of the managers shows the character of the enterprise and certain phases of public opinion : "It is the design of the society to train up the youth intrusted to them from childhood ; to subject them to a steady, mild, and salutary discipline ; to exercise toward them a kind and parental care, guarding them against the approach of every insidious and hurtful influence ; to give them an intimate acquaintance with agriculture or some one of the mechanic arts ; to endow them with virtuous, generous, and honorable sentiments ; in fine, to form the whole character and render it, as far as possible, such as will qualify them to become pioneers in the renovation of Africa. In most of the slave States it is a prevailing sentiment that it is not safe to furnish slaves with the means of instruction. Much as we lament the reasons of this sentiment and the apparent necessity of keeping a single fellow-creature in ignorance, we willingly leave to others the consideration and the remedy for this evil, in view of the overwhelming magnitude of the remaining objects before us. But it is well known that very many masters are desirous to liberate their slaves in such a way as to improve their condition, and we are confident that such masters will rejoice to find the means by which those slaves may be educated by themselves without the danger of exerting an unfavorable influence around them ; and instead of creating disquiet in the country, may carry peace and joy to Africa."

CONCLUSION.

The investigation recorded in the foregoing document was undertaken with a most inadequate estimate of its magnitude, though the writer had for some years been uncommonly conversant with educational matters in the District, and deeply interested in the colored schools. The subject expanded in materials and in importance as the research was pursued, till what was expected at the beginning to fill but a few pages had swelled into a volume. The work was prosecuted in the belief that everything which the colored people have attempted and accomplished for themselves in mental and social improvement in this seat of empire was worth rescuing from oblivion, and that such a chapter would be a contribution to the educational history of the country, peculiarly instructive at this time. It is quite certain that the most of what is gathered into these pages from the first half century of the District would have never been rescued from the past under any other auspices, and from the original, novel, and instructive nature of its character, it has been deemed best to go with much minuteness into details. There is an almost tragic pathos running through the tale of the patient sufferings and sacrifices which these humble and dutiful people have experienced, through so many years of oppression, in their struggles for knowledge.

The facts embraced in the foregoing report have been gathered with an amount of labor that can be adequately estimated only by those who have toiled in a similar field of research. Prior to the rebellion the education of this proscribed and degraded race was held in scorn and derision by the controlling public sentiment of this District, as in the country at large, and schools for the colored people rarely found the slightest record in the columns of the press. After a thorough examination of the various journals published in the District during the first half century of its history, the first reference to any school that can be found is in an article on the city of Washington published in the National Intelligencer August 3, 1816, in which it is stated that "a Sunday school for the blacks has been recently established, which is well attended, and promises great benefit to this neglected part of our species, both in informing their minds and amending their morals." This journal was the only one of established character that alluded in any way to these schools, and a careful examination of its files from 1800 to 1850 has disclosed only the two or three notices already referred to. The remarkable advertisement found in the volume for 1818 of the free colored school on Capitol Hill was a striking fact in itself considered, but was otherwise of the greatest value in this work, because the names of the seven colored men subscribed to the document pointed to the sources from which was procured much of the authentic information pertaining to the first quarter of a century of the District. In this almost total absence of written information it was fortunate to find in the memories of the colored people a wonderful accuracy and completeness of recollection of almost everything pertaining to their schools. In the intercourse with this population which these researches have occasioned, this fact has been a subject of perpetual observation. The aged men and women, even though unable to read a syllable, have almost always been found to know something concerning the colored schools and their teachers. The persecutions which perpetually assailed their schools, and the sacrifices which they so devotedly made for them, seem to have fastened the history of them, with astonishing clearness and precision, in their minds, such as is surely not found among the educated white population pertaining to the white schools of the same period. Another interesting fact is not inappropriate in this connection. There are undoubtedly more colored people of the District of the class free before the war, who own their homes, than are found in proportion to their numbers among the middling classes of the white population. There are also to be found in a multitude of these humble colored homes the same refinements as are found in the comfortable and intelligent white family circles. These interesting developments disclosed in every direction in the preparation of this work have stimulated prolonged research, and made what had otherwise been a wearisome task a most agreeable occupation.

Statesmen and thoughtful public men will discover in these pages facts which put to flight a class of ethnological ideas that have been woven by philosophers into unnumbered volumes of vain theories. The great and imposing truth that the colored race has been for nearly seventy years on a grand trial of their capacity to rise in the scale of human intelligence, such as has not elsewhere in the history of the world been granted them, seems to have entirely escaped observation.   If these records are, as they are confidently believed to be, substantially accurate in all their details, the capabilities of the colored race to rise to superior mental and social elevation, and that too under the most appalling disabilities and discouragements, is illustrated on a conspicuous theatre, and with a completeness that cannot be shaken by any cavil or conjecture.

There is a colored woman in Washington, known and respected for her sterling goodness and remarkable sense. more than half a century a resident of the city, who relates that she used often to see Jefferson during his presidency, in the family of Monroe, in which she was brought up, near Charlottesville, Virginia; that on one occasion, while attending the children in the hall, she heard Jefferson say to Monroe that "he believed *the colored race had as much native sense as the whites,* that they ought to be educated and freed at the age of 21, and that if some plan of this kind should not be adopted, they would in time become self-enlightened, in spite of every oppression assert their liberties, and deluge the south in blood;" to which Mr. Monroe, rising from his seat, with both hands uplifted, exclaimed, "My God, Mr. Jefferson, how can you believe such things?"   This declaration imputed to Jefferson is well substantiated, as it not only comes from a truthful witness, but is in full accordance with the views that he has amply left on record in his writings.   In his celebrated letter to Banneker, the black mathematician and astronomer of Maryland, in elevated and feeling language he expressed to this wonderful, self-taught negro his deep thankfulness for the indisputable evidence which the productions of his genius had furnished, "*that nature has given to our black brethren talents equal to those of the other colors of men;*" and, in apology for the liberty he had taken in transmitting to the President of the French Academy of Sciences the manuscript copy of his first almanac he had sent to the philanthropic statesman as a testimony to the capabilities of his enslaved race, Jefferson went on to say that he had forwarded the remarkable production to that great representative body in the world of letters as an evidence of the intellectual powers of the black man, to which the whole colored race had "a right for their justification against the doubts which have been raised against them." With like ideas may this simple story of patient endurance and of triumph in calamities be submitted to the American people and mankind in vindication of the faith reposed by many good men in the capacity for self-government of a long down-trodden and despised portion of the human family.

The history of these schools, subsequent to the breaking out of the rebellion, records the most remarkable efforts of disinterested contributions, both in money and in labor, which are to be found in the annals of Christian and patriotic beneficence.   The duty of providing for the moral and intellectual enlightenment of a class of people who had been kept hitherto in profound ignorance, directly or indirectly, by the laws and prejudices of the country, pervaded the entire northern mind and heart.

No pains have been spared to ascertain the fields of labor occupied by different associations, and the schools taught by different individuals; but no record can fully describe the self-sacrifice and zeal of that band of noble, refined, and cultivated women who devoted themselves to the education of this neglected class, many of whom fell, as truly martyrs to their patriotic labors as those who perished on the battle field; and not a few of whom are still suffering in their own homes as great a deprivation from the loss of health in this service, as those who will bear to their graves bodies mutilated by the missiles of war.

All of which, with many thanks for your personal and official co-operation in this investigation, is respectfully submitted.

M. B. GOODWIN.

To Hon. HENRY BARNARD,
Commissioner of Education.

To this exhaustive account of the past and present condition of schools for the colored people in the District of Columbia, by Mr. Goodwin, we add a comprehensive survey of the legal status of this portion of the population in respect to schools and education in the several States.—H. B.

PART II.

LEGAL STATUS OF THE COLORED POPULATION IN RESPECT TO
SCHOOLS AND EDUCATION IN THE DIFFERENT STATES.

PART II.

LEGAL STATUS OF THE COLORED POPULATION IN RESPECT TO SCHOOLS AND EDUCATION IN THE DIFFERENT STATES.

LEGAL STATUS OF THE COLORED POPULATION IN RESPECT TO SCHOOLS AND EDUCATION.

DISTRICT OF COLUMBIA.

The only authority to restrain and limit the conduct and privileges of any class of the population in the District is to be found in the charters granted to the municipal corporations and the laws of Maryland and Virginia. Alexandria received its charter originally from Virginia, and Georgetown from Maryland, while Washington was originally incorporated by Congress. The act of Congress of July 16, 1790, establishing the seat of government in this District, provided "that the operation of the laws of the State within such District shall not be affected by this acceptance until the time fixed for the removal of the seat of government, and until Congress shall otherwise by law provide;" and under the act of February 27, 1801, the laws of Virginia and Maryland, as they existed at that date, were continued in full force and effect. In order to understand the condition in which the colored classes were lawfully held in the District during the existence of slavery, or for any period, it is necessary to know the powers existing in the charters of those cities under the State laws at the date last specified, and also the additional enlargements and curtailments of powers subsequently enacted by Congress. Some account of these codes, so far as they pertain especially to education, is also essential to a just estimate of the fortitude with which the colored people have struggled through the long period of darkness over which this history extends

The first settlers of both Maryland and Virginia evidently entertained the idea that a Christian could not be a slave. In "Plantation Laws, London, 1705," a law of 1692 in Maryland is cited as follows:

"Where any negro or slave, being in bondage, is or shall become a Christian and receive the sacrament of baptism, the same shall not, nor ought to be, deemed, adjudged, or construed to be a manumission or freeing of any such negro or slave, or his or her issue, from their servitude or bondage, but that, notwithstanding, they shall at all times hereafter be and remain in servitude and bondage as they were before baptism, any opinion or matter to the contrary notwithstanding."

In 1715 the provision was embodied in a new act with a preamble, and this is the first act found in full in Bacon's Laws, the titles only of the previous laws being given. The act of the Maryland assembly of 1715 declares:

"SEC. 23. And forasmuch as many people have neglected to baptize their negroes, or suffer them to be baptized, in a vain apprehension that negroes by receiving the sacrament of baptism are manumitted and set free: *Be it hereby further declared and enacted by and with the authority, advice, and consent aforesaid,* That no negro or negroes by receiving the holy sacrament of baptism is hereby manumitted or set free, nor hath any right or title to freedom or manumission more than he or they had before, any *law or usage or custom to the contrary* notwithstanding."

In section 36, acts of the Virginia assembly of 1705, is the following clause: "And also it is hereby enacted and declared that baptism of slaves doth not exempt them from bondage." And in 1733 the law was re-enacted in this explicit language:

"Whereas some doubts have arisen whether children that are slaves by birth, and, by the charity and piety of their owners, made partakers of the blessed sacrament of baptisme, should by vertue of their baptisme be made ffree: *It is enacted and declared by this grand assembly and the authority thereof,* That the conferring of baptisme doth not alter the condition of the person as to his bondage or ffreedom; that diverse masters, ffreed from this doubt, may more carefully endeavour the propagation of Christianity by permitting children, though slaves, or those of greater growth, if capable, to be admitted to the sacrament."

In South Carolina there was a law enacted to the same effect in 1712, in which it is curiously declared "lawful for a negro or Indian slave, or any other slave or slaves whatsoever, to receive and profess the Christian faith, and to be therein baptized," and that thereby no slave should be deemed manumitted.

The origin of this singular legislation in Virginia must have arisen from a prevailing apprehension in the public mind upon the subject at that time, 1667; but the enactments of Maryland and South Carolina undoubtedly had, as their immediate producing cause, two judicial investigations which occurred in England in 1686–'87, a short time prior to these enactments. One of these cases, reported in 3 Modern Reports, 120–1, is thus stated:

"Sir Thomas Grantham bought a monster in the Indies, which was a man of that country, who had the perfect shape of a child growing out of his breast, as an excrescency, all but the head. This man he brought hither (to England) and exposed to the sight of the people for profit. The *Indian* turns *Christian* and was baptized, and was detained from his master, who brought a *homine replequiando*, (a writ by which his title to retain the man as property might be legally tested.")

How this case was ultimately disposed of does not appear. In 1696 the question *whether the baptism* of a *negro slave*, without the permit or consent of his master, emancipated the slave, was argued with great research and learning before the King's Bench. In this instance a misconception of the form of action required prevented any decision upon the merits of the case, the matter being thus in both actions left in doubt. The argument of the counsel for the defendant in this latter case is ingenious and curious:

"Being baptized according to the use of the church," says the counsel, "he, the slave, is thereby made a Christian, and Christianity is inconsistent with slavery. And this was allowed even in the time when the popish religion was established, as appears by Littleton; for in those days if a villain had entered into religion, and was professed, as they called it, the lord could not seize him, and the reason there given is, because he was dead in law, and if the lord might take him out of his cloister, then he could not live according to his religion. The like reason may now be given for baptism being incorporated into the laws of the land; if the duties which arise thereby cannot be performed in a state of servitude, the baptism must be a manumission. That such duties cannot be performed is plain, for the persons baptized are to be confirmed by the diocesan when they can give an account of their faith, and are enjoined by several acts of Parliament to come to church. But if the lord hath still an absolute property over him, then he might send him far enough from the performance of those duties, viz., into Turkey or any other country of infidels, where they neither can nor will be suffered to exercise the Christian religion. * * * It is observed among the Turks that they do not make slaves of those of their own religion, though taken in war, and if a *Christian be taken, yet if he renounce Christianity and turn Mahometan, he doth thereby obtain his freedom.* And if this be a custom allowed among infidels, then baptism in a Christian nation, as this is, should be an immediate enfranchisement to them, as they should thereby acquire the privileges and immunities enjoyed by those of the same religion and be entitled to the laws of England."—5 *Modern Reports, Chamberline* vs. *Hervey.*

St. George Tucker, in 1796, while professor of law in the University of William and Mary and one of the judges of the general court of Virginia, delivered in the university and subsequently published a remarkable "*Dissertation on slavery, with a proposal for its abolition in the State of Virginia,*" and in quoting from the act of the Virginia assembly in 1705, above referred to, is provoked to remark that "it would have been happy for this unfortunate race if the same tender regard for their bodies had always manifested itself in our laws as is shown for their souls in this act. But this was not the case, for two years after we meet with an act declaring: 'That if any slave resist his master, or others by his master's orders, correcting him, and by the extremity of the correction should chance to die, such death should not be accounted felony;'" and Professor Tucker adds: "This cruel and tyrannical act, at three different periods enacted with very little alteration, was not finally repealed till 1788, about a century after it had first disgraced our code."

What would this illustrious man now say were he to rise from the dead, and, standing in that university, discourse upon the black code of Virginia as it was in all its atrocious vigor in full force in 1860?

It required a hundred years for the long descent from that first step of barbarism, embodied in the above early statutes, respecting the relation of slaves to Christian profession and baptism, down to that immeasurable infamy which shut with iron bars the gates of knowledge from the whole race, both bond and free, reducing them to the condition of the brute.

And here again the "Dissertation," to which allusion has here been made, is so forcibly suggested that another passage from it cannot be withheld. After depicting "the rigors of the police in regard to this unhappy race," and affirming that it ought to be softened, this great and far-sighted Virginia jurist goes on to inquire if with but 300,000 slaves such things were deemed necessary, what must be the situation of the State when instead of that number there should be more than 2,000,000 in Virginia, concluding with this lofty and prophetic language: "This must happen," he says, in allusion to the increase of the slave population, "within a century, if we do not set about the abolition of slavery. Will not our posterity curse the days of their nativity with all the anguish of Job ? Will they not execrate the memory of those ancestors, who, having it in their power to avert the evil, have, like their first parents, entailed a curse upon all future generations? *We know that the rigor of the laws respecting slaves unavoidably must increase with their number:. What a blood-stained code must that be which is calculated for the restraint of millions held in bondage. Such must our unhappy country exhibit within a century unless we are both wise and just enough to avert f om posterity the calamity and reproach which are otherwise unavoidable.*"

VIRGINIA.

When the act of Congress approved February 27, 1801, organizing the District of Columbia, and providing that the laws of Virginia and Maryland, as those laws at *that date existed*, should continue in force in the portions ceded by those States respectively, became a law, there was no *express* restriction of the education of the colored race upon the statute-books of either State. The earliest legislation aiming at such restrictions are all embraced in the enactments pertaining to gatherings of "slaves, negroes, and mulattoes," denominated in the Maryland statutes "*tumultuous meetings*," and in the Virginia statutes "*unlawful assemblies*," the definition, in common law, of such an assembly being "the meeting of three or more persons to do an unlawful act."

In Virginia, as early as 1680, an act was passed for preventing negro insurrections, declaring that "the frequent meeting of considerable numbers of negroes, under pretence of feasts and burials, is judged of dangerous consequence," and such meetings were forbidden under penalty of *thirty lashes.*

In January, 1804, an act was passed declaring "all assemblages of slaves, under whatever pretext, at any meeting-house, or any other place in the night-time," to be an "unlawful assembly," the offenders to be punished with lashes not exceeding *twenty*. An act explaining and amending the act of January was passed in June, 1805, in which it is provided that nothing in such act shall "prevent masters taking their slaves to places of religious worship conducted by a regularly ordained or licensed white minister."

This act also forbid the overseers of the poor "to require black orphans, bound out, to be taught reading, writing, and arithmetic," showing that hitherto they had required this instruction to be given.

Up to that time *slaves* only were restricted, but in the Revised Code of 1819 all meetings of *free negroes or mulattoes*, associating with slaves in such places, including assemblages at "any school-house or schools for teaching reading or writing, either in the day or night," are embraced in the same interdiction and penalty. The same code also provides that "any *white person*, free negro, mulatto, or Indian, found in such unlawful assembly," is punishable by fine of three dollars and costs, and on failure of present payment, "is to receive *twenty lashes* on his or her bare back, well laid on."

There was no further legislation in the Virginia assembly bearing specially on this matter till the passage of the act of April 17, 1831. The Nat. Turner insurrection, in South Hampton county, occurred in the same year, but not until August, showing that the law was inspired by no special alarm arising from the massacre. The following are the sections relating to education of the colored people :

"SEC. 4. *Be it further enacted*, That all meetings of free negroes or mulattoes, at any school house, church, or meeting-house, or other place, for teaching them reading or writing, either in the day or night, under whatsoever pretext, shall be deemed and considered as an 'unlawful assembly;' and any justice of the county or corporation wherein such assemblage shall be, either from his own knowledge or on the information of others, of such unlawful assemblage or meeting, shall issue his warrant, directed to any sworn officer or officers, authorizing him or them to enter the house or houses where such unlawful assemblage or meeting may be, for the purpose of apprehending or dispersing such free negroes or mulattoes, and to inflict corporal punishment on the offender or offenders, at the discretion of any justice of the peace, not exceeding twenty lashes.

"Sec. 5. *Be it further enacted,* That if any white person or persons assemble with free negroes or mulattoes, at any school-house, church, meeting-house, or other place, for the purpose of instructing such free negroes or mulattoes to read or write, such person or persons shall, on conviction thereof, be fined in a sum not exceeding fifty dollars, and moreover may be imprisoned, at the discretion of a jury, not exceeding two months.

"Sec. 6. *Be it further enacted,* That if any white person, for pay or compensation, shall assemble with any slaves for the purpose of teaching, and shall teach any slave to read or write, such person, or any white person or persons contracting with such teacher so to act, who shall offend as aforesaid, shall for each offence be fined, at the discretion of a jury, in a sum not less than ten nor exceeding one hundred dollars, to be recovered on an information or indictment."

These were the exactions put upon the terrified colored people of Alexandria when the retrocession took effect. The only material change in the law of 1831 was made in 1848, when the act reducing to one the general acts concerning crimes and punishments was enacted, the maximum number of lashes being then increased to 39.

The constitutional convention of Virginia, which met at Alexandria, in 1864, passed a resolution, March 10, declaring slavery to be forever abolished.

MARYLAND.

In Maryland the assembly, in 1695, passed an act "restraining the frequent assembling of negroes within the province."

In 1723 an act was passed to prevent "tumultuous meetings of negroes and other slaves" on Sabbath and other holidays, requiring the appointment of constables to visit monthly all suspected places, and when "negroes or other slaves" are found upon premises to which they did not belong, to break up the "tumultuous assembly," and whip the offenders with lashes upon the bare back, not exceeding 39. A quarter of a century later, in 1748, the assembly of the same State enacted that all persons entertaining any servants or "slaves" upon their premises" during the space of one hour or longer should be fined 100 pounds of tobacco for each hand, and, in default of payment, to receive not exceeding 39 lashes on the bare back. Though this act specifies its purpose to be the prevention of embezzling provisions for such entertainments, and of "many grievous disorders," it is evident that the intelligence awakened by such gatherings was the result mainly deprecated. The provisions of the act are extended, in 1807, to embrace *free negroes* in the prohibition as well as slaves, the constable being required to repress "tumultuous meetings of mulattoes, negroes, and slaves," the penalty to the offending free negro being fine and imprisonment, and to the slave the usual "lashes." In 1831, when Virginia completed its climax of obloquy and turpitude, in shutting up all its colored classes to total ignorance, Maryland, to its honor, did not allow one syllable against the education of either its free or its slave population to find place in its statutes. The policy of her State was at this time to prepare the way for freedom, and a law was in this same year enacted forbidding the introduction of slaves into its territory, and a most liberal and enlightened enterprise organized to encourage the manumission of slaves and their emigration to Liberia. The act of 1831, upon "tumultuous assemblies," provided:

"That it shall not be lawful for any free negro or negroes, slave or slaves, to assemble or attend any meetings for religious purposes unless conducted by a white licensed or ordained preacher, or some respectable white person of the neighborhood, as may be duly authorized by such licensed or ordained preacher, during the continuance of such meeting," and unless conducted in accordance with these provisions all such assemblages were declared to be "tumultuous meetings." It was, however, provided that meetings of slaves or servants upon the premises where they belonged should not be embraced in the prohibitions of the act, and that within the limits of Baltimore city and Annapolis city religious meetings of slaves, free negroes, and mulattoes, held in accordance with the written permission of a white licensed (or) ordained preacher, and dismissed before 10 o'clock at night, should be lawful. It was also provided that the free negroes and mulattoes, for any offence for which slaves were then punishable, should "be subject to the same punishment, and be liable in every respect to the same treatment and penalty as slaves thus offending," the punishment for this offence being not exceeding 39 lashes upon the bare back.

The restrictive policy of 1831, which totally prohibited the introduction of slaves into the State, was modified in 1832, in special cases, and in 1833 every barrier to the introduction of slaves for residence was withdrawn. In 1835 was enacted the law against the publication and circulation of documents tending to inflame discontent and insurrection among the colored population—a law which, everywhere enacted in the slave States, was an instrument of terror and oppression, disheartening to the cause of education. The literature of the country was so largely pervaded with denunciations of slavery at that period, that it was dangerous for a colored man, or a friend of the colored race in a slave State, to have in his possession any of the publications of the day—an old newspaper, used for wrapping purposes in a trunk, often visiting upon its possessor the severest troubles.

THE CHARTER OF GEORGETOWN.

The original act incorporating Georgetown, passed by the general assembly of Maryland 25th December, 1789, contains nothing in the enumeration of the created powers restraining the colored in distinction from the white population, and in the amending act of the assembly, passed January 20, 1798, the only allusion to the colored people distinctively is in the preamble, in which is set forth the want of proper powers in the corporation to restrain by wholesome laws "vagrants, loose and disorderly persons, *free negroes*, and persons having no visible means of support." In the powers conferred by the act which follows the preamble, however, there is no allusion whatever to the colored race; nor is there any distinctive reference of the kind in the amendatory act of Congress of March 3, 1805, the only clause important to note being that which provided that "the said corporation shall have, possess, and enjoy all the rights, immunities, privileges, and powers heretofore enjoyed by them." In 1809 the charter received from Congress another amendment, in which it was declared "that all the rights, powers, and privileges heretofore granted by the general assembly of Maryland, and by the act to which this is a supplement, and which are at this time claimed and exercised by them, shall remain in full force and effect."

GEORGETOWN ORDINANCES.

The first ordinance in Georgetown restricting the assembling of colored people was passed by the councils August 4, 1795, in which were prohibited all "irregular and disorderly meetings of indented servants and slaves," and also "the meeting of servants or slaves exceeding six" on any occasion, with a penalty not exceeding thirty-nine lashes; and in case of interference to prevent the whipping on the part of "master or mistress," a fine for the interference not exceeding £5. October 10, 1796, another ordinance to repress "riotous and disorderly meetings of indented servants and slaves" was enacted, with a special injunction upon the constables to particularly examine all persons of color as to their title to freedom. In this act "the fighting of game-cocks and dunghill fowls" by colored people was specifically prohibited as among disorderly assemblages.

The punishment of whipping was so eagerly and promptly executed by the constable that the councils passed a special ordinance forbidding whipping during market hours.

On the 8th of October, 1831, that year of sorrows to the colored people throughout the slave States, and of shame and infamy to their oppressors, the councils enacted:

"That from this time forth all night assemblages of black or colored persons within the limits of this town, except for religious instruction, conducted by white men of good character, and terminated or dispersed at or before the hour of half past nine o'clock p. m., be and the same are hereby prohibited," the penalty for slaves not more than 39 stripes, and for free colored people not more than 30 days at hard labor in the workhouse.

The same ordinance also prohibits "any negro or mulatto person living in this town from receiving through the post office, or any other mode, or after lapse of ten days from the passage of this act to have in his possession, or to circulate, any newspaper or publication of a seditious and evil character, calculated to excite insurrection or insubordination among the slaves."

"Subscribers to or receivers of a newspaper called 'The Liberator,' published in Boston." are emphatically proscribed; and every free negro or mulatto in any way concerned in the infringement of the act was to be "deemed and adjudged a disorderly person, and a dangerous and unsafe citizen." White persons aiding in the infraction of this law were punished wi h a fine not exceeding $20, or imprisonment not more than 30 days; free negroes and mulattoes failing to pay fine and prison fees were liable to be sold to service not exceeding four months. This section against the free circulation of knowledge was the most oppressive restraint ever imposed upon the colored people. It almost absolutely shut them up from all reading, as they were afraid to have any book in their possession, scarcely even the Bible.

On the 25th of August, 1845, the councils passed an ordinance declaring that—

"From this time forth all assemblages, day or night, of black or colored persons within the limits of this town, except meetings for religious instruction, conducted by white men appointed by either or any of the established churches of the town, and terminated at or before the hour of nine and a half o'clock p. m., and except such other meetings as shall be especially allowed by the mayor, be and the same are hereby prohibited."

The penalty attached to the violation of this ordinance was, in case of a slave, stripes not exceeding 39, and in case of a free negro the punishment was confinement to hard labor at the workhouse not exceeding 30 days, or a fine not exceeding $30; Congress having by act of March 2, 1831, prohibited corporal punishment upon a free man in the District, imprisonment in the county jail for a period not exceeding six months being substituted therefor.

This ordinance of 1845 had no sanction either in the laws of Congress or in those of Maryland. If its provisions had been enforced, colored schools would have been placed at the mercy of the mayor, who, in the case of at least one mayor in the memory of the older residents of the District, would have had no mercy on them, though of this tyranical class Henry Addison, ever a friend of the oppressed. stands forth a very noble exception. These ordinances were never enforced against the schools, though they stood there as an oppressive intimidation, necessarily engendering a spirit of disdain and contempt for the humiliated classes on the part of those, both young and old, whom the enactments made their masters. This was manifested in the persecutions which continually fell upon the colored children on the way to school and returning, it being a common custom for crowds of white boys to congregate at the colored school-houses for the purpose of pelting with stones and maltreating the inoffensive and unresisting children as they would flee towards their humble homes. There were no ordinances in any city of the District to shield these children from such outrages, though the insolent and inhuman practices were always well known to the city authorities.

THE CHARTER OF ALEXANDRIA.

The original charter of Alexandria enacted by the general assembly of Virginia, like that of Georgetown, confers no power exclusively applied to the colored people. The corporate authorities were invested with power "to make by-laws and ordinances for the regulation and good government of said town: *Provided*, such by-laws or ordinances shall not be repugnant to or inconsistent with the laws and constitution of this commonwealth;" and in amending the charter in 1804 Congress conferred upon the city the power "to make all laws which they shall conceive requisite for the regulation of the morals and police of the said town, and to enforce the observance of said laws." In an act still further amending the charter, approved May 13, 1826, substantially the same power is conferred as was embraced in the act amendatory of the charter of Washington, approved May 4, 1812. It enacts that the common council of Alexandria "shall have power to restrain and prohibit the nightly and other disorderly meetings of slaves, free negroes, or mulattoes, and to punish such slaves by whipping, not exceeding 40 stripes, or, at the option of the owner of such slave, by fine or confinement to labor, not exceeding three months for every one offence; and to punish such free negroes or mulattoes for such offences by fixed penalties, not exceeding $20 for one offence; and in case of the failure of such free negro or mulatto to pay and satisfy such penalty and costs, to cause such free negro or mulatto to be confined to labor for any time not exceeding six months for any one offence."

ALEXANDRIA ORDINANCES.

It was under the sanction of the above amending clause that the common council, October 29, 1831, passed an ordinance providing "that all meetings or assemblages of free negroes and mulattoes, or of slaves, free negroes and mulattoes, at any meeting or other house, either in the day or night, under the pretence or pretext of attending a religious meeting, or for any amusement, shall be and the same are hereby prohibited, and any such meeting or assembly shall be considered an unlawful assembly; this act not to be construed to prohibit any slave, free negro, or mulatto from attending any class or other like meeting authorized and required by the present government and discipline of any religious society in the limits of this corporation, for religious services, or at any place of public worship, when and where a white member of the said society, duly authorized by the resident minister of the said religious society to officiate at such meeting; which said meeting is to close, and the persons present to depart to their homes, at or before 10 o'clock: *Provided*, That nothing herein contained shall prohibit any slave, free negro, or mulatto from attending, either day or night, any of the usual places of public worship, when and where a duly authorized white minister shall officiate; but no separate place of worship shall be permitted for slaves, free negroes, or mulattoes."

The ordinance further specifies that nothing in it "shall prohibit any slave, or free apprenticed negro or mulatto meeting on any other lawful occasion, by license in writing from the owner or employer of such slave, or master or mistress of such apprentice, providing such meeting be in the day-time, or if after sunset the same shall not be continued longer than 10 o'clock; nor shall any free negro or mulatto attend any meeting without the written permit of the mayor authorizing such meeting, which meeting is to be under the same limitation as relates to slaves and apprentices."

Section 11 provides "that if any free negro or mulatto person living in this town shall be a subscriber to or receive through the post office, or in any other mode shall, after the lapse of 10 days after the passage of this law, have in possession or circulate any newspaper or other publication, or any written or printed paper, or book, of a seditious and evil character, calculated to excite insurrection or insubordination among slaves or colored people, such free negro or mulatto shall be fined any sum not exceeding $20, or be committed to the workhouse for not less than 30 days, and pay the amount of work-house fees and costs, and give security for his or her good behavior for 12 months, in a sum not exceeding $100, before he or she shall be discharged." In case the fine was imposed, and the offender was unable to pay the amount, he was committed to the work-house, to remain until it was paid.

In February, 1864, Miss Mary Chase, of Alexandria, an excellent colored teacher already mentioned, struck a white boy with a broom-stick because he called her vulgar names as she was sweeping the snow from her door-steps. She was arrested and taken to the mayor's office, and was about to receive sentence without a hearing. She resolutely insisted upon the right to state her case, and was allowed to speak. Her speech closed with these words: "If the boy calls me such names again, I will strike him again; and I will strike anybody else who calls me such names." The mayor replied: "Mary, you had better not talk so;" to which she reiterated her determination; whereupon she was fined "one dollar for costs and fifty cents for the lick."

In the summer of the same year a young woman, for some offence against a white man, was sentenced in Alexandria to receive 39 lashes and be imprisoned 30 days in the county jail. The sentence was rigidly executed; and Miss Julia A. Wilbur often visited her and supplied her with useful employment, and when released furnished her a good home.

THE CHARTER OF WASHINGTON.

In the original charter of Washington, approved May 3, 1802, the enumeration of powers conferred upon the corporation embraces nothing, either expressly or by implication, specifically directed towards the colored people, nor is there any such power given in the supplementary act of 1806. In the act further to amend the charter, approved May 4, 1812, there is, however, a clause to the point, giving the authority " to restrain and prohibit the nightly and other disorderly meetings of slaves, free negroes, and mulattoes, and to punish such slaves by whipping, not exceeding 40 stripes, or by imprisonment not exceeding six calendar months, for any one offence; and to punish such free negroes and mulattoes for such offences by fixed penalties, not exceeding $20 for any one offence;" and in default of paying fine and costs, imprisonment not exceeding six calendar months. In 1820 the original charter, expiring by limitation, was renewed, and the above clause was inserted without alteration.

WASHINGTON ORDINANCES.

The same remarks are applicable to the corporation laws of Washington which have elsewhere been made in regard to those of Georgetown and Alexandria. Every imaginable form of humiliating restriction upon the personal freedom of the colored people, both bond and free, pervades these laws, almost from the first year of its corporate existence. It seems to have been assumed that these humble and patient beings were ready for riot, insurrection, and every species of insubordination and wickedness. They were subjected to the severest penal enactments; and without the slightest legal protection from the abuse of the white race, were at the mercy of inhuman and villainous white people, in their little brief authority, both in and out of corporation office. *No white man can do a wrong to a colored man, and no colored man willingly does right to anybody*, is the ruling temper of all the laws in regard to "slaves, free colored, and mulatto persons," as long as slavery existed in the District.

The first ordinance of the corporation of Washington pertaining to the colored people bears date December 6, 1808, and declares "that no black person, or person of color, or loose, idle, disorderly person shall be allowed to walk about or assemble at any tippling or other house after 10 o'clock at night;" thus classing the whole body of the colored people with the dregs of society; "and any such person being found offending against this law, or *at any time* engaged in dancing, tippling, quarrelling, or in playing at any game of hazard or ball, or making a noise or disturbance, or in assembling in a disorderly or tumultuous manner, shall pay the sum of five dollars for each offence."

Section 9 of this act declares "that it shall not be lawful for any person to entertain a slave or slaves after 10 o'clock p. m.; and for every slave found in the house or dwelling of another after 10 o'clock p. m., the person so entertaining shall forfeit and pay five dollars," unless the slave is found to have been sent on a message by the master or mistress. The fine in every case in this ordinance is to go one-half to the complainant or apprehender, and the other half to the city; one of the most unmerciful features of this law. A striking provision in this ordinance was that in which was legally fixed the value of a constable's services for whipping a negro. The fee, like the duty, was contemptible; yet there is no case on record in which the officer failed, under any ordinance, promptly to administer the "stripes on the bare back, well laid on," and were as impatient to do their brutal business as they were in Georgetown, where the councils were compelled to pass a special ordinance forbidding whipping during market hours. The section fixing the value of the service at half a dollar for each whipping was as follows :

" SEC. 6. *Be it further enacted*, That if any slave shall be convicted under this law the owner of such slave shall be liable for the same, and judgment may be rendered against such owner by any justice of the peace upon the conviction of the slave, but it shall be optional with the owner of such slave to have the whole remitted *except fifty cents*, on condition he or she give directions to have the offending slave whipt according to the judgment of the magistrate, who is hereby directed to remit so much thereof, the residue to go to the person who inflicts the punishment."

The enumerated powers of the original charter of the city, under which this ordinance was enacted, furnishes no authority for the above provisions of the law of 1808, and it was only by the most unjust wrenchings of that instrument that any shadow of authority could have been extorted; yet these provisions were under the same charter of 1802 re-enacted December 16, 1812, with aggravated malignancy, in the following barbarous terms:

" SEC. 4. *And be it further enacted*, That it shall not be lawful for any slave, free black, or mulatto person or persons to assemble in any house, street, or other place, by day or by night, in a disorderly or tumultuous manner, so as to disturb the peace or repose of the citizens.' Penalty: A slave to "receive any number of stripes on his or her bare back not exceeding twenty, and a free black or mulatto to be fined not exceeding $20 and costs, and failing to pay which to go to the work-house not exceeding 90 days." ·

"Sec. 8. If any free black or mulatto person or slave shall have a dance, ball, or assembly at his, her, or their house without first obtaining a permit from the mayor, or other justice of the peace, he, she, or they shall each pay a fine of $20, or be sentenced to confinement and labor for a time not exceeding 30 days; in case of inability or refusal to pay such fine a slave shall receive any number of lashes on the bare back not exceeding ten."

Section 9 provided "that no slave or free black or mulatto person should be allowed to go at large through the streets, or other parts of the said city, at a later hour than 10 o'clock at night from April 1 to October 1, or than 9 o'clock at night from October 1 to April 1, except a slave who had a written permission from his or her master, mistress, or employer." Penalty: slave, not exceeding 39 stripes on his or her bare back; free black or mulatto, fine not exceeding $20 and costs, and failing to pay, not exceeding 90 days at hard labor. The fines in this, as in the law of 1808, went half to the informer or apprehender.

The question is perpetually recurring, while running through these restraining enactments, why the colored people are made the constant and exclusive victims. Why were not white persons prohibited from disturbing the peace and repose of colored persons?

The first sanction given by Congress to this barbarism was when in amending the charter, May 15, 1820, it gave the corporation power "to restrain and prohibit the nightly and other disorderly meetings of slaves, free negroes, and mulattoes, and to punish such slaves by whipping, not exceeding forty stripes, or by imprisonment, not exceeding six calendar months for any one offence." Why the maximum stripes were increased from 39 to 40 it is difficult to conjecture, unless it was to show that barbarism was magnifying itself. The fact that this power was introduced into this amendment of the charter is significant of the fact that the city had been hitherto transcending its authority in the inhuman restraints which had in this regard been enforced by their ordinances

Emboldened by the firmer grasp upon the victims which the enlarged powers of the charter under the amendment of 1820 gave them, the city authorities, April 14, 1821, took a double turn of the screw. In the ordinance of 1812 the free colored people were required simply to exhibit satisfactory evidence of their freedom to the register, who was thereupon to give them license to reside within the limits of the city, the penalty being a fine of $6 or 10 days in the work-house; but the special intent of the ordinance of 1821 was to amplify and make more stringent the whole registry or license system. A thorough examination of the city was ordered, "the city commissioners to make, each in his own ward, diligent inquiry and search for all free persons of color who may then reside or be found in the city," every one to be notified to appear within thirty days at the council chamber "to present for inspection their papers or other evidence of freedom, and shall then subscribe a statement of his or her trade or occupation and means of subsistence." But, in addition to satisfactory proofs of their right to *freedom*, they were obliged to bring "a certificate *satisfactory to the mayor* from at least three respectable white inhabitants, householders, setting forth that they are personally acquainted with such negro, and that he or she live peaceable and quiet lives;" specifying also "their trade or occupation, whether she or he keep an orderly and decent house, and whether they are industrious and honest, and not likely to become chargeable to the corporation."

The ordinance went still further. Every free male person of color residing in the city was required to satisfy the mayor of his title to freedom, and to "*enter into bond with one good and responsible free white citizen*"—a phraseology suggesting that there were *white* citizens *not free*—"as surety, in the penalty of $20, conditioned for the good, sober, and orderly conduct of such person or persons of color and his or her family, for the term of one year following the date of such bond; and that such person or persons, his or her family, nor any part thereof, shall not during the said term of one year become chargeable to the corporation in any manner whatsoever, and that they will not become beggars about the streets."

Parents were also required to give a statement, in writing, showing the name, age, residence, and occupation of each child, and how said child became free ; and the mayor could require, "*in his discretion*," of such parents to give *additional security* for the quiet, peaceable, and orderly behavior of such child, in a sum not exceeding *fifty dollars*, and when any security may, in the *opinion of the mayor*, become insufficient, he may require additional security."

After all these conditions were complied with, and "the license to reside within the city" granted and duly signed by the mayor, countersigned by the register, recorded, and sealed with the seal of the corporation, the ordinance required that it should be renewed, together with the bonds, every year. In case of failure to produce evidence of freedom *satisfactory to the mayor*, the negro was committed to the county jail and dealt with as "an absconding slave." In case of failure to furnish the required sureties and bonds within the 30 days, the penalty was a fine of $5 for the first week, and if still found residing in the city, the man, *together with his wife*, was committed to the work-house for three months, from which they could be discharged, on *satisfying* the mayor that they would "forthwith depart the city." An additional provision was one of greatest cruelty, viz : that "the *children* of such persons committed to the work-house *shall be* bound out to service for such term as the guardians of the poor may think *reasonable*, not exceeding a period at which the males will arrive at the age of 21, the females at the age of 16."

"SEC. 8. It shall be unlawful for any free person of color to receive, entertain, harbor, or conceal any slave, or hire, buy from, sell to, bargain, or in any way trade or barter with any slave, unless by written consent of the owner. Penalty for first offence, fine of $10 ; for second offence. two months in the work-house."

"SEC. 11. When any free negro shall desire to change his residence from one part of the city to another, he shall make known such intention to the register, and produce his license, on which the register shall endorse such intended residence and record the same."

"SEC. 13. It shall be lawful for *any person*, at *any time*, to demand to see the license of any free negro or mulatto, and if within 24 hours he shall not produce such licence, or an official copy thereof, such negro may, in the *discretion* of any justice of the peace, be fined in any sum not exceeding $5."

The determination to prevent, if possible, the increase of the free colored population from without is shown in section 7, which enacted that "all free negroes coming to Washington to reside should not only be subject to all the provisions, terms, and conditions applicable to such persons already residents, but the bond to be given by them shall be in the penalty of *five hundred dollars*, with *two good and responsible free white citizens as sureties*."

Under this ordinance of 1821 the provisions relating to "holding dances, balls, or assemblies," and "all nightly and disorderly meetings of free negroes," were made more stringent, the penalty being extended to every one present at such gatherings, and for the second offence the "license to reside in the city" was forfeited.

The colored people humbly and dutifully rendered obedience to these oppressive enactments, which stood unchanged for the ensuing half a dozen years. On the 31st of May, 1827, an ordinance was enacted which contained all the cruelties embraced in the legislation of the previous quarter of a century, but devised and established additional ones.

The penalty affixed to "idle, disorderly, or tumultuous assemblages," was, in the case of free negroes and mulattoes, the same as in the law of 1812, viz., fine of $20 ; but failure to pay the fine was punished with six months in the work-house, in the place of 90 days, and sureties required to be given for good behavior. For a slave the penalty was increased from 20 to "39 stripes on the bare back ;' the option, however, being given him "to have the whipping *commuted* for the payment of the fine which would be imposed in such cases on free persons of color." This last provision is a notable one, and reveals a dawning conviction, on the part of the law-makers, of the barbarism of the slave code.

The fine of $20 affixed, in 1812, as the penalty for free negroes and mulattoes for "having a dance, ball, or assembly," was reduced to $10; but the penalty for non-payment was extended from 90 days in the work-house to six months ; for a slave the number of stripes was increased from 10 to 39, and commutation of punishment as above was allowed.

A similar change was made in the ordinance prohibiting the "going at large after 10 o'clock at night without a permit," viz : the fine reduced from $20 to $10, and work-house time doubled; but the penalty in case of a slave remained unchanged, it being 39 stripes in 1812 as well as 1827.

The ordinance relating to "having a dance, ball, or assembly," required a permit from the mayor, in which must be mentiond the place, time of meeting, number of guests, and hour of breaking up; and a violation of any one of the conditions embodied in the permit exposed the offending party to the full penalty.

In the ordinance of 1827 the provisions touching the registry and "residence license" were not essentially different from those of 1821, except in the penalty. Failure to pay the fine imposed for not complying with the provisions necessary to a license was made punishable with *six months* in the work-house, instead of three; and in the case of new comers who failed to present the required two *"freehold sureties* in the penalty of *five hundred* dollars for his good and orderly conduct," no fine was imposed, but they were "to depart the city forthwith," or be sent to the work-house for *twelve* months instead of three.

In 1829 an ordinance was passed containing the provision that colored persons should not frequent the Capitol square, the penalty being a fine not exceeding $20, or 30 days in the work-house. This enactment was peculiarly oppressive, because it was so totally destitute of decent pretext. Its operation is illustrated in the case of Alexander Hays, the colored schoolmaster and teacher of music. He had a great anxiety to hear the music of the marine band in the Capitol grounds, and venturing, with a colored friend, to step a few yards inside the gate, was seized violently by a brutal officer upon the grounds, led at arm's length to the gate, and, with a thrust, directed to "be off." In the same year, 1849, the same man attempted to get near enough on the occasion to hear General Taylor, at the inauguration services. He crept up under the steps in a concealed place, and when General Taylor was about taking the oath was again grasped by the rough hand of a policeman, and dragged like a dog through the crowd and bid "begone." These incidents are given on the authority of Mr. Hays, who is known in this city as an upright and useful man.

These enactments, however, did not grind these poor people to the entire satisfaction of their torturers, for nine years later some of the exactions were greatly increased, and even doubled. In an ordinance supplementary to that of 1827, dated October 29, 1836, the climax of infamous legislation was reached. The following selections from the act contain the leading features:

"SECTION 1. Every free negro or mulatto, whether male or female, and every colored person who may be manumitted or made free in any manner, shall forthwith exhibit to the mayor satisfactory evidence of his or her title to freedom, and shall enter into bond, with *five* good and sufficient freehold sureties, in the penalty of *one thousand dollars*, conditioned for his or her good and orderly conduct, and that of every member of his or her family, and that they, or either of them, do not become chargeable to this corporation, which bond shall be renewed every year; and on failure to comply with the provisions of this section, shall pay a sum not exceeding *twenty dollars*, and shall be ordered by the mayor to depart *forthwith* from the city, and on failure to do so shall be committed to the work-house until such conditions shall be complied with, not exceeding six months."

"SEC. 3. It shall not be lawful for the mayor to grant a license for any purpose whatsoever to any free negro or mulatto, or to any person acting as agent or in behalf of any free negro or mulatto, except licenses to drive carts, drays, hackney carriages, or wagons; nor shall it be lawful to grant a license *for any purpose whatsoever* to any free negro or mulatto who shall not, *before the passage of this act,* be a resident of this city, and be registered as such.

"SEC. 4. Nor shall any free negro or mulatto, nor any person acting for any free negro or mulatto, keep any tavern, ordinary, shop, porter-cellar, refectory, or eating-house of any kind, for profit or gain," &c., the penalty affixed being a fine of *twenty dollars.*

"SEC. 5. All secret or private meetings or assemblies whatsoever, and all meetings for religious worship beyond the hour of 10 o'clock at night, of free negroes, mulattoes, or slaves, shall be unlawful; and any colored person found at such unlawful assemblages or meetings, or who may continue at any religious meeting after 10 o'clock at night, shall pay the sum of *five dollars;* and, in the event of any such meeting or assemblage, it shall be the duty of any police constable to use and employ all lawful and necessary means immediately to disperse the same, and in case any police constable, after full notice and knowledge of such meetings, shall neglect or refuse to execute the duty hereby enjoined, he shall pay the sum of *fifty dollars.*"

But in spite of this latter provision the policemen were not unfrequently bought off, and many a colored resident can witness to having paid and seen paid sundry dollars and larger sums to sundry policemen, when returning home, a few minutes after 10 o'clock, from an evening meeting or party—an hour when those officials were sure to be awake and on time. These perquisites were, quite probably, of more value than the fees for whipping.

There is also a most interesting petition in the files of the city councils illustrating the bearing of this particular feature of this inhuman legislation in Washington.

In 1833 Joseph Jefferson, the illustrious comedian and the father of the eminent living comedian of that name, was, in connection with another gentleman, the lessee of the Washington Theatre, and all the citizens of Washington, who remember that day and appreciate what is greatest in the dramatic art, have vivid and delightful recollections of that theatre. On the 15th day of July, 1833, Jefferson and Mackenzie, as the lessees, addressed the following appeal to the city councils :

"DEAR SIR : Permit us to take the liberty of representing to you a burden that oppresses us most heavily, and of requesting your kind endeavors so to represent the case before the mayor and council that we may obtain all the relief that it is in their power to grant.

"You must be aware that we pay nightly to the city a tax of $6 for permission to perform in the theatre; in the year 1832 this amounted to nearly $1,400 in the aggregate; we pay this tax cheerfully, and all we ask in return is a liberal protection and support from the city authorities.

"There is at present a law in force which authorizes the constables of the city to arrest the colored people if on the street after 9 o'clock without a pass. A great proportion of our audience consists of persons of *this caste*, and they are consequently deterred from giving us that support that they would otherwise do.

"Can there be any modification of that law suggested, or will the mayor and council authorize us to give passes to those colored persons who leave the theatre for the purpose of proceeding directly to their homes?

"In the city of Baltimore, where we have a theatre, and pay a smaller license than we do here, the law, as regards the colored people, is not acted upon when they are coming or going to the theatre.

"In a pecuniary point of view, we look upon this law as a detriment to us of $10 nightly, and we have great reason to hope that a law that rests so heavily upon us alone may meet with the kind consideration of the mayor and council, and be so modified as to relieve us from the heavy loss that it causes us at present to incur.

"We have the honor to be, dear sir, your obedient servants,
"JEFFERSON & MACKENZIE,
"*Managers of the Washington Theatre.*"

From 1836 there was no further legislation of consequence upon this subject for 14 years. On the 13th of December, 1850, the infamous requirement of the bond demanding "*five good and sufficient freehold sureties in the penalty of* $1,000," in the ordinance of 1836, had been so thoroughly exposed in its odiousness that a relaxation of its unexampled rigor was enacted, by which "one good and sufficient freehold surety" in the penalty of $50 only was demanded. It was, however, demanded that every head of a family should give "a like bond and surety for each and every member of his or her family between the ages of 12 and 21 years." This tenderness, however, was more than neutralized in section third of the same act, which required, after its passage, that every free negro or mulatto, whether male or female, within five days after arriving in the city, and on the tenth day of December thereafter annually, to "record his or her name and the names of every member of his or her family on the books of this corporation, and at the same time pay for himself, herself, and every member of his or her family the sum of fifty dollars, upon which registration and payment the mayor is authorized to grant a permit of residence; and on failure to comply with the provisions of this section shall pay a sum not less than ten dollars nor exceeding twenty dollars, and shall be ordered to depart forthwith from this city."

These enactments as a general rule were inexorably enforced. Especially was this the case while the ordinances gave to the police officers—"the hounds," as they were called by the poor victims whom they hunted down—one-half the fine for their detestable work. The councils seem also to have been perpetually vigilant, re-enacting almost every year some resolution looking to the enforcement of the requirements pertaining to the bond. As an illustration of this official fidelity the case of Mr. William Syphax, now chairman of the board of trustees of colored schools, is in point. After a residence in the city for 12 years, with a character as unblemished as that of any man in the District, he was summoned in 1847 before a magistrate by one of these vigilant "hounds," and, as a non-resident, fined

$10 and compelled to enter into the bond under the law of 1836, "with five good and suffi-cient freehold sureties in the penalty of $1,000." Mr. Seaton, editor of the National Intelligencer, was one of his bondsmen.

There is a curious and significant commentary on this legislation to be found in the files of the corporation of Washington. In 1839 this restriction began to make labor scarce in the city—returning with its atrocities to plague the inventors. A petition was therefore sent to the city councils, signed by some hundred of the prominent business men of the city, who were wont to employ colored labor, setting forth that the colored people of the city who had given their *thousand-dollar bond* had apparently combined to control the price of labor by informing on all colored laborers who came into the city without giving bonds, thus preventing competition. The petition prays, therefore, that the law may be modified; not that the grasp of the brutal policemen may be removed from their humble, inoffensive victims, but that the white capitalists of the city may have power to grind them the more effectually in their wages, which at best was but a pittance. The names upon this petition, if inserted in this connection, would make many living men ashamed.

One of the most oppressive of the restraints introduced into the ordinance of 1836 was that which prohibited the mayor from issuing a license to a free negro or mulatto to do any business except "to drive carts, drays, hackney carriages, or wagons," and expressly forbidding any license to an agent of any colored person.

The prohibition of "all secret or private meetings or assemblages whatsoever" beyond the hour of 10 o'clock p. m. was peculiarly oppressive and also inhuman, because directed against the various charitable and self-improving associations, including the Masonic, Odd-Fellow, and Sons of Temperance brotherhoods which the colored people had organized, and the meetings of which, to be dispersed before 10 o'clock, could be of but comparatively little benefit to the members. These societies in those years were more or less educational in character, and an important means of self-improvement to these inoffensive people, and those who made enactments were fully sensible of that fact. These restrictions were, moreover, rigorously enforced. and it was but a few years before the war that a company of the most respectable colored men of the District, on their return from the Masonic lodge a few minutes of 10 o'clock, were seized by the scrupulous police, retained at the watch-house till morning, and fined.

The prohibition forbidding a colored person to be abroad after 10 o'clock at night without a pass, under a penalty of " a fine, "confinement to hard labor," or "stripes upon the bare back," well laid on," must at a glance impress every candid mind with surprise, and yet it is only upon considerate reflection that its atrociousness is revealed. A poor colored man finds a member of his family in a dying condition at midnight, and on his way for a doctor is seized by a wretch in the garb of a policeman, carried to a watch-house, and, without friends or money, is sent next day to the work-house. A colored man has a store containing a heavy stock of goods; it takes fire in the night, and his sons start for the rescue of their property, are seized by a relentless officer, and held, as in the other case, till morning at police head-quarters. These are not imaginary cases, and yet this was a mild restraint compared with many others found in the corporation ordinances of all three cities.

It will, however, be seen that the ordinances of Washington were less stringent in their restraints upon the assembling of colored people than those of Alexandria and Georgetown, and that they were less severe in Alexandria while that city was in the District than in Georgetown. This is peculiarly surprising from the fact that while the laws of Virginia were absolutely prohibitory of education to every class of its colored population, the statutes cf Maryland contain not a word of positive prohibition even against *teaching slaves.*

THE DISENTHRALMENT.

Thus stood this barbarous, execrable system of tyrannical legislation in the District when the Moloch of slavery marshalled its forces to overthrow the best government that human wisdom had ever devised. Under the operation of these hateful and inhuman enactments the liberty of a free colored person was but a delusion. "A free colored or mulatto person" was not a free individual, neither in the spirit nor in the phraseology of this legislation, and the change which the mere abolition of slavery in the District wrought in the condition of the bondmen was scarcely less than an aggravation of their miseries, while to those who were not slaves it brought no relief at all.   General Henry Wilson, of Massachusetts, who had carefully studied the history of this vile legislation, and with pain and indignant emotions witnessed the deplorable condition of its victims, was the foremost to engage in the work of emancipation.   The earliest movement looking to the repealing and annulling of the black codes of the District after the rebellion opened was the introduction into the Senate, by Mr. Wilson, of a resolution "that all laws in force relating to the arrest of fugitives from service, and *all laws concerning persons of color within the District*, be referred to the Committee on the District of Columbia, and that the committee be instructed to consider the expediency of abolishing slavery in the District."   The chairman of the committee was Mr. Grimes.   On the 16th of December, 1861, twelve days after this resolution was offered, Mr. Wilson, apparently impatient with the delay of the committee, introduced a bill to abolish slavery in the District, and on the 24th of February, 1862, brought in a bill to abrogate and annul the black codes, which he very appropriately affirmed to be only a measure following up the bill abolishing slavery in the District.

When these two measures were under discussion in the Senate, in March, 1862, General Wilson, on the 25th of that month, addressed that body in an elaborate and powerful speech in their favor, reviewing the black codes with indignant and impressive eloquence.   After declaring that these infamous codes had outraged the moral sense of the American people; that the fame of the nation had been soiled and dimmed by the deeds of cruelty perpetrated in the interests of slavery in its capital, he breaks forth in language forcible, feeling, and just, as follows:

"In what age of the world, in what land under the whole heavens, can you find any enactment of equal atrocity to this iniquitous and profligate statute; this legal presumption that color is evidence that a man made in the image of God is an absconding slave?   This monstrous doctrine, abhorrent to every manly impulse of the heart, to every Christian sentiment of the soul, to every deduction of human reason, which the refined and Christian people of America have upheld for two generations, which the corporation of Washington enacted into an imperative ordinance, has borne its legitimate fruits of injustice and inhumanity, of dishonor and shame."   In relation to the fact that "the oath of the black man afforded no protection whatever to his property, to the fruits of his toil, to the personal rights of himself, his wife, his children, or his race," he said: "Although the black man is thus mute and dumb before the judicial tribunals of the capital of Christian America, his wrongs we have not righted here will go up to a higher tribunal, where the oath of the proscribed negro is heard, and his story registered by the pen of the recording angel.   *   *   *   These colonial statutes of Maryland, reaffirmed by Congress in 1801; these ordinances of Washington and Georgetown, sanctioned in advance by the authority of the federal government, stand this day unrepealed.   Such laws and ordinances should not be permitted longer to insult the reason. pervert the moral sense, or offend the taste of the people of America.   Any people mindful of the decencies of life would not longer permit such enactments to linger before the eye of civilized man."

The denunciation of these measures by members who had been familiar with slavery all their lives was exceedingly violent, and to the coarse exclamation of one of these senators, "Why do you not go out into this city and hunt up the blackest, greasiest, fattest old negro wench you can find, and lead her to the altar of Hymen?" Senator Harlan was provoked to reply in these words:

"I regret very much that senators depart so far from the proprieties, as I consider it, of this chamber, as to make the allusions they do. It is done merely to stimulate a prejudice which exists against a race already trampled under foot.   I refer to the allusions to white people embracing colored people as their brethren, and the invitations by senators to white men and white women to marry colored people.   Now, sir, if we were to descend into an investigation of the facts on that subject, it would bring the blush to the cheeks of some of these gentlemen.   I once had occasion to direct the attention of the Senate to an illustrious example from the State of the senator who inquired if 'any of us would marry a greasy old wench.' It is history that an illustrious citizen of his State, who once occupied officially the chair that you, sir, now sit in, lived notoriously and publicly with a negro wench, and raised children by her. * * * I refer to a gentleman who held the second office in the gift of the American people; and I never yet have heard a senator on this floor denounce the conduct and the association of that illustrious citizen of our country. I know of a family of colored or mulatto children—the children, too, of a gentleman who very recently occupied a seat on the other side of the chamber—who are now at school in Ohio; yes, sir, the children of a senator who very recently (not to exceed a year) occupied a seat on this floor, a senator from a slave State."

The allusion in the first of these cases was to Richard M. Johnson, who, it is well known, brought a colored woman with him when he came here as senator from Kentucky. It is due Mr. Johnson to say that he acknowledged his children, educated them, and left them free. The senator from Delaware might also have been reminded of a decision made in 1838 by the highest legal tribunal of his State, declaring that a *father cannot hold his child as a slave.* "We ought not," says the court in Tindal *vs.* Hudson, (1838, 2d Harrington, 441,) "to recognize the right of a father to hold his own children in slavery. Humanity forbids it. The natural rights and obligations of a father are paramount to the acquired rights of the master." The second allusion made by Mr. Harlan was to Senator Hemphill, of Texas, and the school referred to was the Wilberforce University, at Xenia, Ohio, founded by the Cincinnati conference of the Methodist Episcopal church "for the special benefit of colored youth;" but in 1863 transferred to the African Methodist Episcopal church, and Bishop D. A. Payne made president. "While under the care of the Cincinnati conference it was supported," the annual report says, "mainly by southern slaveholders, who *sent their children* there to be educated." The following brief statement was recently made by an officer of that institution:

"Senator Hemphill came to Wilberforce University late in the autumn of 1859, having with him three children, a lad of about 18, and two girls, of about 12 and 10 years of age. The lad, who was evidently his son, he took to Washington. His two daughters, Theodora and Henrietta, remained with us until 1862, when the pressure of the civil war constrained the trustees (the younger) to suspend the operations of the institution, and they went to Cincinnati, where Henrietta (the younger) died of consumption. Theodora was, at the last time we heard of her, living in Cincinnati. The young ladies were both beautiful. Their complexion proclaimed their mother to have been a black woman. She died before they were brought to Wilberforce. They were well supported by Senator Hemphill, who kept up his correspondence with them, both by letters and presents, till he left Washington to perform his part in the drama of the rebellion. The last time we heard from their brother he wrote to me from California touching the condition and wants of his sisters."

The recital of the black laws of this District which has been made in these pages furnishes ample reason for the solicitude which was manifested by "the slaves, free negroes, and mulatto persons," when the above bills were under discussion, and when the bill abolishing slavery in the District became a law, April 16, 1862, all classes of the colored people, bond and free, gave expression to their sense of gratitude by assembling in their churches and offering up homage to God for the great deliverance; and when the black codes were, thirty-five days subsequently, swept into the receptacle of the wretched things that were, the feeling of relief and thankfulness was hardly less deep and universal. The mode in which this measure was accomplished was interesting.

On the 29th of April, 1862, Mr. Grimes introduced into the Senate a bill providing for the education of colored children in the city of Washington; and on the 30th of the same month, when the subject was under discussion in the Senate, General Wilson moved to amend the bill by adding the following section:

"Sec. 4. *And be it further enacted,* That all persons of color in the District of Columbia, or in the corporate limits of the cities of Washington and Georgetown, shall be subject and amenable to the same laws and ordinances to which free white persons are or may be subject or amenable; that they shall be tried for any offences against the laws in the same manner as free whites are, or may be tried for the same offences; and that upon being legally convicted of any crime or offence against any law or ordinance, such persons of color shall be liable to the same penalty or punishment, and no other, as would be imposed or inflicted upon free white persons for the same crime or offence; and all acts or parts of acts inconsistent with the provisions of this act are hereby repealed."

The object of the bill, which was simply to secure to the colored people of the District the exclusive use of the tax levied upon their property, for the education of their children, failed, as has been seen in a previous part of this history, by reason of the fact that the municipal authorities, in whose hands the execution of the law was reposed, were hostile to its humane and just designs. This amendment, however, did its work promptly and effectually in all particulars. In support of his amendment, after alluding to the odious old laws of Maryland and of Washington and Georgetown, which were admitted by everybody to be very oppressive to the colored people, he said: "As we are now dealing with their educational interests, I think we may as well at the same time relieve them of these oppressive laws, and put them, so far as crime is concerned, and so far as offences against the laws are concerned, upon the same footing, and have them tried in the same manner and subject them to the same punishment as the rest of our people." The bill, as amended, passed the Senate May 9, and, reported by E. H. Rollins, of New Hampshire, from the House District Committee, passed that body and received the approval of the President May 21, 1862, as already stated. The colored people of this District, who are sensible of the great practical service which Mr. Wilson has in many ways done them here and in the country at large, have repeatedly, on public occasions, since this bill became a law, signified their profound gratitude for this release, by specially designating this measure in connection with the author's name.

There was a singular fitness, as has been intimated, in the mode by which this great deliverance was consummated. It had been the chief and essential idea of all this odious and barbarous legislation to shut its unhappy victims out from every highway and by-way of learning, to put out the eye of the understanding, and to doom a whole race, made in the image of God and endowed with immortal longings for knowledge, to brutal and besotted ignorance. It was, therefore, a just and signal providence which made the very cause of education, against which these infamous enactments had been formed, the avenging instrument in the destruction of the accursed system. The circumstance that this was the first measure for the education of the colored race ever enacted by Congress renders this providential coincidence still more striking.

Negro testimony.—The original bill for the abolition of slavery, which, introduced into the Senate December 16, 1861, became a law May 16, 1862, contained a provision securing to the person claimed to owe service or labor the right to testify before the commissioners who were to be appointed under the law. This provision was expanded by an amendment incorporated into the bill on motion of Mr. Sumner, April 3, 1862, which empowered the commissioners to take testimony " without the exclusion of witnesses on account of color;" "to assess the sum to be paid for each slave claimed to owe service or labor: to examine and take the testimony, in the pending cases, *of colored witnesses, free or slave.*" These were the initial steps which resulted, in July following, in the full recognition of the rights of the colored people in the matter of their testimony before the legal tribunals of the District. On the 7th of July Senator Wilson's supplementary bill for the release of certain persons held to labor or service in the District of Columbia was passed, and approved on the 12th, having been amended, on motion of Mr. Sumner, by adding as a new section: " *That in all judicial proceedings in the District of Columbia there shall be no exclusion of any witness on account of color.*" This just measure was followed up by Mr. Sumner, who, on the 25th of June, 1864, moved an amendment to the civil appropriation bill, by adding "that in the *courts of the United States* there shall be no exclusion of any witness on account of color." On the 2d of July, 1864, this bill, thus amended, became a law, and since then no distinction on account of color has been recognized in the federal courts. It remains for the just people of the American nation, by constitutional amendment, to extend this principle to every State tribunal of the land.

Rights of colored people in the cars.—Mr. Sumner persistently followed up his efforts to secure to the colored people the privileges in the District which reason and humanity alike dictated as their due. In the Senate, February 27, 1863, on his motion, an amendment to the House bill to extend the charter of the Washington and Alexandria Railroad Company was added, providing "that no person shall be excluded from the cars on account of color," and this became a law March 3, 1863. On the 16th of March, 1864, Mr. Sumner moved an amendment to the bill, then before the Senate, incorporating the Metropolitan Railroad Company: "That there shall be no regulation excluding *any* persons from *any* car on account of color," and this bill, with the amendment, was passed and approved July 1, 1864.

But the Washington and Georgetown railroad was not yet reached. This road was chartered May 17, 1862, and not being able to exclude colored people from the cars, had set aside certain cars, so designated by a sign on the outside, for such persons. It was in one of these placarded cars that the writer had the pleasure, in the autumn of 1863, of seeing Charles Sumner and Henry W. Longfellow riding up the avenue. In June, 1864, a bill being before the Senate to amend the bill incorporating the above-named railroad, Mr. Sumner moved to add a provision corresponding to the one in the original charter of the Metropolitan railroad, viz: "That there shall be *no exclusion* of *any person* from *any* car on account of color." The amendment was carried in the Senate June 21 by the close vote of 17 to 16, but was lost in the controversy between the two branches of Congress; but February 4, 1865, a similar provision, though of still wider application, was moved by Mr. Sumner in committee of the whole as a separate section, to be added to a bill amendatory of the charter of the Metropolitan railroad. The motion was lost, 20 to 19. The bill, with certain other amendments, was then passed, and thus coming before the Senate, Mr. Sumner, with his wonted promptness and parliamentary skill, renewed his motion, and two days after the vote was reached and the amendment adopted—yeas 26, noes 10. The section reads as follows, and went into effect March 3, 1865:

"SEC. 5. *And be it further enacted*, That the provision prohibiting any exclusion from any car on account of color, already applicable to the Metropolitan railroad, is hereby extended to every other railroad in the District of Columbia." Approved March 3, 1865.

These amendments produced animated debates in both houses, especially when before them March 17, 1864. Mr. Saulsbury, Mr. Powell, Mr. Hendricks, and Mr. Willey, in the Senate, being very determined and bitter in their opposition, while Mr. Sumner, Mr. Wilson, Mr. Morrill, of Maine, and Mr. Grimes supported them with rare force of argument. Mr. Morrill's speech was elaborate in discussion and eloquent in language. Mr. Reverdy Johnson, like Mr. Trumbull and some others, though in favor of the object of the amendment, at first voted against it as unnecessary, maintaining in a speech of much power the right of a colored person, under the legal guarantees already secured, to ride in any railroad car in the District, and in that speech he also replied to Senator Saulsbury in a defence of the colored race in character and mental ability. He finally gave his vote for the amendment. Mr. Conness, of California, also objected to the provision as unnecessary, it being included, as he said, in a bill already before the Senate. Mr. Sumner replied, "I am in favor of getting what I can as soon as I can, and not postponing to an indefinite future."

Colored mail carriers.—The law prohibiting persons of color from carrying the mails was passed and approved March 3, 1825, and, as Mr. Wickliffe stated in the discussion on the motion for its repeal, "was originally enacted to exclude some men in the south who were in the habit of obtaining mail contracts and employing their negroes to drive their stages and carry the mails." The act reads as follows:

"That no other than a free white person shall be employed in conveying the mail, and any contractor who shall employ or permit any other than a free white man to convey the mail shall for every offence incur a penalty of $20."

The following facts as to the origin of this offensive legislation make the subject appropriate to this history. When Gideon Granger was Postmaster General, in 1802, he wrote a letter to James Jackson, senator from Georgia, in which, after stating that "an objection exists against employing negroes or people of color in transporting the public mails of a nature too delicate to engraft into a report which may become public," he proceeds to explain as follows:

"The most active and intelligent negroes are employed as post riders. These are the most ready to learn and the most able to execute. By travelling from day to day and hourly mixing they must, they will, acquire information. *They will learn that a man's rights do not depend on his color.* They will in time become teachers to their brethren. They become acquainted with each other on the line. Whenever the body or a portion of them wish to act they are an organized corps, circulating our intelligence openly, their own privately."

The words placed in italics assert a fact which it was the purpose of every black law and ordinance to subvert, the law under consideration being peculiarly of that nature. On the 18th of March, 1862, Mr. Sumner introduced a bill in the Senate providing "that from and after its passage *no person by reason of color* should be disqualified from employment in carrying the mails." It was referred to the Committee on Post Offices and Post Roads, and on March 27, 1862, it was reported back by Mr. Collamer without amendment, passing the Senate April 10 by a very large majority, but was defeated in the House by an equally decided vote. Mr. Colfax, May 20, 1862, reported it from the House Post Office Committee, with the recommendation that it do not pass. In assigning reasons for the action of the committee, he said: "It will throw open the business of mail contracting, and of thus becoming officers of the Post Office Department, not only to blacks, but also to the Indian tribes, civilized and uncivilized, and to the Chinese, who have come in such large numbers to the Pacific coast."

This argument, the best that could be urged, was sufficient—astonishing now to contemplate—to carry the House two to one against the bill. On the 18th of January, 1864, however, Mr. Sumner again introduced the subject to the Senate, and Mr. Collamer reported the old bill with an amendment, providing "that in the courts of the United States there shall be *no exclusion of any witness* on account of color, it being necessary for the protection of the mail service that all mail carriers should be allowed to testify in the federal courts. The bill met with bitter opposition from the pro-slavery party, opposed also by some of the true friends of freedom, but passed and was approved March 3, 1865, and henceforth color is no disqualification in carrying the mails.

To secure, still more thoroughly, to the colored population of the District full political rights, the present Congress passed the following act, which was approved by President Grant March 18, 1869 :

AN ACT for the further security of equal rights in the District of Columbia.

Be it enacted by the Senate and House of Representatives of the United States of America in Congress assembled, That the word " white." wherever it occurs in the laws relating to the District of Columbia, or in the charter or ordinances of the cities of Washington or Georgetown, and operates as a limitation on the right of any elector of such District, or of either of the cities, to hold any office or to be selected and to serve as a juror, be, and the same is hereby, repealed, and it shall be unlawful for any person or officer to enforce or attempt to enforce such limitation after the passage of this act.

This bill had twice before passed both houses, first in July, 1867, and again in December of the same year ; but in both cases failed to receive President Johnson's signature.

Thus was consummated by bold and faithful statesmen the series of measures which have cleared away the manifold disabilities and execrable exactions of the black codes that for more than sixty years had disgraced this District and shed infamy upon the whole country.

ALABAMA.

With the exception of a small portion of her territory, which belonged to Florida, Alabama was originally within the jurisdiction of Georgia, but became a part of the territory of Mississippi in 1800, and an independent State in 1820, her constitution having been adopted in 1819, by the provisions of which the privileges of citizenship and education were confined to the white population only. Prior to the organization of the State government, the territorial legislation of Mississippi respecting the unlawful meeting of slaves, and trading with or by them, included Alabama.

There was little State legislation relating to the colored people previous to the act of 1832, which provided that "Any person or persons who shall attempt to teach any free person of color or slave to spell, read, or write, shall, upon conviction thereof by indictment, be fined in a sum not less than $250, nor more than $500." This act also prohibited with severe penalties, by flogging, "any free negro or person of color" from being in company with any slaves without written permission from the owner or overseer of such slaves; it also prohibited the assembling of more than five male slaves at any place off the plantation to which they belonged; but nothing in the act was to be considered as forbidding attendance at places of public worship held by white persons. No slave or free person of color was permitted to "preach, exhort, or harangue any slave or slaves or free persons of color, except in the presence of five respectable slave-holders," or unless the person preaching was licensed by some regular body of professing Christians in the neighborhood, to whose society or church the negroes addressed properly belonged.

In 1833, the mayor and aldermen of the city of Mobile were authorized by law to grant licenses to such persons as they might deem suitable, to instruct for limited periods the free colored creole children within the city and in the counties of Mobile and Baldwin, who were the descendants of colored creoles residing in said city and counties in April 1803; provided, that said children first received permission to be taught from the mayor and aldermen, and had their names recorded in a book kept for that purpose. This was done, as set forth in the preamble to the law, because there were many colored creoles there whose ancestors, under the treaty between France and the United States, in 1803, had the rights and privileges of citizens of the United States secured to them; and because these creoles had conducted with uniform propriety, and were anxious that their children should be educated.

The constitution adopted September 30, 1865, provides that the general assembly shall, from time to time, make necessary and proper laws for the encouragement of schools and education; take proper measures to preserve from waste or damage any lands granted by the United States for the use of schools, and apply the funds derived from them to that object; place the school fund under the control and management of a superintendent of education, requiring such a superintendent to be appointed for the whole State; provide for a county superintendent of free public schools in each county, and for the appointment of three trustees of free public schools in each township.

In accordance with the provisions of the constitution, the revised code, adopted February 19, 1867, provides that "every child between the ages of six and twenty years shall be entitled to admission into and instruction in any of the free public schools of the township in which he or she resides, or to any school in any adjacent township." Color is not mentioned in the chapter relating to the public school system.

SCHOOLS FOR THE FREEDMEN SINCE 1864.

Under the auspices of the assistant commissioner for the Freedmen's Bureau, for the State of Alabama, (General Swayne,) a great amount of local good feeling was enlisted in that State towards establishing schools for the colored population. School buildings were provided and kept in repair at the expense of the Freedmen's Bureau. By a bill introduced into the legislature in 1867, to establish a common school system, it was provided that the board of directors of each township in the State should "establish separate schools for the education of negro and mulatto children, and persons of African descent between the ages of six and twenty-one years, whenever as many as thirty pupils in sufficient proximity for school purposes claim the privilege of public instruction, and the fund for that purpose is sufficient to support a school for four months in the year." This movement, on the part of the citizens and legislature of Alabama, was seconded by northern societies, and schools were opened particularly at Mobile, Montgomery, Huntsville and other places, in the northern part of the State. Among the societies thus giving aid may be mentioned the American Missionary Association, the Freedmen's Aid Society of the Methodist Episcopal Church, and the American Freedmen's Union Commission, operating through its Pennsylvania, Cleveland, western and northwestern branches, the latter of which had 11 teachers in its employment in 1866. In order to train their beneficiaries up to a system of self-reliance and support, all of these schools in Alabama, while closing their doors to none, enforced the principle of requiring a small tuition fee from such as might be able to pay.

In this educational work the important duty of providing for the training of teachers has not been overlooked, and two normal schools have been established, one at Talladega and the other at Mobile.

THE TALLADEGA NORMAL SCHOOL.

This institution was opened in 1867, commencing its first session with 140 pupils, under the superintendence of Rev. H. E. Brown. By the aid of the government, a fine piece of property was procured, consisting of 34 acres of land and a handsome three-story brick building, 100 feet long by 60 feet in width. This building was erected before the war for college purposes, at a cost of $23,000.

EMERSON INSTITUTE AT MOBILE.

The Emerson Institute is the name of the other school, which occupies a large brick edifice, with four acres of land, fronting upon Government street, in Mobile. This property was procured by the aid of the Freedmen's Bureau and the liberality of two gentlemen of Rockford, Illinois, in compliment to one of whom it received its name. The property was formerly the seat of the " Blue College," and is estimated to be worth more than $60,000. The institute is now conducted by a corps of able instructors, having under their charge more than 500 pupils, in rooms amply supplied with furniture of approved modern construction, and with a complete equipment of chemical and philosophical apparatus.

SWAYNE SCHOOL.

The Swayne school, Montgomery, so named in honor of General Swayne, was erected under the auspices of the American Missionary Association, and was dedicated April 21, 1869. This is a handsome edifice, three-stories in height, built by Henry Duncan in a thorough and workmanlike manner, and provided with convenient and ample means for ventilation by Isaac Frazier, both of whom are skillful colored mechanics. There are six recitation rooms, with modern seats, desks, and blackboards; and by the liberality of friends at the north an ample supply of outline maps, tablets, and other educational appliances have been provided, as well as an organ, costing $200. Here, in this neat and comfortable edifice the freed children of Montgomery find an agreeable change from " Fritz & Frazer's Trade House," where, within a few years past, they conned their lessons; or in earlier and darker days many of them may have been put up as merchandise for sale.

The following tables, compiled by Professor Vashon, exhibits the progress and condition of the schools for the colored population in Alabama from 1865 to 1868:

Number of schools, teachers, and scholars, 1865 to 1868.

Year.	Number of schools.			Number of teachers.			Number of scholars.			Average attendance.	Per cent.
	Day.	Night.	Total.	White.	Colored.	Total.	Male.	Female.	Total.		
1865			13			15			817		
1866			28			31			3,338	3,065		91
1867	122	53	175	126	24	150	4,373	5,426	9,799	8,123	82
1868	62	22	84	77	32	109	2,055	2,260	4,315	3,297	76

Studies and expenditures, 1867 and 1868.

Year.	Number of scholars in different studies pursued.							Expenditures in support of schools.		
	Alphabet.	Easy reading.	Advanced readers.	Writing.	Geography.	Arithmetic.	Higher branches.	By freedmen.	By others.	Total.
1867	3,390	4,385	2,314	3,447	1,782	2,888	813	$2,974	$14,801	$17,775
1868	519	2,873	2,292	1,698	1,197	1,861	390	4,207	4,682	8,889

ARKANSAS.

The province ceded by France in 1803, under the general designation of Louisiana, was in in 1804 organized by Congress into two parts—the Territory of Orleans and the district of Louisiana. The latter embraced the country out of which was constituted in 1805 the Territory of Louisiana, which was again reorganized in 1812 into the Territory of Missouri, the southern part of which erected into a distinct jurisdiction as Arkansas Territory in 1819, and as a State in 1836, and another portion into the State of Missouri in 1821. The laws governing the colored population were nearly the same in both States. The first statute relating to them was passed by the governor and judges of the district of Indiana Territory in 1806, and provided that no slave should go from the plantation of his master, or other person with whom he lived, without a pass, under penalty of "stripes at the discretion of the justice of the peace;" and if found on any other plantation without leave in writing from his owner, it was lawful for the owner or overseer "to give or order such slave 10 lashes on his or her bare back for every such offence." It forbid the master, mistress, or overseer to suffer meetings of slaves alone for more than four hours at any one time, or to go abroad to trade, on penalty of $3 for each offence. All trading with slaves or allowing slaves to trade was forbidden under severe penalties. All assemblages of the slaves of different estates in the night or on Sunday, except at the church ot white people, were forbidden.

The first act relating to slaves after Arkansas became a State was passed in 1838, in which their owners were authorized to permit slaves "to labor for themselves on Sunday, if such labor is done voluntarily by such slaves and without the coercion of the master, and for the sole use of the slave." As this was the only day allowed for such religious instruction as the slave could receive, this provision cannot be regarded as being beneficent. This act forbids any white persons, or free negro, being found in company of slaves at any unlawful meeting, on severe penalty for each offense. In 1843 all migration of free negroes and mulattoes into the State was forbidden : but no law is found on the statute book directly prohibiting teaching slaves or persons of African descent.

In the constitution adopted in 1836, all the privileges of citizenship were confined to the whites. In the constitution adopted in 1864, it is provided that "neither slavery nor involuntary servitude shall hereafter exist in this State," and "that no act of the legislature prohibiting the education of any class of the inhabitants thereof shall have the force of law." In the constitution adopted by the people of the State, March 13, 1868, the language of that instrument recognizes no distinction in citizenship on account of color. The first section of article IX, relating to education, reads as follows :

"A general diffusion of knowledge and intelligence among all classes being essential to the preservation of the rights and liberties of the people, the general assembly shall establish and maintain a system of free schools for the gratuitous instruction of all persons in this State between the ages of five and twenty-one years."   *   *   *

In the "Act to establish and maintain a system of free common schools for the State of Arkansas," approved July, 23, 1868, the State board of education, (composed of the State and circuit superintendents) is directed "to make the necessary provisions for establishing separate schools for white and colored children and youth," and to adopt such other measures as shall be deemed expedient for carrying the system into effectual and uniform operation, and provide as nearly as possible for the education of every youth.

EDUCATION AND SCHOOLS FOR THE FREEDMEN SINCE 1864.

For reasons that will be apparent from the remarks that follow, fewer schools for colored persons have been established in Arkansas since 1864 than in any other of the formerly slave-holding States. Yet the educational work was commenced there while the war for the Union was still raging ; and, from its commencement, it has been prosecuted in such a spirit as promises the most satisfactory results in the future. In the third year of the rebellion, several thousands of persons liberated by President Lincoln's proclamation of freedom had sought protection within the military lines of the government, and were congregated in camps at Helena, Pine Bluff, Little Rock, and other points within the limits of this State. Destitute of all the comforts and necessaries of life, they immediately aroused the sympathy of benevolent individuals throughout the northwestern portion of the country. Associations for the relief of their physical wants were speedily formed : but these soon discovered that the mental and moral needs of these unhappy creatures were fully as pressing as their hunger and nakedness. To break through the barriers raised by legislation in the interest of the slave power, and carry food to those starving souls as well as to their bodies, was an evident duty. In its performance, schools were established at these different camps ; and self-denying men and women, braving the manifold perils of those unsettled times, willingly assumed their charge. Prominent among the philanthropists who labored in this section of the country were the Friends, constituting what is known as the Indiana Yearly Meeting. First to enter upon this Christian work, they have at no time since relaxed their generous exertions ; and they now have the satisfaction of seeing them rewarded by the establishment at Little Rock and elsewhere of several graded schools, which, in their appointments and in the improvement made by their pupils, will compare favorably with those of any other localities.

At the outset, these schools were, as might naturally be expected, very deficient in everything needful for the pleasant pursuit of learning. Within the rudely-constructed shanty which served as the school-room, the only books usually found were a few tattered primers, spelling-books, and Testaments, which had already done good service for other children in far happier circumstances. But for this dearth of facilities in the acquisition of knowledge the patient assiduity of teacher and the earnest application of pupils made ample amends ; so that, in spite of all obstacles, an astonishing progress in the primary studies was a frequent, indeed an ordinary, result. It was not long, however, before the kindness of northern friends supplied the wants of those humble establishments ; and, by the time that these eager scholars were ready for the use of slates, maps, and appropriate books in the different branches of learning, these articles were furnished to them quite liberally. The number of these schools, too, was increased by a timely measure on the part of the government. In ts efforts to restore the industrial interests of the south, and to regulate the relations between employers and the emancipated laborers, it established a system by which abandoned plantations were leased out upon certain conditions, one of which required, for every lot of 500 acres so leased, the employment of at least one teacher for the freedmen who cultivated them.

The colored people thus benefited showed themselves deserving of the interest taken in their behalf by the willingness which they manifested to do everything in their power for the support of these schools. Indeed it will be remembered to their credit that they established the first free schools that ever were in Arkansas. This they did at Little Rock, where, after paying tuition for a short time, they formed themselves into an educational association, paid by subscription the salaries of the teachers, and made their schools free.

Notwithstanding this willingness on the part of the freed people of Arkansas to co-operate with those desirous of educating them, that State has fared somewhat indifferently in the matter of schools, from the fact that it has no important commercial centers, and that, from a want of good roads, its interior is difficult of access. These circumstances render it an uninviting field for teachers. Still, quite a number of these have seconded the efforts made by the educational officers of the Freedmen's Bureau to establish schools, and have cheerfully endured the dangers and fatigues of travel, in going even as far as the Red River country in the extreme southwestern part of the State, by almost impassable roads and in the rudest conveyances, to enter upon their duties. The planters of Arkansas, too, have quite generally exhibited a commendable friendliness towards any movements touching the instruction of their laboring hands, by inviting the establishment of schools in their localities, and engaging to provide board and suitable accommodations for teachers who might come among them. Under these favorable circumstances, and through the aid of the congressional appropriation for building schools, nearly $30,000 of which was allotted to Arkansas, quite an increased activity marked educational affairs there during 1867 and 1868. This was in some measure checked by political disturbances, and by the privations incident to a succession of scanty harvests; but it is to be hoped that with the prevalence of good order, and the return of prosperity, the schools for colored people in Arkansas will again begin to increase in number and to improve in condition.

The following tables, prepared by Prof. Vashon, exhibit the progress of the schools from 1866 to 1868:

Number of schools, teachers, and scholars, 1866 to 1868.

Year.	Number of schools.			Number of teachers.			Number of scholars.			Average attendance.	Per cent.
	Day.	Night.	Total.	White.	Colored.	Total.	Male.	Female.	Total.		
1866	.....	.....	30	23	5	28	.....	.....	1,584	1,209	.....
1867	25	10	35	33	7	40	950	1,042	1,992	1,625	81
1868	22	5	27	31	12	43	715	822	1,537	1,225	79

Distribution of studies and expenditures.

Year.	Number of scholars in different studies pursued.							Expenditures in support of schools.		
	Alphabet.	Easy reading.	Advanced readers.	Writing.	Geography.	Arithmetic.	Higher branches.	By freedmen.	By others.	Total.
1867	364	1,197	494	629	347	805	198	$2,987	$7,982	$10,969
1868	201	811	573	787	386	783	55	3,415	7,232	10,647

CALIFORNIA.

By the census of 1860 the population of California was 379,994, of which number 4,086 were free colored.

In the constitution of California, adopted in 1849, prior to its admission into the Union as a State in 1850, the right of suffrage is limited to white male citizens, but the establishment of slavery or involuntary servitude, except for crime, is prohibited.

In the revised school law, approved March 24, 1866, the following sections apply to colored children:

SEC. 57. Children of African or Mongolian descent, and Indian children not living under the care of white persons, shall not be admitted into public schools, except as provided in this act: *Provided*, That, upon the written application of the parents or guardians of at least 10 such children to any board of trustees or board of education, a separate school shall be established for the education of such children, and the education of a less number may be provided for by the trustees in any other manner.

SEC. 58. When there shall be in any district any number of children, other than white children, whose education can be provided for in no other way, the trustees, by a majority vote, may permit such children to attend school for white children: *Provided*, That a majority of the parents of the children attending such school make no objection, in writing, to be filed with the board of trustees.

SEC. 59. The same laws, rules, and regulations which apply to schools for white children shall apply to schools for colored children.

The superintendent of public instruction, Hon. John Swett, in his annual report for 1867, reports as follows:

Number of negro children in the State between 5 and 16 years of age................ 709
Number of separate schools... 16
Number of pupils in attendance... 400

"The people of the State are decidedly in favor of separate schools for colored children."

CONNECTICUT.

In 1860 the free colored population of Connecticut was 8,627, out of a total of 460,147 inhabitants.

The constitution of 1818 limits the privilege of the elector to white male citizens, but the public schools of the State have never been restricted to any class on account of color, although in the city of Hartford, in 1830, a separate school was established under legislative permission granted on application made by the school committee at the request of the colored people of the city.

This example was followed in two or three towns, but the system of separate schools, under special legislation or the action of school committees, was broken up by the legislature in 1868, and the old practice of "schools good enough for all" revived and established by law.

The legislature in 1833, under the lead of a few influential men, passed a law which illustrated the extent to which the prejudices of the community could be enlisted against the colored people, but this law was repealed in 1838, having accomplished its object in a manner no way creditable to the State.

PRUDENCE CRANDALL AND THE CANTERBURY SCHOOL.

The following account of the efforts made by Miss Prudence Crandall, in the town of Canterbury, to establish a boarding and day school for young women of African descent, is abridged from the "Recollections of the Anti-Slavery Conflict," by Rev. Samuel J. May:

In the summer of 1832, Miss Prudence Crandall, an excellent, well-educated Quaker young lady, who had gained considerable reputation as a teacher in the neighboring town of Plainfield, purchased, at the solicitation of a number of families in the village of Canterbury, Connecticut, a commodious house in that village, for the purpose of establishing a boarding and day school for young ladies, in order that they might receive instruction in higher branches than were taught in the public district school. Her school was well conducted, but was interrupted early in 1833, in this wise : Not far from the village a worthy colored man was living, by the name of Harris, the owner of a good farm, and in comfortable circumstances. His daughter Sarah, a bright girl, 17 years of age, had passed with credit through the public school of the district in which she lived, and was anxious to acquire a better education, to qualify herself to become a teacher of the colored people. She applied to Miss Crandall for admission to her school. Miss Crandall hesitated, for prudential reasons, to admit a colored person among her pupils; but Sarah was a young lady of pleasing appearance and manners, well known to many of Miss Crandall's present pupils, having been their classmate in the district school, and was, moreover, a virtuous, pious girl, and a member of the church in Canterbury. No objection could be made to her admission except on account of her complexion, and Miss Crandall decided to receive her as a pupil. No objection was made by the other pupils, but in a few days the parents of some of them called on Miss Crandall and remonstrated; and although Miss Crandall pressed upon their consideration the eager desire of Sarah for knowledge and culture and the good use she wished to make of her education, her excellent character, and her being an accepted member of the same Christian church to which they belonged, they were too much prejudiced to listen to any arguments—"they would not have it said that their daughters went to school with a nigger girl." It was urged that if Sarah was not dismissed, the white pupils would be withdrawn; but although the fond hopes of success for an institution which she had established at the risk of all her property, and by incurring a debt of several hundred dollars, seemed to be doomed to disappointment, she decided not to yield to the demand for the dismissal of Sarah; and on the 2d day of March, 1833, she advertised in the Liberator that on the first Monday in April her school would be open for "young ladies and little misses of color." Her determination having become known, a fierce indignation was kindled and fanned by prominent people of the village, and pervaded the town. In this juncture, the Rev. Samuel J. May, of the neighboring town of Brooklyn, addressed her a letter of sympathy, expressing his readiness to assist her to the extent of his power, and was present at the town meeting held on the 9th of March, called for the express purpose of devising and adopting such measures as "would effectually avert the nuisance or speedily abate it if it should be brought into the village."

The friends of Miss Crandall were authorized by her to state to the moderator of the town meeting that she would give up her house, which was one of the most conspicuous in the village, and not wholly paid for, if those who were opposed to her school being there would take the property off her hands at the price for which she had purchased it, and which was deemed a reasonable one, and allow her time to procure another house in a more retired part of the town.

The town meeting was held in the meeting-house, which, though capable of holding a thousand people, was crowded throughout to its utmost capacity. After the warning for the meeting had been read, resolutions were introduced in which were set forth the disgrace and damage that would be brought upon the town if a school for colored girls should be set up there, protesting emphatically against the impending evil, and appointing the civil authority and selectmen a committee to wait upon "the person contemplating the establishment of said school and persuade her, if possible, to abandon the project."

The resolutions were advocated by Rufus Adams, esq., and Hon. Andrew T. Judson, who was then the most prominent man of the town, and a leading politician in the State, and much talked of as the democratic candidate for governor ; and was a representative in Congress from 1835 to 1839, when he was elected judge of the United States district court, which position he held until his death in 1853, adjudicating, among other causes, the libel of the Amistad and the 54 Africans on board. After his address on this occasion, Mr. May, in company with Mr. Arnold Buffum, a lecturing agent of the New England Anti-Slavery Society, applied for permission to speak in behalf of Miss Crandall but their application was violently opposed, and the resolutions being adopted, the meeting was declared, by the moderator, adjourned.

Mr. May at once stepped upon the seat where he had been sitting and rapidly vindicated Miss Crandall, replying to some of the misstatements as to her purposes and the character of her expected pupils, when he gave way to Mr. Buffum, who had spoken scarcely five minutes before the trustees of the church ordered the house to be vacated and the doors to be shut. There was then no alternative but to yield.

Two days afterwards Mr. Judson called on Mr. May, with whom he had been on terms of a pleasant acquaintance, not to say of friendship, and expressed regret that he had applied certain epithets to him ; and went on to speak of the disastrous effect on the village from the establishment of " a school for nigger girls." Mr. May replied that his purpose was, if he had been allowed to do so, to state at the town meeting Miss Crandall's proposition to sell her house in the village at its fair valuation, and retire to some other part of the town. To this Mr. Judson responded : " Mr. May, we are not merely opposed to the establishment of that school in Canterbury, we mean there shall not be such a school set up anywhere in the State."

Mr. Judson continued, declaring that the colored people could never rise from their menial condition in our country, and ought not to be permitted to rise here ; that they were an inferior race and should not be recognized as the equals of the whites ; that they should be sent back to Africa, and improve themselves there, and civilize and christianize the natives. To this Mr. May replied that there never would be fewer colored people in this country than there were then ; that it was unjust to drive them out of the country ; that we must accord to them their rights or incur the loss of our own ; that education was the primal, fundamental right of all the children of men ; and that Connecticut was the last place where this should be denied.

The conversation was continued in a similar strain, in the course of which Mr. Judson declared with warmth : " That nigger school shall never be allowed in Canterbury, nor in any town of this State ;" and he avowed his determination to secure the passage of a law by the legislature then in session, forbidding the institution of such a school in any part of the State.

Undismayed by the opposition and the threatened violence of her neighbors, Miss Crandall received early in April 15 or 20 colored young ladies and misses from Philadelphia, New York, Providence, and Boston ; and the annoyances of her persecutors at once commenced ; all accommodations at the stores in Canterbury being denied her, her pupils being insulted whenever they appeared on the streets, the doors and doorsteps of her house being besmeared, and her well filled with filth ; under all of which, both she and her pupils remained firm. Among other means used to intimidate, an attempt was made to drive away those innocent girls by a process under the obsolete vagrant law, which provided that the selectmen of any town might warn any person, not an inhabitant of the State, to depart forthwith, demanding $1 67 for every week he or she remained after receiving such warning ; and in case the fine was not paid and the person did not depart before the expiration of ten days after being sentenced, *then he or she should be whipped on the naked body not exceeding ten stripes.*

A warrant to that effect was actually served upon Eliza Ann Hammond, a fine girl from Providence, aged 17 years ; but it was finally abandoned, and another method was resorted to, most disgraceful to the State as well as the town. Foiled in their attempts to frighten away Miss Crandall's pupils by their proceedings under the obsolete " pauper and vagrant law," Mr. Judson and those who acted with him pressed upon the legislature, then in session, a demand for the enactment of a law which should enable them to accomplish their purpose ; and in that bad purpose they succeeded, by securing the following enactment, on the 24th of May, 1833, known as the "*black law.*"

" Whereas attempts have been made to establish literary institutions in this State for the instruction of colored persons belonging to other States and countries, which would tend to the great increase of the colored population of the State, and thereby to the injury of the people : Therefore,

"*Be it enacted, &c.*, That no person shall set up or establish in this State any school, academy, or other literary institution for the instruction or education of colored persons, who are not inhabitants of this State, or harbor or board, for the purpose of attending or being taught or instructed in any such school, academy, or literary institution, any colored person who is not an inhabitant of any town in this State, without the consent in writing, first obtained, of a majority of the civil authority, and also of the selectmen of the town in which such school, academy, or literary institution is situated, &c.

"And each and every person who shall knowingly do any act forbidden as aforesaid, or shall be aiding or assisting therein, shall for the first offense forfeit and pay to the treasurer of this State a fine of $100, and for the second offense $200, and so double for every offense of which he or she shall be convicted; and all informing officers are required to make due presentment of all breaches of this act."

On the receipt of the tidings of the passage of this law, the people of Canterbury were wild with exultation; the bells were rung and a cannon was fired to manifest the joy. On the 27th of June Miss Crandall was arrested and arraigned before Justices Adams and Bacon, two of those who had been the earnest opponents of her enterprise; and the result being predetermined, the trial was of course brief, and Miss Crandall was "committed" to take her trial at the next session of the supreme court at Brooklyn, in August. A messenger was at once dispatched by the party opposed to Miss Crandall to Brooklyn to inform Mr. May, as her friend, of the result of the trial, stating that she was in the hands of the sheriff, and would be put in jail unless he or some of her friends would "give bonds" for her in a certain sum.

The denouement may be related most appropriately in the language of Mr. May:

"I calmly told the messenger that there were gentlemen enough in Canterbury whose bond for that amount would be as good or better than mine, and I should leave it for them to do Miss Crandall that favor." 'But,' said the young man, 'are you not her friend?' 'Certainly,' I replied, 'too sincerely her friend to give relief to her enemies in their present embarrassment, and I trust you will not find any one of her friends, or the patrons of her school, who will step forward to help them any more than myself.' 'But, sir,' he cried, 'do you mean to allow her to be put in jail?' 'Most certainly,' was my answer, 'if her persecutors are unwise enough to let such an outrage be committed.' He turned from me in blank surprise, and hurried back to tell Mr. Judson and the justices of his ill success.

"A few days before, when I first heard of the passage of the law, I had visited Miss Crandall with my friend, Mr. George W. Benson, and advised with her as to the course she and her friends ought to pursue when she should be brought to trial. She appreciated at once and fully the importance of leaving her persecutors to show to the world how base they were, and how atrocious was the law they had induced the legislature to enact—a law, by the force of which a woman might be fined and imprisoned as a felon in the State of Connecticut for giving instruction to colored girls. She agreed that it would be best for us to leave her in the hands of those with whom the law originated, hoping that, in their madness, they would show forth all their hideous features.

"Mr. Benson and I, therefore, went diligently around to all who he knew were friendly to Miss Crandall and her school, and counseled them by no means to give bonds to keep her from imprisonment, because nothing would expose so fully to the public the egregious wickedness of the law and the virulence of her persecutors as the fact that they had thrust her into jail.

"When I found that her resolution was equal to the trial which seemed to be impending, that she was ready to brave and to bear meekly the worst treatment that her enemies would venture to subject her to, I made all the arrangements for her comfort that were practicable in our prison. It fortunately happened that the most suitable room, unoccupied, was the one in which a man named Watkins had recently been confined for the murder of his wife, and out of which he had been taken and executed. This circumstance we foresaw would add not a little to the public detestation of the *black law.* The jailor, at my request, readily put the room in as nice order as was possible, and permitted me to substitute for the bedstead and mattress on which the murderer had slept, fresh and clean ones from my own house and Mr. Benson's.

"About 2 o'clock, p. m. another messenger came to inform me that the sheriff was on the way from Canterbury to the jail with Miss Crandall, and would imprison her unless her friends would give the required bail. Although in sympathy with Miss Crandall's persecutors, he saw clearly the disgrace that was about to be brought upon the State, and begged me and Mr. Benson to avert it. Of course we refused. I went to the jailor's house and met Miss Crandall on her arrival. We stepped aside. I said: 'If now you hesitate—if you dread the gloomy place so much as to wish to be saved from it, I will give bonds for you even now.' 'O, no,' she promptly replied, 'I am only afraid they will not put me in jail.'

Their evident hesitation and embarrassment show plainly how much they deprecate the effect of this part of their folly, and therefore I am the more anxious that they should be exposed, if not caught in their own wicked devices.'

"We therefore returned with her to the sheriff and the company that surrounded him to await his final act. He was ashamed to do it. He knew it would cover the persecutors of Miss Crandall and the State of Connecticut with disgrace. He conferred with several about him, and delayed yet longer. Two gentlemen came and remonstrated with me in not very seemly terms : 'It would be a ——— shame, an eternal disgrace to the State, to have her put into jail—into the very room that Watkins had last occupied.'

"'Certainly, gentlemen,' I replied, 'and this you may prevent if you please.'

"'O !' they cried, 'we are not her friends ; we are not in favor of her school ; we don't want any more ——— niggers coming among us. It is your place to stand by Miss Crandall and help her now. You and your ——— abolition brethren have encouraged her to bring this nuisance into Canterbury, and it is ——— mean in you to desert her now.'

"I rejoined : 'She knows we have not deserted her, and do not intend to desert her. The law which her persecutors have persuaded our legislators to enact is an infamous one, worthy of the dark ages. It would be just as bad as it is whether we would give bonds for her or not. But the people generally will not so soon realize how bad, how wicked, how cruel a law it is unless we suffer her persecutors to inflict upon her all the penalties it prescribes. She is willing to bear them for the sake of the cause she has so nobly espoused. If you see fit to keep her from imprisonment in the cell of a murderer for having proffered the blessings of a good education to those who in our country need it most, you may do so ; *we shall not.*'

"They turned from us in great wrath, words falling from their lips which I shall not repeat.

"The sun had descended nearly to the horizon ; the shadows of night were beginning to fall around us. The sheriff could defer the dark deed no longer. With no little emotion, and with words of earnest deprecation, he gave that excellent, heroic, Christian young lady into the hands of the jailor, and she was led into the cell of Watkins. So soon as I had heard the bolts of her prison door turned in the lock and saw the key taken out, I bowed and said : 'The deed is done, completely done. It cannot be recalled. It has passed into the history of our nation and our age.' I went away with my steadfast friend, George W. Benson, assured that the legislators of the State had been guilty of a most unrighteous act, and that Miss Crandall's persecutors had also committed a great blunder ; that they all would have much more reason to be ashamed of her imprisonment than she or her friends could ever have.

"The next day we gave the required bonds. Miss Crandall was released from the cell of the murderer, returned home, and quietly resumed the duties of her school until she should be summoned as a culprit into court, there to be tried by the infamous '*Black Law of Connecticut.*' And, as we expected, so soon as the evil tidings could be carried in that day, before Professor Morse had given to Rumor her telegraphic wings, it was known all over the country and the civilized world that an excellent young lady had been imprisoned as a criminal—yes, put into a murderer's cell—in the State of Connecticut, for opening a school for the instruction of colored girls. The comments that were made upon the deed in almost all the newspapers were far from grateful to the feelings of her persecutors. Even many who, under the same circumstances, would probably have acted as badly as Messrs. A. T. Judson & Co., denounced their procedure as "unchristian, inhuman, anti-democratic, base, mean."

On the 23d of August, 1833, the first trial of Miss Crandall was had in Brooklyn, the seat of the county of Windham, Hon. Joseph Eaton presiding at the county court.

The prosecution was conducted by Hon. A. T. Judson, Jonathan A. Welch, esq., and I. Bulkley, esq. Miss Crandall's counsel was Hon. Calvin Goddard, Hon. W. W. Elsworth, and Henry Strong, esq.

The judge, somewhat timidly, gave it as his opinion "that the law was constitutional and obligatory on the people of the State."

The jury, after an absence of several hours, returned into court not having agreed upon a verdict. They were instructed and sent out again, and again a third time, in vain ; they stated to the judge that there was no probability that they could ever agree. Seven were for conviction and five for acquittal, so they were discharged.

The second trial was on the 3d of October, before Judge Daggett of the supreme court, who was a strenuous advocate of the black law. His influence with the jury was over-powering, insisting in an elaborate and able charge that the law was constitutional, and, without much hesitation, the verdict was given against Miss Crandall. Her counsel at once filed a bill of exceptions, and took an appeal to the court of errors, which was granted. Before that, the highest legal tribunal in the State, the cause was argued on the 22d of July, 1834. Both the Hon. W. W. Elsworth and the Hon. Calvin Goddard argued with great ability and eloquence against the constitutionality of the black law. The Hon. A. T. Judson and Hon. C. F. Cleaveland said all they could to prove such a law consistent with the *Magna Charta* of our republic. The court reserved a decision for some future time; and that decision was never given, it being evaded by the court finding such defects in the information prepared by the State's attorney that it ought to be quashed.

Soon after this, an attempt was made to set the house of Miss Crandall on fire, but without effect. The question of her duty to risk the lives of her pupils against this mode of attack was then considered, and upon consultation with friends it was concluded to hold on and bear a little longer, with the hope that this atrocity of attempting to fire the house, and thus expose the lives and property of her neighbors, would frighten the instigators of the persecution, and cause some restraint on "the baser sort." But a few nights afterwards, about 12 o'clock, being the night of the 9th of September, her house was assaulted by a number of persons with heavy clubs and iron bars; and windows were dashed to pieces. Mr. May was summoned the next morning, and after consultation it was determined that the school should be abandoned. Mr. May thus concludes his account of this event, and of the enterprise.

"The pupils were called together and I was requested to announce to them our decision. Never before had I felt so deeply sensible of the cruelty of the persecution which had been carried on for 18 months in that New England village, against a family of defenseless females. Twenty harmless, well behaved girls, whose only offense against the peace of the community was that they had come together there to obtain useful knowledge and moral culture, were to be told that they had better go away, because, forsooth, the house in which they dwelt would not be protected by the guardians of the town, the conservators of the peace, the officers of justice, the men of influence in the village where it was situated. The words almost blistered my lips. My bosom glowed with indignation. I felt ashamed of Canterbury, ashamed of Connecticut, ashamed of my country, ashamed of my color. Thus ended the generous, disinterested, philanthropic, Christian enterprise of Prudence Crandall, but the law under which her enterprise was defeated was repealed in 1838."

The principal championship of the repeal of the "Canterbury Law," as the act of 1833 was called, in the legislature of 1838, was made by Hon. Francis Gillette, then and always an earnest member of the house from Bloomfield:

"This law is unwise, impolitic, and preposterous. Colored children, and any other persons, may come into this State in any numbers, and for any other purpose than that of acquiring knowledge—no matter what they are, idlers, thieves, vagabonds, the very sweepings of the globe; but if an innocent child comes into this State for the purpose of attending school, and that child's complexion is a little dashed, if it has not the Caucasian dye, that child is liable, by this law, to be treated as a vagrant pauper, and hurried out of the State, as though its very breath was contagion and death. Notwithstanding, if it will throw away its books, and turn to some menial employment; if it will abandon the pursuit of knowledge and become a waiter or a boot-black, it may, forsooth, tarry within the State, unmolested by this or any other law. It may, indeed, remain for any other purpose than to prepare itself to become an intelligent and worthy citizen; but across the path of knowledge it finds the Canterbury black act, snake-like distended. We admit the vicious and degraded, while we reject the pure-hearted and aspiring.

"Connecticut has ever shown herself deeply sensible of the value of education to all classes, and of its inseparable connection with her prosperity, happiness, and glory. Her munificent school fund attests it; her school-houses dotting thickly her surface evince it; her general policy from her earliest settlement confirms it; but we here find in her recent legislation a law diametrically opposed to her past policy, and conflicting with her whole system of measures for pouring the light of knowledge over the youthful mind, and thus enriching herself, not with pelf, but with the treasures of cultivated intellect.

"In vain shall we look for a parallel to this legislation in any modern free State; but in an earlier and darker age it is recorded of the inhabitants of Mitylene that they forbade the people of a tributary province to give the least instruction to their children, they having learned the close connection between light and liberty. Let us be mindful of our obligation to treat the children of this unfortunate race—the victims of ages of barbarous cruelty—with some little justice and humanity; and when they come to us asking for the bread of knowledge, let us not give them a stone, and thrust them from our presence, but cheer their wounded hearts with kindness and compassion, and welcome them to participate with us in the blessings of knowledge, of wise government, and impartial laws."

SCHOOLS FOR COLORED CHILDREN IN HARTFORD.

The following letter from Rev. W. W. Turner, to the Commissioner of Education, gives the history and present status of the colored population in respect to public schools not only in Hartford but in the State generally:

DEAR SIR: Until the year 1830 no separate schools for colored children had ever been organized in this town. From the beginning they had been received into the schools for other children, with equal privileges and advantages for instruction, support being derived from school funds and public taxation, and no distinction was recognized between them and the white children in the same school. Such in general was the fact throughout this State and the whole of New England.

About the year above specified, the colored people expressed a desire that one or more separate schools for their own children should be formed in the city of Hartford, on which should be expended that part of the public school money which would be drawn by them according to their number. A mutual agreement to that effect was entered into, and the legislature, by request of the School Society of Hartford, passed a law authorizing within its limits one or more separate colored schools, and the appropriation to them of their share of the public money. This arrangement was consummated the same year, and was continued without any special change until the autumn of 1846. A memorial or petition was then sent to the School Society by the pastor of the colored congregational church showing that since the separation above described nothing had been done for the colored schools by said society beyond the paying over of their share of the public fund every year. No school-houses had been built or furnished, and excepting small contributions from a few benevolent persons, not a farthing had been given for the payment of their teachers and the support of their schools by the white citizens of Hartford. The colored population from want of means had been unable to procure suitable rooms, or competent teachers, and consequently the education of their children had been exceedingly irregular, deficient and onerous—much of the time being without any schools at all. The School Society promptly voted to raise a tax sufficient to support two schools for colored children with suitable rooms and teachers, and appointed a committee to receive and apply the money raised for that purpose. This arrangement was entirely satisfactory to all concerned, and its results were especially beneficial to the colored population of the city. By the natural increase of this class of children, the rooms occupied by their schools some years after had become quite too small; and as graded schools had been established for other children, patrons of the colored schools of the city felt that the time had come when a suitable building for the accommodation of their schools should be built for them at the public expense. A petition to that effect was sent by many of the principal colored residents of Hartford to the School Society, which appointed a committee to investigate and report on the whole subject. As a preliminary step to all future action, this committee called a meeting of the colored people to discuss and to decide for themselves the question whether they would have their children taught in future with the white children, or in schools of their own as heretofore. After a free and full deliberation upon the matter, they came almost, if not quite, unanimously to the conclusion that they preferred to have their children taught in separate schools in a building sufficiently large and properly arranged for classification to accommodate them all. The committee reported in favor of the plan, and the society authorized the erection of such a building in April, 1852. From that time until August of last year the colored schools, in common with all the public schools of the city, have been supported by tax on the property of our citizens, without any other expense to the parents of the children; and the full benefits of this judicious policy have been experienced by all classes of the community. In 1868 a law was enacted by the legislature of Connecticut providing that "the public schools of this State should be open to all persons between the ages of four and sixteen; and that no person should be denied admittance to and instruction in any public school in the school district where such person resides, on account of race or color." This law permitted the colored parents of this city to send their children to any of the public schools of the districts in which they resided—a privilege denied them in some of these districts, and one which they very much desired to enjoy. They had for a good while been certain that the white population of the city would not furnish for them as good school accommodations as they had already done for their own children; and that it was impossible for the colored people to establish and keep up such schools as were regarded essential to the thorough training of their children for the new fields of usefulness now opening before them. Immediately, therefore, on the passage of the law referred to, they concluded with entire unanimity to avail themselves of its provisions. They gave up their separate schools, and sent their children to the public schools of their respective districts. The new law and the new arrangement obtained the cheerful acquiescence of the teachers and scholars of these schools; the colored parents made special efforts to clothe and otherwise prepare their children for the new positions assigned them ; and up to the present time the plan has worked admirably, and has already devoloped a rapid improvement in learning, and in the deportment and self-respect of the colored children for whose benefit mainly the law was enacted."

The act of 1868, referred to in the foregoing communication, is as follows :

"The public schools of this State shall be open to all persons between the ages of four and sixteen years, and no person shall be denied admittance to and instruction in any public school in the school district where such person resides, on account of race or color, any law or resolution of this State heretofore passed to the contrary notwithstanding."

DELAWARE.

Out of a population of 112,216, in 1860, there were in Delaware 21,627 blacks, of which number 19,829 were free.

In 1739, free negroes or mulattoes were forbidden by law to harbor or entertain any slave without the consent of the owner of such slave, under severe penalties; and this was the only legislative action by this State, relating exclusively to the colored people, during the colonial period. Nearly one hundred years later, in 1832, an act was passed, providing that no congregation or meeting of free negroes or mulattoes, of more than 12 persons, should be held later than 10 o'clock in the night, except under the direction of three respectable white men, who were to be present during the continuance of the meeting, under a penalty of $10 for each offense ; and on failing to pay, the offender was to be sold into slavery for a term not to exceed three years. It was also further enacted, that no free negro or mulatto, not a resident of the State, should "attempt or presume to hold any meeting for the purpose of religious worship, or for the purpose of, or under the pretense of, preaching or exhortation, without the license of some judge or justice of the peace in this State, granted upon the rec ommendation of five respectable and judicious citizens." The penalty was a fine of $50 and costs ; and on failure to pay, to be sold "to the highest bidder for a term not exceeding seven years."

In 1833 a law was passed requiring the owner of any slave to pay $5 for a license to sel the same to a person in Maryland : and in the case of the importation of a slave from Maryland, $10 was to be paid ; and the sums thus paid were to be added to the fund for the education of the children of the white population.

The laws respecting free negroes and mulattoes remained essentially unchanged until 1852; and they did not, in express language, forbid the establishment of schools for their instruction ; nor was the instruction of the slaves expressly forbidden, though the Revised Statutes of 1852 provided for the taxation of all the property of the State for the benefit of schools for the children of whites'alone.

In 1863 a positive enactment was made against all assemblages for the instruction of colored people, and forbidding all meetings except for religious worship and the burial of their dead. The penalty for each offense was a fine of $10 and costs, and on failure to pay, to be sold into slavery not exceeding seven years, to any person residing in the county.

While the free colored people were taxed to a certain extent for school purposes they could not enjoy the privileges of public instruction thus provided, and were left for many years to rely principally upon individual efforts among themselves and their friends for the support of a few occasional schools. In 1840 the Friends formed the African School Association, in the city of Wilmington ; and by its aid two very good schools, male and female, were established in that place.

In 1866 the Delaware Association for the Moral Improvement and Education of the Colored People of the State was organized through the efforts of General E. M. Gregory, an earnest and efficient assistant commissioner of the Freedmen's Bureau. He was aided therein by Judge Hugh M. Bond and Francis T. King, of Baltimore, Maryland ; and also by the Right Reverend Alfred Lee, Bishop of the Protestant Episcopal Church of Delaware.

The latter gentleman penned an appeal to the public, in which he urgently pressed the considerations that should influence all classes to give to this movement their sympathy and co-operation. These considerations were alleged to be: 1st. The manifest equity of no longer excluding any class of the community from the advantages of mental culture; 2d. The rescue of a large number of the young from indolence and vice; 3d. The general social improvement which might be expected in the State; 4th. The certain benefits to productive industry; and, 5th. The satisfaction of doing something to redress a great wrong, and so pay a debt long overdue to the poor and defenseless. To the association thus founded and advocated the African School Association transferred its school property in Wilmington, valued at about $4,000, and also the income of its funds, in trust, that the former should establish and maintain on the premises transferred as high an order of schools for the colored people as their condition permitted. The Delaware Association also took charge of a school in Wilmington, which had been sustained previously by private contributions, and opened another in the school-room of the African Zion church. Besides these, it speedily established schools in the following places, viz: Dover, Milford, Seaford, Smyrna, Odessa, Christiana, New Castle, Laurel, Georgetown, Milton, Newark, Delaware City, Lewis, Camden, Newport, Williamsville, and Port Penn. These schools have generally been well conducted, and attended with very satisfactory results. In their establishment the association was largely indebted to the Freedmen's Bureau, which contributed over $10,000 in furnishing building materials; and in their support it has, also, had the co-operation of the colored people themselves, who have contributed about $8,000 in payment of tuition, teachers' board, purchase of books, and erection of school buildings.

On the 3d of October, 1867, two normal schools, male and female, were opened in the old African Association building, which had been altered to suit their purposes. Of these schools Professor William Howard Day, an educated colored gentleman, who is superintendent of education under the Freedmen's Bureau for the States of Maryland and Delaware, speaks in very commendable terms. The following statistics for the years 1867 and 1868 present the educational work done in the State of Delaware during that period:

Number of schools, teachers, and pupils—1867-'68.

Year.	Number of schools.			Number of teachers.			Number of scholars.			Average attendance.	Per cent.
	Day.	Night.	Total.	White.	Colored.	Total.	Male.	Female.	Total.		
1867	20		20	4	16	20	269	443	712	581	81
1868	32	3	35	10	25	35	767	510	1,277	904	71

Studies and expenditures for schools—1867-'68.

Year.	Number of scholars in different studies pursued.							Expenditures in support of schools.		
	Alphabet.	Easy reading lessons.	Advanced readers.	Writing.	Geography.	Arithmetic.	Higher br's.	By freedmen.	By others.	Total.
1867	338	265	189	203	133	282		$5,800	$34,963	$40,763
1868	158	570	433	545	587	551	25	2,299	6,191	8,490

FLORIDA.

By the census of 1860 Florida had 140,425 inhabitants, of whom 62,677 were blacks, and of these 61,747 were slaves.

While Florida was still a Territory, in 1832, the immigration of any free negro or mulatto into its jurisdiction was forbidden by legal enactment; and at the same time an act was passed forbidding any of the same class of persons, resident in the Territory, "to assemble at any time or place" for any purpose except for labor—not even for a funeral. They might, however, "attend divine worship at any church, chapel, or other place of congregated white persons for that purpose."

In 1846, one year after the admission of Florida as a State, "all assemblies and congregations of slaves, free negroes, and mulattoes, consisting of four or more, met together in a confined or secret place," were declared to be unlawful, and the most stringent measures were used to prevent them; but no "church or place of public worship," where any religious society should be assembled, " a portion of whom" were white, could be broken into or disturbed " at any time before 10 o'clock in the evening."

December 28, 1848, an act was passed "to provide for the establishment of common schools," and giving to any person, liable to taxation on his property for the erection of school-houses, the right to vote at the district meetings; but white children only, of a specified age, were entitled to school privileges.

In the same year an act was passed providing that the school fund should consist of "the proceeds of the school lands," and of all estates, real or personal, escheating to the State, and " the proceeds of all property found on the coast or shores of the State." In 1850 the counties were authorized to provide, by taxation, not more than four dollars for each child within their limits of the proper school age. In the same year the amount received from the sale of any slave, under the act of 1829, was required to be added to the school fund. The common school law was revised in 1853, and the county commissioners were authorized to add from the county treasury any sum they thought proper for the support of common schools.

January 18, 1866, an act establishing common schools for freedmen was passed, providing for a tax of one dollar each upon "all male persons of color between the ages of 21 and 45" for the support of such schools, which were placed under the care of a superintendent appointed by the governor. In 1869, by act approved January 30, a common school law was established, in which no reference is made to the complexion of the pupils.

EDUCATION OF THE FREEDMEN.

Among the various agencies engaged in the work of educating the freedmen of the South are two consisting of colored people in the northern States, and known respectively as the African Civilization Society and the Home Missionary Society of the African Methodist Episcopal Church. Both of these societies have shown no lack of interest in the great matter of improving the condition of their formerly enslaved brethren, and both of them have labored zealously, as far as their means would permit, either independently or in co-operation with others, in the establishment of schools at different points in the southern States. Several of these schools were opened at Tallahassee and other places in Florida shortly after the close of the war, and have proved important and successful instrumentalities for good.

More sparsely settled than the other States, and lacking in the advantages of convenient roads, this State has not furnished so inviting a field to philanthropic effort as others; yet, in spite of these obstacles, the northern societies have not been without their representatives here, the New York branch of the American Freedmen's Union Commission having the greatest number of teachers employed in this section. As elsewhere, their labors have been blessed in the improvement of their pupils both in school learning and in the general conduct of life. Besides the schools already mentioned there were yet others, amounting, perhaps, to one-half of the entire number of schools in the State. These last were taught by freed persons who had acquired a little learning in their bondage. However poorly qualified they may have been to act as instructors, the existence of their schools was evidence both of their desire to labor in the elevation of their brethren and of the necessity felt by the latter for acquiring some knowledge, were it only the merest rudiments of learning. It is to be hoped, then, that even these schools were not wholly destitute of their wished-for fruit. Through the three several agencies already mentioned 30 schools were in existence in Florida at the close of 1865.

Early in the following year, January 16, 1866, the State legislature created a public

22

system of education for the freedmen of the State.   This enactment proivdes for the appointment of a superintendent, whose duty is to "establish schools for freedmen, when the
number of children of persons of color shall warrant the same," and to employ competent
teachers for them.   For the support of these schools it also provides that, besides a tuition
fee of 50 cents per month to be collected from each pupil, a fund, "to be denominated the
common school fund for the education of freedmen," shall be raised by levying a tax of $1
upon all male persons of color between the ages of 21 and 55 years.   The good effects of
this law were apparent in the increased number of schools during that year and the following.

The action of the legislature was heartily seconded by the freedmen themselves, who, in a
number of instances, erected school-houses at their own expense, besides contributing from
their scanty means towards the support of teachers.   Here, too, as in other States, the Freedmen's Bureau proved itself their efficient friend.   In order to enable them to secure for themselves school-houses as well as schools, it advised the formation of "school societies," and
suggested a course of procedure upon compliance with which its assistance would be extended
to them.   It stipulated that each society should acquire, by gift or purchase, the perfect title
to an eligible lot of ground not less than one acre in extent, to be vested in a board of trustees for school purposes, and that it should then secure good pledges of labor and money
sufficient to provide for all the work required in the erection of the school-house and in
making needed improvements of the property.   Upon these conditions it agreed to supply
all the lumber and other materials necessary for the construction of the building.   Not only
did the freedmen accede to this plan, but also quite a number of the landed proprietors entered
cordially into it, readily furnishing the school lots required.

The reports of 1868 showed, in the diminished number of schools, that Florida had not
been exempt from the sufferings which hard times had entailed upon other States.   With all
the advantages just mentioned, it became evident, in the stringency of money matters, that
its public school system, however judicious and commendable it may be, cannot be a complete success until years of patient and earnest labor shall be blessed with that prosperity
which such labor must inevitably secure.

The following table, compiled by Professor Vashon, presents the statistics of these
schools from 1865 to 1868 :

Number of schools, teachers, and scholars, 1865 to 1868.

Year.	Number of schools.			Number of teachers.			Number of scholars.			Average attendance.	Per cent.
	Day.	Night.	Total.	Whites.	Colored.	Total.	Male.	Female.	Total.		
1865			30			19			1,900		
1866			38			51			2,663		
1867	42	29	71	32	32	64	1,053	1,175	2,228	1,815	81
1868	33	21	54	24	37	61	1,032	1,150	2,182	1,619	74

Studies and expenditures, 1867 and 1868.

Year.	Number of scholars in different studies pursued.							Expenditures in support of schools.		
	Alphabet.	Easy reading.	Advanced reading.	Writing.	Geography.	Arithmetic.	Higher branches.	By freedmen.	By others.	Total.
1867	418	1,047	432	562	208	481	19	$608	$20,392	$21,000
1868	212	1,163	683	1,040	485	898	50	629	18,571	19,200

The State superintendent of public instruction, in a report submitted to Governor Reed January 9, 1869, remarks, respecting the schools conducted under the auspices of northern benevolent associations :

" Many of the ladies who assumed the duties of teachers were persons of wealth and high social positions at home. Coming at a time when the freed children were cast suddenly at the threshold of a new life, unused to the responsibilities and ignorant of the duties thus thrust upon them, they were welcomed with great joy, and labored with sincere Christian devotion, amidst hardships and privations. The teachers have changed, but most of the schools are still maintained."

GEORGIA.

By the census of 1860 the population of Georgia was 1,057,286; and of this number 465,698 were black, of whom all but 3,500 were slaves.

The Province of Georgia, in 1770, adopted the law of South Carolina, passed in 1740, providing a lighter penalty only for teaching slaves to write—a fine of £20 instead of £100. The same law provided that any magistrate or constable must " disperse any assembly or meeting of slaves which may disturb the peace and endanger the safety of his Majesty's subjects ;" and any slave found at such meeting might, by order of the magistrate, be immediately corrected, *without trial*, by whipping on the bare back " twenty-five stripes with a whip, switch, or cowskin." The reason for the passage of this provision of the law was, as stated, because " the frequent meeting of slaves, under the pretense of feasting, may be attended with dangerous consequences." The " feasting" referred to was the love feast of the Methodist church.

In 1829 the following law was enacted : " If any slave, negro, or free person of color, or any white person, shall teach any other slave, negro, or free person of color to read or write either written or printed characters, the said free person of color or slave shall be punished by fine and whipping, or fine or whipping, at the discretion of the court ; and if a white person so offend, he, she, or they shall be punished with a fine not exceeding $500 and imprisonment in the common jail at the discretion of the court."

In December, 1833, the penal code was consolidated, and in it a provision from the act of 1829 was embodied, providing a penalty not exceeding $100 for the employment of any slave or free person of color in setting up type or other labor about a printing office requiring a knowledge of reading or writing. This penal code continued in force until swept away by the events of the late war.

In 1833 the city of Savannah adopted an ordinance " that if any person shall teach or cause to be taught any slave or free person of color to read or write within the city, or who shall keep a school for that purpose, he or she shall be fined in a sum not exceeding $100 for each and every such offense ; and if the offender be a slave or free person of color he or she may also be whipped, not exceeding thirty-nine lashes." And yet, in the face of such ordinances, instruction was imparted by persons of color in the city of Savannah, and individuals were to be found who a few years later advocated a more humane and liberal policy toward the entire laboring class of the State.

In the summer of 1850 a series of articles by Mr. F. C. Adams appeared in one of the papers of Savannah, advocating the education of the negroes as a means of increasing their value and of attaching them to their masters. The subject was afterwards taken up in the Agricultural Convention which met at Macon in September of the same year. (See the Macon Journal and Messenger, Chapman, editor.) The matter was again brought up in September, 1851, in the Agricultural Convention, and after being debated, a resolution was passed that a petition be presented to the legislature for a law granting permission to educate the slaves. The petition was presented to the legislature, and Mr. Harlston introduced a bill in the winter of 1852, which was discussed and passed in the lower house, to repeal the old law, and to grant to the masters the privilege of educating their slaves. (See Milledgeville Recorder.) The bill was lost in the senate by two or three votes.

SCHOOLS FOR THE BLACKS IN GEORGIA.

The following account of the efforts to establish schools in Georgia since 1865 was prepared by Professor Vashon:

Among the many secret things brought to light by the opening of the southern prison-house, there was one at least which did not challenge the public regard by its atrocity, but rather by the evidence which it afforded of the futility of oppressive enactments in crushing out the soul's nobler aspirations. This was a school for colored persons in Savannah, Georgia. For upwards of 30 years it had existed there, unsuspected by the slave power, and sucessfully eluding the keen-eyed vigilance of its minions. Its teacher, a colored lady by the name of Deveaux, undeterred by any dread of penalties, throughout that long period silently pursued her labors in her native city, in the very same room that she still occupies; and she now has the satisfaction of knowing that numbers who are indebted to her for their early training are, in these more auspicious days, co-workers with her in the elevation of their common race. It is not a matter for surprise that a city favored with such an establishment as Miss Deveaux's should prove a field ripe for the harvesters, or that its colored residents should hail with appreciative joy the advent of a better time. Within a few days after the entrance of Sherman's army, in December, 1865, they opened a number of schools having an enrolment of 500 pupils, and contributed $1,000 for the support of teachers. In this spontaneous movement they were fortunate in having the advice and encouragement of the Rev. J. W. Alvord, then secretary of the Boston Tract Society, and of other friends who were with the invading forces. Two of the largest of these schools were in "Bryant's Slave Mart;" and thus the very walls which had, but a few days before, re-echoed with the anguish of bondmen put up for sale, now gave back the hushed but joyous murmurs of their children learning to read. In a very little while this effort attained to such a development as to compel an appeal for outside assistance. To the Macedonian cry, "Come over and help us," the American Missionary Association and also the Boston and New York societies responded, both by sending additional teachers and by engaging to pay the salaries of those already on the ground. Schools were also established at Augusta, Macon, and other places thoughout the State; so that, at the close of the year, there were 69 schools in existence, with as many teachers, 43 of whom were colored, and with over 3,600 pupils in attendance.

The same spirit that prompted the negroes of Georgia to open these schools was still manifested by them in a continuance and enlargement of the good work. In January, 1866, they organized the Georgia Educational Association, whose object was to induce the freedmen to establish and support schools in their own counties and neighborhoods; and, in furtherance of this end, it provided for the formation of subordinate associations throughout the State. The purpose of its projectors was to act in harmony with agencies already in the field, with the educational officers of the Freedmen's Bureau, and with all other parties who were willing to assist them in the moral and mental culture of their race. Thus, they hoped, by this union of effort, to accomplish much immediate good, and to lay deeply and permanently the foundation of a system of public instruction which should, in time, place an education within the reach of all the citizens of Georgia. The plan thus proposed met with an approving response from the people, and schools were rapidly opened in many counties of the State. In many quarters, however, great opposition was offered to this new order of things; and the newspapers, in alluding to the female teachers, would descend to the most abusive ribaldry. In frequent instances, too, this opposition did not stop short of acts of violence and outrage. During the year 1866 seven school buildings were destroyed by white incendiaries; and, at a number of points, teachers were forced either to close their schools or to appeal to the bureau for protection. In the following year, however, Mr. G. L. Eberhart, the State superintendent of education under the bureau, reported a wonderful change in this matter, in the following words: "At the beginning of the current school year scarcely any white persons could be found who were willing to '*disgrace*' themselves by '*teaching niggers*;' but, as times grew hard, and money and bread scarce, applications for employment became so numerous that I was obliged to prepare a printed letter with which to answer them. Lawyers, physicians, editors, ministers, and all classes of white people applied for employment; and while a few by their letters evinced only tolerable qualifications —none of them first class—a vast majority were unable to write grammatically or to spell the most simple and common words in our language correctly. Not a few appeared to think that ' *anybody can teach niggers.*'" This change in popular sentiment rendered it possible to establish schools to a much greater extent in the country districts; and the result was that at the close of the school year, in 1867, 191 day schools and 45 night schools were reported as existing. Of these schools 96 were supported either wholly or in part by freedmen, who also owned 57 of the school buildings. The poverty which had contributed so much towards diminishing the prejudices of the white residents, had, on the other hand, an unfavorable effect on the prosperity of the schools. Through its pressure many of the subordinate societies ceased to exist, and the schools supported by them were discontinued; and as the northern associations deemed it to be the better policy to confine their work to the cities in the training of prospective teachers, the rural districts suffered somewhat, and the exhibit of schools for 1868 was about 100 less than in the preceding year. Some compensation for this, however, was found in the establishment by the American Missionary Association of three permanent institutions of a higher grade, with brief notices of which this sketch shall be closed.

THE GEORGIA UNIVERSITY, ATLANTA.

Early in the year 1867 the Georgia University was incorporated, $10,000 having been contributed from the educational fund of the Freedmen's Bureau towards establishing its normal department. A desirable tract of land, consisting of 53 acres within the city limits, and known as Diamond Hill, was purchased and two brick buildings erected thereon. These are to be used as dormitories, after the completion of the main edifice, which it is the intention of the trustees to put up at as early a date as their means will permit.

THE BEACH INSTITUTE, SAVANNAH.

The Beach Institute, at Savannah, was established in 1867, and was thus named in honor of Alfred E. Beach, esq., editor of the Scientific American, who generously donated the means for purchasing the lot upon which it stands; and it is a neat and substantial frame structure, erected by the Freedmen's Bureau at a cost of $13,000. This building, which rests upon brick foundations, is 55 feet by 60 feet, and has, at the north and south ends, two Ls, each 10 feet by 35 feet. On the first floor are four large school-rooms, all of which can be converted into one when desired, by means of sliding doors and windows. Four other school-rooms and an ante-room are on the second floor. All of these rooms have high ceilings, and are well lighted, and furnished with substantial desks, seats, black-boards, &c. A staircase at each end furnishes ready egress from the upper story. On the east side of this building stands the "Teachers' Home," a neat and comfortably arranged two-story frame house, erected by the association at a cost of $3,000. There are 600 pupils in the institution, which is under the charge of Mr. O. W. Dimick, assisted by nine female teachers, eight of whom are white and one colored.

THE LEWIS SCHOOL, MACON.

The Lewis School, at Macon, was dedicated, with appropriate exercises, to God, and to the Christian education of the freed people of Georgia, on the 26th day of March, 1866. It is named in honor of General John R. Lewis, inspector of the Freedmen's Bureau, and is a handsome two-story building 80 feet long by 60 in width, affording accommodations for over 500 pupils. The school-rooms are neatly finished with Georgia pine, and furnished with cherry desks, and all the other most approved modern educational appliances. With a corps of teachers, intelligent, refined, and thoroughly capable, there is no doubt that the Lewis School will justly continue to be, as it is now the pride of its founders and of the colored people of Macon.

Number of schools, teachers, and pupils—1865-'68.

Year.	Number of schools.			Number of teachers.			Number of scholars.			Average attendance.	Per cent.
	Day.	Night.	Total.	White.	Colored.	Total.	Male.	Female.	Total.		
1865...........	....	....	69	26	43	69	....	....	3,603	....	....
1866...........	....	....	79	....	....	113	....	....	7,792	....	....
1867...........	191	45	236	148	91	239	6,033	7,448	13,481	10,231	76
1868...........	103	26	132	127	47	174	4,035	4,507	8,542	6,708	78

Studies and expenditures—1867-'68.

Year.	Number of scholars in different studies pursued.								Expenditures in support of schools.		
	Alphabet.	Easy reading.	Advanced readers.	Writing.	Geography	Arithmetic.	Higher branches.		By freedmen.	By others.	Total.
1867..............	2,600	8,987	2,318	3,020	1,854	2,810	139		$35,224	$40,000	$91,096
1868..............	1,560	4,592	2,366	3,573	2,361	3,102	253		21,596	31,000	52,596

ILLINOIS.

Out of a total population of 1,711,951 in 1860 there were returned 7,628 free colored inhabitants. By the constitution of 1847 the right of suffrage is restricted to white male citizens, and the benefits of the school law are by implication extended exclusively to children of white parents. Hon. Newton Bateman, in his exhaustive, elaborate, and every way excellent report as superintendent of public instruction, submitted to the governor December 15, 1868, introduces the subject of schools for the colored population, as follows:

"The number of colored persons in the State under 21 years of age, as reported for 1867, was 8,962, and the number reported for 1868 was 9,781. The number between the ages of 6 and 21 years, or of lawful school age, was in 1867, 5,492, and in 1868 the number of school-going colored children reported in the State was 6,210.   *   *   *

"I have made every effort to obtain reliable statistics in respect to this element of our population, but there is good reason to believe that the actual number of colored persons in the State is much greater than is exhibited in the above statement. As children of color are not included in the numerical basis upon which either the county superintendent or the township trustees apportion the school fund, there is no special or pecuniary motive to care and diligence in taking this census, as there is in taking that of white children, as previously shown. Indifference and other causes have also operated, in some portions of the State, to prevent a faithful effort to collect and report the desired information in regard to these people. Taking the figures as reported and comparing them, it will be seen that the number of colored persons under 21 has increased 1,565, or over 18 per centum, in the last two years; and that the number between 6 and 21 has increased 1,279, or 26 per centum. I have no doubt that the actual number of colored children in the State, between 6 and 21, is at least 7,000, and probably more. Indeed this is demonstrated from the statistics which are given. The number under 21 reported is 9,781. Of these, the number under six must be deducted. The ratio of 6 to 21 is two-sevenths; hence, the number between 6 and 21 should be very nearly five-sevenths of the whole number under 21; but five-sevenths of 9,781 is 6,987, being an inconsiderable fraction under 7,000. While, for reasons previously given, the number reported as under 21 is undoubtedly too small, yet, being more easily taken than the number between 6 and 21, it is no doubt the more nearly correct of the two. At all events, it is not too large, and if there are 9,731 colored people in the State under 21, it is absolutely certain that there are not less than 7,000 between 6 and 21, being a little less than one per centum of the number of white children between the same ages."

"In remarking upon the condition of these people in respect to school privileges, in the last biennial report, the following language was used: 'For the education of these 6,000 colored children the general school law of the State makes, virtually, no provision. By the discriminating terms employed throughout the statute, it is plainly the intention to exclude them from a joint participation in the benefits of the free school system. Except as referred to by the terms which imply exclusion, and in one brief section of the act, they are wholly ignored in all the common school legislation of the State. The purport of that one section (the 80th) is that the amount of all school taxes collected from persons of color shall be paid back to them; it does not say what use shall be made of the money so refunded, although the intention (if there was any) may be presumed to be that it should be used for separate schools for colored children. But if that was the object it has not been attained, except in a few instances, for two reasons: first, the school taxes paid by persons of color are not generally returned to them; and, second, even when they are refunded, there are not colored children enough, except in a few places, to form separate schools. In some of the cities and larger towns, where the schools are under special acts and municipal ordinances, the education of colored children is provided for in a manner worthy a just and Christian people; and in many other instances the requirements of the law are faithfully observed, and the efforts of the colored people to provide schools for their children are heartily seconded. But the larger portion of the aggregate number of colored people in the State are dispersed through the different counties and school districts, in small groups of one, two, or three families, not enough to maintain separate schools for themselves, even with the help of the pittance paid for school taxes by such of them as are property holders. This whole dispersed class of our colored population are without the means of a common school education for their children; the law does not contemplate their co-attendance with white children, and they are without recourse of any kind. I think it safe to say that at least one-half of the 6,000 colored children, between the ages of 6 and 21, are in this helpless condition with respect to schools. They are trying, by conventions, petitions, and appeals, to reach the ears and hearts of the representatives of the people and the law-making power of the State, to see if anything can be done for them. I have tried to state their case; I think it is a hard one. I commend the subject to the attention of the general assembly, as demanding a share of public regard.'

" I desire again to call attention to the fact that, as I understand the law, those people are excluded from all participation in the benefits of the public schools, except by common consent, or as a matter of sufferance. The recurrence throughout the statute of the restrictive word 'white' leaves no room for doubt that it was the intention to provide for the education of white children only, in the free schools of the State, and upon this principle the school law has been interpreted, and the system administered, from the first. I approve the resolution adopted by the State Teachers' Association, 'that the distinctive word "white," in the school law and the 80th section of the same, are contrary to the true intent of the principle on which the school system is based, and should be repealed.' I regard the longer presence in the school law of this great and free commonwealth, of provisions which now exclude 7,000 children of lawful school age from all the blessings of public education, and which, if not repealed, will continue to exclude them and the thousands which may hereafter be added to the number, as alike impolitic and unjust; the opprobium and shame of our otherwise noble system of free schools. No State can afford to defend or perpetuate such provisions, and least of all the State that holds the dust of the fingers that wrote the proclamation of January 1, 1863. Let us expunge this last remaining remnant of the unchristian 'black laws' of Illinois and proclaim in the name of God and the Declaration of Independence, that *all* the school-going children of the State, without distinction, shall be equally entitled to share in the rich provisions of the free school system. Nor need any one be scared by the phantom of blended colors in the same school-room. The question of co-attendance, or of separate schools, is an entirely separate and distinct one, and may safely be left to be determined by the respective districts and communities to suit themselves. In many places there will be but one school for all; in many others there will be separate schools.. That is a matter of but little importance, and one which need not and cannot be regulated by legislation. Only drive the spirit of caste from its *intrenchments in the statute*, giving all equal educational rights *under the law*, and the consequences will take care of themselves.''

COLORED SCHOOLS IN CHICAGO.

From the following note of Mr. Packard, superintendent of public schools in Chicago, addressed to the State superintendent of public instruction in Indiana, it appears that the experiment of a separate school for the colored children was tried without satisfactory results. Why the school was abolished by the legislature does not appear:

"For one year, 1864 and 1865, the experiment of a separate colored school was tried. The school was disorderly and much trouble existed in the vicinity of the school. The legislature in 1864–'5 abolished this school, and since that time colored children have been admitted to the public schools on an equality with other children. Not a word of complaint has come, with perhaps one or two individual exceptions, arising from seating pupils—a matter which is easily remedied. Colored children are admitted to our high school: one graduated last year; others will graduate this year. All difficulty with the children of color has disappeared, except such as may be common to all children who have had no better advantages than themselves; we certainly have less frequent complaints than in the separate system.''

INDIANA.

By the census of 1860 the population of Indiana was 1,350,428, and of this number 11,428 were free colored; and towards this class a violent and persistent hostile legislation has been pursued from the earliest history of the State.

The constitution in 1851 provides that "no negro or mulatto shall have the right of suffrage" and after the date of its adoption, "no negro or mulatto shall come into or settle in the State," and "all contracts made with such persons are declared void;" and "any person who shall employ such negro or mulatto, or otherwise encourage him to remain in the State, shall be fined in any sum not less than $10 nor more than $500, such fines to be appropriated to the colonization of such negroes as desire to leave the State." The general assembly are directed to pass laws to give effect to these provisions. The utterly un-American, undemocratic and unchristian character of these provisions has been frequently exposed, and particularly by the State superintendents of public instruction. Professor Hoss, in his report to the general assembly dated December 31, 1866, remarks:

"I am fully aware of the public sensitiveness on this subject, hence conscious of the difficulty of preventing it. If the time ever was in Indiana when it was honestly believed, that the colored man could be kept out of the State by stringent legislation, that time has passed and that belief cannot exist now, unless in an illiberal or prejudiced mind. The severe logic of events proves the truth of this assertion. These events and agencies, such as the abolition of slavery, the enactment of the civil rights bill, the nullification of the 13th article of the constitution of Indiana, and the changed and changing tone of public sentiment concerning the colored man, are all of too recent a date and of too great a magnitude to require presentation here.

"Therefore, whereas it is clear, first, that the colored man is to remain with us, i. e., in our State; second, that he is being, and is to be, clothed with new and larger powers of citizenship, it follows that he is becoming a greater force in both society and the State. Any force generated in, or injected into, the social or political organism at once suggests the necessity of guidance or control; uncontrolled, evil if not ruin will ensue. But in a popular government like ours, human force in the aspect now under consideration is most easily controlled for the good of society and the State when the party possessing and exerting such force is educated. The constitution of our State broadly and explicitly recognizes the above truth as applied to governments. The constitution holds the following: 'knowledge and learning generally diffused throughout a community, being *essential* (italicizing mine) to the preservation of a free government,' it becomes the duty of the legislature to provide a system of common schools and other means of securing popular intelligence, also to encourage 'moral, intellectual, and scientific improvement.'

"Therefore, the above granted true, it follows that the welfare of the government, i. e., the State, requires the education of all the community, hence of the colored man. A non-sequitur can hardly be pleaded here by saying the negro is not a citizen. If such were true, it is not material to the argument, as the constitution speaks not narrowly of citizens only, but of members of community in general. Hence under the narrowest logic and most prejudiced definition of terms, the constitution includes the colored man as an element of that community throughout which 'knowledge and learning are to be diffused.' Therefore, the above true, the constitution seems clearly to contemplate the education of colored children.

"But, granting the above all true, we are in the lower story of the argument, namely, among policies and expediencies, which look to the 'preservation of a free government.' Let none suppose that I do not regard this a great, a glorious object. It is both great and glorious, yet justice may be as great and glorious.

"The question occurs, how far justice will sustain the State in closing, or at least refusing to open, the avenues of knowledge to the eager minds of several thousand members of the community.

"Independent of recent events, I submit that these children are as clearly entitled to their share of the congressional township revenue as any children in the State. Congress in granting this land did not use the now ambiguous term 'citizen,' but the plainer term 'inhabitant,' saying that 'section numbered 16 in every township   *   *   *   shall be granted to the inhabitants of such township for the use of schools.' Consequently, every colored child resident of the State, being an 'inhabitant' of some one of the congressional townships, is entitled to its pro rata of the congressional revenue of that township.

"Second and higher, I suppose it will be granted that there are claims higher than the claims of mere inhabitancy, namely the claims of a human being as such. The claims of a colored man are the claims of a human being with human responsibilities, human aspirations, with human hopes and sympathies, and bearing as others bear, marred by sin, the image of his Creator. Hence both State policy and justice say that he should be educated.

"Deference to the extreme sensitiveness of public opinion may say, wait for a more opportune time. If it be true that this be not the time, the time is coming, and coming surely if not speedily. 'The mills of God grind slowly, but surely.' Justice, like truth, bides her time, but executes her mission.

"If the legislature shall deem it wise to inaugurate a movement looking to the above end, I would respectfully submit the following in aid of this result :

"1. That the school trustees open separate schools for colored children, when a given number of such children of school age reside within attending distance. Probably that number could not safely be less than 15.

"2. In case in any neighborhood the number of children be less than 15, then the distributive share of revenue due each colored child shall be set apart for the education of such child in such manner as the proper school trustee shall provide.

"3. Make it specially obligatory upon the trustee to make some provision for the education of the children to the extent of the money set apart for the same, as provided in case second."

Mr. Hobbs, in his annual report submitted December 31, 1868, remarks:

"We cannot avoid the grave consideration, that there is a large colored population in the State who have hitherto submitted patiently to the ordeal of adverse public sentiment and the force of our statutes, in being denied participation in the benefits of our public school funds, while at the same time no bar can be discovered to their natural and constitutional right to them. By the grants of Congress, whence mainly we derive these funds, no exclusion is made. They were evidently designed for the citizens of the State without regard to color. Whatever additions our States may have made, they are still known as one 'common school fund.' But whatever distinctions may have been made in the rights and privileges of citizens by our laws, they have been set aside by the emendations of our national constitution and the 'civil rights bill.' All citizens are now equal before the law. Colored citizens, while hitherto deprived of their natural and constitutional rights, have been *subject to the special school tax* for township purposes in common with *white citizens*, and have thus paid their proportion of expense for building school-houses for white children. After being denied all privilege to the school funds and thus taxed, they have been under the necessity of levying on themselves an additional tax to build their own school-houses and for the entire cost of their tuition. The historian will find this a dark chapter in our history.

"Whatever elements of ignorance and incompetency the population of a State may contain, is so much that may damage its prosperity and safety. How can we inspire these people with gratitude and patriotism, and win them to the support of law and virtue, when we repel them by cold indifference and deny them their natural and constitutional rights ?"

To reach a safe decision, founded on the experience of other States, as to the true policy of dealing with this portion of the population, the superintendent ascertained by correspondence the practice of other free States in this regard, and finds that "Illinois and Indiana are alone of States north of Mason and Dixon's line" in denying educational privileges to colored citizens, and urges that "the deeply seated prejudices in the minds of many citizens should yield to duty, justice, and humanity."

IOWA.

Iowa had in 1860 a population of 674,913 inhabitants, of whom 1,069 were free blacks. By the constitution of 1857 the right of suffrage was limited to white male citizens; "but by sundry amendments," writes the late Franklin D. Wells, superintendent of public instruction, to the superintendent of schools in Indiana, "to our State constitution submitted to the people, and by them adopted at the election on the 3d of November, 1868, by nearly 30,000 majority, a man's rights and privileges are no longer determined by the color of his skin. Colored citizens of Iowa are entitled to vote, to hold office, and hold property ; are a part of the militia, and are entitled to the benefits of our public school system on the same footing with white citizens. Wherever the word 'white' occurred in the constitution it has been stricken out."

KANSAS.

In 1860 Kansas had a population of 107,206, of which number 625 were free colored persons.

By the constitution adopted July 29, 1861, the right of suffrage is restricted to white male persons; but the first school law provides that equal educational advantages "shall be extended to all children in the State." A clause in the law leaves it to the discretion of the board of directors to establish separate schools for the colored children ; but the legislature, in 1867, provided that when any children are denied admittance to a public school by vote or action of the directors, the members of such board shall each pay a fine of $100 for any school month the children are thus excluded.

The people of this State have from its earliest settlement been imbued with the spirit of freedom ; and their legislation in reference to educational matters has consequently been free from invidious discriminations as to the several races. Their schools are generally open to black and to white children alike ; and it is only at a few points, where large numbers of negro emigrants are to be found, that schools for colored children exist separately. About 15 of these schools have been established and maintained through benevolent agencies ; among which may be mentioned the American Missionary Association, the Michigan and the Northwestern branches of the American Freedmen's Union Commission, and the General Assembly of the Presbyterian church, old school. The last of these, operating through a standing committee originally formed in 1864, and reorganized in the following year, has labored with praiseworthy efficiency not only in this State but also in Tennessee, Virginia, Maryland, North Carolina, South Carolina, Georgia, Arkansas, and the District of Columbia. Its mission in Kansas is located at Quindaro, where, under the superintendence of the Rev. E. Blachly, D. D.,

THE QUINDARO HIGH SCHOOL

has been established. This institution, situated on the western bank of the Missouri river, and on the line of the Pacific railroad, is readily accessible from every quarter. In the face of great discouragements it has gone quietly forward, and had, at the date of its last catalogue, 180 students, 95 of whom were males and 85 females. Colonel F. A. Seely, the superintendent of education under the Freedmen's Bureau, in speaking of this institution says : "In respect to orderly conduct, thoroughness of instruction, and advancement in study, this school is unsurpassed." It is the purpose of its trustees to establish a department of theological instruction, and to this end they are desirous to secure the services of an efficient teacher in that branch. The property of the institution, valued at $6,200, consists at present of a commodious seminary building and three dwelling houses for teachers. Besides this, the trustees hope to secure 200 acres of land, so as to add a manual labor feature to their promising institution.

KENTUCKY.

Out of a population of 1,555,684, in 1860, 336,167 were blacks, and of these 10,684 were free and 225,483 were slaves.

In 1738 Kentucky was included in what was then formed into the county of Augusta, in Virginia. In 1769 Botetourt county was cut off from the county of Augusta ; in 1772 Fincastle was cut off from Botetourt ; and in 1776, the first year of the commonwealth of Virginia, Fincastle was divided into three counties, Washington, Montgomery, and Kentucky, the latter constituting what is now the State, and which was originally the hunting and battle ground of the savages, north and south, from whom it received the name Cane-tuck-ee, signifying "the dark and bloody ground."

In the compact with Virginia, in 1789, by which Kentucky was empowered to originate an independent State, "free male inhabitants above the age of 21 years" were designated as electors ; and the constitution, adopted June 1, 1800, declared "every free male citizen, negroes, mulattoes, and Indians excepted," of the age of 21 years, to be electors. It also prohibited the emancipation of slaves by the general assembly, without the consent of the owner, but gave to slaves the right of "an impartial trial by a petty jury" in charges of felony.

The first legislation in the State, on the subject of the colored people, declared that no persons should be slaves in the State, except those who were slaves on the 17th of October, 1785, and their descendants ; and in other respects the laws were essentially the same as those of Virginia, in relation to the colored population, until 1792. In 1816, and also in 1830, stringent laws were enacted to prevent cruelty in the treatment of slaves, and in 1833 the importation of slaves was forbidden under a penalty of $600 for each offense. No laws are found on the statute books of Kentucky forbidding the instruction of slaves.

In 1830 a school system was established, by which school districts had the power to tax the inhabitants of the district for school purposes. In this provision the property of colored people was included, although they could not vote nor have the benefits of the school. The provision for a full tax not exceeding 50 cents was, however, confined to "every *white* male inhabitant over 20 years of age; but the right to vote in the school district meeting was in certain cases extended to white females over 21 years of age. The Revised Statutes of 1852 provided that "any widow, having a child between six and 18 years of age should be allowed to vote in person, or by written proxy." But colored children were excluded from the district school, even though their parents were taxed for its support.

In 1864 the school laws were revised, but the benefits of the system were still confined to free white children. In 1867, however, an act was passed and approved March 9, "for the benefit of the negroes and mulattoes" of the State, providing that all taxes collected from negroes and mulattoes shall be set apart and constitute a separate fund for their use, one-half, if necessary, to be applied to the support of their paupers and the remainder to the education of their children. An additional tax of $2 was also to be levied upon every male negro 18 years of age, for this fund. Separate schools may be established in each district, for the support of which they are to receive their proportion of the appropriate fund. As to the operation of this law the State superintendent, (Z. F. Smith,) in his annual report, dated March 25, 1868, remarks as follows:

"The new law, approved March 9, 1867, has not operated to the satisfaction of its framers, as was hoped. I think the following extract from a letter of one of our commissioners explains the chief ground of difficulty:

"'There were no colored schools taught in my county in 1867, under the supervision of trustees; consequently none reported. The trustees have all been apprised of the fact that the law makes it their duty to have colored schools taught. But they reply "the law says they *may* have, but don't say they *shall* have, colored schools taught in their districts." The trustees therefore are perfectly indifferent in regard to colored schools.'"

"There is nothing obligatory in the law making the trustees responsible for neglecting its enforcement. They have no personal interest in its operations, and to leave its execution to the chance impulses of the spirit of philanthropy is a very doubtful reliance for the application of a general law. The difficulties are magnified, also, by the fact that there exists yet in some quarters much of morbid and unreasonable prejudice against legislating in any way for the benefit of the colored population, and especially for the education of their children. Trustees do not like always to encounter this prejudice, especially when they conclude that they have no personal interest in so doing, and the law is left to become a dead letter.

"I prepared some amendments to the law, which, I thought, would make it practicable and efficient; but these did not seem to meet the approval generally of the legislators, and were not adopted. But another amendment was introduced, and became a law, which requires all the revenues from taxes collected of negroes and mulattoes to be used, first, for pauper purposes; and, if there should be any excess, for school purposes. The amendment is published as part of this report. With the embarrassing provisions of the original law, it virtually destroys the practicability of existing legislation to furnish the colored people with any educational advantages. I think there is little hope of accomplishing anything for the education of the negroes until a law, independent of any pauper scheme, is passed, and the execution of such law left, in its details, to agencies from among their own people."

SCHOOLS FOR FREEDMEN.

The attempts to establish schools for colored children have encountered greater obstacles, perhaps, in Kentucky than in any other of the former slave States. As it did not engage in the rebellion as a State, slavery only ceased there upon the official announcement, on the 10th day of December, 1865; and until then no colored child within its limits was by law permitted to go to school. On account of its *quasi* loyalty, the Freedmen's Bureau has had but little power there, while the opposition prompted by intense local prejudice to the education of the blacks has deterred northern benevolent societies from sending their teachers to a quarter where they could not expect adequate protection. Then, too, the freedmen who had enlisted in great numbers in the Union army returned to their homes at the close of the war, with a manful worthiness well attested by courage on the battle-field, and by their eager desire for mental improvement, but hampered by a degree of poverty that hindered them in many instances from doing anything to secure instruction for themselves or their children. Yet, in spite of all these obstacles, the educational work which had been begun in the camps of colored troops, at such brief intervals as are afforded by a soldier's life, found its continuance, on the return of peace and the subsequent proclamation of liberty.   More than 30 schools with an attendance of over 4,000 pupils were soon in operation at different points in the State.   Most of these schools were taught by colored teachers, and mainly supported by the freed people themselves.   In Lexington, Frankfort, Danville, and, perhaps, one or two other places, public opinion looked somewhat favorably upon this innovation ; but elsewhere great opposition to it was manifested not only in opprobrious words, but often in acts of violence.   Still, in the face of all these discouragements, the work of enlightenment went on increasing, until, at the close of the school-year in 1868, 178 schools were reported in Kentucky, with an enrolment of 8,189 pupils.

For a time it seemed that liberal views would influence the legislation of this State in behalf of the education of its freedmen.   By an act approved February 16, 1866, it was provided that the taxes collected from negroes and mulattoes should be " set apart as a separate fund for their use, one-half, if necessary, to go to the support of their paupers, and the remainder to the education of their children."   Under this law, which permitted separate schools for colored children, but failed to make their establishment obligatory, a few hundred dollars were appropriated in accordance with its provisions, during the year following its enactment.   In 1867, it was amended so as to entitle each colored child attending school for at least three months during the year to receive $2 50 from taxes collected within its county. But the assembly of 1868 rescinded the doings of the preceding assemblies and directed that all taxes collected from negroes and mulattoes should be devoted only to the support of their paupers.

It is well that in this desert there is an oasis or two for the eye to rest upon.   Such an oasis is

BEREA COLLEGE.

Berea College was established in Madison county in 1858, and which was an outgrowth of the missionary work of the Rev. John G. Fee, a native Kentuckian, and of his co-laborers, under the care of the American Missionary Association.   From its commencement its founders took quiet but firm ground against the spirit of caste ; and it is, therefore, not to be wondered at that in the popular agitation consequent on the John Brown raid this school fell a prey to lawless fanaticism.   Its teachers were driven into exile and its students scattered.   The rebellion soon followed ; and, after the war which crushed out both the rebellion and slavery, its cause, most of the Berea exiles returned to their homes.   The school was re-opened January 1, 1866 ; and, although its trustees steadfastly adhered to their position not to tolerate distinctions of color and race, its success has exceeded the sanguine expectations of its friends.   The last catalogue showed 301 students in attendance, about one-third of whom were white, and the remainder colored.

Berea College has an able corps of instructors, made up as follows, viz : Rev. J. G. Fee, A. M., president and lecturer on Biblical Antiquities and the Evidences of Christianity.

Rev. J. A. R. Rogers, A. M., principal, and teacher of Latin and Mathematics.

Rev. W. E. Lincoln, teacher of Greek, Rhetoric, &c.

Teachers : Mrs. Louie M. Lincoln, Miss Eliza M. Snedeker, Miss Louisa Kaiser, Miss Jennie Donaldson.

THE ELY NORMAL SCHOOL, LOUISVILLE.

The Ely normal school was formally dedicated April 6, 1868, with appropriate exercises, including addresses by the Rev. Messrs. Hayward, Cravath, Right Rev. B. B. Smith, Bishop of Kentucky, the Hon. Bland Ballard, the Hon. James Speed, and others.   It received its name in compliment to General John Ely, who, as chief superintendent of freedmen's affairs, first organized the bureau in this State, and by faithful labors in behalf of the freedmen, both in redressing their wrongs and in securing their just prerogatives, had merited their lasting gratitude.

This school is delightfully situated.   It is located on a corner lot having one front of 100 feet on Broadway, the finest street in the city, and another of 220 feet on 14th street.   In point of convenience and simple architectural beauty the building has no superior in the city. It is a two-storied structure, built of the best quality of brick, is 50 by 70 feet in extent, and contains nine rooms suitably furnished for its purposes. The total cost of this handsome property was $20,000, of which sum the government appropriated the sum of $12,300.

This institution is under the control of the American Missionary Association, and has an attendance of over 400 pupils. Mr. A. H. Robbins, a graduate of Oberlin College is its superintendent.

The following tables, prepared by Professor Vashon, give the number of scholars and attendance, as well as teachers and studies for 1867–'68.

Table giving the number of schools, teachers, scholars, and attendance.

Year.	Number of schools.			Number of teachers.			Number of scholars.			Average attendance.	Per cent.
	Day.	Night.	Total.	White.	Colored.	Total.	Male.	Female.	Total.		
1866.........	....	....	35	....	....	58	....	....	4,122	....	......
1867.........	88	14	107	36	98	124	2,765	3,606	6,371	5,396	84
1868.........	155	23	178	37	155	190	3,741	4,441	8,182	6,236	76

Table showing the number in different studies, and cost of maintaining schools.

Year.	Number of scholars in different studies pursued.							Expended in support of schools.		
	Alphabet.	Easy reading.	Advanced reading.	Writing.	Geography.	Arithmetic.	Higher branches.	By freedmen.	By others.	Total.
1867..............	834	3,160	1,883	2,310	1,332	2,355	388	$21,736	$10,027	$31,763
1868..............	984	3,584	2,476	2,810	1,770	2,810	490	17,138	20,996	38,134

LOUISIANA.

By the census of 1860 there were 708,002 inhabitants, of whom nearly one-half were blacks, viz: 331,726 slaves, and 18,647 free ; a total of 350,373.

By the treaty of Paris, April 30, 1803, for the purchase of the province of Louisiana, it was stipulated that "the inhabitants of the ceded territory" should be admitted to "all the rights, advantages, and immunities of *citizens* of the United States." As early as January, 1805, a law was enacted by the territorial legislature of Orleans, containing a provision as to the mode of selling slaves at auction ; and in May of that year an act was passed "for the punishment of crimes and misdemeanors," which declared that nothing in the act should be construed to extend to slaves, but that they should be punished for the specified offenses by "the laws of Spain for regulating her colonies." The "Black Code," approved June 7, 1806, was rigorous, but protected slaves from outrage. By it slaves were to have the enjoyment of Sundays ; or, if employed, to receive 50 cents a day. But by the same code it was declared that "no slave can possess anything in his own right or dispose of the proceeds of his industry without the consent of his master." No slave was permitted to go out of the plantation to which he belonged without written permission, under a penalty of 20 lashes. Free people of color were never "to presume to conceive themselves equal to the whites ; but they ought to yield to them in every occasion, and never speak to or answer them disrespectfully," under the penalty of imprisonment, according to the nature of the offense ;" for the third offense of striking a white man, the slave might suffer death.

In 1814 a law was passed forbidding any free negro or mulatto to settle in the Territory, or remain in it more than two weeks after coming into it from another State ; and as a penalty, if unable to pay the fine and costs, he was to be sold to pay them.

Louisiana was admitted into the Union April 30, 1812, and in September of that year an act was passed authorizing the organization of "a corps of militia," from among the free creoles who had paid a State tax. The commander of the corps was to be a white man, and the corps was to consist of four companies of 64 men each. In January, 1815, "an auxiliary troop of free men of color" was authorized to be raised in the parish of Natchitoches, not exceeding 80 men, who were to furnish themselves with arms and horses. Each member of the corps was to be the owner or the son of the owner "of some real property of the value of at least $150." In 1830 the prohibitions of the act of 1814 against the immigration of free people of color were re-asserted, with additional provisions of greater rigor. This act also provided that whoever should "write, print, publish, or distribute anything having a tendency to produce discontent among the free colored population, or insubordination among the slaves," should, on conviction, be imprisoned "at hard labor for life, or suffer death, at the discretion of the court." Whoever used language having a similar tendency, or was "instrumental in bringing into the State any paper, book, or pamphlet having such tendency," was to "suffer imprisonment at hard labor, not less than three years nor more than 21 years, or death, at the discretion of the court." It was also provided that "all persons who shall teach, or permit or cause to be taught, any slave to read or write, shall be imprisoned not less than one month nor more than 12 months."

From the headquarters, seventh military district, at Mobile, on the 21st of September, 1814, General Andrew Jackson addressed a proclamation to the free colored inhabitants of Louisiana, inviting them to participate in the military movements of that section of the country, "as a faithful return for the advantages enjoyed under her mild and equitable government," with the same pay in bounty money and land received by white soldiers. On the 18th of December he reviewed the troops, white and colored, and in the address calculated to awaken their enthusiastic ardor, he said to the colored soldiers: "I expected much from you, for I was not uninformed of those qualities which must render you so formidable to an invading foe. I knew that you could endure hunger and thirst, and all the hardships of war. I knew that you loved the land of your nativity, and that, like ourselves, you had to defend all that is most dear to man. But you surpass my hopes. I have found in you, united to those qualities, that noble enthusiasm which impels to great deeds."

In 1847 a system of public schools for "the education of white youth" was established, by which "one mill on the dollar, upon the *ad valorem* amount of the general list of taxable property," might be levied for its support. The income from the sale of the public lands donated by Congress was given for the same purpose. In 1857 an act was passed forbidding the emancipation of slaves; and this was the last legislation on the subject previous to the rebellion.

By the act of January 3, 1864, the article of the then existing civil code which declared that there were in the State "two classes of servants, to wit, free servants and the slaves," was changed so as to declare "there is only one class of servants in this State, to wit, free servants." In 1867 an act establishing a system of free schools in Baton Rouge limited the taxation for their support and their benefits to the white population. By the constitution, ratified April 23, 1868, all discrimination based on race, color, or previous condition, are prohibited in the public schools. Under the operations of this provision $70,000 were appropriated to the support of schools for colored children.

FREEDMEN'S SCHOOLS.

For the following account and tables of the schools for colored children in Louisiana, since 1865, we are indebted to Professor Vashon:

Prior to the rebellion the only schools for colored children in Louisiana, were a few private ones in the city of New Orleans, among that somewhat favored class of mixed blood known as "Creoles." Even these schools, although not in contravention of any specific law, were barely tolerated by a community whose criminal code declared, that to teach a slave to read and write, was an offense "having a tendency to excite insubordination among the servile class, and punishable by imprisonment at hard labor for not more than 21 years, or by death at the discretion of the court." Thus, even the wealthy tax-paying persons of the proscribed race, as well as its less fortunate members, were debarred from any participation in the benefits of the system of public instruction provided by law.

Only one attempt to open a school for the poor of the colored people of this State is to be noted. Mrs. Mary D. Brice, of Ohio, a student of Antioch College, went with her husband to New Orleans in December, 1858, feeling that she was called by heaven to make this attempt. Poor and unaided, she was unable to begin her school until September, 1860; and so great was the popular outcry against the proceedings, that she was compelled to close it the following year. After the lapse of five months, receiving, as she believed, a divine intimation that she would be sustained, she reopened her school; and in spite of frequent warnings and threats, persisted in teaching until the triumph of the Union forces under Farragut, in April, 1862, made it safe for her to do so. With the advent of these forces, too, a few other private teachers appeared in response to the urgent call of the colored people for instruction.

In October, 1863, the first public colored schools were established by the commissioners of enrolment, created by order of Major General Banks, then commanding the Department of the Gulf. Soon seven of these were in operation under the charge of 23 teachers, and having an average attendance of 1,422 scholars. On March 22, 1864, General Banks issued his general order No. 38, which created a board of education for freedmen in the Department of the Gulf, with power to establish common schools, employ teachers, erect school houses, regulate the course of studies, and have, generally, the same authority that assessors, supervisors and trustees have in the northern States, in the matter of establishing and conducting common schools. The purpose of this order was stated to be "for the rudimental instruction of the freedmen of the department, placing within their reach those elements of knowledge which give intelligence and greater value to labor." And for the accomplishment of this purpose the board was empowered to assess and levy upon all real and personal property, taxes sufficient to defray the expense of the schools established, for the period of one year. On the first day of the following month, the schools already established were transferred to this board, which also accepted other schools that had been recently opened under the auspices of benevolent societies, and provided additional ones in 14 other parishes. In the performance of its duties the board encountered great difficulties, not only in obtaining suitable school accommodations, but also in taking measures to guard against attacks by guerilla bands, and to repress the opposition of persons professedly loyal. But it labored energetically, and in December, 1864, it reported as under its supervision 95 schools, 162 teachers, and 9,571 scholars.

The system of schools thus established continued to progress satisfactorily until November 7, 1865, when the power to levy the tax was suspended. This suddenly deprived the schools of nearly all their support. Through the restoration of property to pardoned rebels too, many of the buildings used for school purposes had to be given up. The consequence of all this was that the number of colored schools in Louisiana, which had increased to 150, was speedily cut down to 73. In this sad juncture of affairs the freedmen manifested the most profound solicitude, and thousands of them expresed a willingness to endure, and even petitioned for increased taxation, in order that the means for supporting their schools might be obtained.

But the depression in educational matters thus caused did not long continue. The northern benevolent societies came to the rescue, and labored with increased zeal in this crisis. The freedmen, too, strenuously insisted upon the fullfilment of the contracts which required planters to provide means of instruction for their children, while the planters themselves found their manifest profit in aiding to build school houses, thus securing willing and industrious laborers. Through the operation of these combined causes, the schools of Louisiana not only regained their highest number under the system created by military authority, but even doubled it, thus manifesting a prosperity which, it is hoped, will long continue.

Number of schools, teachers, and pupils, 1865 *to* 1868.

Year.	Number of schools.			Number of teachers.			Number of scholars.			Average attendance.	Per cent.
	Day.	Night.	Total.	White.	Colored.	Total.	Male.	Female.	Total.		
1865..........	....	....	150	....	....	265	....	....	19,000	....	....
1866..........	....	....	73	....	....	90	....	....	3,338	2,093	62
1867..........	195	105	300	142	152	294	5,640	5,063	10,703	9,383	87
1868..........	162	63	225	151	122	273	5,622	5,123	10,745	8,265	76

Studies and expenses, 1867 *and* 1868.

Year.	Number of scholars in different studies pursued.								Expenditures in support of schools.		
	Alphabet.	Easy reading.	Advanced readers.	Writing.	Geography.	Arithmetic.	Higher branches.		By freedmen.	By others.	Total.
1867..............	2,636	4,067	3,044	3,951	2,150	3,356	501		$39,230	$7,537	$46,767
1868..............	1,718	4,229	3,374	3,696	2,974	4,026	513		52,866	7,150	60,016

MAINE.

By the census of 1860 the population of Maine was 628,279, of whom 1,327 were free blacks.

By the constitution of 1820 the right of suffrage is not affected by color or race, and the common school is open to all children of the community for which it is established.

MARYLAND.

By the census of 1860 Maryland had 687,049 inhabitants, of whom 171,131 were blacks, viz: 87,189 slaves and 83,942 free.

By constitutional provision from 1776 down to 1867, the right of suffrage has been restricted to white male citizens having certain qualifications.

By early legal enactments, the earliest in 1638, the poor negro slave was treated as not to be numbered among the Christian inhabitants, and in 1692 it was provided that the sacrament of baptism should not be construed to work the freedom or manumission of any negro or slave. In 1695 "the frequent assembling of negroes within the province" was prohibited, and in 1723 this restriction was specifically extended "to the Sabbath and other holidays." Although numerous enactments of similar character were made down to the abolition of slavery, no statute of Maryland that we have read ever expressly prohibited the instruction of either its free or slave colored population. And there were not wanting at all times in her history men, like Bacon, Bray, and Boucher, who urged the duty of preparing the way for the emancipation of the slaves and of mitigating its evils by Christian teaching.

By the constitution of 1864 it is made imperative on the general assembly, at its first session after the adoption of this fundamental law, "to provide a uniform system of free public schools," and "to levy at each regular session an annual tax of not less than 10 cents on each $100 of taxable property, for the support of free public schools," to be distributed to the several counties "in proportion to their respective population between the ages of 5 and 20 years."

One of the earliest schools for colored children in Baltimore was the St. Frances academy, established in 1831, in connection with the Oblate Sisters of Providence Convent, some account of which has been given already.

The Wells school, so called in memorial of Nelson Wells, a colored man, who left by will to trustees the sum of $7,000, the income alone to be applied to the education of free colored children, was opened about 1835, and has been maintained as a free school ever since.

In 1864 an association was formed in Baltimore, comprised principally of members of the Society of Friends, "for the moral and educational improvement of the colored people," and before the close of their first year's operations it had 7 schools in the city and 18 schools in the county in successful operation, with an aggregate of about 3,000 scholars, at an expense of $9,566; and at the end of the second year there were 79 schools, with 7,300 pupils, at an expense of $52,551.

In submitting a bill for "*a uniform system of public instruction for the State of Maryland,*" Dr. Van Bokkelen, the State superintendent, provided for the establishment of separate schools for children and youth of African descent, in all respects equal to schools designed for the education of other children and subject in every particular to the same rules as to teachers, text-books, &c. On these provisions he makes the following comments :

"Maryland has given freedom to or removed the stain of degraded servility from more than one-fourth of her people. It remains for her to vindicate the policy and humanity of this act of emancipation, by fitting its recipients for their new privileges and obligations. Shall we leave these colored people in ignorance and permit them to degenerate until they become worthless and vicious, inmates of almshouses or of jails? or shall we educate them, make them intelligent, virtuous, useful? Upon the action of the general assembly depends the fact whether freedom shall be fraught with richest blessings, or leave the freedman no better than when he was a slave, unless he avails himself of his new facilities for change of residence and leaves us for a more favored latitude.

" I have no doubt as to what duty demands, no doubt but that duty will be our guide. These freedmen and those who have been degraded because of the same color as the slave, must be educated ; they must be made intelligent and skillful, according to their capacity ; they must have every opportunity that intelligent legislation and a sense of moral obligation can give them. It is their right as much as that of white children, for they have to do their part to develop the resources of the State, and they have to bear their full proportion of taxation upon every dollar of property which they own or may earn. Hence it is proposed that they shall have schools; schools adapted to their wants; schools as good as any in the State, and have a fair opportunity to show what they can do when they have a fair chance.

" Private benevolence has commenced the work which properly belongs to the State, and agencies are now in successful operation to which the taxes collected from colored persons can be paid over for the benefit of their own children.

" I am informed that the amount of school tax paid annually by these people to educate white children in the city of Baltimore for many years has been more than $500. The rule of fair play would require that this be refunded, unless the State at once provides schools under this title."

These recommendations were not heeded, but the superintendent, in his first annual report after the inauguration of the system, dated December 30, 1865, urges immediate and liberal action in the following earnest language :

" By the friends of universal education our system of public instruction will not be recog nized as such, unless it provides for all the children in the State. Knowledge is better than ignorance, and virtue is better than vice, and therefore it is wise that the opportunity of instruction shall be proffered to all who have minds to be cultivated or moral sentiments to be developed. If ignorance leads to idleness and crowds our almshouses with paupers—if vice tends to crime and fills our jails and penitentiaries with wretched convicts—then it is good policy to open the school-house to every child whom ignorance may degrade or vice corrupt. It matters not what may be the color of the skin or the land of nativity, the shape of the cranium or the height of the cheek-bones, whether the child be of Indian or African, European or Asiatic descent ; his ignorance will be a blight and his vice a curse to the com munity in which he lives.

" Whether the pauper be white or black, the tax to support him is equally great ; and it costs as much to conduct the trial by which an Americo-African or a Chinese is convicted of crime, as it would were he of the superior race. All the economic arguments, therefore, which are advanced for the education of the white child are equally applicable to the black. They are even more forcible, because the colored race, having been so long degraded by ignorance, needs education the more.

" We cannot reconcile it to sound judgment that any portion of our thinking population be deprived of instruction ; if knowledge be good for any, it is good for all. Yet we record the fact that Maryland, while devising a uniform system of what is termed public instruction, closed the school door against one-fourth of her people, they representing one-half of her laboring population.

" We all know that the prosperity of our State and the development of her vast resources depend upon the skill and intelligence of the industrial classes. The labor of Maryland is her wealth. The more persevering and expert the labor, the greater and more valuable its

23

product. The virtue of the laboring class is the strongest incentive to preserving industry, and the only certain assurance that the gains of diligence will be well applied and frugally consumed.

"What, then, must be the result if, through prejudice or because of a short-sighted policy. we cramp the minds and thus pervert the morals of one-half of our laborers? what if, instead of energizing the mass of muscle by an active brain, we withhold the influences of education? what if, instead of developing those moral sentiments which counsel temperance and frugality, we give the low vices a chance to grow in the rank soil of ignorance? Will the State become any richer by such a course? Will it be more desirable as a home? Will the poor-tax and jail-tax be lessened? Will property be more valuable or shall we be more honored because we have kept a portion of our people down? These are questions for citizens of Maryland to ponder. They have a very significant claim upon our thoughts. They involve our interests and even our dignity as a civilized and progressive community of intelligent and liberal-minded men. They are directly, intimately, connected with the education of the colored persons who are among us, who intend to remain with us, and whose services we need; the services of every one of them, and even more; for the cry from all sections of the State is that labor is scarce, and industrious workmen can find prompt and abundant work.

"Other reasons may be urged why schools ought to be opened for colored children. These people for many years have been to us faithful servants they have tilled our fields; and worked in our dwellings, performing acceptably all those duties which increase the conveniences and comforts of social life. They have been our hewers of wood and drawers of water. Generation after generation has followed our bidding and helped to earn for us what we possess. In our homes their kind hearts have attracted the love of our children, and the faithful nurse is remembered with affection and treated even with respect. Now that they are free and provide for themselves—and this by no act of theirs, but by our will—our duty is to educate them, to give them knowledge enough to know how to provide for themselves. Grant them at least this much of the inheritance, that they may be able to take care of themselves and their families, and become valuable members of the community. This we owe to the colored people. To educate them is our duty as well as our interest.

"The constitutional provision by which the school money is divided according to population, without regard to color, I think imposes upon us a legal obligation to educate all children without reference to caste, class, or condition; and therefore, in framing the bill which was presented to the general assembly, I considered it my duty, as under the constitution, to provide separate schools for colored children, just as I would for any other class that I found in the State which could not mingle with the white children.

"Money is appropriated and therefore ought to be used for colored schools. According to the constitution, all the money received from the 15-cent State tax is divided by the total number of persons between 5 and 20 years, white and black. Thus, $1 68 per year was apportioned to each person, and that sum multiplied by the total population between 5 and 20 years gave the amount received by each county. Charles county, for instance, has 6,466 persons between 5 and 20, she therefore receives $10,883 47. But by act of legislature she is released from the responsibility of educating 4,384 of those persons, they being black, and use the entire school money for the education of 2,082, thus receiving $5 for each. On the other hand, Alleghany county receives $18,264 24 for a population of 10,851, nearly all of whom have to be educated, there being only 464 colored children in the county; thus receiving only $1 94 for each pupil.

"This is an unjust discrimination in favor of certain counties. It alone would furnish sufficient reason for requiring separate schools to be opened for colored children, even were there no arguments upon economic and general grounds.

"If the money is given for a specific purpose, it is the duty of legislators to require its faithful application.

"While the State is holding back, an association of citizens, influenced by philanthropic motives, is endeavoring to make up our lack of duty. Their report shows 34 schools in the different parts of the State maintained by private liberality. The plan of operations for 1866 embraces 116 schools, at an expense of $56,000. If nothing more can be done, this association ought at least to be authorized to draw from the treasury the amount paid for each colored child, but I trust the general assembly will put into the law the sections reported by me last February, directing that separate schools shall be established for the instruction of youth of African descent, whenever as many as 40 claim the privileges of public instruction; these schools to be under the control of the board of school commissioners.

"No person of intelligence pretends to doubt the capacity of colored children to acquire knowledge. The experience of the past three years settles this point very satisfactorily; not only in our midst, but even in those portions of the south where slavery was more exacting, and the negroes were worked in large bodies upon the rice and cotton plantations, having very little intercourse with persons of any degree of intelligence. Our labor then will not be in vain, and I invoke the general assembly to manifest its wisdom and philanthropy by proffering the blessings of education to a class of children long neglected, whose parents have rendered faithful service, and by whose labor millions of dollars have been added to our wealth.

"I leave politicians to discuss the question of suffrage, but this much may be asserted, that while it is very doubtful whether the colored man is to be trusted with the ballot, there can be no doubt that he ought to have the spelling book."

In his second annual report, dated December 15, 1867, the superintendent submits the following remarks and statistics respecting schools for colored children :

"No public organized plans have been adopted for the education of this class of children, except in the city of Baltimore, as reported last year. Schools have been continued in the counties under the direction of the Baltimore Association for the Moral and Mental Improvement of Colored Persons, supported by contributions from benevolent associations, and the payment of tuition fees by the parents or friends of the children educated.

"The extent and efficiency of this work are indicated by the following statistics furnished by the actuary of the Baltimore association:

Summary of statistics of schools for colored persons for year ending June 30, 1867.

Total number of schools for colored persons	84
In the city of Baltimore	22
In 19 counties	62
Number of pupils registered	8,600
In the city	2,800
In the counties	5,800
Average attendance	6,600
Number of teachers	89
Number of months schools were open	9
Total expense of 84 schools, including books, furniture, and supervision	$61,808 50
Average cost of each school	734 62
Average salary of each teacher	364 46
Cost of each different pupil	7 19
Cost of each average pupil	9 35
Cost of each different pupil per month	80
Contributions to sustain the schools were received from—	
Citizens of Baltimore	$3,305 16
Appropriation of city council	20,000 00
Associations in other States	10,787 97
Friends in England and Ireland	1,144 23
Colored people in the State	23,371 14
Loan	3,200 00

"A normal school has been established in the city of Baltimore, in which teachers for colored schools are trained for their special work, and subjected to a rigorous examination before taking charge of a school. A large building has been purchased and furnished with all requisites for the success of the institution.

"The schools for colored people in the city of Baltimore were adopted by the city council in September, 1867, and are now conducted under the supervision of the city school commissioners.

"The large amount contributed by the colored people towards the support of their schools, being more than one-third the whole income, is proof of their interest in the education of their children, and is worthy of special commendation. It is the best guarantee that they will use faithfully whatever facilities may be given them for establishing a school system.

"Upon this important topic I have nothing to add to the views presented in previous reports. The opinions then advocated have been strengthened by observation during official visits. Whatever prejudice may have existed in the minds of some of our citizens on this subject is rapidly disappearing, and I think it may be asserted that, while there is not at present a willingness to educate colored children at the public expense, there is a readiness to grant them such facilities and encouragements as will not prove a burden upon the resources of the State."

The general school law adopted in 1865, in pursuance of Article VIII in the constitution as revised in 1867, by which the system established in 1865 is abolished, dispenses with a State superintendent, but provides for an annual report by the principal of the State normal school on the condition of the schools based on the reports of the county school commissioners. The legislature by special act relating to the colored population, passed March 30, 1868, provides as follows :

"Section 1. The total amount of taxes paid for school purposes by the colored people of any county, or in the city of Baltimore, together with any donations that may be made for the purpose, shall be set aside for the maintaining the schools for colored children, which schools shall be conducted under the direction of the board of county school commissioners or the board of commissioners of public schools of the city of Baltimore, and shall be subject to such rules and regulations as said respective board shall prescribe."

Professor Newell, in the report required of him on the condition of schools in the State for the year ending September 30, 1868, embraces the following items and statements respecting the colored schools :

"In the city of Baltimore there were 13 public schools for colored children with 1,312 pupils on the roll, under 29 teachers. These schools were maintained at an expense of $22,166, of which sum $2,856 were paid by the pupils in tuition."

The school commissioners of Frederick county, after referring with just pride to the action of the State in extending liberal aid to the instruction of the blind, of the deaf mute, of the orphan, of the juvenile offender, and the adult criminal, remark:

"And with all this her labor of amelioration is not complete, nor can it be until she meets squarely the question of State policy, which demands some attention to the mental and moral culture of her negro population. Shall this large and increasing population continue in its present ignorant and vicious condition? Does not every consideration of morality and enlarged benevolence, and indeed self-protection, plead the cause of the poor abject negro?

" Torn from his relation to his master by a violent political convulsion, in which he acted no voluntary part; thrown upon the world in his weakness, poverty, and ignorance, among a race with which, with equal advantages, he can never compete; is it wise, is it politic, that he should be left to grope back to his original barbarism? This is a question of grave importance, and should be met promptly and without prejudice. Its postponement will only increase the burden; its neglect is cruel : he is tantalized with a personal liberty, whilst the shackles of ignorance and vice are riveted upon his mind and soul. To ameliorate his condition he is powerless. Give him education or take back that which has been thrust upon him—his personal liberty—which is but the instrument of his extermination."

The school commissioner of Dorchester county remarks:

" In obedience to the order of the board last summer, I visited the Jenifer Institute, a school for colored children in the town of Cambridge. My report of the admirable condition of the school, the perfect discipline maintained, the evidences of real progress made by the pupils, induced the board to take some action with regard to these schools. In a short time trustees were nominated to the board by the patrons of these schools, and confirmed, so that we have had a sort of oversight of them. The colored people seem most anxious to be under the control of the board, and the warm interest taken in their schools by the commissioners and the examiner is evidently most grateful to them. The amount of their school tax will be divided between the schools, but this amount is so small that they continue to help themselves, with such assistance as they can get from the Baltimore association."

The following tables, prepared by Professor Vashon, will exhibit the progress of the schools for colored children, from 1865 to 1868:

Table giving the number of schools, teachers, scholars, and attendance.

Year.	Number of schools.			Number of teachers.			Number of scholars.			Average attendance.	Per cent.
	Day.	Night.	Total.	White.	Colored.	Total.	Male.	Female.	Total.		
1865.........	....	....	47	24	27	51	....	....	4,016	....	.....
1866.........	....	....	86	....	....	101	....	....	8,144	....	.....
1867.........	69	38	107	28	75	103	3,390	2,657	6,047	4,220	69
1868.........	102	32	134	44	110	154	2,882	2,576	5,458	4,547	83

Table showing the numbers in different studies and cost of maintaining schools.

Year.	Number of scholars in different studies pursued.							Expended in support of schools.		
	Alphabet.	Easy reading.	Advanced reading.	Writing.	Geography.	Arithmetic.	Higher branches.	By freedmen.	By others.	Total.
1867...............	638	3,004	1,940	2,837	1,755	2,426	118	....	....	$92,781
1868...............	393	2,174	2,526	3,241	1,680	3,241	497	....	....	....

MASSACHUSETTS.

In Massachusetts, out of a population of 1,231,066, in 1860, there were 9,602 free colored persons. By the constitution and laws of the State, the right of suffrage, eligibility to office, and the advantages of the public schools of every grade, are open to all citizens without distinction of color.

SEPARATE SCHOOLS FOR COLORED CHILDREN PROHIBITED.

In Boston, as early as 1798, a separate school for colored children was established in the house of Primus Hall, a respectable colored man, and taught by Elisha Sylvester, a white man, at the expense of the parents sending to it. In 1800 a petition was presented to the school committee by 66 colored persons, praying for the establishment of a public school for their benefit. The petition was referred to a sub-committee, who reported in favor of granting the petition; but the request was refused by the town at a special meeting, in the call for which a notice that this question would be acted upon was inserted.

The private school, first taught by Elisha Sylvester, was continued until 1806 by two gentlemen, Messrs. Brown and Williams, from Harvard College. In 1806, the African meeting-house in Belknap street was erected, and the lower story was fitted up as a school-room for colored children, to which place the school kept in Mr. Hall's house was transferred, where it was continued until 1835, when a school-house was erected out of a fund left by Abiel Smith, known as the Smith school-house. Towards this school the town made an annual appropriation of $200, the remainder of the expense being defrayed by the parents, those who were able to do so paying 12½ cents per week. The erection of the Smith school-house was deemed at the time of sufficient importance to be marked by appropriate public exercises, as part of which Hon. William Minot delivered an address.

From 1809 to 1812 this school was taught by the well-known Prince Sanders, who was brought up in the family of a lawyer in Thetford, Vermont, and who in 1812 became a civil and diplomatic officer in the service of Christophe, Emperor of Hayti. He was brought to the city by the influence of Dr. Channing and Mr. Caleb Bingham, and was supported by the liberality of benevolent persons in Boston.

The African school in Belknap street was under the control of the school committee from 1812 to 1821, and from 1821 was under the charge of a special sub-committee. Among the teachers was John B. Russworm, from 1821 to 1824, who entered Bowdoin college in the latter year, and afterwards became governor of the colony of Cape Palmas in southern Liberia.

The first primary school for colored children in Boston was established in 1820, two or three of which were subsequently kept until 1855, when they were discontinued as separate schools, in accordance with the general law passed by the legislature in that year, which provided that, " in determining the qualifications of scholars to be admitted into any public school, or any district school in this commonwealth, no distinction shall be made on account of the race, color, or religious opinions of the applicant or scholar." "Any child, who, on on account of his race, color, or religious opinions should be excluded from any public or district school, if otherwise qualified," might recover damages in an action of *tort*, brought in the name of the child in any court of competent jurisdiction, against the city or town in which the school was located.

MICHIGAN.

The population of Michigan in 1860 was 749,113, of whom 6,799 were colored. Under a decision of the Supreme Court, a man with not over one-fourth negro blood is a "white man;" but for 15 years colored men (and women if liable to taxation) have been legal voters in school meetings, on an equality with whites. Colored children are included in the school census, and the public money is apportioned upon all between 5 and 20 years of age, the public schools being free to all alike.

MISSISSIPPI.

Mississippi had a population of 791,305 in 1860, of whom more than half were slaves, the number being 436,631; and the number of free colored people was only 773.

This State was originally principally embraced in the charter of Georgia of 1732, which ex ended to the Mississippi river. Its early laws pertaining to the colored race were almost exact transcripts of the laws of Louisiana Territory of 1804. An early act, July 20, 1805, prohibited the emancipation of any slave, except for some meritorious act for the benefit of his owner or of the Territory. An act of 1807 prohibited slaves from going from home without a pass, the penalty being limited to "20 stripes." Unlawful assemblies were to be atoned for by a penalty of 39 stripes. White men, free negroes, and mulattoes, found in company with slaves at an unlawful meeting, were fined $20 and costs for each offense. In 1817 the western ern portion of the Territory became a State, and in 1819 a law was passed forbidding the immigration of any free negro or mulatto into the State. In 1818 provision was made for a separate burial place for "the bodies of slaves and colored persons" in the city of Natchez, with a penalty not exceeding $50 for the burial of any slave or colored person in any other place than the one designated. In 1822 the several acts relating to colored people were arranged together, and a provision was introduced declaring it to be unlawful for any slave to possess in his or her own right, any horse, mare, gelding, mule, or any other cattle, sheep, or hogs whatever;" or to cultivate cotton for his own use. Any negro or mulatto, bond or free, might be a "good witness" in cases where free negroes or mulattoes alone were interested; but the law adds, "if any negro or mulatto shall be found, upon proof made to any county or corporation court of this State, to have given false testimony, every such offender shall, without further trial, be ordered by said court to have one ear nailed to the pillory, and there to stand for the space of one hour, and then the said ear to be cut off, and thereafter the other ear nailed in like manner and cut off at the expiration of one other hour, and moreover to receive 39 lashes on his or her bare back, well laid on, at the public whipping-post, or such other punishment as the court shall think proper, not extending to life or limb." This law remained in force until the period of the rebellion.

By an act of January, 1823, all meetings of slaves, free negroes, or mulattoes, above the number of five, at any place of public resort or meeting-house, in the night; or at any schoolhouse, for teaching, reading, or writing, in the day or night, was to be considered an unlawful assembly; and the penalty was lashes, "not exceeding 39." With the permission of their master or overseer, however, slaves might attend a meeting for religious worship, conducted by a regularly ordained or licensed white minister, or attended by at least two discreet and reputable white persons, appointed by some regular church or religious society.

In 1831 "every free negro or mulatto in the State, under the age of 50 years, and over the age of 16 years," was peremptorily ordered, within 90 days from the date of the passage of the act, to "remove and quit the State," and not to return on any pretense. The penalty for such a person remaining in the State was to be sold into slavery for five years. But exceptions were made in cases where licenses to remain were obtained from the court, founded upon evidence of "good character and honest deportment." By the same act it was "unlawful for any slave, free negro, or mulatto, to preach the gospel," under a penalty of 39 lashes, except to slaves upon the plantation where the one preaching belonged, and with the permission of the owner.

In March, 1846, an act was passed to establish a system of common schools, and creating a fund from "all escheats and all fines and forfeitures and amercements;" from licenses to hawkers; and all incomes from school lands. The several counties were authorized to levy a special tax, not exceeding the State tax, for common school purposes. In 1848 another act was passed to provide for common schools in certain counties in which a tax equal to 25 per cent. of the State tax was annually levied upon all the taxable property of the county, to constitute a common school fund for such counties. All acts prescribed that the schools were for the education of "white youth between the ages of 6 and 20 years."

FREEDMEN'S SCHOOLS.

The work of establishing schools for the freedmen has not been as successful in the State of Mississippi as in some of the other States, owing to the unsettled condition of public affairs; but at different points schools have been established, some under the direction of northern associations, some under the auspices of the churches, and some through the efforts of the freedmen themselves, who have manifested great eagerness to learn to read and write. Several of the largest landed proprietors have taken up the subject and are establishing schools for the children of persons employed on their estates.

The following statistics have been prepared by Professor Vashon from the reports of the Freedmen's Bureau:

Number of schools, teachers, and scholars—1865 to 1868.

Year.	Number of schools.			Number of teachers.			Number of scholars.			Average attendance.	Per cent.
	Day.	Night.	Total.	White.	Colored.	Total.	Male.	Female.	Total.		
1865			34			68			4,310		
1866			50			80			5,407		
1867	53	27	80	80	19	99	2,689	3,019	5,708	4,449	77
1868	102	32	134	94	46	140	3,090	3,663	6,753	5,226	77

Studies and expenditures—1867–'68.

Year.	Number of scholars in different studies pursued.							Expenditures in support of schools.		
	Alphabet.	Easy reading.	Advanced readers.	Writing.	Geography.	Arithmetic.	Higher branches.	By freedmen.	By others.	Total.
1867	443	2,833	2,532	2,426	1,242	2,426	156	$2,020	$5,588	$7,608
1868	838	2,960	2,796	2,509	1,677	4,384	257	5,689	5,143	10,832

MISSOURI.

There were in this State, in 1860, 1,182,012 inhabitants, 118,503 of whom were colored; of these 114,931 were slaves, and 3,572 were free.

The province ceded by France to the United States in 1803, under the general name of Louisiana, was organized by Congress in 1804, by the names of the Territory of Orleans, and the District of Louisiana, the latter embracing the territory now forming the States of Arkansas, Missouri, Iowa, the greater part of Minnesota, and the region west of these States to the Rocky mountains. In 1805 the District of Louisiana was called the Territory of Louisiana; and this name was again changed in 1812 to that of the Territory of Mississippi. The first legislation relating to the colored people in Missouri was while it was in a territorial condition, by the governor and judges of the Indian Territory, who were authorized by Congress to make laws for the district. This act of 1804 provided that no slave should go from the tenements of his master "without a pass or some letter or token;" the penalty was "stripes at the discretion of the justice of the peace." If a slave presumed to go upon any other plantation than that of his master, without leave in writing from his or her owner, not being absent upon lawful business, the penalty was "10 lashes."

No master or mistress of slaves was permitted to suffer the meeting of slaves upon his or her plantation above four hours at any one time, without leave of the owner or owners. The penalty was $3 for each offense, increased by $1 for each negro present at the meeting, above the number five. Any white person, free negro, or mulatto, who should be found in company with slaves at any unlawful meeting, was fined $3 for each offense; and, on failure to

pay the fine and costs, he was to receive "20 lashes well laid on by order of the justice.'
All trading with or by slaves was strictly forbidden, "except with the consent of the master,
owner, or overseer."

In 1817 the general assembly of the Territory of Missouri passed a more stringent act against
slaves traveling without permission. In 1822, after Missouri was admitted as a State, more
severe penalties were attached to the offense of trading with slaves; and in 1833 "slaves
or free persons of color" were forbidden to assemble at any store, tavern, grocery, grog or
dram shop" at any time by night or day, "more especially on the Sabbath day, commonly
called Sunday."

In 1845 free negroes and mulattoes were forbidden to remain in the State except on license.
Three days were allowed to depart, and one additional day for every 20 miles travel was
allowed, to escape to some free State, on the penalty of fine, imprisonment, and lashes. In
1847 it was enacted that "no person shall keep or teach any school for the instruction of
negroes or mulattoes in reading or writing, in this State." No meetings were allowed for
religious worship, where the services were conducted by negroes or mulattoes, unless some
sheriff or other officer or justice of the peace were present, "to prevent all seditious speeches
and disorderly and unlawful conduct of every kind." Such meetings, held in violation of
these provisions, were deemed unlawful, and the penalty was a "fine not exceeding $500 or
imprisonment not exceeding six months, or both fine and imprisonment." No free negro or
mulatto was henceforth to be permitted to come into the State.

By the present constitution and laws of the State, provision is made for a free public
school system; for the appointment of a State superintendent of schools. In each county a
county superintendent is elected every two years. Each congressional township composes a
school district, under the control, in matters of education, of a board of education. Smaller
divisions are regarded as sub-districts, under the management of local directors. The excellent system of public schools in the city of St. Louis includes a normal school, a high school,
31 district schools, and three colored schools.

The following table, prepared by Professor Vashon, gives the progress of schools for colored youth from 1865 to 1868:

Table giving the number of schools, teachers, scholars, and attendance.

Year.	Number of schools.			Number of teachers.			Number of scholars.			Average attendance.	Per cent.
	Day.	Night.	Total.	White.	Colored.	Total.	Male.	Female.	Total.		
1865..........	....	....	24	....	....	31	....	....	1,925	....	....
1866..........	....	....	38	....	....	46	....	....	2,698	....	....
1867..........	44	11	55	32	30	62	1,290	1,469	2,759	1,918	69
1868..........	49	11	60	39	31	70	2,196	2,016	4,212	3,009	71

Table showing the numbers in different studies, and cost of maintaining schools.

Year.	Number of scholars in the different studies pursued.							Expended in support of schools.		
	Alphabet.	Easy reading.	Advanced readers.	Writing.	Geography.	Arithmetic.	Higher branches.	By freedmen.	By others.	Total.
1867..............	237	1,074	604	881	523	837	87	....	....	....
1868..............	757	1,623	2,029	2,520	1,698	1,995	695	....	....	....

NEW YORK.

By the census of 1860 the total population of the State of New York was 3,880,735, of which number 49,005 were free colored.

By the constitution of 1777 the right of suffrage was extended to every male inhabitant of full age, without respect to color; but in the revision of 1821 this right was so far abridged that "no man of color, unless he shall have been for three years a citizen of this State and for one year next preceding any election shall be seized and possessed of a freehold estate of $250 over and above all debts and incumbrances charged thereon, and shall have been actually rated and paid a tax thereon, shall be entitled to vote at any such election. And no person of color shall be subject to direct taxation unless he shall be seized and possessed of such real estate as aforesaid." In 1846 and in 1850 the question of equal suffrage to colored persons was submitted separately, on the adoption of each revised constitution of those dates, and rejected by large majorities on both occasions. In 1867 the convention for revising the constitution adopted an article giving equality of suffrage to colored people, to be voted upon separately.

By act of 1841 the legislature authorized any school district, with the approbation of the school commissioners of the town in which the district was situated, to establish a separate school for the colored children of such district. This was not intended to deny them the privileges of the regular school, to which they were declared by the superintendent to be equally with all others entitled. In the revised school code of 1864 the school authorities of any city or incorporated village organized under special acts may establish separate schools for children and youth of African descent resident therein; "and such schools shall be supported in the same manner and to the same extent as the schools supported therein for white children; and they shall be subject to the same rules and regulations and be furnished with facilities for instruction equal to those furnished to the white schools therein."

EARLY EFFORTS OF ELIAS NEAU AT NEW YORK.

A school for negro slaves was opened in the city of New York in 1704 by Elias Neau, a native of France, and a catechist of the "Society for the Propagation of the Gospel in Foreign Parts." After a long imprisonment for his public profession of faith as a Protestant, he founded an asylum in New York. His sympathies were awakened by the condition of the negroes in slavery in that city, who numbered about 1,500 at that time. The difficulties of holding any intercourse with them seemed almost insurmountable. At first he could only visit them from house to house, after his day's toil was over; afterwards he was permitted to gather them together in a room in his own house for a short time in the evening. As the result of his instructions at the end of four years, in 1708, the ordinary number under his instruction was 200. Many were judged worthy to receive the sacrament at the hands of Mr. Vesey, the rector of Trinity church; some of whom became regular and devout communicants, remarkable for their orderly and blameless lives.

But soon after this time some negroes of the Carmantee and Pappa tribes formed a plot for setting fire to the city, and murdering the English, on a certain night. The work was commenced but checked, and after a short struggle the English subdued the negroes. Immediately a loud and angry clamor arose against Elias Neau, his accusers saying that his school was the cause of the murderous attempt. He denied the charge in vain; and so furious were the people that, for a time, his life was in danger. The evidence, however, at the trial proved that the negroes most deeply engaged in the plot, were those whose masters were most opposed to any means for their instruction. Yet, the offense of a few was charged upon the race; and even the provincial government lent its authority to make the burden of Neau the heavier. The common council passed an order forbidding negroes "to appear in the streets after sunset, without lanthorns or candles;" and as they could not procure these, the result was to break up the labors of Neau. But at this juncture Governor Hunter interposed and went to visit the school of Neau, accompanied by several officers of rank, and by the society's missionaries; and he was so well pleased that he gave his full approval to the work, and in a public proclamation called upon the clergy of the province to exhort their congregations to extend their approval also. Vesey, the good rector of Trinity church, had long watched the labors of Neau and witnessed the progress of his scholars, as well as assisted him in them ; and finally the governor, the council, mayor, recorder, and two chief justices of New York joined in declaring that Neau " in a very eminent degree deserved the countenance, favor and protection of the society." He therefore continued his labors until 1722, when, " amid the unaffected sorrow of his negro scholars and the friends who honored him for their sake, he was removed by death."

The work was then continued by " Huddlestone, then schoolmaster in New York ;" and he was succeeded by Rev. Mr. Wetmore, who removed in 1726 to Rye ; whereupon the Rev. Mr. Colgan was appointed to assist the rector of Trinity church, and to carry on the instruction of the negroes. A few years afterwards Thomas Noxon assisted Mr. Colgan, and their joint success was very satisfactory. Rev. R. Charlton, who had been engaged in similar labor at New Windsor, was called to New York in 1732, where he followed up the work successfully for 15 years, and was succeeded by Rev. Samuel Auchmuty. Upon the death of Thomas Noxon, in 1741, Mr. Hildreth took his place, who in 1764 wrote that " not a single black admitted by him to the holy communion had turned out badly, or in any way disgraced his profession." Both Auchmuty and Hildreth received valuable support from Mr. Barclay, who, upon the death of Mr. Vesey, in 1746, had been appointed to the rectory of Trinity church.

OTHER EARLY LABORERS FOR THE SLAVES.

The labors of Neau and others in New York, for a period of half a century, had their counterpart in many other places by other laborers. Taylor and Varnod, missionaries of the society in South Carolina, bestowed diligent care in giving religious instruction to the slaves; and they gratefully confess to have received assistance from the masters and mistresses, which was the more welcome, on account of the ill will and opposition which any attempt to ameliorate the condition of slaves provoked among most of the British planters of that day. In the ranks of the Pennsylvania missionaries was Hugh Neill, once a distinguished Presbyterian minister in New Jersey. During the 15 years of his ministry he labored with zeal and success for the instruction of the negroes. Dr. Smith, provost of the college of Philadelphia, engaged in the same work, and at the death of Neill, in 1766, was placed on the list of the society's missionaries. Dr. Jenney was rector of St. Peter's and Christ church in Philadelphia from 1742 to 1762, and during his incumbency the society appointed a catechetical lecturer in that church for the instruction of negroes and others. William Sturgeon, a student of Yale College, was selected for that office and sent to England to receive ordination. He entered upon his duties in 1747, and discharged them for 19 years. In 1763 a complaint of neglect of duty was brought before the society against him, in not catechizing the negro children ; but, upon a full investigation by the rector and four vestrymen its falsehood was shown and his stipend was increased.

In 1706 Dr. Le Jean, a missionary of the society, was appointed to the mission at Goose creek, near Charleston, South Carolina, where he labored 11 years, especially among the negroes, and he succeeded in carrying on a systematic course of instruction. Dr. Le Jean was preceded in the same work by Rev. Mr. Thomas, in 1695, who had not only taught 20 negroes to read and write, but induced several ladies to engage in the work ; among them was Mrs. Haige Edward, who instructed several of her slaves. I hope, writes Rev. Mr. Taylor, their example will provoke some masters and mistresses to take the same care with their negroes.

Bishop Gibson, who presided over the See of London from 1723 to 1748, did not hesitate to urge forward the work of Christian love in behalf of the negro slave. He wrote two public letters upon this subject in 1727 ; one exhorting masters and mistresses of families " to encourage and promote the instruction of their negroes in the Christian faith ;" and the other, urging and directing the missionaries to assist in the work.

The bishop of London, in 1727, published a letter to the masters and mistresses of families in the English plantations abroad, exhorting them to encourage and promote the instruction of the negroes in the Christain faith, and in it remarks : " Considering the greatness of the profit there is received from their labors, it might be hoped that all Christian masters—those especially who are possessed of considerable numbers—should also be at some small expense in providing for the instruction of those poor creatures, and that others, whose numbers are less, and who dwell in the same neighborhood, should join in the expense of a common teacher for the negroes belonging to them."

In the year 1733, among other Africans consigned to Michael Denton, of Annapolis, Maryland, was one of delicate constitution, who was sold to a gentleman 'living on the eastern shore. One day a white boy found him in the woods apparently engaged in prayer, and mischievously disturbed him by throwing sand in his face. Rendered unhappy by this and similar treatment, he ran away to a neighboring county, where his dignified but melancholy bearing excited attention. An old negro was at last found who understood his language, and from him it was discovered that the slave had been a foulah in Africa. He had in his possession slips of paper on which were written certain characters, which being sent to Oxford proved to be in the Arabic language. General Oglethorpe became deeply interested in the man and redeemed him from captivity. On his arrival in England he was treated with marked attention, dined with the Duke of Montague, received a gold watch from the Queen, and assisted Sir Hans Sloane in the translation of Arabic manuscripts. This romantic occurrence led to much discussion as to the duty of planters to the negro, and in 1735, when Oglethorpe was member of Parliament, an act was passed prohibiting the importation of black slaves or negroes into the province of Georgia.

In 1749 the Rev. Thomas Bacon, of Talbot county, Maryland, delivered some remarkable discourses to masters and mistresses, as well as to his "beloved black brethren and sisters," which were published in London, and in the present century reprinted at Winchester, Virginia, by the late Bishop Meade.

Williams, bishop of Chichester, in a discourse before the Society for Foreign Parts, says:

"These negroes are slaves, and for the most part treated as worse, or rather by some as if they were a different species, as they are of a different color, from the rest of mankind. The Spaniards are reproached for driving the poor Americans to the fort like the cattle of the field, but our slaves, on the other hand, are driven from it."

Bishop Butler, author of the Analogy of Religion, declared in a discourse that the slaves of the British colonies ought not to be treated "merely as cattle or goods, the property of their master. Nor can the highest property possible to be acquired in these servants cancel the obligation to take care of their religious instructions. Despicable as they may appear in our eyes, they are the creatures of God."

Archbishop Secker, in 1741, recommended the "employing of young negroes, prudently chosen, to teach their countrymen," and Dr. Bearcroft, in 1744, alludes to this project in a discourse before the Society for Propagating the Gospel in Foreign Parts, in these words:

"The society had lately fallen upon a happy expedient by the purchase of two young negroes, whom they have qualified by a thorough instruction in the principles of Christianity, and, by teaching them to read well, to become schoolmasters to their fellow-negroes. The project is but of yesterday, but the reverend person who proposed, and under whose care and inspection the two youths are placed, hath acquainted the society that it succeeds to his heart's desire; that one school is actually opened at Charles Town, South Carolina, which hath more than 60 young negroes under instruction, and will annually send out between 30 and 40 of them well instructed in religion and capable of reading their Bibles, who may carry home and diffuse the same knowledge which they shall have been taught among their poor relations and fellow-slaves. And in time schools will be spread in other places and in other colonies to teach them to believe in the Son of God, who shall make them free indeed."

Bishop Warburton, in 1766, says:

"From the free savages I come now to the savages in bonds. By those I mean the vast multitudes yearly stolen from the opposite continent and sacrificed by the colonists to their great idol, the god of gain. But what, then, say these sincere worshippers of mammon? They answer: 'They are our own property which we offer up.' Gracious God! talk as of herds of cattle, of property in rational creatures, creatures endowed with all our faculties, possessing all our qualities but that of color, our brethren both by nature and grace, shocks all the feelings of humanity and the dictates of common sense."

Bishop Lowth, formerly professor of poetry in the Oxford University, speaking of negroes in America, said:

"From their situation they are open and accessible to instruction, and by their subjection are under the immediate influence and in the hands of those who ought to be their instruct-ors. These circumstances, so favorable in appearance, have not been productive of the good effects which might have been expected.   If their masters, tyrannizing over this people with a despotism beyond example, are determined to keep their minds in a state of bondage still more grievous than that in which they hold their bodies ; should not suffer them to be instructed ;   *   *   *   *   should this in reality be a common practice among their masters, ' Woe unto you.' "

Bishop Porteus, whose mother was a native of Virginia, and whose father had resided there many years, in one of his discourses alludes to plantation negroes as being generally considered as mere machines and instruments to work with, rather than beings with minds to be enlightened and souls to be saved.

Bishop Wilson (Sodor and Man) was another distinguished clergyman, who watched for the opportunity to aid the missionaries who were laboring in the colonies for the instruction of the Indians and negroes ; and in 1740 he published an " Essay towards the Instruction for the Indians," the germ of which was written by him in 1699, on " The Principles and Duties of Christianity," for the use of the people of the Isle of Man, and was the first book ever printed in the Manx language.   He bequeathed £50 for the education of negro chil-dren in Talbot county.

In 1711 Bishop Fleetwood preached the anniversary sermon before the society, in which he urged the duty of instructing the negroes, the effect of which afterwards, on the heart of a prejudiced planter in North Carolina, is shown by an extract from a letter by Giles Rains-ford, one of the society's missionaries. "By much importunity," he says, "I prevailed on Mr. Martin to let me baptize three of his negroes.   All the arguments I could make use of would scarce effect it, till Bishop Fleetwood's sermon preached before the society turned the scale."   These are a few only of the many instances going to show the prevailing sentiment of the laborers of a century and a half ago.

SCHOOLS FOR COLORED CHILDREN BY THE MANUMISSION SOCIETY.

The first school for colored children in the city of New York, established by the Manumis-sion Society, was denominated "The New York African Free School."

It appears that in the years 1785 and 1786 the business of kidnapping colored people and selling them at the south was carried on in this city and vicinity to such an extent as to pro-voke public attention to the necessity of taking some measures to check this growing evil.

In the city of Philadelphia a society had already been formed to protect the blacks from similar dangers there.   A deputation was sent from New York to that society for infor-mation, and to procure a copy of its constitution, which assisted much in the organization of "The New York Society for Promoting the Manumission of Slaves, and Protecting such of them as have been, or may be, Liberated."   The following are the names of the mem-bers of this society, who composed the first board of trustees of the "New York African Free School:"

Melancthon Smith, Jno. Bleecker, James Cogswell, Lawrence Embree, Thomas Burling, Willett Leaman, Jno. Lawrence, Jacob Leaman, White Mattock, Mathew Clarkson, Na-thaniel Lawrence, Jno. Murray, junior.

Their school, located in Cliff street, between Beekman and Ferry, was opened in 1786, taught by Cornelius Davis, attended by about 40 pupils of both sexes, and appears, from their book of minutes, to have been satisfactorily conducted.   In the year 1791 a female teacher was added to instruct the girls in needlework, the expected advantages of which measure were soon realized, and highly gratifying to the society.   In 1808 the society was incorporated, and in the preamble it is recorded that "a free school for the education of such persons as have been liberated from bondage, that they may hereafter become useful mem-bers of the community," has been established.   It may be proper here to remark that the good cause in which the friends of this school were engaged was far from being a popular one.   The prejudices of a large portion of the community were against it; the means in the hands of the trustees were often very inadequate, and many seasons of discouragement were witnessed; but they were met by men who, trusting in the divine support, were resolved neither to relax their exertions nor to retire from the field.

Through the space of about 20 years they struggled on; the number of scholars varying from 40 to 60, until the year 1809, when the Lancasterian, or Monitorial, system of instruc tion was introduced, (this being the second school in the United States to adopt the plan, under a new teacher, E J. Cox, and a very favorable change was produced, the number of pupils, and the efficiency of their instruction being largely increased.

Soon after this, however, in January, 1814, their school-house was destroyed by fire, which checked the progress of the school for a time, as no room could be obtained large enough to accommodate the whole number of pupils. A small room in Doyer street was temporarily hired, to keep the school together till further arrangements could be made, and an appeal was made to the liberality of the citizens and to the corporation of the city, which resulted in obtaining from the latter a grant of two lots of ground in William street, on which to build a new school-house; and in January, 1815, a commodious brick building, to accommodate 200 pupils, was finished on this lot, and the school was resumed with fresh vigor and increasing interest. In a few months the room became so crowded that it was found necessary to engage a separate room, next to the school, to accommodate such of the pupils as were to be taught sewing. This branch had been for many years discontinued, but was now resumed under the direction of Miss Lucy Turpen, a young lady whose amiable disposition and faithful discharge of her duties rendered her greatly esteemed, both by her pupils and the trustees. This young lady, after serving the board for several years, removed with her parents to Ohio, and her place was supplied by Miss Mary Lincrum, who was succeeded by Miss Eliza J. Cox, and the latter by Miss Mary Ann Cox, and she by Miss Carolina Roe, under each of whom the school continued to sustain a high character for order and usefulness.

The school in William street increasing in numbers, another building was found necessary, and was built on a lot of ground 50 by 100 feet square, on Mulberry street, between Grand and Hester streets, to accommodate 500 pupils, and was completed and occupied, with C. C. Andrews for teacher, in May, 1820.

General Lafayette visited this school September 10, 1824, an abridged account of which is copied from the Commercial Advertiser of that date:

Visit of Lafayette to the African school in 1824.

"At 1 o'clock the general, with the company invited for the occasion, visited the African free school, on Mulberry street. This shcool embraces about 500 scholars; about 450 were present on this occasion, and they are certainly the best disciplined and most interesting school of children we have ever witnessed. As the general was conducted to a seat, Mr. Ketchum adverted to the fact that as long ago as 1788 the general had been elected a member of the institution (Manumission Society) at the same time with Grenville Sharp and Thomas Clarkson, of England. The general perfectly remembered the circumstance, and mentioned particularly the letter he had received on that occasion from the Hon. John Jay, then president of the society. One of the pupils, Master James M. Smith, aged 11 years, then stepped forward and gracefully delivered the following address:

"'GENERAL LAFAYETTE: In behalf of myself and fellow schoolmates, may I be permitted to express our sincere and respectful gratitude to you for the condescension you have manifested this day in visiting this institution, which is one of the noblest specimens of New York philanthropy. Here, sir, you behold hundreds of the poor children of Africa sharing with those of a lighter hue in the blessings of education; and while it will be our pleasure to remember the great deeds you have done for America, it will be our delight also to cherish the memory of General Lafayette as a friend to African emancipation, and as a member of this institution.'

"To which the general replied, in his own characteristic style, 'I thank you, my dear child.'

"Several of the pupils underwent short examinations, and one of them explained the use of the globes and answered many questions in geography."

PUBLIC SCHOOLS FOR COLORED CHILDREN.

These schools continued to flourish, under the same management, and with an attendance varyig from 600 in 1824 to 862 in 1832, in the latter part of which year the Manumission Society, whose schools were now in part supported by the public fund, applied to the Public School Society for a committee of conference to effect a union. It was felt by the trustees that on many accounts it was better that the two sets of schools should remain separate, but, fearing further diversion of the school fund, it was desirable that the number of societies participating should be as small as possible, and arrangements were accordingly made for a transfer of the schools and property of the elder society. After some delay, in consequence of legislative action being found necessary to give a title to their real estate, on the 2d of May, 1834, the transfer was effected, all their schools and school property passing into the hands of the New York Public School Society, at an appraised valuation of $12,130 22.

The aggregate register of these schools at the time of the transfer was nearly 1,400, with an average attendance of about one-half that number. They were placed in charge of a committee with powers similar to the committee on primary schools, but their administration was not satisfactory, and it was soon found that the schools had greatly diminished in numbers, efficiency, and usefulness. A committee of inquiry was appointed, and reported that, in consequence of the great anti-slavery riots, and attacks on colored people, many families had removed from the city, and of those that remained many kept their children at home; they knew the Manumission Society as their special friends, but knew nothing of the Public School Society; the reduction of all the schools, but one, to the grade of primary, had given great offense; also the discharge of teachers long employed, and the discontinuance of rewards, and taking home of spelling books; strong prejudices had grown up against the Public School Society. The committee recommended a prompt assimilation of the colored schools to the white; the establishment of two or more upper schools in a new building; a normal school for colored monitors, and the appointment of a colored man as school agent, at $150 a year. The school on Mulberry street at this time, 1835, was designated Colored Grammar School No. 1. A. Libolt was principal, and registered 317 pupils; there were also six primaries, located in different parts of the city, with an aggregate attendance of 925 pupils.

In 1836 a new school building was completed in Laurens street, opened with 210 pupils, R. F. Wake, (colored,) principal, and was designated Colored Grammar School No. 2. Other means were taken to improve the schools, and to induce the colored people to patronize them; the principal of No. 1, Mr. Libolt, was replaced by Mr. John Paterson, colored, a sufficient assurance of whose ability and success we have in the fact that he has been continued in the position ever since. A "Society for the Promotion of Education among Colored Children" was organized, and established two additional schools, one in Thomas street, and one in Center, and a marked improvement was manifest; but it required a long time to restore the confidence and interest felt before the transfer, and even up to 1848 the aggregate attendance in all the colored schools was only 1,375 pupils.

In the winter of 1852 the first evening schools for colored pupils were opened; one for males and one for females, and were attended by 379 pupils. In the year 1853 the colored schools, with all the schools and school property of the Public School Society, were transferred to the "Board of Education of the City and County of New York," and still further improvements were made in them; a normal school for colored teachers was established, with Mr. John Paterson, principal, and the schools were graded in the same manner as those for white children. Colored Grammar School No. 3 was opened at 78 West Fortieth street, Miss Caroline W. Simpson, principal, and in the ensuing year three others were added; No. 4, in One Hundred and Twentieth street, (Harlem,) Miss Nancy Thompson, principal; No. 5, at 101 Hudson street, P. W. Williams, principal; and No. 6, at 1167 Broadway, Prince Leveridge, principal. Grammar Schools Nos. 2, 3, and 4, had primary departments attached, and there were also at this time three separate primary schools, and the aggregate attendance in all was 2,047. Since then the attendance in these schools has not varied much from these figures. The schools themselves have been altered and modified from time to time, as their necessity seemed to indicate; though under the general management of the Board of Education, they have been in the care of the school officers of the wards in which they are located, and while in some cases they received the proper attention, in others they were either wholly, or in part, neglected. A recent act has placed them directly in charge of the Board of Education, who have appointed a special committee to look after their interests, and measures are being taken by them which will give this class of schools every opportunity and convenience possessed by any other, and, it is hoped, will also improve the grade of its scholarship.

The organization and attendance of these schools in 1868 is shown in the following table, compiled from information received from the city superintendent of schools, Mr. S. S. Randall:

Schools.	Date of organization.	Teachers.				Pupils.		Location.
		Principals.	Assistants.	Of music.	Of drawing.	Whole number registered.	Average attendance.	
No. 1—Boys' department ..	1820	John Peterson ...	5	1	1	399	149	135 Mulberry street, 14th
Girls' department...		Eliza Gwynne ...	5			380	142	ward.
No. 2—Boys' department ..	1836	Ransom F. Wake.	2	2	1	(*)	(*)	51 and 53 Laurens street,
Girls' department...		Fanny Tompkins.	5			147	64	8th ward.
Primary departm't .		Sarah Ennalls ...	3			470	122	
No. 3—Grammar departm't.	1853	Chas. L. Reason..	3	1	1	102	46	78 West Fortieth street,
Primary departm't .		Cath. A.Thomps'n	2			207	62	20th ward.
No. 4—Grammar departm't.	1840	S. J. S. Tompkins.	5	1	1	310	143	98 West Seventeenth street,
Primary departm't .		Elizabeth Pierce .	3			....	.....	16th ward.
No. 5	1854	Mary E. Tripp...	....	....	....	41	11	One-hundred-and-twenti'th st., (Harlem,) 12th ward.
No. 6	1868	Mary M. Moreau.	1	....	....	(*)	(*)	155 Stanton st., 17th ward.
Evening schools.								
No. 1..............	1852	S. J. S. Tompkins.	....	....	....	(*)	(†)	In building of school No. 2.
No. 2.....................	1852	Ransom F. Wake.	....	....	....	(*)	(†)	In building of school No. 4.
No. 3.....................	1868	Mary M. Moreau.	....	....	....	(*)	(†)	In building of school No. 6.
Normal school	1854	Chas. L. Reason..	....	....	....	.....	......	In building of school No. 1,
		Carol'e Hamilton.						on Saturdays.
Total.............	......	....	34	....	....	2,056	739	

GRADE OF SCHOLARSHIP.—Colored boys' grammar schools, 78; colored girls' grammar schools, 71½; colored primary schools, 76½; total of all the schools in the city, 80 3-7. (Whole number of sessions, 430 in each.)

* No report.   † About 45 in each.

In addition to and independent of these schools there are four primaries in connection with the Colored Orphan Asylum at One hundred and fifty-first street. Their aggregate register last year was 264 pupils. There are also two or three small private primary schools for colored children in the city, and these, with the before-mentioned, comprise all those now in existence. The teachers in these schools are, with but two exceptions—the principal of No. 6 and the assistant principal of No. 1—of the same race as their pupils. The pupils are, for the most part, children of laboring people; many of them are put out to service at an early age, and only get a chance to go to school when they are out of a situation; while very few are able, or take sufficient interest to attend regularly all of the time; which in part accounts for the low grade of scholarship in this class of schools; but there has been an improvement in this respect of late, and, in view of the efforts being made in their behalf, we are encouraged to believe that their future history will show a brighter record.

GERRITT SMITH'S SCHOOL AT PETERBORO'.

In any historical survey of the progressive development of schools for colored people, the timely and liberal aid and efforts of Hon. Gerritt Smith, of Peterboro', New York, should not be omitted. This eminent philanthropist was one of the earliest to extend liberal aid to several, as well as the assurance of his sympathy to all, institutions which opened their doors to children and youth of the colored population. He established and maintained for a number of years in his own village a school, which was attended by colored pupils from different parts of the country. He was an early and very liberal patron of Oneida Institute, the doors of which were ever open to pupils without respect to complexion or race. He gave to it between $3,000 and $4,000 in cash, and 3,000 acres of land in Vermont. He did even more for Oberlin College, in Ohio, *because* of its hospitality to colored pupils. He gave it a few thousand dollars in money and 20,000 acres of land in Virginia, which brought to the institution probably more than $50,000. The New York Central College, at McGrawville, where colored and white young men and women were instructed together, cost Mr. Smith several thousand dollars more.

NORTH CAROLINA.

The total population of North Carolina in 1860 was 992,622, of whom 361,522 were colored; and of these 331,059 were slaves, and 30,463 free. It was not until 1729 that any law relating to assemblies of slaves, free negroes, and mulattoes was enacted in North Carolina, when slaves were also forbidden to hunt or range over the lands not belonging to their owner; and when thus trespassing, the owner of the land on which they were found was authorized to whip them, "not exceeding 40 lashes." And, by the same law, " if any loose, disorderly, or suspected person, not being a white person," was found drinking, eating, or keeping company with slaves in the night time," he was liable to a penalty of 40 lashes, unless he could give a "satisfactory account of his behavior." If negroes belonging to one man were found in the quarters or kitchens of the negroes of another man, they were liable to a penalty of 40 lashes, while those who entertained them were subject to 20. In 1741 slaves not wearing a livery were forbidden to leave the plantation to which they belonged. In 1777 it was enacted that no negro or mulatto slave should be set free, "except for meritorious services." Among other enactments of about this period were those forbidding free negroes or mulattoes to entertain any slave during the Sabbath, or to trade with slaves, the penalties for either offense being severe. In 1812 slaves were forbidden to act as pilots on the coast of the State, and in 1830 it was provided that the owner of any slave consenting to such service should forfeit the value of the slave. This law was still in force in 1860.

Until the year 1835 public opinion permitted the colored residents of this State to maintain schools for the education of their children. These were taught sometimes by white persons, but more frequently by teachers of the same race as their pupils. After this period colored children could be educated only by finding a teacher within the circle of their own family, or out of the limits of the State; in which latter event they were regarded as expatriated, and prohibited by law from returning home. The public school system of North Carolina declared that no descendant from negro ancestors, to the fourth generation inclusive, should enjoy the benefit thereof. Thus matters continued until the success of the Union forces opened a way for educational effort. In 1863 thousands of freedmen had taken refuge at Newbern and on Roanoke island, and to both of these places the American Missionary Association sent teachers who opened schools. As in Virginia, so, too, in North Carolina other schools followed close upon the march of the United States troops. Immediately upon the entry of the latter into Wilmington, in 1865, the teachers of the association also made their appearance there, and were hailed by the negro population with indescribable delight. Mr. Coan, one of these teachers, thus describes the scene: "By appointment, I met the children at the church vestry the next morning. They were to come at 9 o'clock; by 7 the street was blocked, the yard was full. Parents, eager to get 'dese yer four children's name tooken,' came pulling them through the crowd. 'Please, sir, put down des yer.' 'I wants dis gal of mine to jine; and dat yer boy hes got no parents, and I jes done and brot him.' . . . The same evidences of joy inexpressible were manifest at the organization of evening schools for adults. About 1,000 pupils reported themselves in less than one week after our arrival in Wilmington." This thirst for knowledge, which was common to the freed people throughout the entire south, was met by efforts on the part of various benevolent agencies to satisfy it. Upon the cessation of hostilities schools were opened in different localities, and before the end of the year nearly 100 were in operation, with an attendance of more than 8,000 pupils. Each successive year since then has been marked by an increase in the number of these schools, in spite of the obstacles which presented themselves, in the scarcity of teachers, and of suitable school buildings, and, too often, in the unfriendly opposition of white residents. To overcome these obstacles the freedmen themselves have earnestly seconded the efforts of philanthropy in their behalf. In the depth of their poverty they have sustained a large portion of the schools, and cheerfully contributed to the support of others. In 1867 Mr. F. A. Fiske, the State superintendent of education under the Freedman's Bureau, reported, that many instances had come under his notice where the teachers of a self-supporting school had been sustained till the last cent the freedmen could command was exhausted, and where these last had even taxed their credit in the coming crop to pay the bills necessary to keep up the school. As evidence of the great interest manifested in acquiring knowledge, the same officer mentioned a fact connected with one of the schools under his supervision which is, perhaps, without a parallel in the history of education. Side by side, commencing their alphabet together, and continuing their studies until they could each read the Bible fluently, sat a child of six summers, her mother, grandmother, and great-grandmother, aged 75 years, the representatives of four generations in a direct line.

The following tables, prepared by Professor Vashon, give the condition of the schools for the years specified:

Number of schools, teachers, and pupils, 1865 to 1868.

Year.	Number of schools.			Number of teachers.			Number of scholars.			Average attendance.	Per cent.
	Day.	Night.	Total.	White.	Colored.	Total.	Male.	Female.	Total.		
1865.........	....	....	86	....	....	119	....	....	8,506	....	.....
1866.........	....	....	136	....	....	158	....	....	10,971	....	.....
1867.........	130	60	190	139	88	227	5,922	6,351	12,273	8,714	71
1868.........	238	104	342	146	221	367	8,531	8,879	17,410	11,078	63

Studies and expenditures, 1867 and 1868.

Year.	Number of scholars in different studies pursued.							Expenditures in support of schools.		
	Alphabet.	Easy reading.	Advanced readers.	Writing.	Geography.	Arithmetic.	Higher branches.	By freedmen.	By others.	Total.
1867.............	1,363	7,425	3,462	4,005	2,879	3,872	321	$3,671	$48,249	$51,920
1868.............	1,286	6,310	4,043	6,200	3,652	5,455	711	15,510	69,258	84,768

There are two high schools in North Carolina, one at Wilmington, and another at Beaufort. These were established by the American Missionary Association.

Among the other benevolent educational agencies operating in this State, mention should be made of the American Freedmen's Union Commission, working principally through its New York and New England branches, and the Friends Association of Philadelphia. The last mentioned society, besides ministering largely to the relief of physical wants and suffering among the freedmen, since its organization on the 11th of November, 1863, has, also, maintained schools at different points throughout the south. Nineteen of these were within the limits of North Carolina.

The Protestant Episcopal church, too, has found here a field for its Christian labor; and its freedmen's committee has under its charge, at Raleigh,

THE ST. AUGUSTINE NORMAL SCHOOL.

This institution was incorporated in July, 1867, and opened in the following January for the admission of pupils, of whom 26 were enrolled. Its principal is the Rev. J. Brainton Smith, D. D. The trustees have now on hand and in pledges a fund of about $4,300, which they purpose to set apart as a permanent endowment. Besides, they have already purchased a tract of land, consisting of 100 acres, pleasantly situated just outside of the city limits. Here, in a beautiful grove, they are now erecting a commodious edifice that will, when completed, readily accommodate 150 pupils; they also intend to erect a boarding hall to serve as a home for pupils coming from a distance.

There is another academical school at Charlotte.   24

THE BIDDLE MEMORIAL INSTITUTE.

This institution was founded by a generous donation from the widow of the late Henry J. Biddle, of Philadelphia, and is, indeed, a fitting monument to the memory of that gentleman, who gave his life to his country in efforts to crush the slaveholders' rebellion. For this reason the Biddle institute appeals peculiarly to the regard of the freedmen, and they have not been deaf to its claims. It has been duly incorporated under the laws of North Carolina ; and through the liberality of Colonel W. R. Myers, of Charlotte, has been made the recipient of a beautiful tract of eight acres in the immediate neighborhood of the city. Upon this site two houses intended for professors' residences have been erected and paid for, and the main building is now in process of erection. To complete the entire work $8,000 are required, which, it is confidently hoped, will be readily made up by the freedmen and their friends. The first session of the institute opened on the 16th of September, 1867, and 43 students were admitted during its first school year. Great care is exercised in the admission of students, and all of them are required to devote a part of their time to teaching among the people.

This institution was established under the auspices of the general assembly's committee on freedmen of the Presbyterian church, (old school,) whose praiseworthy labors in Kansas and elsewhere have already been adverted to, and who have, since 1865, supported 22 other schools at different points in the State of North Carolina.

The present constitution of North Carolina, adopted in April, 1868, provides for " a general and uniform system of free public schools." The governor, lieutenant-governor, secretary of State, treasury, auditor, superintendent of public works, superintendent of public instruction, and attorney general, constitute a State board of education, which succeeds to all the powers and trusts of the president and directors of the literary fund of North Carolina ; and has full power to legislate and make all needful rules and regulations in relation to free public schools and the educational fund. The superintendent of public instruction has the charge of the schools. Each county is divided into school districts, in each of which one or more public schools must be maintained at least four months in the year. The schools of each county are under the control of county commissioners, elected biennially.

OHIO.

By the census of 1860 the population of Ohio was 2,339,511, of which number 36,673 were free colored. By repeated votes of the people the right of suffrage has been denied to this portion of the population unless they have a preponderance of white blood.

The superintendent of common schools (John A. Norris) writes to the superintendent of public instruction in Indiana as follows : " Colored youths of legal school age, i. e., between the ages of 5 and 21 years, are entitled to the privileges of the public school fund. Colored youth cannot of legal right claim admittance to our common schools for white youth. The local school authorities may, however, admit a colored youth to the public schools for white youth, and as a matter of fact in the larger part of the State the colored youth are admitted on equal terms with the white youth to the common or public schools." According to his report for 1869 there were, in 1868, employed in the colored schools of the State, 241 teachers, (male, 104 ; female, 137.) The number of schools was 189, having 10,404 pupils enrolled, (males 5,409 ; females, 4,995.) The average number in daily attendance was 5,246, (males, 2,730 ; females, 2,516.)

THE COLORED SCHOOLS OF CINCINNATI.

The first schools exclusively for colored persons were established in the year 1820, and by colored men. One of these schools was located in what was known as " Glenn's old pork house," on Hopple's alley, near Sycamore street. This school did not last long. Another was established, in the same year, by a colored man named Schooley. It was kept somewhere in the neighborhood of Sixth street and Broadway, which vicinity was then called " The Green," which has long since disappeared. Mr. Wing, who kept a private school near the corner of Vine and Sixth streets, admitted colored students to his night school. During the period of time extending from 1820 to 1835 no school was regularly kept, teachers being few and patronage slack. Owen T. B. Nickens, a colored man, who still teaches at New Richmond, Ohio, was one of the prominent educators of that period.

About 1835 came the begining of the anti-slavery discussion among the people of Cincinnati. A number of young men and women, filled with a hatred to slavery and a desire to labor for a down-trodden race, came to Cincinnati and established several schools. One in the colored Baptist church, on Western row, was taught at various times by Messrs. Barbour, E. Fairchild, W. Robinson, and Augustus Wattles. Of the ladies, there were the Misses Bishop, Matthews, Lowe, and Mrs. Merrell. They were all excellent teachers, and deeply imbued with a desire to do good, and are remembered with gratitude by those who received instruction at their hands.

They were, of course, subjected to much contumely. Boarding-house keepers refused to entertain them, placing their trunks upon the sidewalks and telling them that they "had no accommodations for nigger teachers." They were obliged to club together, rent a house, and board themselves. Frequently the schools were closed because of mob violence.

A part of the salary of these teachers was paid by an educational society, consising of benevolent whites (many of whom have lived to witness the triumph of principles which they espoused amid so much obloquy) and the better class of colored people. Among the colored men who co-operated heartily in the work, may be named Baker Jones, Joseph Fowler, John Woodson, Dennis Hill, John Liverpool, and William O. Hara.

These schools continued with varying fortunes until 1844, when Rev. Hiram S. Gilmore, a young man of good fortune, fine talents, and rare benevolence, established the "Cincinnati high school," which was, in some respects, the best school ever established in Cincinnati for the benefit of the colored people. Its proprietor, or patron rather, spared no expense to make it a success. Ground was purchased at the east end of Harrison street and a commodious building of five large rooms and a chapel was fitted up. In the yard, an unusual thing at that time in any Cincinnati school, was fitted a fine gymnasium. Good teachers were employed to give instruction in the branches usual to a full English course of study, besides which, Latin, Greek, drawing, and music were taught.

The number of pupils at times rose to 300 ; but the receipts never equalled the expenses.

Some of the pupils displayed such proficiency in singing, declamations, and the like, that regularly, every vacation, classes of them, in charge of the principal, journeyed through the States of Ohio and New York giving concerts. The profits realized by these expeditions were devoted to clothing and furnishing books to the poorer pupils of the school. In some cases the time of such poor pupils as gave sign of ability was hired from their parents. Never did a nobler soul exist than that which animated the breast of Hiram S. Gilmore! The teachers of this school were : Mr. Joseph H. Moore, Thomas L. Boucher, David P. Lowe, lately police judge of our city, and finally Dr. A. L. Childs; the musical proficiencies of the pupils was due to their thorough training by W. F. Colburn, their instructor in music. In 1848 the school passed into the hands of Dr. A. L. Childs, who was its principal at the time of its discontinuance.

PUBLIC SCHOOLS FOR COLORED CHILDREN.

The law authorizing the establishment of schools for colored children at the public expense was passed in 1849. An attempt to organize schools under the law was made in 1850. Trustees were elected, teachers employed, and houses hired, but the money to pay for all this was not forthcoming from the city treasury. The law orders that so much of all the funds belonging to the city of Cincinnati as would fall to the colored youth, by a *per capita* division, should be held subject to the order of the colored trustees. The city declared that the colored trustees, not being electors, were not and could not be qualified as office-holders under the constitution of the State of Ohio, hence they could draw no money from the city treasury. They refused, therefore, to honor the drafts of the school board. The schools were closed after continuing three months, the teachers going unpaid. The colored school board, inspired by the appeals and counsels of the late John I. Gaines, called a meeting of the colored people, and laid the case before them. It was resolved to raise money and employ counsel to contest this decision of the city officials. The legal proceeding was in the nature of an application for *mandamus.* The case was placed in the hands of Flamen Ball, esq. The colored people were victors, though not till the case had been carried to the supreme court by the contestants.

In 1851 the schools were again opened, but the accommodations were wretched. The amount falling to the colored schools was small. Good houses were needed, but eminent legal gentlemen declared there was no authority anywhere to build school-houses for colored children. The school board was proceeding cautiously in the matter, when, suddenly, by a change in the law, they were thrown out of power. The control of the colored schools was vested in the board of trustees and visitors which had control of the public schools for white children. This board was authorized by the new law to appoint six colored men, to whom the task of managing the schools was intrusted, except in the matter of controlling the funds. The leading colored men held aloof from this arrangement, feeling that if colored men were competent to manage the schools in one particular they were in all, and if colored men could manage the schools, colored men could select the managers as well or better than white men could.

The law was again altered in 1856, giving to the colored people the right of electing their own trustees. Thus it stands to-day.

The first school-house was erected and occupied in 1858. It was built by Nicholas Longworth and leased to the colored people, with privilege of purchasing in 14 years. It has been paid for several years ago. It cost $14,000. In 1859 the building on Court street, for the western district, was erected. Since then three other buildings, two of them small, have been completed. The total value of all the property used by the colored schools is about $50,000. The rooms will accommodate about 700 pupils. The title to this, as with other school property, is vested in the city of Cincinnati.

The schools are classified as primary, intermediate, and high school. Seventeen teachers are employed, all of whom are colored and former pupils, except two, who are Germans, and are employed, one in teaching the German language, the other in teaching music. The salaries paid are not so high as are paid in the other public schools of the city. The receipts for the year ending June 30, 1869, were about $24,000. The number of pupils enrolled in all departments was 1,006 ; average belonging, 522 ; average attendance, 475.

WILBERFORCE UNIVERSITY.

The earliest collegiate institution in the United States, founded and owned by colored men, is Wilberforce University, which originated in 1863, during the heat of the great rebellion. Although designed for the special training of colored youth, it is prohibited by its charter from making any distinctions on account of race or color, among its trustees, its instructors, or its students. The present faculty consists of five persons, three of whom are colored and two white. It is located three and a half miles east of Xenia, in Greene county, Ohio, and is under the management of members of the African Methodist Episcopal church.

The first establishment of Wilberforce University, however, is due to another body of Christians. In 1853 some of the ministers and members of the Methodist Episcopal church saw and felt the necessity of a more liberal and concentrated effort to improve the condition of the colored people in Ohio and other States, and to furnish the facilities of education to them. Deeming that colored men must be, for the most part, the educators and elevators of their own race in this and other lands, they conceived the idea of an institution wherein many of that class should be thoroughly trained for professional teaching, or for any other pursuit in life. At the session of the Cincinnati conference, in 1855, this movement culminated in the appointment of the Rev. John F. Wright as general agent to take the incipient steps for establishing such a college. This gentleman, with others, entered into negotiations for the purchase of the Xenia Springs property, which had been previously fitted up as a fashionable watering place, at a cost of some $50,000. This property consisted of 52 acres of land, in a beautiful and healthy region, upon which there had been erected a large edifice with numerous rooms, well adapted to the purposes of a collegiate institution. Besides this principal building, there was a number of cottages upon the place well suited to the use of private families. Mr. Wright and his associates were fortunate enough to find about half a dozen wealthy and philanthropic gentlemen to second them in their efforts, and in May, 1856, the purchase was concluded for $13,500. In the following August application was duly made for incorporation under the general law of the State of Ohio, and every legal requisition having been complied with, the institution was organized and constituted a body corporate under the name of the Wilberforce University. It was kept in successful operation from October, 1856, until June, 1862, at which time, as it was supported mainly by southern slaveholders who sent their children there to be educated, the war cut off the greater portion of its patronage and compelled a suspension of its operations. The institution was then laboring under an indebtedness of $10,000 ; and for this sum the trustees offered to sell out all their right, title, and interest to the African Methodist Episcopal church, whose co-operation in this enterprise had been requested and declined as early as 1856. This offer was accepted ; thus the *present* Wilberforce University came into being. The credit for this result is largely due to the Rt. Rev. Daniel A. Payne, one of the bishops of the African Methodist Episcopal church, who had favored co-operation with the white Methodists, and who has ever since been an untiring worker in behalf of this educational enterprise.

In the course of the two following years the new proprietors reduced their indebtedness to $3,000, having received aid from their white friends only to the extent of $260. The gratifying success attendant thus far upon the establishment of this unique institution was destined to encounter quite a serious check. On the 14th day of April, 1865—a day sadly memorable in the annals of our country as that of President Lincoln's assassination—the college edifice fell a prey to incendiarism ; but the ardor of the friends of Wilberforce was quickened instead of being diminished by this misfortune. The amount of insurance upon the burnt building ($8,000) enabled them to discharge the obligations existing against them, and to reserve $5,000 as a fund for rebuilding. With this amount at their command, they confidently laid the foundation of a new structure 160 feet in length by 44 feet in width, at an anticipated cost of $35,000, and made appeal to their friends to aid them in their endeavors. Their call for assistance has been quite favorably responded to both by members of their own denomination and other parties ; among the latter of whom may be mentioned the executors of the Avery estate, and the Society for the Promotion of Collegiate and Theological Education at the West. They are now enabled to show as the result of their persevering energy a handsome building, sufficiently advanced towards completion to accommodate their students, about 80 in number, equally divided between the two sexes. The prospects are quite flattering, too, for the endowment of their requisite number of professorships, and for making additions to their scientific apparatus and to their library, now already numbering about 2,500 volumes.

Wilberforce is designed to be a university complete in all the ordinary faculties. Those of literature, medicine, and theology have already been established, and additional ones in the department of science and law are contemplated. The several courses of instruction are full and thorough ; and two features included in them are deserving of especial mention as showing the laudable spirit of its board of trustees. These are, first, that, in view of anticipated missionary effort in Hayti, particular attention is paid to the study of French; and, second, that, with the design of training teachers for labor among the freedmen, a normal day and Sunday school has been instituted.

The corps of instruction now employed at Wilberforce University is as follows, viz : Rt. Rev. Daniel A. Payne, D. D., President and Professor of Christian Theology, Mental Science, and Church Government; John G. Mitchell, A. M., Professor of Greek and Mathematics; Rev. William Kent, M. D., Professor of Natural Sciences; Theodore E. Suliot, A. M., Professor of English, Latin, and French Literature, and Associate Professor of Mathematics.

Medical Department.—William Kent, M. D., Professor of Practical and Analytical Chemistry ; —— Williams, M. D.; J. P. Marvin, M. D.; Alexander T. Augusta, M. D.

OBERLIN COLLEGE.

In any account of the higher education of colored youth in this country, Oberlin College must not be omitted. That institution, established in 1833, opened its doors to deserving applicants without distinction of sex, race, or color, and as early as 1836 had several colored students. The first colored graduate of the college was George B. Vashon, subsequently professor of languages in Avery College, at Pittsburg. The whole number of colored graduates is 20, three of whom are females. The whole number of colored graduates in the teachers' course is 16; in the theological department, 1. Before the war the ratio of colored students to the whole number was five per cent. for a period of nearly 20 years; since the war it has amounted to nearly eight per cent., making an average of nearly 50 colored students during the last 25 years.

PENNSYLVANIA.

By the census of 1860 there were returned, out of a population of 2,906,115, in Pennsylvania, 56,849 free blacks. By the constitution of the State the right of suffrage is restricted to whites; but by the school law the privileges of a public school education are extended to all children, whether white or black; and, by an act passed in 1854, the school directors of the several districts are authorized and required "to establish, within their respective districts, separate schools for the tuition of negro and mulatto children, whenever such schools can be so located as to accommodate 20 or more pupils; and whenever such separate schools shall be established and kept open four months in any year, the directors or controllers shall not be compelled to admit such pupils into any other schools of the district: *Provided*, That in cities and boroughs the board of controllers shall provide for such schools out of the general funds assessed and collected by uniform taxation for educational purposes."

To the members of the Society of Friends, in Philadelphia, and to associations originating under the auspices of that religious body, are the blacks of this country indebted for the earliest permanent and best developed schools for their children.

SCHOOLS FOR BLACK PEOPLE BY ANTHONY BENEZET.

Rev. George Whitefield—who visited America in 1739, partly to found an orphan house after the model of that of Franké, at Halle, purchased in 1740 a tract of land of about 5,000 acres in Upper Nazareth township; but in view of making a location further south, (in Georgia,) transferred his title to the Moravian brethren in 1843—contemplated, it is said, the establishment of a school for negro children, but accomplished nothing.[*]

The earliest school of any kind for the education of the children of negroes, in Philadelphia, so far as we can ascertain, was established as an evening school, by Anthony Benezet, about the year 1750, and taught by him gratuitously. This remarkable man, who was the first on this continent to plead the cause of the oppressed African race, and whose publications were instrumental in enlisting the energies of Clarkson and others in the abolition of the slave trade, was born at St. Quentin, France, December 31, 1713, (old style.) His parents were among the most noted and wealthy persons of the place, but, on becoming Pro-

---

[*] It is stated in Sypher's "School History of Pennsylvania" that Rev. George Whitefield commenced the erection of a school-house for colored children at Nazareth. We do not have at hand the authorities to confirm or refute this statement; but we find in Anderson's "Colonial Church" that Whitefield, on the occasion of his visit to Georgia, in 1740, censured Oglethorpe and others, who had got introduced into the charter a clause prohibiting the importation of negro slaves into the colony of Georgia. "To prohibit people from holding lands, except under the conditions which those laws prescribed, or to require them to carry on the work of cultivation in a hot climate without negro labor, was little better, he said, than to tie their legs and bid them walk. He maintained that to keep slaves was lawful; else how was the Scripture to be explained which spoke of slaves being born in Abraham's house, or purchased with his money? He denied not that liberty was sweet to those who were born free; but argued that, to those who had never known any other condition, slavery might not be so irksome. The introduction, also, of slaves into Georgia, would bring them, he believed, within the reach of those means of grace which would make them partakers of a liberty far more precious than any which affected the body only; and, upon such grounds, he hesitated not to exert himself to obtain a repeal of that part of the charter which forbade the importation of slaves."

testants, their estate was confiscated, and they withdrew from their native country and took refuge in Holland. From thence the family removed to London, and the father having engaged in commercial pursuits there, he recovered, to some extent, his lost fortune.

In 1731 the family removed to Philadelphia, where they were permanently established; and in 1736 Anthony married Joyce Marriott, of Wilmington, Delaware, with whom he lived 50 years "in love and peace." Declining to engage in commerce, from motives of a religious nature, he turned his attention to mechanical pursuits, which proving unfavorable to his health, at the age of 26 he engaged as a teacher at Germantown, in the vicinity of Philadelphia.

In 1742 he became usher in the public school formed under a charter from William Penn, in which school he continued 12 years. In 1755 he opened a school for the instruction of girls, which was attended for 30 years by the daughters of the most affluent and respectable inhabitants of the city. His methods of instruction and of discipline were far in advance of those of the teachers of that period, by which he attached his pupils to himself for his gentleness and regard for their happiness; among other privileges granting them a room as a place of amusement during the intervals of study. His views of education are expressed in the following paragraphs:

"With respect to the education of our youth, I would propose, as the fruit of 40 years' experience, that when they are proficients in the use of their pen, and become sufficiently acquainted with the English grammar and the useful parts of arithmetic, they should be taught mensuration of superficies and solids, as it helps the mind in many necessary matters, particularly the use of the scale and the compass, and will open the way for those parts of the mathematics which their peculiar situations may afterwards make necessary. It would also be profitable for every scholar, of both sexes, to go through and understand a short but very plain set of merchant's accounts in single entry, particularly adapted to the civil uses of life. And in order to perfect their education in a useful and agreeable way, both to themselves and others, I would propose to give them a general knowledge of the mechanical powers, geography, and the elements of astronomy; the use of the microscope might also be profitably added, in discovering the minute parts of creation; this, with the knowledge of the magnitude and courses of those mighty bodies which surround us, would tend to exalt their ideas.

"Such parts of history as may tend to give them a right idea of the corruption of the human heart, the dreadful nature and effects of war, the advantage of virtue, &c., are also necessary parts of an education founded upon Christian and reasonable principles. These several instructions should be inculcated on a religious plan, in such a way as may prove a delightful rather than a painful labor, both to teachers and pupils. It might also be profitable to give lads of bright genius some plain lectures upon anatomy, the wondrous frame of man, deducing therefrom the advantage of a simple way of life, enforcing upon their understanding the kind efforts of nature to maintain the human frame in a state of health, with little medical help but what abstinence and exercise will afford. These necessary parts of knowledge, so useful in directing the youthful mind in the path of virtue and wisdom, might be proposed by way of lectures, which the pupil should write down, and when corrected should be copied in a neat bound book, to be kept for future perusal."

While teaching this school for girls he prepared and published two of the earliest school-books printed in this country; one a spelling-book and primer, and a grammar. The sentiments expressed in these books were such as grew out of his efforts to promote the education of youth on the basis of a true estimate of human life, "whence obedience and love to God, benignity to man, and a tender regard for the whole creation would necessarily flow;" and also from his desire to give to youth "as easy and compendious a knowledge of their own language, and such other useful parts of learning, as their respective situations may make necessary to answer all the good purposes of life."

In the year 1750 he became interested in the iniquity of the slave trade, and from this time he devoted himself strenuously to the amelioration of the condition of the black people till the end of his life. In this direction he took special interest in the education of their youth, establishing for them, as has been stated, the first evening school, which he taught himself gratuitously; and he subsequently engaged in soliciting funds for the erection of a building for a day school for their instruction. From the experience derived from his own school, and from his intercourse with the blacks, he formed and expressed a more favorable opinion of their dispositions and mental capacities than had been previously generally entertained. On these points he says: "I can with truth and sincerity declare that I have found among the negroes as great variety of talents as among a like number of whites, and I am bold to assert that the notion entertained by some, that the blacks are inferior in their capacities, is a vulgar prejudice, founded on the pride or ignorance of their lordly masters, who have kept their slaves at such a distance as to be unable to form a right judgment of them."

When the education of colored youth was taken up by the Society of Friends, Benezet volunteered to assist the teacher; and on several occasions, when there was a failure to procure a teacher, he himself continued the school. Without dwelling further on the labors of Benezet to promote the abolition of slavery in his own State, and to ameliorate the condition of the colored people everywhere, the following extract from his will exhibits his desire to continue his work in their behalf after his death:

"I give my above said house and lot, or ground rent proceeding from it, and the rest and residue of my estate which shall remain undisposed of after my wife's decease, both real and personal, to the Public School of Philadelphia, founded by charter, and to their successors forever, in trust, that they shall sell my house and lot on perpetual ground rent forever, if the same be not already sold by my executors, as before mentioned, and that as speedily as may be they receive and take as much of my personal estate as may be remaining, and therewith purchase a yearly ground rent, or ground rents, and with the income of such ground rent proceeding from the sale of my real estate hire, and employ a religious-minded person, or persons, to teach a number of negro, mulatto, or Indian children to read, write, arithmetic, plain accounts, needle-work, &c. And it is my particular desire, founded on the experience I have had in that service, that, in the choice of such tutors, special care may be had to prefer an industrious, careful person, of true piety, who may be or become suitably qualified, who would undertake the service from a principle of charity, to one more highly learned, not equally disposed; this I desire may be carefully attended to, sensible that from the number of pupils of all ages, the irregularity of attendance their situation subjects them to, will not admit of that particular inspection in their improvement usual in other schools, but that the real well-doing of the scholars will very much depend upon the master making a special conscience of doing his duty; and shall likewise defray such other necessary expense as may occur in that service; and as the said remaining income of my estate, after my wife's decease, will not be sufficient to defray the whole expense necessary for the support of such a school, it is my request that the overseers of the said Public School shall join in the care and expense of such a school, or schools, for the education of negro, mulatto, or Indian children, with any committee which may be appointed by the monthly meetings of Friends in Philadelphia, or with any other body of benevolent persons who may join in raising money and employing it for the education and care of such children; my desire being that, as such a school is now set up, it may be forever maintained in this city."

Benezet died on the 3d of May, 1784, and his funeral was attended by the widows and orphans and the poor of all descriptions, including many hundreds of blacks, all of whom 'mourned for the loss of their best friend."

SCHOOLS FOR BLACK PEOPLE BY THE SOCIETY OF FRIENDS.

To the Society of Friends in particular is the African slave in America indebted for the earliest efforts for his enlightenment and for the most persistent struggles for his emancipation and the abolition of the slave trade. George Fox, from the time of landing in 1672, on the banks of the Patuxent, in Maryland, never failed to impress upon those who controlled the negro the importance of raising him above the brute. In an epistle to Friends in America, written in 1679, he says: "You must instruct and teach your Indians and negroes, and all others, how that Christ, by the grace of God, tasted death for every man." The journals of the Quaker preachers who succeeded him show they were animated by the same spirit. One of their number, a man of fine classical education, and educated as a lawyer, says: "The morning that we came from Thomas Simons's my companion, speaking some words of truth to his negro woman, she was tendered, and as I passed on horseback by the place where she stood weeping I gave her my hand, and then she was much more broken.   *   *   She stood there, looking after us and weeping as long as we could see her. I inquired of one of the black men here how long they had come to meetings. He says they had always been kept in ignorance and disregarded, as persons who were not to expect anything from the Lord, till Jonathan Taylor, who had been there the year before discoursing with them, had informed them that the grace of God, through Christ, was given also to them." On the 25th of the second month, at Pocoson, not far from Yorktown, Virginia, he was "entertained in much friendship and tender respect by Thomas Nichols and his wife, but by her especially, who, though a mulatto by extraction, was not too tawny for the divine light of the Lord Jesus Christ."

On the 26th of January, 1770, through the influence of Anthony Benezet, a committee was appointed at a monthly meeting of Friends, in Philadelphia, "to consider on the instruction of negro and mulatto children in reading, writing, and other useful learning suitable to their capacity and circumstances;" and, on the 30th of May of the same year, they decided to authorize a special committee of seven Friends to employ a schoolmistress of prudent and exemplary conduct "to teach, not more at one time than 30 children, in the first rudiments of school learning and in sewing and knitting." The school was to be opened to white children if a sufficient number of children of negroes and mulattoes did not apply for admission. In June a male teacher was employed—Moles Patterson—who had a salary of £80 a year and an additional sum of £11 for one-half of the rent of his dwelling-house. While instruction was gratuitous to the poor, those who were able were requested to pay, "at the rate of 10s. a quarter for those who write and 7s. 6d. for others."

The scholars having been found on examination to have made good progress, the monthly meeting authorized the construction of a school-house for the express uses of the school. On the resignation of Patterson, David Estaugh was employed as the teacher, "he having spent some time to improve himself under our friend Anthony Benezet, who, having frequently met with us and assisted us in the trust committed to us, now kindly offered to attend daily and give his assistance to David in the school."

With reference to the capacity of the children gathered in this school, the testimony of those who examined it was that it was equal to that of other children. Jacob Lehré succeeded David Estaugh in 1774, the latter having resigned, "finding the employment too heavy." In 1775 the committee agreed to admit 10 or 12 white children, because there was a probability that the school would otherwise be small in the winter season, and in April 40 colored and six white children were in the school. No record of the transactions of the committee from the early part of 1777 to 1782, because, as is stated, "a part of this period was remarkable for commotion, contending armies taking, evacuating, and repossessing this city, and schools kept within the compass thereof were generally for a time suspended." John Haughton was the teacher at the latter period, and continued in that service five years, when he resigned on account of failing health, and his place was filled by Anthony Benezet, with "the entire approbation of the committee," until his death, in May, 1784. Just before his death he addressed the following to the "overseers of the school for the instruction of the black people:"

"My friend Joseph Clark having frequently observed to me his desire, in case of my inability of continuing the care of the negro school, of succeeding me in that service, notwithstanding he now has a more advantageous school, by the desire of doing good to the black people makes him overlook these pecuniary advantages, I much wish the overseers of the school would take his desires under their peculiar notice and give him such due encouragement as may be proper, it being a matter of the greatest consequence to that school that the master be a person who makes it a principle to do his duty."

The overseers decided that "the strongest proof of their love and good-will to their departed friend, they think, will be to pay regard to the advice and recommendation contained in the said letter."

In 1784 William Waring was placed in charge of the larger children, at a salary of £100, and Sarah Dougherty of the younger children and girls, in teaching spelling, reading, sewing, &c., at a salary of £50. · In 1787 aid was received from David Barclay, of London, in behalf of a committee for managing a donation for the relief of Friends in America; and the sum of £500 was thus obtained, which, with the fund derived from the estate of Benezet, and £300 from Thomas Shirley, a colored man, was appropriated to the erection of a school-house. In 1819 a committee of "women Friends," to have exclusive charge of the admission of girls and the general superintendence of the girls' school, was associated with the overseers in the charge of the school. In 1830, in order to relieve the day school of some of the male adults who had been in the habit of attending, an evening school for the purpose of instructing such persons gratuitously was opened, and has been continued to the present time. In 1844 a lot was secured on Locust street, extending along Shield's alley, now Aurora street, on which a new house was erected in 1847, the expense of which was paid for in part from the proceeds of the sale of a lot bequeathed by John Pemberton. Additional accommodations were made to this building, from time to time, as room was demanded by new classes of pupils.

From a report published by direction of the committee of the "schools for black people and their descendants," it appears that up to the year 1867, covering a period of over 96 years, about 8,000 pupils had been instructed in these schools. In 1866 there were upwards of 4,000 colored children in the city of Philadelphia of the proper school age, of whom 1,300 were in the public schools, 800 in seminaries supported by charitable bequests and voluntary subscriptions, and 200 in private schools.

In 1849 a statistical return of the condition of the people of color in the city and districts of Philadelphia shows that there was then one grammar school, with 463 pupils; two public primary schools, with 339; and an infant school, under the charge of the Pennsylvania Abolition Society, of 70 pupils, in Clifton street; a ragged and a moral reform school with 81 pupils. In West Philadelphia there was also a public school, with 67 pupils; and, in all, there were about 20 private schools, with 300 pupils; making an aggregate of more than 1,300 children receiving an education.

In 1859, according to Bacon's "Statistics of the Colored People of Philadelphia," there were 1,031 colored children in public schools, 748 in charity schools of various kinds, 211 in benevolent and reformatory schools, and 331 in private schools, making an aggregate of 2,321 pupils, besides four evening schools, one for adult males, one for females, and one for young apprentices. There were 19 Sunday schools connected with the congregations of the colored people, and conducted by their own teachers, containing 1,667 pupils, and four Sunday schools gathered as mission schools by members of white congregations, with 215 pupils. There was also a "Public Library and Reading Room" connected with the "Institute for Colored Youth," established in 1853, having about 1,300 volumes, besides three other small libraries in different parts of the city. The same pamphlet shows that there were 1,700 of the colored population engaged in different trades and occupations, representing every department of industry.

CHARITY, BENEVOLENT, AND REFORMATORY SCHOOLS.

In 1822 an "Orphan's Shelter" was established by an association of women "Friends;" in 1850 a "House of Refuge" for children found guilty of offenses against the law; in 1855 a "Home for Colored Children;" and in 1852 a high school or "Institute for Colored Youth." In 1858 the Sheppard school was established at the House of Industry.

In a historical memoir of this society, published in 1848, it is stated that "the condition of the colored population of the city and adjoining districts, although far in advance of what it was at the organization of this society, is also a subject which still occupies its close attention. The schools already instituted for the education of colored children have largely contributed to benefit the people as a class, and will demand the vigilant attention of the society, under whose fostering care it is hoped much may be effected towards the elevation of the colored youth of our city. It would not be difficult to point to many families amongst them whose intelligence and moral standing in the community is justly referable to the early training they received in these schools, and it has afforded encouragement to many members of this society to hear the acknowledgment of many respectable individuals, that to these schools they were, under the divine blessing, mainly indebted for their success in life. Hence, also, has arisen that thirst for knowledge amongst the colored population which has led to the formation of societies for promoting the exercise of their intellectual faculties, and for the pursuit of literary and scientific subjects."

The teachers of the Institute for Colored Youth, and of all the private schools, are of their own complexion; the others are generally white. No register is kept in any school denoting standard of scholarship, nor is there any system of rewards for exciting emulation.

One of the results of the education of this class of the population has been to elevate their self-respect and to promote habits of thrift and economy, as well as to break up the habit of congregating in so large numbers in the narrow and crowded streets of the city, and to create a desire to possess houses and gardens in the suburbs. As they have become educated they have risen more and more from the condition of mere day laborers into that of skillful and industrious artisans and tradesmen, until in 1867 it was found, as a result of statistical inquiry, that they were engaged in more than 130 distinct occupations, having a fair representation in all the principal mechanical industries of the city.

From an inquiry instituted in 1837 it was ascertained that, out of the 18,768 colored people in Philadelphia, 250 had paid for their freedom the aggregate sum of $70,612, and that the real and personal property owned by them was near $1,500,000. There were returns of several chartered benevolent societies for the purpose of affording mutual aid in sickness and distress, and there were 16 houses of public worship, with over 4,000 communicants.

SCHOOLS OF THE PENNSYLVANIA ABOLITION SOCIETY.

The Pennsylvania Abolition Society established a school for children of the blacks, in 1794, taught by a well-qualified black teacher. In 1809 they erected for the use of the school a house at a cost of $4,000, to which, in 1815, they gave the name of "Clarkson Hall." In 1813 a board of education was organized, consisting of 13 persons, with a visiting committee of three, who were to visit the school once each week. In 1818 the board of education, in their report, speak in the highest terms of the beneficial effect of the Clarkson schools, which they say "furnish a decided refutation of the charge that the mental endowments of the descendants of Africa are inferior to those possessed by their white brethren. We can assert, without fear of contradiction, that the pupils of this seminary will sustain a fair comparison with those of any other institution in which the same elementary branches are taught."

PUBLIC SCHOOLS FOR COLORED CHILDREN.

In 1820 this society applied to the comptrollers of the public schools to obtain for the children of colored parents a share of the school education to which they were entitled by the law of Pennsylvania providing for the schooling of all the poor children of the commonwealth at the public expense. In 1822 the comptrollers, admitting that the benefits of the law should be extended to the colored as well as to poor white children, opened a school in Lombard street for the education of the children of both sexes of indigent persons of color; and in 1841 a primary school was opened in the same building. In 1833 the "Unclassified school" in Coates street, and from time to time afterwards several additional schools of the same class in West Philadelphia were established. These schools are maintained in the same way as the public schools generally.

INSTITUTE FOR COLORED YOUTH.

By the will of Richard Humphreys, a member of the Society of Friends, who died in 1832, the sum of $10,000 was devised to certain trustees, to be paid over by them to such benevolent society or institution as might be established for the purpose of instructing "descendants of the African race in school learning in the various branches of the mechanic arts and trade, and in agriculture." At this time the idea of giving instruction to the colored race was very unpopular, even in Philadelphia, and no society was formed to carry out the design of Mr. Humphreys until five years afterwards. Thirty members of the Society of Friends then formed themselves into an association, and took measures to establish an institution in accordance with the design of the legacy. In the preamble to the constitution adopted by them they say:

"We believe that the most successful method of elevating the moral and intellectual character of the descendants of Africa, as well as of improving their social condition, is to extend to them the benefits of a good education, and to instruct them in the knowledge of some useful trade or business, whereby they may be enabled to obtain a comfortable livelihood by their own industry; and through these means to prepare them for fulfilling the various duties of domestic and social life with reputation and fidelity, as good citizens and pious men."

To enable the youth to receive instruction in "mechanic arts and agriculture," the association, in 1839, purchased a piece of land in Bristol township, Philadelphia county, and educated a number of boys in farming, and to some extent in shoe-making and other useful occupations. In 1842 the institute was incorporated; and in 1844 there was an addition to its treasury of $18,000 from the estate of another member of the Society of Friends, Jonathan Zane, and several other small legacies. After the experiment of the combined literary, agricultural, and manual labor school for a time, in consequence of certain unfavorable circumstances, it was finally concluded, though with much regret, in 1846, to suspend the experiment for a time; and the farm and stock were sold, the only endeavor of the managers to carry out the objects of their trust, during the next six years, being by apprenticing colored lads to mechanical occupations, and maintaining an evening school for literary education.

In 1850 a day school was contemplated, but not established for the want of a proper building until 1851, when a lot was secured in Lombard street and a building erected, in which a school was opened in the autumn of 1852 for boys only, under the care of Charles L. Reason, of New York; but in the same year the girls' school was opened, the pupils being selected from those of a standing above that of the ordinary schools.

These schools proved successful, giving a good English and classical education to many active youth, thus fulfilling the design of Mr. Humphreys in qualifying many useful teachers, of both sexes, who are now scattered over the country engaged in elevating the character of the colored people. The growing want of the school for increased accommodations was met in part, in 1863, by the appropriation of $5,000 to a building fund, from the estate of Josiah Dawson, who had been a member of the corporation. Soon after two other donations of $5,000 each were made by Friends, provided $30,000 could be raised by the board to complete the building fund. This step was immediately taken and resulted successfully.

The institute under the charge of Professor E. D. Bassett, (recently appointed United States commissioner and consul general to Hayti and San Domingo,) a graduate of the State Normal School at New Britain, Connecticut, would compare favorably with any institution of the same class and grade in the city. According to the last published catalogue there were on the rolls of all the departments of the institute 223. In the boys' high school there were 52; in the girls', 100; in the boys' preparatory school, 35; and in the girls', 36; total, 223. The library of the institute contains about 2,500 volumes. The total number of graduates of the institute is 48, of whom 44 are now living. Of these, 32 are engaged in teaching.

AVERY COLLEGE, ALLEGHENY CITY.

We are indebted to Professor Vashon, who was for a time connected with this college as professor, for the following notice of this institution, and of its founder and benefactor, Rev. Charles Avery:

Immediately after entering the main gateway of Allegheny cemetery, in Pittsburg, Pennsylvania, the eye of the visitor is arrested by a piece of sculpture which, representing a man erect upon an elevated pedestal, and attired in the costume of the present day, is indisputably the most noted of all the artistic adornments of that resting place of the dead. This lifelike statue recalls, in its finished details, the well-known personal appearance of the one whom it is designed to commemorate, the late Rev. Charles Avery, a native of the State of New York, but during the greater part of a long and honored life a resident of western Pennsylvania. Starting in life without any of the aids of fortune, he became, through efforts always characterized by the greatest probity, the possessor of ample wealth; and never, perhaps, was wealth more worthily bestowed; for, in his hands, it was but the means of doing good. His private charities were cheerfully and lavishly dispensed; and, among his public ones, may be mentioned the building of at least two neat and commodious churches for the Protestant Methodist connection, in which he was a local preacher. At his death, too, which occurred in January, 1858, his estate passed, by his last will, into the hands of his executors, who were enjoined, after satisfying various testamentary provisions in favor of his widow and other surviving relations, to devote the residue of his estate, amounting to $300,000, to educating and christianizing persons of the African race. One-half of this residue was directed to be employed in behalf of that class upon the continent of Africa, and the other half for the benefit of such as were in this country. It is understood that, as to the first half, the executors made choice of the American Missionary Society as the instrumentality for its employment; and that they themselves have, in the execution of their trust as to the second, made large donations to Oberlin College, Lincoln, and Wilberforce Universities, and other institutions that are earnestly laboring for the educational advancement of our colored population.

But the statue before mentioned is not the proudest monument to the memory of the Rev. Charles Avery. That monument is to be found in Avery College, an institution which is located in Allegheny City, Pennsylvania, and of which he was the sole generous benefactor. Having obtained an act of incorporation for it from the legislature of Pennsylvania, in 1849, he donated to the trustees named in its charter a portion of land upon North street, extending from Avery to Liberty street, and running back over 100 feet. Upon this land he had caused to be erected a handsome, substantial, and well-finished brick edifice, admirably suited to the purposes for which it was intended. The amplitude of this edifice may be inferred from the following brief description of it :

Its ground floor is divided off into a lecture room and two recitation rooms; and its second story into four rooms, two of which are fitted up for school purposes, a third set apart for the use of literary societies, while the remaining one, elegantly carpeted and furnished, is arranged as a library and apparatus room. There is still a third story, loftily ceiled, which is appropriated to the use and occupancy of a congregation belonging to the African Methodist Episcopal Zion connection, and which is known as the Avery Mission church. The entire structure is surmounted by a gracefully proportioned cupola with its clock and bell.

Mr. Avery donated to this offspring of his generosity a complete set of apparatus needful to illustrate all the various branches of natural science, physics, chemistry and astronomy.

Mr. Avery generously met the wants of the new institution by directing the selection and purchase of about 700 volumes, comprising books of reference, scientific treatises, histories, travels, and works of general literature by standard British and American authors. The selection was judiciously made ; and thus a small but excellent library was established for the benefit, not only of the college students, but also of any of the colored people of Pittsburg and Allegheny cities. This library was increased by the addition of about 300 volumes more at the death of the donor's widow, in 1865. Besides this library, Mr. Avery also donated a collection of about 300 volumes of such text-books as are used in the institution. This latter collection is known as the Avery College Beneficent Library, and is open to the use of students upon the payment of a small fee per term.

For the support of this institution the lamented founder provided an endowment of about $25,000, which has thus far, through safe and profitable investment, sufficed for that end. The board of trustees charged with its control consists of nine members, of whom three are white and the rest colored. The following gentlemen constitute this board at present, viz: Dr. C. G. Hussey, president : Rev. John Peck, vice-president ; Alexander Gordon, treasurer ; Samuel A. Neale, secretary ; P. L. Jackson, E. R. Parker, Barclay Preston, Matthew Jones, and A. I. Billows.

Avery College was first opened for the admission of students in April, 1850, with the Rev. Philotas Dean, A. M., and M. H. Freeman, A. M , as senior and junior professors. Upon the retirement of Professor Dean, in 1856, Professor Freeman became the principal, and continued to act in that capacity until the latter part of 1863, when he was succeeded by George B. Vashon, A. M. Both of these gentlemen had as an assistant Miss Emma J. Woodson, a graduate of the institution. After the resignation of Professor Vashon, in July, 1867, the operations of Avery College were suspended until April, 1868, when its corps of instructors was reorganized as follows, viz :

Rev. H. H. Garnett, D. D., president and professor of history, rhetoric, logic, mental and moral philosophy, and political economy ; B. K. Sampson, A. M., professor of mathematics, natural sciences, and languages ; Miss Harriet C. Johnson, principal of the preparatory and ladies' departments ; and Miss Clara G. Toop, teacher of vocal and instrumental music. All of these ladies and gentlemen, with the exception of Professor Dean, are colored persons.

In its religious aspect Avery College is free from any sectarian organization ; but its charter provides that all its officers shall be professors of Christianity. Its discipline is strict, yet mild and parental ; and its courses of study, collegiate and academical, which are the same as are ordinarily adopted by other colleges and academies in our country, are open to worthy persons of color of either sex. The number of its students at present is upwards of 70, of whom the greater portion are females. The tuition fee is put down at the low rate of $2 per term; the academical year commencing on the 2d Monday in September, and being divided into three terms of 15, 13, and 12 weeks, respectively.

Avery College has had a number of graduates from its academical course, but none as yet from its collegiate department. It is, however, fully empowered to confer the usual degrees in the arts and sciences; and there is now reason to hope that, in the course of a year or two, it will be able to reckon several baccalaureates among its alumni.

ASHMUN INSTITUTE—LINCOLN UNIVERSITY.

At a stated meeting of the Presbytery of New Castle, October 5, 1853, after discussion, it was determined that "There shall be established within our bounds, and under our supervision, an institution, to be called the Ashmun Institute, for the scientific, classical, and theological education of colored youth of the male sex."

In pursuance of this determination, J. M. Dickey, A. Hamilton, R. P. Dubois, ministers, and Samuel J. Dickey and John M. Kelton, ruling elders, were appointed a committee to carry out this determination, by collecting funds, selecting a suitable site, and erecting plain and convenient edifices for the purpose; also, to take steps to procure a charter from the State of Pennsylvania. On the 14th of November following this committee agreed to purchase 30 acres of land for $1,250, appointed a sub-committee to prepare a copy of the charter, and took other measures for carrying out the plan.

At the session of the legislature in 1854 the charter was granted, establishing "at or near a place called Hinsonville, in the county of Chester, an institution of learning for the scientific, classical, and theological education of colored youth of the male sex, by the name and style of the "Ashmun Institute." The trustees of this institute were John M. Dickey, Alfred Hamilton, Robert P. Dubois, James Latta, John B. Spottswood, James M. Crowell, Samuel J. Dickey, John M. Kelton, and William Wilson.

By the provisions of this charter the trustees had power "to procure the endowment of the institute, not exceeding the sum of $100,000;" "to confer such literary degrees and academic honors as are usually granted by colleges;" and it was required that "the institute shall be open to the admission of colored pupils of the male sex, of all religious denominations, who exhibit a fair moral character, and are willing to yield a ready obedience to the general regulations prescribed for the conduct of the pupils and the government of the institute."

On the 31st of December, 1856, the institute was formally opened and dedicated; and retained the name first given in its charter until the dedication of the new chapel, May 23, 1867, when the name "Lincoln University" was given. In the address of the president of the trustees, on that occasion, he says: "We were compelled, on the day of our first dedication, to go to Africa for a name; we could designate our new institution for the colored man by no name of any one who had labored for his freedom or for the salvation of his soul, but as foreshadowing his removal to Africa as his home. But now we take another name, the name of the martyr whose emancipation proclamation has not only closed the black man's days of bondage, but become the prelude to his full citizenship." "By the name, Lincoln, therefore, we call this chapel and this university, and dedicate both to the Triune God, Father, Son and Holy Ghost."

The board of trustees at present consists of 21 members, chosen by the Presbytery of New Castle. The officers of the board are a president, secretary, and treasurer. The faculty consists of the president, professors, and tutors. The present faculty in the collegiate department consists of Rev. I. N. Randall, president; Rev. Alonzo Westcott, Rev. E. R. Bower, Rev. E. E. Adams, and S. B. Howell, M. D., professors of mathematics, Greek, belles lettres, and natural sciences, respectively; and C. Geddes, M. D., tutor in Greek, and Latin; and Albert D. Minor, tutor in mathematics.

The number of students, as reported by the catalogue of 1868-9, was 114, of whom 14 were in the theological department, 17 in the preparatory class, and 83 in the collegiate department. Of the students now in the university, 48 are preparing for the ministry and 41 for teaching. The institution has a small library of about 1,200 volumes ; and is dependent upon donations from its friends for additions to it.

Eighty thousand dollars have recently been added to the endowment fund, securely invested, and devoted to the following objects : $20,000 for the endowment of the presidency, and named the Mary Dickey professorship ; $20,000 contributed by Hon. W. E. Dodge, and named the Dodge professorship of sacred rhetoric ; $20,000 conveyed in invested funds by J. C. Baldwin, esq., of New York city, named the Baldwin professorship of theology ; and $20,000 assigned by the trustees of the Avery estate, Pittsburg, Pennsylvania, and named the Avery professorship of Lincoln University.

RHODE ISLAND.

Out of a population of 174,620, in 1860, there were 3,952 free colored persons in Rhode Island, and by the census in 1865 these had increased to 4,087. As far back as 1708 the blacks constituted one-fourth of the whole population. Their social position and standing here has at all times been better than in any other portion of the country. During the war of the Revolution the negroes were permitted to enlist in the Rhode Island regiment, and many of them did so and received their freedom. At the close of the war, February 23, 1784, an act was passed providing that all children born after the first of March following of slave mothers should be free. By the first constitution of Rhode Island, which went into operation in May, 1843, the negroes were allowed to vote on the same conditions as the native American white citizens, and since that date they have enjoyed all the facilities for progress which the right of voting could give.

In the year 1828 a separate school was established, on their own petition, in Providence, with one male teacher, although the children were not forbidden to attend any of the public schools in their vicinity. By an act of the legislature in 1864 all separate schools for colored children were abolished.

SOUTH CAROLINA.

South Carolina had, in 1860, a population of 703,708, of whom more than one-half were blacks, viz : 402,406 slaves and 9,914 free, or a total of 412,120. This State took the lead in legislating directly against the education of the colored race ; in 1740, while yet a British province, its assembly enacted this law : " Whereas the having of slaves taught to write, or suffering them to be employed in writing, may be attended with inconveniences, *Be it enacted,* That all and every person and persons whatsoever, who shall hereafter teach or cause any slave or slaves to be taught, or shall use or employ any slave as a scribe in any manner of writing whatever, hereafter taught to write, every such person or persons shall for every such offense forfeit the sum of £100 current money."

In 1800 the State assembly passed an act, embracing free colored people as well as slaves in its shameful provisions, enacting " That assemblies of slaves, free negroes, mulattoes, and mestizoes, whether composed of all or any such description of persons, or of all or any of the same and a proportion of white persons, met together for the purpose of *mental* instruction in a confined or secret place, or with the gates or doors of such place barred, bolted, or locked, so as to prevent the free ingress to and from the same," are declared to be unlawful meetings ; the officers dispersing such unlawful assemblages being authorized to " inflict such corporeal punishment, not exceeding 20 lashes, upon such slaves, free negroes, mulattoes, and, mestizoes, as they may judge necessary for deterring them from the like unlawful assemblage in future." Another section of the same act declares, " That it shall not be lawful for any number of slaves, free negroes, mulattoes, or mestizoes, even in company with white persons, to meet together and assemble for the purpose of mental instruction or religious worship before the rising of the sun or after the going down of the same." This section was so oppressive that, in 1803, in answer to petitions from certain religious societies, an amending act was passed forbidding any person before 9 o'clock in the evening " to break into a place of meeting wherever shall be assembled the members of any religious society of the State, provided a majority of them shall be white persons, or other to disturb their devotions, unless a warrant has been procured from a magistrate, if at the time of the meeting there should be a magistrate within three miles of the place: if not, the act of 1800 is to remain in full force."

It was not, however, till nearly a third of a century later that the State took open and direct action against the education of its free colored population under all circumstances. On the 17th of December, 1834, the climax of infamy was attained in an act, of which the following is the introductory section:

"SECTION 1. If any person shall hereafter teach any slave to read or write, or shall aid or assist in teaching any slave to read or write, or cause or procure any slave to be taught to read or write, such person. if a free white person, upon conviction thereof shall, for each and every offense against this act, be fined not exceeding $100 and imprisonment not more than six months; or if a free person of color, shall be whipped not exceeding 50 lashes and fined not exceeding $50, at the discretion of the court of magistrates and freeholders before which such free person ot color is tried; and if a slave, to be whipped, at the discretion of the court, not exceeding 50 lashes, the informer to be entitled to one-half the fine and to be a competent witness. And if any free person of color or slave shall keep any school or other place of instruction for teaching any slave or free person of color to read or write, such free person of color or slave shall be liable to the same fine, imprisonment, and corporeal punishment as by this act are imposed and inflicted on free persons of color and slaves for teaching slaves to write."

The second section, following up the detestable purpose of the act to doom its victims to besotted ignorance, forbids with severe penalties the employment of colored persons as "clerks or salesmen in or about any shop, store, or house used for trading." The third section makes it a grave misdemeanor "to sell, exchange, give, or in any otherwise deliver any spirituous liquors to any slave except upon the written and express order of the owner or person having the care and management of such slave. This section completes the infamy of the measure, in placing the dispensing of mental instruction to a slave in the same category of crimes with that of selling them intoxicating liquors, as is seen in the penalty which declares that "any free person of color or slave shall for each and every such offense incur the penalties prescribed for free persons of color or slaves for teaching slaves to read and write." All these acts, including the old province act of 1740, stood in full force when the rebellion came.

SCHOOLS FOR THE FREEDMEN.

The following account of the efforts to establish schools for colored children since 1861 was drawn up by Professor Vashon:

This State, famous in American annals as being the most determined advocate of the servitude of the African race and foremost in the secession movement made to secure its perpetuity, was, through the retributive workings of Divine justice, the next one after Virginia to witness the efforts of philanthropy in behalf of its oppressed free colored residents and of its peeled, broken, and imbruted bondmen. It is true that South Carolina had never, like other slave States, formally prohibited by law the maintenance of schools for free colored persons; but, by a statute enacted December 17, 1834, it had forbidden any individual of that class to keep such a school, and it visited with severe pains and penalties any one guilty of the offense of teaching a slave to read or write. The thick clouds of moral darkness thus formed were destined, however, to be rent and dissipated by the fierce-flashing lightnings of war, and that, too, before secession was a year old. In the month of November, 1861, the Port Royal islands were captured, and, on the 8th day of the following January, the Rev. Solomon Peck, D, D., of Boston, with the sanction of the military authorities, opened a school at Beaufort. In the latter part of the same month Mr. Barnard K. Lee, jr., a superintendent of "contrabands," opened another one at Hilton Head. The destitution upon which these schools cast the first cheering ray was indeed forlorn. All of the whites had fled from these islands, leaving there about 8,000 negroes, steeped in ignorance and want. Their deplorable condition appealed strongly to the officers of the government for relief, and did not appeal in vain. Early in January, 1862, Edward L. Pierce, esq., was sent out by Secretary Chase, of the Treasury Department, to examine the condition of the abandoned plantations on these islands; and, about the same time, the Rev. Mansfield

French was deputed by the government to examine the condition of the negroes along the whole southern coast. He was accompanied by a teacher of the American Mission Association, who opened another school at Beaufort on the 1st of February, 1862. About the middle of the same month other schools were opened on Hilton Head island by three teachers whose services had been secured in reply to appeals addressed by Mr. Pierce to the Revs. E. E. Hale and J. M. Manning, D. D., of Boston. Upon Mr. French's return he brought with him letters from General T. W. Sherman and Commodore Dupont urging the benevolent of the north to bestir themselves in behalf of the destitute within the limits of their command. In response public meetings were held at once in Boston, New York, and Philadelphia, which resulted in the formation of three freedmen's aid societies, viz, the Boston Educational Commission, on February 7th; the Freedmen's Relief Association, at New York, on February 22d; and the Port Royal Relief Commission, on March 3, 1862. On the same day that this last society was organized in Philadelphia 52 teachers, missionaries and superintendents (40 men and 12 women) sailed from New York for Port Royal. Twenty-nine of these (25 men and 4 women) were under the commission of the Boston society. To these persons transportation and boarding were furnished by the government, which also, after a short time, paid the salaries of the superintendents. Upon their arrival at their field of labor schools were immediately established, the salaries of the teachers being paid by the societies which had sent them out. Other teachers were soon sent out by the Philadelphia society, and, in the following June, 86 persons were reported in the field. On the 28th of the last mentioned month this work was transferred to the War Department and placed under the supervision of General Rufus Saxton, then military governor of South Carolina.

Words would fail to depict the noble devotion and self-sacrifice of these sea island teachers as they carried on their philanthropic labors during the remaining years of the war. With a courage worthy of comparison with that of their brothers on the tented field, they remained at their posts, braving all the perils and privations of their situation. Heaven smiled upon their efforts, and, although they were called upon to instruct beings whom oppression had degraded almost to the intellectual level of the brute, they were enabled to attain to results which might be triumphantly compared with those of other educators in far more favorable spheres. Those results are their highest praise, and doubtless the same God who blessed their labors will also bestow upon them their merited reward.

With the capture of Charleston a new and extended impulse was given to educational work in South Carolina. Immediately thereafter Mr. James Redpath was appointed superintendent of education for that city, and entered upon his duties with laudable energy and zeal. On the 4th of March, 1865, he took possession of the public school buildings and reopened them for the use of black and white children in separate rooms. He invited all former teachers of these schools to continue their labors, and sent at once to the northern societies for experienced teachers to aid in their reorganization and instruction. Within a week's time he reported 300 white children and 1,200 colored ones as being in attendance. The societies which he had appealed to became responsible for the salaries of the southern teachers, of whom 68 were employed, a large proportion being colored. Other teachers were sent on from the north, and, at the expiration of the school term in July of that year, an enrollment of 4,000 pupils was reported.

The creation of the Freedmen's Bureau, March 3, 1865, with General O. O. Howard, the indefatigable and impartial friend of white and black, as Chief Commissioner; the recommendation of the national council of Congregational churches, held in Boston in the following June, that $250,000 should be raised for the work among the freedmen, with its indorsement of the American Missionary Association as an agency providentially fitted for its employment, and the final concentration of the various freedmen's aid societies of the north and west into the American Freedmen's Union Commission were all circumstances productive of salutary effects upon the schools in South Carolina as well as elsewhere throughout the south. The several societies already mentioned in this paper have since been known as the New England, New York, and Pennsylvania Branches of the Union Commission. The increase in the number of schools established and of teachers employed by them in 1867, proved that their energy and efficiency were not diminished by their coalition. South

Carolina has been fortunate, too, in having, in the person of Mr. Reuben Tomlinson, a State superintendent of education under the Freedmen's Bureau, an officer whose hearty co-operation and sympathy with the various agencies at work there rendered its schools as great a success as the means at command would permit of. And, although a comparison of these schools in 1868 with their condition in the preceding year shows a falling off, that result is attributable to the greater poverty of the freedmen themselves rather than to any diminution of effort or zeal on the part of their friends. In spite of this falling off, the following statement, made in March, 1868, by Mr. Arthur Sumner, a teacher employed by the New England branch, makes quite an interesting exhibit of the schools in Charleston at that time:

The Shaw school, (New England branch F. U. C.,) 360 pupils.

Mr. F. L. Cardozo's school, (American Missionary Association,) 360 pupils.

Zion Church school, (Presbyterian,) 525 pupils.

Franklin Street school, (Episcopalian,) 665 pupils.

Tivoli Garden school, (Baptist,) 150 pupils.

Morris Street school, (municipal,) 500 pupils.

It is to be remembered that to the 2,560 children then in those schools are to be added about 500 others who belonged to private schools. And, speaking with reference to educational matters in the entire State, it is also to be remembered that this sketch of the South Carolina schools is by no means a perfect measure of the enlightenment there. The Rev. J. W. Alvord, general superintendent of schools under the Freedmen's Bureau, made the following statement in his third semi-annual report, January, 1867: "From information at our command, it is safe to assert that at least 30,000 colored persons, men, women, and children, have learned to read during the last year." And there is no doubt that every year since the close of the rebellion the number of colored persons who have learned to read and write in South Carolina has been far in excess of the number reported as attending the schools.

In conclusion, the following description, copied from a Charleston paper, of a school recently established there and dedicated with appropriate exercises on May 7, 1868, may prove interesting:

THE AVERY INSTITUTE, CHARLESTON.

"This new and handsome school building is named in honor of the late Rev. Charles Avery, of Pittsburg, Pennsylvania, from whose bequest $10,000 were given to the American Missionary Association, and applied by it to the purchase of the lands on which this edifice stands, and to the erection of a mission home. The normal school edifice was built for the association by the Freedmen's Bureau at a cost of $17,000.

"The building is 88 feet long, 68 feet wide, 50 feet high, and to the top of the flag-staff, 90 feet. It is raised on brick pillars, with spacious brick basements and a large cistern underneath. On the first floor are four large class rooms, two for the first class of boys and two for the first class of girls. Two of these rooms are of double size, divided by sliding glass doors, and intended, when built, for the preparatory and higher classes of a normal department. Each of the class rooms is capable of accommodating from 50 to 75 pupils, and is fitted up with handsome desks. The hall-way is also furnished with convenient closets and racks for the reception of hats, cloaks, &c. On the second floor is a commodious assembly hall, with four long rows of seats, and a desk and platform for the principal. On this floor are also two large class rooms, and running round the walls of the class rooms is a composition blackboard. On either side of the building are spacious piazzas running the entire length, and opened upon from the class rooms. The building is finely ventilated on a new and improved plan."

The following tables exhibit the statistics of the colored schools from 1865 to 1868:

Number of schools, teachers, and pupils, 1865 to 1868.

Year.	Number of schools.			Number of teachers.			Number of scholars.			Average attendance.	Per cent.
	Day.	Night.	Total.	White.	Colored.	Total.	Male.	Female.	Total.		
1865.........	....	....	48	[52	24	176	....	....	10,000	....	......
1866.........	....	....	113	98	90	188	....	....	12,017	....	......
1867.........	124	36	160	139	95	234	7,963	8,687	16,650	13,289	79
1868.........	87	26	113	128	75	203	7,167	7,733	14,900	9,606	64

Studies and expenditures, 1867 and 1868.

Year.	Number of scholars in different studies pursued.							Expenditures in support of schools.		
	Alphabet.	Easy reading.	Advanced readers.	Writing.	Geography.	Arithmetic.	Higher branches.	By freedmen.	By others.	Total.
1867...............	3,750	5,835	6,196	9,902	2,850	8,934	574	$12,200	$80,800	$93,000
1868...............	1,898	4,097	6,107	5,918	3,602	6,810	442	6,838	50,162	57,000

TENNESSEE.

There were in this State, in 1860, 283,019 colored persons, out of a population of 1,109,801, of whom 275,719 were slaves and 7,300 free.

The territory constituting the State of Tennessee was a part of North Carolina until ceded to the United States, in 1790; and the laws of North Carolina then in force were to continue till superseded by the legislation of the proper authorities. Among the laws which continued in force down to 1821 was one enacted in 1741 by North Carolina, forbidding the whipping of "a Christian servant naked, without an order from the justice of the peace," on penalty of 40 shillings; and another, enacted in 1779, punishing "the stealing of slaves with intent to sell them" by "death, without benefit of clergy." Another law enforced in Tennessee was that of 1787, that "if any free negro or mulatto shall entertain any slave in his or her house during the Sabbath or in the night, between sunset and sunrise," he or she might be fined $2 50 for the first two and $5 for every subsequent offense. Tennessee became a State in 1796, and in 1799 an act was passed "to prevent the willful and malicious killing of slaves." There was no specific act forbidding the assemblies of slaves until 1803, when such assemblies were forbidden, without a written permission from the owner, under a penalty of $10. In 1806 "any white person, free negro, or mulatto" attending any such unlawful meeting, or "harboring or entertaining any slave, without the consent of the owner," might be fined not more than $20 nor less than $10 for each offense; and the negroes so found were to receive "15 stripes on the bare back, well laid on, under the direction of the patrol." In 1831 "all assemblages of slaves in unusual numbers or at suspicious times and places, not expressly authorized by the owners," were to be deemed unlawful.

In 1836 an act was passed concerning incendiary publications and speeches, forbidding "words or gestures, with intent to excite any slave or free person of color to insubordination, insurrection, or rebellion;" also "the circulation or publication of seditious pamphlets," the penalty for which was confinement in the penitentiary from 5 to 10 years for the first and from 10 to 20 years for any subsequent offense.

The revised code of 1858 retains all these severe restrictions.

In 1838 a system of common schools was established, according to which the scholars were designated as "white children over the age of six years and under 16;" but in 1840, in the act amending this system, discrimination of color is not mentioned, but it is provided that " all children between the ages of 6 and 21 years shall have the privilege of attending the public schools ;" and the act of 1862 also comprehended all children. This State never enacted any law positively forbidding the instruction of colored people ; but, notwithstanding the language of the law, the benefits of the common school system were confined exclusively to white children. The school fund of the State was composed of the proceeds of certain school lands, bonuses from the banks and other incorporated companies, from licenses, fines, and taxes, to which the free colored people contributed no inconsiderable share. The fund, in 1858, consisted of $1,500,000 deposited in the Bank of Tennessee, together with property given by will for the purpose ; the proceeds of sales or rents of escheated lands, or lands bought by the State at tax sales, and of the personal effects of intestates having no kindred entitled by the laws thereto ; besides taxes on certain mineral lands.

In March, 1867, an act was passed " to provide for the reorganization, supervision, and maintenance of free common schools," which declares that the school fund for annual distribution shall consist of the school funds already provided by law, together with a tax of two mills on the dollar of all taxable property, and an addition of 25 cents to the poll-tax previously levied by law, which fund shall be for "the benefit of all the youth of the State." The distribution of the income of this fund is made in proportion to the number of school children in each district. By the same act the boards of education and other officers having authority, in each district or city, were authorized and required to establish within their respective jurisdictions one or more special schools for colored children, when there are more than 25, so as to afford them the advantages of a common school education, the schools so established to be under the control of the board of education or other school officers having charge of the educational interests of other schools. If at any time the number of children attending the school should fall below 15 for any one month, the school may be discontinued for a period not exceeding five months at one time.

The following statistics give the condition of the colored schools for the years specified :

Number of schools, teachers, and pupils, 1866 to 1868.

Year	Number of schools.			Number of teachers.			Number of scholars.			Average attendance.	Per cent.
	Day.	Night.	Total.	White.	Colored.	Total.	Male.	Female.	Total.		
1866.........	......	......	42	......	......	125	......	......	9,114	6,279	68
1867.........	109	19	128	111	43	154	4,245	5,206	9,451	6,377	67
1868.........	146	32	178	131	72	203	5,190	5,580	10,770	7,758	71

Studies and expenditures, 1867 and 1868.

Year.	Number of scholars in different studies pursued.							Expenditures in support of schools.		
	Alphabet.	Easy reading.	Advanced readers.	Writing.	Geography.	Arithmetic.	Higher branches.	By freedmen.	By others.	Total.
1867..............	1,344	4,501	3,691	3,306	2,092	3,308	557	$10,152	$61,575	$71,727
1868..............	1,509	4,507	4,615	4,025	3,168	4,609	691	12,235	59,426	71,661

TEXAS.

In 1860 there were in Texas 182,921 colored people, out of the whole population of 604,215, of whom only 355 were free, 182,566 being slaves.

Slavery existed in Texas while it was a Mexican province, but different from that in the United States. In a decree of the congress of Coahuila and Texas, September 15, 1827, it is provided that "in each change of owners of slaves, in the nearest succession even of heirs apparent, the tenth part of those who are to pass to the new owner shall be manumitted," the manumission being determined by lot. This provision is to be understood only in connection with the fact that slaves in Mexico were transferred with the real estate. By the same decree it was declared that "the ayuntamientos, under the most rigid responsibility, shall take particular care that free children, born slaves, receive the best education that can be given them, placing them, for that purpose, at the public schools and other places of instruction, wherein they may become useful to society." The ayuntamientos correspond to mayors and aldermen.

In 1827 there was another decree that the slave who, for convenience, wished to change his master should be permitted to do so, "provided the new master indemnify the former for what the slave cost him, agreeably to the consequence."

In 1836, in accordance with the express provisions of their constitution, the congress of Texas made the penalty for introducing any "Africans or negroes" into the republic, except from the United States, to be an offense to be punished with "death, without benefit of clergy;" and by the same act the introduction of Africans or slaves from the United States, except such as were legally held as slaves in the United States, was declared to be piracy, and punishable in the same manner. In 1837 it was enacted that "free Africans and descendants of Africans" who were residing in the republic at the date of the declaration of independence might remain free. At the same time a law was passed forbidding any slave or free person of color from using insulting or abusive language to or threatening any white person, under a penalty of "stripes, not exceeding 100 and not less than 25." In 1840 free persons of color were forbidden to immigrate into the republic, under a penalty of being sold into slavery ; and the same act gave two years' time for all free persons of color to remove from the republic, at the same time providing that those found in the republic at the expiration of that period might be sold as slaves. In 1841 and in 1845 a few were excepted from the provisions of this act by special enactment. This was the nature of the legislation in 1845, when Texas came into the Union.

At the first session of the legislature of the State of Texas, in May, 1846, an act was passed forbidding any one to allow slaves to go at large more than one day in a week, except at the Christmas holidays, the penalty being a fine of not more than $100. "All negroes and Indians, and all persons of mixed blood descended from negro ancestry, to the third generation, though one ancestor of each generation may have been a white person," were declared incapable of being witnesses, "except for or against each other." The last act of legislation relating to the free colored people, previous to the rebellion, was one in 1851 permitting one Thomas Cevallas, a free man of color who had resided in the State since 1835 and been wounded in the defense of the country, "to remain a resident of the county of Bexar."

There is nothing in relation to the education of colored people, free or slave, on the statute books of the State. As the free colored people were generally banished, there was no necessity for any enactments in regard to their education.

The new constitution of the State, adopted in the convention April 2, 1866, declares that "Africans and their descendants shall be protected in their rights of person and property by appropriate legislation." The legislature, in 1866, took care to protect the school fund of the State, so far as it remained, and took measures to establish a system of common schools. But by an act passed in 1867, providing for the education of indigent white children, it appears that the "system" is not entitled to be called a common school system. It provides that "the police courts—at their discretion—of the several counties may levy and collect a tax annually, not to exceed one-half of the State tax, and upon the same subjects of taxation, (Africans and the descendants of Africans, and their property, excepted,) to be applied solely to the education of *indigent white children*."

The following tables, compiled by Professor Vashon, exhibits the condition of the schools under the superintendents of the Freedmen's Bureau:

Number of schools, teachers, and scholars, 1865 to 1868.

Year.	Number of schools.			Number of teachers.			Number of scholars.			Average attendance.	Per cent.
	Day.	Night.	Total.	White.	Colored.	Total.	Male.	Female.	Total.		
1865.........	10	6	16	....	....	10	....	....	1,041	....	......
1866.........	....	....	90	....	....	43	....	....	4,590	....	......
1867.........	68	34	102	58	40	98	1,960	2,238	4,198	2,923	6?
1868.........	51	25	76	55	26	81	1,235	1,369	2,604	2,176	8?

Studies and expenditures, 1867 and 1868

Year.	Number of scholars in different studies pursued.							Expenditures in support of schools.		
	Alphabet.	Easy reading.	Advanced readers.	Writing.	Geography.	Arithmetic.	Higher branches.	By freedmen.	By others.	Total.
1867..............	682	1,765	1,696	1,607	486	1,263	77	$11,340	$823	$12,16?
1868..............	254	888	1,183	1,259	602	1,077	240	2,093	5,739	7,83?

VIRGINIA.

By the census of 1860 the population of Virginia, including the territory since occupied as West Virginia, was 1,596,318, of whom 548,907 were colored, and of these 490,865 were slaves and 58,042 were free.

To Virginia belongs the bad pre-eminence of having been, if not the birthplace and nursery, the great commercial mart of involuntary domestic servitude, and of having fixed the legal status of slavery in the slave States of this Union. By the several acts already cited the information and culture which are the results of travel, the free intercourse with others more intelligent and refined, the printed page, the living views of educated teachers and preachers, the choice and practice of varied mechanical, as well as agricultural labor, and all the inspiring motives of political privileges and the responsibilities generally of business and of family and social position, were denied.

Fifty years after the introduction of slaves into Virginia, Sir William Berkley reports the population of the province at 40,000, of whom 2,000 were black slaves. Continual importations from Africa increased the number rapidly, and in the reign of George the First alone not less than 10,000 were brought into the colony. At the beginning of his reign, out of the population of 95,000 in the colony, 23,000 were negroes; and in 1756, when the population reached 293,000, the negroes amounted to 120,000. But in that early day the church of Virginia was careful to give to the slaves the benefit of Christian instruction, inasmuch as an act was passed October, 1785, declaring "that baptism of slaves doth not exempt them from bondage."

The difficulties in the way of instructing the slaves, even when permission was given, as in this early period, were very great, since Sunday was the only day of rest for them, and the great distances of the plantations from each other made it impracticable for a teacher to keep up any systematic plan of visitation. In addition to this was the indifference or opposition of most planters, who considered the negroes as little above the brutes, and that to attempt to give them moral and intellectual culture was worse than useless.

REV. MORGAN GODWYN AND EARLY LABORERS FOR THE SLAVE.

Virginia was not without early witnesses to the evils of slavery and advocates for the amelioration of its condition. Rev. Morgan Godwyn, who was a student of Christ church,

Oxford, and for several years an ordained minister of the Church of England, in Virginia, and afterwards for a few years in Barbadoes; and Rev. Jonathan Boucher, rector of Hanover, and subsequently of St. Mary's parish, in Virginia, and dean of Queen Ann's parish, in Maryland.

Godwyn, in a pamphlet published by him in London, in 1680, and written while he was in Barbadoes, entitled "The Negroes and Indians' Advocate, suing for them admission into the church, &c.," in the preface of this work, states that his efforts to baptize and train negroes in the knowledge of Christian truth had been opposed; (1) by those who declared it to be impracticable; (2) by those, who regarded it as a work savoring of Popish supererogation, and utterly needless; and (3) by those, the most numerous, who condemned it as likely to be subversive of their own interests and property, and strove to put it down by ridicule. The planters vindicated their treatment of the negro by saying that, although he bore the resemblance of a man, he had not the qualities of a man— a conceit of which Godwyn boldly asserts, "atheism and irreligion were the parents, and avarice and sloth the foster nurses." The Quakers of that time also upbraided the church for the continuance of the evils of slavery, and issued "a petty reformado pamphlet" on the subject, in which the question was asked, "who made you ministers of the Gospel to the white people only, and not to the tawneys and blacks also?"

Godwyn, in his sermon, maintains the following propositions: "(1) that the negroes, both slaves and others have naturally an equal right with other men to the exercise and privileges of religion, of which it is most unjust in any part to deprive them; (2) that the profession of Christianity absolutely obliging to the promoting of it, no difficulties nor inconveniences, how great soever, can excuse the neglect, much less the hindering or opposing of it, which is, in effect, no better than a renunciation of that profession; (3) that the inconveniences here pretended for this neglect, being examined will be found nothing such, but rather the contrary."

The delivery of this sermon exposed its preacher to the most barbarous usage, and another of the clergy, who, upon another occasion, urged from the pulpit the like duty, was treated with severity by the planters. The negroes, also, in consequence of these efforts on the part of the clergy of Barbadoes to help them, were exposed to still more brutal treatment. In one case a negro, whose crime was neither more nor less than receiving baptism on a Sunday morning at his parish church, from the hands of the minister, was reproved by the brutish overseer, and given to understand "that that was no Sunday work for those of his complexion; that he had other business for him, the neglect whereof would cost him an afternoon's baptism in blood, as in the morning he had received a baptism with water; which he accordingly made good. Of which the negro afterward complaining to the minister, and he to the governor, the miserable wretch was forever after so unmercifully treated by that inhuman devil, that, to avoid his cruelty, betaking himself to the woods, he there perished."

Godwyn represents that the persevering, "officious" Quaker incurred the enmity of the authorities of the island, who secured in 1676 and 1678 the passage of several acts for the express purpose of preventing Quakers, under severe penalties, from bringing negroes to their meetings. One of these acts (1676) contained a clause that no person should be allowed to keep a school unless he first took an oath of allegiance and supremacy; a precaution perhaps not impolitic in a colony where labor was of more utility than learning. The clergyman who administered the rite of baptism in the case referred to was obliged to vindicate himself in a tone of apology for having done that act of ministerial duty.

To Morgan Godwyn belongs the credit of having first borne his testimony against the lawfulness of trading in the persons of men; although Bishop Sanderson, about the same period, gave his testimony against it, as well as Baxter, in his Christian Directory, where he gives rules for the masters of slaves in foreign plantations to give their slaves instructions.

Mr. Godwyn also published a sermon in 1685, entitled "Trade Preferred before Religion," which was first preached at Westminster Abbey, and afterwards in divers churches in London, and dedicated to the King. In this dedication he states that the end and design of his discourse was "to stir up and provoke your Majesty's subjects abroad, (and even at home also,) to use at least some endeavors for the propagation of Christianity among their domestic slaves and vassals." In his preface he notes the spreading of the leprosy of mammonism and irreligion, by which the efforts to instruct and Christianize the heathen were paralyzed, and even the slaves who were the subjects of such instruction became the victims of still greater cruelty; while the ministers who imparted the instructions were neglected or even persecuted by the masters.

Among the motives presented for the English people and the English church to take up the subject of instruction of the slaves were the following, as set forth in his own language as printed: "This ought to be reformed in respect of the *dishonor* from thence redounding to our *church* and *nation* and even to the *whole* Reformation. First, to the *church;* for it occasions her *enemies to blaspheme.* Hence a certain *Romanist* demands of us, *where are the indefatigable missioners* sent by you to *the remotest parts of the world for the conversion of heathens? a noble function wherein the Catholic* (that is their *Roman) church only and most justly glories; whilst you like lazy drones sit at home not daring to wet a foot, &c.* And by another it is objected against both *ourselves* and our equally *zealous* neighbors, *that never anything for the propagation of Christianity in foreign parts hath by either nation been at any time attempted.* And from thence a third person very roundly infers the *nullity* of our *church* and religion, viz: *Because we have no zeal,* therefore *no faith,* and therefore *no church nor religion among us."*

"Again, when the great industry of our people in *New England* shall be rehearsed, their converting of *nations,* turning the *whole Bible into the Indian tongue;* their *college built and endowed* for the *education of Indian youth;* their *missioners* sent forth and *lands purchased* for their maintenance; and all this out of a barren soil some 60 years since no better than a *rocky* wilderness; whilst ours, out of *better* conveniences and more happy *opportunities,* (such are our *grateful* returns!) have not produced the *least grain of harvest* to God's glory in those parts; but upon all occasions *shifting it off* with the unfitness of the season and pretending that *the time is not come;* proclaiming it *impracticable* and impossible, though effected by others of smaller abilities; or, like *Solomon's* sluggard, setting up *lions* and *tigers* in the way; raising obstructions and *creating* difficulties, when upon experience there are *no such* to be found. Now when these mighty works shall be hereafter rehearsed, how will that glorious name of the *Church of England* stand as it were in *disgrace,* not only among those *primitive* worthies who at first so cheerfully entered upon this work and afterwards endured the *heat* of the day? but when compared even with these moderns, whom we bespeak as *schismatics* and *idolaters,* yet do each of them give those testimonies of their *zeal* and *charity* which are equally requisite and would be no less *commendable* in us also."

JONATHAN BOUCHER.

The evils of slavery, both in its moral and economical aspects, were clearly seen and forcibly presented by Rev. Jonathan Boucher, in a discourse "On the Peace in 1763," preached in Hanover parish, King George's county, Virginia. After pointing out the objections to war, Mr. Boucher dwells on the advantages, pursuits, and duties of peace. Among the latter he urges an immediate improvement in the present practice of agriculture, by which all the varied advantages of climate and soil are neglected for the culture of a single staple, which, he says, he is "at some loss how to characterize, either as a necessary of life or a luxury. A necessary it certainly is not, since it can neither be used as food nor raiment; neither is it a luxury, at least in the sense of a gratification, being so nauseous and offensive that long habit alone can reconcile any constitution to the use of it." Such culture as is now going on, he adds, in the language of Scripture, will "make a fruitful land barren, for the wickedness of them that dwell therein." He sums up his views on this part of the subject by citing the opinion of "an ancient," who, in drawing the picture of a happy people, says: "It is necessary peace and good laws should prevail; that the ground should be well cultivated; children well educated; and due homage paid to the gods."

The next duty of a state of peace, he says, is to attempt the civilization of the Indian tribes, whom, he says, the white men have made it a kind of religion to exterminate; but whom he believes "it is in our power to convert into freemen, useful subjects, and good Christians." He concludes thus: "But Indians are by no means the sole or chief objects of our present attention; the united motives of interest and humanity call on us to bestow some consideration on the case of those sad outcasts of society, our negro slaves; for my heart would smite me, were I not, in this hour of prosperity, to entreat you (it being their unparalleled hard lot not to have the power of entreating for themselves) to permit them to participate in the general joy. Even those who are the sufferers can hardly be sorry when they see wrong measures carrying their punishment along with them. Were an impartial and competent observer of the state of society in these middle colonies asked, whence it happens that Virginia and Maryland (which were the first planted, and which are superior to many colonies, and inferior to none, in point of natural advantage) are still so exceedingly behind most of the other British trans-atlantic possessions in all those improvements which bring credit and consequence to a country? he would answer—they are so, because they are cultivated by slaves. I believe it is capable of demonstration that, except the immediate interest which every man has in the property of his slaves, it would be for every man's interest that there were no slaves; and for this plain reason, because the free labor of a free man, who is regularly hired and paid for the work he does, and only for what he does, is, in the end, cheaper than the extorted eye-service of a slave. Some loss and inconvenience would, no doubt, arise from the general abolition of slavery in these colonies; but were it done gradually, with judgment, and with good temper, I have never yet seen it satisfactorily proved that such inconvenience would either be great or lasting. North American or West Indian planters might, possibly, for a few years, make less tobacco, or less rice, or less sugar; the raising of which might also cost them more; but that disadvantage would probably soon be amply compensated to them by an advanced price, or (what is the same thing) by the reduced expense of cultivation." * * * " If ever these colonies, now filled with slaves, be improved to their utmost capacity, an essential part of the improvement must be the abolition of slavery. Such a change would hardly be more to the advantage of the slaves than it would be to their owners. An ingenious French writer (Montesquieu) well observes, ' the state of slavery is, in its own nature bad; it is neither useful to the master nor to the slave. Not to the slave, because he can do nothing through a motive of virtue; not to the master, because, by having an *unlimited* authority over his slaves, he insensibly accustoms himself to the want of all moral virtues, and from thence grows fierce, hasty, severe, voluptuous, and cruel.'

" I come now, in the last place, to exhort you not to disappoint the pious wishes which our pious king had in thus publicly summoning us to hail *the Lord of lords and King of kings with songs of deliverance*, for having *given his people the blessing of peace*." "And notwithstanding all that a discontented party has said, or has written, on the idea that the conditions of the peace are inadequate to our great success, so far as they concern us we can have no objection to them."

SCHOOLS IN NORFOLK AND RICHMOND.

Of all the States in the American Union, Virginia is, on several accounts, peculiarly associated with the history of the colored people of this country. Upon its shores, in 1620, a Dutch vessel landed the first cargo of human merchandise that had ever been brought from the ill-fated continent of Africa into a British colony. Through the slave labor thus introduced, its eminent agricultural resources were developed during the following century and a half so largely that, at the epoch of the Revolution, it ranked first in importance among the 13 original constituents of the confederation since known as the United States of America. Its slave population, too, had increased to such an extent as to enable it to supply from its excess of laborers the requirements of the other slaveholding States; and thus Virginia became and continued to be, during all the days of servitude, the great breeding slave mart of the Union.

But the curse thus destined to work so much ill both to Africa and America did not prove to its immediate victims one of entirely unmitigated severity. In Virginia, as elsewhere, the relation of master and slave soon led to the existence of a class in whose veins the blood of the oppressed was mingled with that of the oppressor; and, in behalf of this class, the voice of nature did not in many cases plead in vain. Besides, the constant and daily intercourse of slaveholding families with that portion of their property known as house servants was frequently illustrated by such marked instances of devoted fidelity upon the part of the latter as appealed successfully for a grateful recognition from their owners, in return. To these fortunate individuals, either the offspring or the favorites of their masters, the rudiments of a common education were often imparted. Through manumission, too, and the privilege granted to slaves to purchase their freedom, quite a large free colored population was added to society in Virginia; and, in Richmond, Norfolk, and other of the principal cities, a few schools were tolerated for the benefit of this class. These schools were generally taught by colored persons who had acquired sufficient education for that purpose; and, through their instrumentality, a knowledge of reading and writing and the other common branches of learning was quite extensively disseminated. About 40 years ago there were two excellent schools of this description in the city of Petersburg, one of which was taught by a Mr. Shepherd, and the other by the Rev. John T. Raymond, a Baptist minister, living in Boston, Massachusetts, in 1869.

These schools existed for several years, although in the midst of a continually growing feeling of dissatisfaction in regard to them on the part of the white portion of the community. It was suspected that, in addition to the influence which they might have in rendering the slaves discontented, they were also the means of enlightening some of them, as well as their free brethren. This led to the enactment by the general assembly of Virginia, on the 2d of March, 1819, of a law prohibiting "all meetings or assemblages of slaves, or free negroes, or mulattoes, mixing and associating with such slaves, at any meeting-house or houses, or any other place or places, in the night, or at any school or schools for teaching them reading and writing, either in the day or night." For the violation of this law any justice of the peace was authorized to inflict the penalty of 20 lashes upon each and every offender against its provisions. But, although the instruction of slaves was thus guarded against, schools for free colored people were still allowed until the occurrence of Nat Turner's insurrection had aroused terror and dismay throughout the entire south. Then public opinion almost universally demanded the prohibition of these establishments. Accordingly, on the 7th day of April, 1831, the general assembly of Virginia enacted a law with the following among other provisions, viz:

"SEC. 4. *And be it enacted*, That all meetings of free negroes or mulattoes at any schoolhouse, church, meeting-house, or other place, for teaching them reading or writing, either in the day or night, under whatsoever pretext, shall be deemed and considered an unlawful assembly; and any justice of the county or corporation wherein such assemblage shall be, either from his own knowledge, or on the information of others of such unlawful assemblage or meeting, shall issue his warrant directed to any sworn officer or officers, authorizing him or them to enter the house or houses where such unlawful assemblage or meeting may be, for the purpose of apprehending or dispersing such free negroes or mulattoes, and to inflict corporal punishment on the offender or offenders, at the discretion of any justice of the peace, not exceeding 20 lashes.

"SEC. 5. *And be it enacted*, That if any white person or persons assemble with free negroes or mulattoes at any school-house, church, meeting-house, or other place, for the purpose of instructing such free negroes or mulattoes to read or write, such person or persons shall, on conviction thereof, be fined in a sum not exceeding $50, and, moreover, may be imprisoned, at the discretion of a jury, not exceeding two months.

"SEC. 6. *And be it enacted*, That if any white person, for pay or compensation, shall assemble with any slaves for the purpose of teaching, and shall teach any slave to read or write, such person, or any white person or persons contracting with such teacher so to act, who shall offend as aforesaid, shall, for each offense, be fined at the discretion of a jury in a sum not less than $10 nor exceeding $100, to be recovered on an information or indictment."

Upon the revision of the criminal code of the Commonwealth of Virginia, the laws already referred to and quoted were retained, with a few alterations, under the head of "Offenses against the public policy." Nor was this law prohibiting colored schools a mere *brutum fulmen*, as it was made apparent in 1854, when Mrs. Margaret Douglass, a white lady, born in South Carolina, was imprisoned in the common jail of the city of Norfolk for having violated its provisions, although ignorant of their existence when she began her school, in 1851.

That vindication of the laws may have served its purpose by putting a stop to any open instruction of colored children; but, from the time of the first prohibition until then, schools for that purpose were secretly maintained in the principal cities of Virginia, although the colored aspirants after knowledge were constrained to keep their books and slates carefully hidden from every prying eye, and to assume the appearance of being upon an errand as they hurried along and watched their chance to slip unnoticed into the sedulously concealed school-room. Such was the thirst for enlightenment on the part of the proscribed children of Virginia, and such the determined severity of that State towards them, at the very time when she was beginning to awaken to the necessity of securing the benefit of a common school system for her white people.

SCHOOLS FOR FREEDMEN.

It was reserved for Virginia herself to abrogate all this iniquitous legislation by her consenting to become a party in the movement to break up the federal Union. It was reserved for her shores, that had witnessed the inception of the wrong, to behold also the first step in the expiation. In the close neighborhood of the very spot where the first cargo of slaves had been disembarked stands the little brown building that served as the first school-house for the freedmen. Securely it nestled under the guns of Fortress Monroe, with the military power of the nation pledged for its maintenance. Six months had not yet elapsed since the clouds of war had gathered when this earliest sunbeam of a dawning civilization burst through to relieve their gloom. On the 17th day of September, 1861, the school was opened. It had an appropriate and, at the same time, a competent teacher in Mrs. Mary S. Peake, a lady of whom one of the ancestors on the maternal side might possibly have come over to this country on the Dutch vessel already alluded to. The honor of its establishment is due to the American Missionary Association, which had labored, even before the war, for the educational advancement of the colored people in Kentucky and elsewhere, and whose keen-eyed philanthropy eagerly caught sight of this "opening of the prison-house to those who were bound."

With the advance of the Union armies in the ensuing years of the war the labors of these friends of humanity kept steady pace. In 1862 their efforts in the State of Virginia secured the establishment of four additional schools, one of which was at Norfolk, two at Newport News, and the fourth one opened in the old court-house at Hampton. Besides establishing these they sent books to another school, begun by a colored man in Suffolk. They were aided, too, in their noble work by the Boston Education Commission, organized in the early part of that year under the presidency of the late Governor John A. Andrew. This latter association sent south more than 70 teachers, three of whom opened schools at Norfolk and Craney island.

The year 1863 was ushered in by the emancipation proclamation of President Lincoln, which conferred legal freedom upon all the slaves of the nation except those of certain specified localities, and actual freedom upon all such as might come within the lines of the national armies. The consequent enlargement of the area of philanthropic labor was followed by a corresponding increase in the number of earnest and efficient laborers. Hundreds of ladies, tenderly nurtured, and refined by all the accomplishments of modern culture, hastened to this field, now whitening for the harvest, and, braving privation and the vicissitudes of war, eagerly enrolled themselves among the teachers of the freedmen. In the State of Virginia the schools already established increased largely in the number of their pupils, while many others were opened in different localities to meet the importunity of those newly liberated thirsters after knowledge. The abandoned homes of "the first families" were in many instances pressed into the service of their former bondmen, and their elegant mansions were occupied—like that of ex-Governor Henry A. Wise—as schools for colored children and homes for their instructors. It is safe to say that the number of these schools, including those held at night, was at least 50. One of them, in the city of Norfolk, was so large within the first week of its establishment as to compel the employment of 15 colored assistants, and, in the course of the year, its attendance attained to the number of 1,200 pupils. In the following year—1864—additional schools were opened and the force of teachers at least doubled.

The pecuniary outlays necessitated by these operations were cheerfully made by numerous freedmen's associations throughout the north, acting generally as auxiliaries to the two agencies already mentioned.

The year 1865 was marked by the fall of Richmond and the close of the rebellion. The extended opportunity thus offered for philanthropic labors was straightway embraced, and schools were opened at every feasible point. The aid of the government also was secured for their maintenance. On the 3d of March, of this year, the Freedmen's Bureau had been created by act of Congress, and through the kind ordering of an Ali-wise Providence, Major General O. O. Howard, the gallant Christian soldier, was, in the following month of May, assigned to duty as its Commissioner. In his circular No. 2, dated May 19, 1865, he said : "The educational and moral condition of the people will not be forgotten. The utmost facility will be offered to benevolent and religious organizations and State authorities in the maintenance of good schools for refugees and freedmen, until a system of free schools can be supported by their organized local governments." But the co-operation of the Commissioner with these benevolent agencies did not stop here. He gave them efficient aid by turning over for school purposes the disused government buildings, and those seized from disloyal owners, which were under his charge ; by affording transportation for teachers, books, and school-furniture, and by assigning quarters and rations to all engaged in the work of instruction, at the same time that protection was given to them through the department commanders. By his directions, too, the " refugee and freedmen's fund " was used to assist in the maintenance of schools supported, in part, by the freedmen themselves, and in each State superintendents of schools were appointed, whose duty it was " To work as much as possible in connection with State officers who may have had school matters in charge, and to take cognizance of all that was being done to educate refugees and freedmen, secure protection to schools and teachers, promote method and efficiency, and to correspond with the benevolent agencies which were supplying his field." Thus, under the beneficent administration of General Howard, this bureau has been, in the matter of education, as in many other respects, of efficient service to the freedmen, and has helped to prepare them for a right exercise of the franchises with which they are now invested as citizens. To bring about this result, too, the various religious denominations of the country have all labored, to a greater or less extent, with commendable zeal ; and to aid in securing it, the American Freedmen's Union Commission, which unites in its organization the various undenominational freedmen's aid societies of the land, with the exception of the American Missionary Association, has shown itself the worthy co-adjutor of that body. This commission was formed on the 16th day of May, 1866, and its object, as stated in its constitution, is "To aid and co-operate with the people of the south, without distinction of race or color, in the improvement of their condition, upon the basis of industry, education, freedom, and Christian morality."

In all the advantages that have been mentioned the State of Virginia has participated, and, as a consequence of the several influences at work, its schools have increased in number, and have prospered greatly, every year since the close of the rebellion. True, they have had to contend with much prejudice and opposition on the part of a large majority of the white population. But there is reason to believe, from present indications, that these hostile sentiments are gradually diminishing, and that many, who are bitterly opposed to the political equality of the negro, admit the expediency and justice of providing for his education.

The following tables, which present a statistical view of these schools for the last three years, will, on examination, give a very satisfactory exhibit of their increase, cost of maintenance, and the advancement of the pupils in the several studies pursued during that period :

Number of schools, teachers, and pupils, 1866 to 1868.

Year.	Number of schools.			Number of teachers.			Number of scholars.			Average attendance.	Per cent.
	Day.	Night.	Total.	White.	Colored.	Total.	Male.	Female.	Total.		
1866	....	....	123	....	....	200	....	....	11,784	8,951	76
1867	195	56	251	197	98	295	8,076	8,039	16,115	10,890	68
1868	239	45	284	206	155	361	8,180	8,528	16,708	11,816	71

Studies and expenditures, 1867 *and* 1868.

Year.	Number of scholars in different studies pursued.							Expenditures in support of schools.		
	Alphabet.	Easy reading.	Advanced readers.	Writing.	Geography.	Arithmetic.	Higher branches.	Bo freedmen.	By others.	Total.
1867......	1,986	7,953	5,162	7,119	4,221	6,409	960	*$7,352 13	*$85,792 57	*$93,144 70
1868......	1,397	7,532	6,750	8,240	6,214	7,877	754	12,472 15	84,079 28	96,551 43

* Estimated upon reports of the Bureau Superintendent of Education, for six months of the year.

A brief account of two normal schools recently established will form an appropriate conclusion to this sketch of school matters among the colored population of Virginia. The first of these in the order of their establishment is—

THE RICHMOND NORMAL AND HIGH SCHOOL

This institution was opened for the admission of pupils in October, 1867, having been duly incorporated, with a board of trustees consisting of five members, by charter granted by the circuit court. The principal building, which is a handsome new brick edifice, erected at a cost of about $5,000, is 52 feet long by 32 feet wide, and two stories in height. Substantially built and amply provided with school furniture of the best modern styles, philosophical apparatus valued at $350, and a judiciously selected library of about 500 volumes, it is rendered still better adapted to its purposes by having its different rooms adorned with historical paintings and other works of art. It accommodates 100 pupils, whose studies are directed by the principal, Mr. Andrew Washburn, aided by two assistant teachers. The course of study prescribed is that which is usual in our normal schools; and the moral effect of the institution is apparent, not only in the wholesome instruction and discipline afforded to its pupils, but in its influence upon the community at large, awakening the nobler aspirations of colored youth, and diminishing the blind and unreasoning prejudice entertained against them by their white fellow-citizens. This school derives its support from the normal school fund of the English Friends, the Peabody fund, the city council, and the Freedmen's Bureau. The ulterior design of its founders is to prepare competent teachers for the hoped-for public school system, which is to follow in the train of reconstruction in Virginia.

THE HAMPTON NORMAL AND AGRICULTURAL INSTITUTE,

of which Mr. S. C. Armstrong is principal, is also designed to take part in raising up teachers; its purpose (as stated in a circular issued shortly after its establishment) being to prepare "youth of the south, without distinction of color, for the work of organizing and instructing schools in the southern States." It was opened in April, 1868, under the auspices of the American Missionary Association, and was duly incorporated in the following September. It is also a manual labor school, and connected with it is a farm of 120 acres provided with all the appliances needful for the instruction of its students, in both the theory and the practice of the most profitable methods of agriculture.

All of the house-work, too, in the boarding department is performed by the female students. The circular further states that "this 'Whipple farm' lies upon Hampton Roads. The school and home buildings, valued at $20,000, occupy a beautiful site upon the shore. They are so furnished and arranged as to offer to the students the helps to right living which belong to a cultivated Christian home." There is a three years' course of study, embracing, among other branches, English grammar and composition, arithmetic and bookkeeping, geography and natural science, lectures, physiology, agriculture and agricultural chemistry, with analysis of soils and experiments by pupils, &c., &c. Opportunities for enabling students to acquire experience in imparting instruction are enjoyed through actual teaching in the Butler and Lincoln model schools, which are in the vicinity of the institution. Thus far this new enterprise has been attended with the most gratifying results.

Its students have earned, upon an average, a small amount per week above expenses to them; and its gross sales of produce in the northern markets have been over $2,000. It possesses, too, the well-selected nucleus of a library; for enlarging which, as well as for providing scientific apparatus, together with cabinets of minerals and of natural history, it hopes to find the means in its own income, aided by the generous co-operation of friends.

The following report to the American Missionary Association, drawn up by President Hopkins, of Williams College, Massachusetts, calls special attention to this institution :

I. *Location.*—In this there is a historical fitness. It is within the capes, and not far from the spot where the first slaves brought to this country were landed. It is where General Butler first refused to deliver up the fugitives, calling them " contraband of war," and where a city of refuge was provided to which they thronged by boat loads, and wagon loads, and in caravans, and were housed and fed by the government. It was here, too, that the first school for freedmen was established. It was the site of the hospital barracks of McClellan's and Grant's armies, where fifteen thousand sick and wounded were under treatment at one time, and the farm connected with the institute includes the United States cemetery containing the bodies of nearly six thousand United States soldiers, together with the granite monument to those martyrs in the cause of freedom, which is in full view from the institute. Not far distant is seen the flag of Fortress Monroe, and it is within sight of the spot where the battle was fought between the Monitor and the Merrimac.

The location has also advantages as regards convenience, economy and the coast. It is accessible by water, and so by the cheapest possible transportation, from the region of the Chesapeake Bay, of the Potomac, York and James Rivers, and of the Pamlico and Albemarle Sounds, a region including a colored population which has been, if it be not now, of greater relative density than any other. With a steamboat landing on the farm it has ready access to the principal sea-board cities of the North, both as markets and as sources of supplies. It is also relatively beautiful, having the advantages of sea breeze and opportunities for sea bathing. The place was indeed formerly the seat of a large female seminary, and was a summer resort for health and recreation.

II. *History.*—As has been said, this was the site of the first school for freedmen, and here the Butler school is still kept in the large building originally built for it on the premises, and is taught by pupils from the institute. This, however, did not involve the idea of the institute as a normal school and a seminary of a high order. That was originated by General Armstrong, who had charge of the freedmen's bureau at this point, and who first comprehended the facilities afforded by the place, and the greatness of the work that might be done here. At his suggestion, and chiefly through his efforts, the American Missionary Association heartily co-operating, the estate now called the Whipple Farm, including a hundred and twenty-five acres of excellent land, together with the mansion used by the United States officers for their headquarters, the Butler school-house, and the hospital barracks, was purchased. The whole cost, including improvements, has been about $45,000.

III. *Object and plan.*—The object of the institute, as stated in its act of incorporation, is " to prepare youth of the South, without distinction of color, for the work of organizing and instructing schools in the southern States." Its object is the diffusion throughout the South, where normal and agricultural schools have not been established as yet, of the best methods and advantages of education; and if the benefit of the colored people be more immediately anticipated, it is only from the apprehended unwillingness of others to avail themselves of the advantages of the institute. Whatever provision may or may not be made for the general education of the South, it is clearly among the most imperative duties both of the North and of the South to provide in the best manner practicable for the enlightenment, the more perfect christianization, and the full manhood of the freedmen. This is now the point of trial for this nation before Him who has begun to vindicate the rights of a long-suffering people, and scarcely more for their sakes than for our own, and for the sake of the whole African race, should this duty be accepted by us.

But if the duty be accepted, it is not seen how it can be performed without some institution which shall combine, as this institute proposes to do, education and training with opportunity for self-help. In these two, education and self-help, we have the object and plan of the institute. It would provide a body of colored teachers, the best and the only available agency for the work, thoroughly trained, not only in the requisite knowledge and in the best methods of teaching, but also in all that pertains to right living, including habits of intelligent labor. Emotional in their nature, unaccustomed to self-control, and improvident by habit, the freedmen need discipline and training even more than teaching; and the institute would avoid the mistake sometimes made on missionary grounds of so training teachers as to put them out of sympathy with the people in their present condition and in the struggle that is before them, if they are to rise. It would, therefore, make much of the feature of self help, not only as relieving the benevolent from a burden, but as inspiring self-reliance, and as tending to a consistency and solidity of character that are especially needed. It would aim at reaching (and to be effectual it must reach) those who cannot pay their way except by their own labor.

With these views a large agricultural interest has been organized both for instruction and profit. So far this has succeeded well in both respects, and with suitable management it cannot fail to do so in future. The soil is rich and varied, adapted both to fruits and vegetables. On the farm are large quantities of muck and sea mud and fish guano from the neighboring fisheries. It is intended to make the culture varied, and to introduce improved methods to be put in practice wherever the pupils may go. The farm, thus furnishing food for the school, in connection with the adjacent fisheries, which make living cheap, will enable the poorest youth to meet all his necessary expenses, and, at the same time, receive good educational advantages. This department is under the superintendence of Mr. F. Richardson, who is admirably qualified for the position.

The farm is for the men; but, as at the North so at the South, and more and more, the teaching is to be done by the women, and for their education and training too ample provision cannot be made. Young women at the institute are on equal footing in all respects with the young men, except that their opportunities for supporting themselves by their own labor are not as good. Something, much, indeed, has been done. An industry has been organized by which the pupils are paid for making up garments, which are sold at a small profit. This is beneficial in every way. About twenty can also be employed the greater part of the year in teaching. This department needs and should receive efficient aid.

IV. *Present condition and prospects.*—Of these we do not hesitate to speak with satisfaction and high hope. The school was opened in April, 1868, and there have since been sixty-six pupils in attendance, of whom fifty-two were boarders. Of these, eight have been employed as teachers in freedmen's day schools, doing, under careful superintendence, the work done in previous years by northern teachers, and giving good satisfaction in it, and thus, while keeping up with their classes in the normal school, paying their necessary expenses. Three hundred children have thus been taught during the past year by under-graduates of the institute, and it is expected that twice that number will be thus taught during the year to come. In the present vacation, including July and September, twelve pupils have gone out to teach, and will not have less than five hundred children in their schools.

The closing examination and exercises of the school indicated a thoroughness and faithfulness on the part of the teachers that nothing but missionary zeal could have inspired. Hitherto the teachers of the institute have all been ladies, and here, as in many places throughout the South, northern ladies of high character have done and are doing a most Christian and heroic work, looking for their richest reward in the thanks of the lowly and the smile of Him who came that the Gospel might be preached to the poor. On the part of the scholars there was indicated a diligence and proficiency quite remarkable, and that would have done credit to students similarly situated of any race or color. Not only has the teaching been diligent but of the highest order, and the results correspond. There was great correctness in reading and spelling. Nearly all wrote a good hand, and the blackboard exercises in map-drawing, with the new method of triangulation, would have been creditable to the pupils of any normal school at the North. The whole results furnish the fullest encouragement to future effort.

We are thus doing for the freedmen through this institute, with such modifications as their condition demands, just what we are doing for ourselves in those States that are furthest advanced in education : and if the southern people could but wisely co-operate, the experiment with the freedmen could at once be fairly made. Fortunate in its position, and comprehensive in its aims, the institute is adapted to do a great work for the African race, both in this and their fatherland. It is just the agency needed through which benevolent individuals and the fund of Mr. Peabody, now so magnificently enlarged, may work. In the plan of it nothing is wanting; to carry it out, executive ability and business talent of a high order will be needed, especially at first. These we think it now has in those at the head of each of its departments, and we heartily commend the enterprise to the confidence, to the prayers, and to the benefactions of the good people of the whole country.

WEST VIRGINIA.

The legislature of West Virginia, at its first session, December 9, 1863, passed an act forbidding slaves to be introduced into the State or removed from it, with intent to deprive them of the right to freedom guaranteed by the constitution. An act was also passed at the same session establishing a system of free schools, providing for the enumeration of " all the youth between the ages of 6 and 21 years, distinguishing between males and females." The township boards of education were authorized and required to establish one or more separate schools for free colored children when the whole number enumerated exceeded 30, the schools so established to be under the control of the board of education; but when the average attendance of free colored children was less than 15 for any one month, the school might be discontinued for a period not exceeding six months at one time; and the money raised on the number of free colored children, in case the attendance was less than 15 and the number enumerated was less than 30, was to be reserved to be appropriated for the education of colored children in such a way as the township should direct.

In 1865 the school law was revised, and the word "free" in connection with the colored people was struck out. In 1866 township boards of education were authorized to furnish school-houses for their respective towns, and to levy a tax, not exceeding $7 on the $100 of the taxable property for that purpose; but this proviso was added: "Provided colored children shall not attend the same school or be classified with white children."

The following tables exhibit the condition of the freedmen's schools:

Number of schools, teachers, and scholars, 1867 and 1868.

Year.	Number of schools.			Number of teachers.			Number of scholars.			Average attendance.	Per cent.
	Day.	Night.	Total.	White.	Colored.	Total.	Male.	Female.	Total.		
1867.........	10	2	12	4	8	12	295	280	575	486	84
1868.........	11	1	12	4	8	12	326	304	630	545	86

Studies and expenditure of schools, 1867 and 1868.

Year.	Number of scholars in different studies pursued.							Expended in support of schools.		
	Alphabet.	Easy reading.	Advanced readers.	Writing.	Geography.	Arithmetic.	Higher branches.	By freedmen.	By others.	Total.
1867	48	287	143	299	247	278	23	$30	$5,915	$5,945
1868	56	395	198	387	375	392	33	861	6,315	7,176

WISCONSIN.

This State had a population in 1860 of 775,881, of whom only 1,171 were colored. There are no constitutional or legal restrictions upon the colored people which are not shared alike by the whites. The colored people exercise the franchise in the same manner as others; their children attend the public schools with the white children, there being no separate schools for either class.

VERMONT.

There were in Vermont only 709 colored persons in 1860 out of a population of 315,093. The declaration of rights, after asserting that all men are born equally free and independent, concludes as follows: "Therefore, no male person, born in this country or brought from over the sea, ought to be holden by law to serve any person as a servant, slave, or apprentice, after he arrives to the age of twenty-one years, nor female, in like manner, after she arrives to the age of eighteen years, unless they are bound by their own consent after they arrive to such age, or bound by law for the payment of debts, damages, fines, costs, or the like." The constitution declares every man of the full age of twenty-one years, with certain conditions alike applied to all, to be entitled to all the privileges of a freeman; and the laws make no distinction in regard to color.

NEW HAMPSHIRE.

There were in New Hampshire in 1860 only 494 colored persons out of a total population of 326,073. The constitution of this State makes no distinction in its provisions in regard to race or color, and the "bill of rights" declares that "all men are born equally free and independent;" but, in face of this declaration, in 1835, when the principal of the academy at Canaan admitted colored pupils to his classes, a mob could be raised, without rebuke and without resistance by the town or the State, to remove the building from its site and transfer it to a neighboring swamp.

NEW JERSEY.

This State had a population in 1860 of 672,035, of whom 25,336 were colored, and of these 18 were slaves. By the constitution the right of suffrage is limited to white male citizens of the United States of the age of twenty-one years; but it is provided that the funds for the support of public schools shall be applied for the equal benefit of all the people of the State. Colored children are entitled to the privileges of this fund and are admitted into the public schools.